WHAT IS A PARENT?
A SOCIO-LEGAL ANALYSIS

D1352347

What is a Parent?
A Socio-Legal Analysis

Edited by
ANDREW BAINHAM, SHELLEY DAY SCLATER,
AND MARTIN RICHARDS

FOR THE CAMBRIDGE SOCIO-LEGAL GROUP

·HART·
PUBLISHING

OXFORD – PORTLAND OREGON
1999

Hart Publishing
Oxford and Portland, Oregon

Published in North America (US and Canada) by
Hart Publishing
c/o International Specialized Book Services
5804 NE Hassalo Street
Portland, Oregon
97213-3644
USA

Distributed in the Netherlands, Belgium and Luxembourg by
Intersentia, Churchillaan 108
B2900 Schoten
Antwerpen
Belgium

Distributed in Australia and New Zealand by
Federation Press
John St
Leichhardt
NSW 2000

Hart Publishing Ltd is a specialist legal publisher based in Oxford, England.
To order further copies of this book or to request a list of other
publications please write to:

Hart Publishing Ltd, 19 Whitehouse Road, Oxford, OX1 4PA
Telephone: +44 (0)1865 434459 or Fax: +44 (0)1865 794882
e-mail: mail@hartpub.co.uk

British Library Cataloguing in Publication Data
Data Available
ISBN 1 84113–058–3 (cloth)
1 84113–043–5 (paperback)

Typeset by Hope Services (Abingdon) Ltd.
Printed in Great Britain on acid-free paper
by Biddles Ltd, Guildford and Kings Lynn.

Contents

Acknowledgements

This collection of essays is the product of a series of seminars held under the auspices of the newly-formed Cambridge Socio-Legal Group. The editors owe an enormous debt of gratitude to Jill Brown, Secretary of the Centre for Family Research for her invaluable assistance with the editorial work and in producing the manuscript. They would like to thank Julie Jessop and Frances Murton for their helpful contribution as discussants, and to the former for indexing and the latter for subediting of the text. They would also like to record their thanks to Sally Roberts for providing helpful technical assistance.

The Editors
Cambridge, June 1999

Notes on the Contributors

Andrew Bainham is a Fellow of Christ's College, Cambridge and University Lecturer in Law. He is Editor of the *International Survey of Family Law* (Martinus Nijhoff) and the author of a leading text on children and the law, *Children: The Modern Law* 2nd edn. (Jordans, 1998).

Stuart Bridge is a Fellow of Queens' College, Cambridge. Called to the Bar in 1981, he practised for some years before joining the Faculty of Law at the University of Leeds. He has been a University Lecturer at the University of Cambridge since 1990, teaching land law, family law and associated subjects. He has written mainly on property law (particularly landlord and tenant— *Residential Leases* (Blackstone Press, 1994), *Assured Tenancies* (Blackstone Press, 1999), but is also the co-author of a statutory guide to the Children Act 1989. He was a Visiting Professor at Cornell Law School in the 1994 fall semester.

Carol Brayne is a lecturer in Epidemiology and Honorary Consultant in Public Health Medicine, University of Cambridge. She was one of the Principal Investigators on both the MRC Multi-centre Study of Cognitive Function and Ageing and its Healthy Ageing component. She has been working on longitudinal studies for thirteen years, examining issues related to the ageing population, concentrating most particularly on dementia, cognitive decline and healthy ageing.

Rachel Cook is a Senior Lecturer in Health Psychology at Anglia Polytechnic University, Cambridge. She is a psychologist with research interests in infertility and its consequences, particularly in relation to donation and surrogacy. She has recently been involved in the BMA working party on surrogacy and was a contributing author to its report, *Changing Conceptions of Motherhood* 1996.

Shelley Day Sclater has taught Psychosocial Studies at the University of East London since 1993. Formerly a solicitor, she spent seven years in private practice, specialising in family law. She has recently completed an ESRC-funded study on the psychological aspects of divorce and dispute resolution. She is author of *Divorce: A Psychosocial Study* (Ashgate, 1999) and co-editor of *Undercurrents of Divorce* (Ashgate, 1999) and *Lines of Narrative* (Routledge, forthcoming). She is currently working on collaborative projects on disputed contact cases and surrogacy and developing her theoretical and methodological work on narrative methods in the social sciences.

Margaret Ely is a Statistician at the Centre for Family Research, University of Cambridge with an interest in the effect of attrition and missing data on estimates derived from cohort studies. She has worked on divorce data from the Twenty-07 Study and the NCDS and BS70 cohort studies.

Loraine Gelsthorpe is a Fellow of Pembroke College, Cambridge, University Lecturer in Criminology, University of Cambridge and Director of the Ph.D. Programme in the Institute of Criminology. Her particular research interests revolve around discretion and discrimination in the delivery of criminal justice, and in youth justice. Current research includes discretion and the detention of asylum seekers, and social exclusion, crime and justice. Her published work includes numerous essays and articles on youth justice, *Feminist Perspectives in Criminology*, co-edited with Allison Morris (Open University Press, 1990), *Minority Ethnic Groups in the Criminal Justice System* (Cropwood Series, 1993) and *Understanding the Sentencing of the Female Offender*, co-edited with Carol Hedderman (Home Office, 1997).

Susan Golombok is Professor of Psychology and Director of the Family and Child Psychology Research Centre at City University. She has for the past twenty years carried out research on the effects on children of being raised in non-traditional families. Her books include *Gender Development* (Cambridge University Press, 1995) and *Growing Up in a Lesbian Family* (Guilford Press, 1997).

Jack Goody was formerly Professor of Anthropology at the University of Cambridge and is a Fellow of St. John's College. He is author of *The Development of Marriage and the Family in Europe* (1983) and other books on the comparative study of family and kinship.

Jonathan Herring is a Fellow in Law at New Hall and Affiliated Lecturer in the Faculty of Law, University of Cambridge. He teaches criminal and family law and is co-author with M. Cremona of *Criminal Law*, 2nd edn. (1998). He was formerly Lecturer in Law at Christ Church, Oxford.

Felicia Huppert is a Lecturer in the Psychology of Ageing in the Department of Psychiatry, University of Cambridge. Her principal research interest is the relationship between health, cognitive function and the social environment in the ageing population, and she has published extensively in the areas of health psychology and neuropsychology as they apply to the ageing process. Dr. Huppert is Co-Director of the newly established Cambridge Interdisciplinary Research Centre on Ageing (CIRCA).

Allison James is Reader in Applied Anthropology and Co-Director of the Centre for the Social Study of Childhood, University of Hull. Recent publications include *Theorising Childhood*, with C. Jenks and A. Prout (Policy Press, 1998).

Julie Jessop is currently a Ph.D.student at the Centre for Family Research, University of Cambridge, conducting research into parenthood and new partners. She has previously worked on an ESRC funded project on the psychology of divorce and a Joseph Rowntree project on children's definitions of family.

Martin Johnson is Professor of Reproductive Sciences, University of Cambridge, co-author of *Essential Reproduction* (Blackwell, 1999 5th Edition) and a member of the Human Fertilisation and Embryology Authority.

Bridget Lindley is a solicitor specialising in family and child-care law since qualifying in 1986. She has worked at the Family Rights Group for nine years advising and advocating for families who are involved with Social Services about the care of their children, and undertaking socio-legal research on their perspectives in this field. She is also involved in lobbying for improvements in law and practice, especially in relation to the adoption law review. She has recently begun working at the Centre for Family Research, University of Cambridge, on a project funded by the Nuffield Foundation which is evaluating the efficacy of advocacy for families in the child protection process.

Mavis Maclean is a Senior Research Fellow in the Faculty of Law at Oxford and has written extensively on family law and family politics. Her most recent publication, with John Eekelaar, is *The Parental Obligation* (Hart, 1997).

Juliet Mitchell is a Lecturer in Gender and Society, University of Cambridge and Fellow of Jesus College. She is a Member of the International Psychoanalytical Association and a practising psychoanalyst. Her most recent book

Frances Murton was formerly a local authority social worker specialising in work with children and families including foster care and adoption. She has worked on several research projects at the Centre for Family Research, University of Cambridge and is a practising family mediator.

Ros Pickford is a Research Associate at the Centre for Family Research, University of Cambridge. She has recently completed a project on non-married fathers and the law funded by the Joseph Rowntree Foundation.

Martin Richards is Director of the Centre for Family Research and Professor of Family Research at the University of Cambridge. His research interests include parental divorce and children and psycho-social consequences of the new human genetics. Books include *The Troubled Helix* edited with Theresa Marteau (Cambridge University Press, 1996), *Children of Social Worlds*, edited with Paul Light (Polity Press, 1986) and *Sexual Arrangements: Marriage and Affairs*, with Janet Reibstein (Heinemann, 1992).

Wendy Solomou is a Research Associate at the Centre for Family Research, University of Cambridge. Her research interests include the long-term effect of divorce and the psychological aspects of prenatal detection of fetal abnormality.

Candida Yates is a psycho-social studies lecturer in the Department of Human Relations at the University of East London. Her field of research includes the psychoanalytic sociology of the emotions, and the construction of sexual difference in consumer culture. She is currently completing her doctoral thesis on "The formations of male jealousy in late modernity".

Table of Cases

1

Introduction

SHELLEY DAY SCLATER, ANDREW BAINHAM
and MARTIN RICHARDS*

What is a parent? This book presents an interdisciplinary exploration of the nature of parenthood and its various manifestations in contemporary society. The contributors to this book consider this question in the context of the background of their own disciplines; ideas about parents which derive from law, sociology, psychology, biology, history and criminology are explored. As we shall see, "parent" emerges from this book as a contested concept; definitions are various and fluid, parenting practices are by no means fixed, and ideologies which frame who parents are and what they do are subject to disruptions from several quarters. In short, this book shows the ways in which "parent", like "child", is a term with a shifting meaning. "Parenthood", like "childhood", refers to a fluid set of social practices and expectations that are historically and culturally situated, and its meaning is contingent upon broader social, political and economic exigencies.

Importantly, this book suggests that we make a mistake if we try to think about parents in isolation from broader historical and social changes, particularly those concerning "the family". Crucially, too, parents and children emerge as mutually constituted in relation to each other; to ask the question "what is a parent?", as this book does, is also to beg the question of "what is a child?" As the contributors to this book show, it is of no small significance that these questions are being asked at this time in our history. In the late modern world, older ideas about both parents and children are being challenged by social and demographic changes in families, by new political rhetoric, social policies and legal provisions, by innovations in biomedical technologies and by new outlooks in the social sciences.

The terrain of what constitutes a "parent" is now, perhaps more than ever, a highly contested one and there is no consensus on either what parents are or what they should be. At the heart of the debates are three linked issues: first, that of the relative importance of and status to be accorded to "biological" and "social" parents. Who has the most legitimate claim to the title "parent", and what are the rights and responsibilities that should appropriately attach to each?

* We wish to thank Heather Price, Barry Richards and Candida Yates for their helpful comments on an earlier draft of this chapter.

Secondly, there is the question of the role of law in the regulation of parenting practices; in what circumstances, to what extent and in what ways can and should the state intervene in families and in reproductive and child-care decisions? How effective are social prescriptions for parenting likely to be anyway? Thirdly, there is the issue of gender;[1] can parenting ever be a truly gender-neutral activity, or is the ideal of the gender-neutral parent likely to be subverted by socio-economic realities, by the gendered discourses of motherhood and fatherhood, and by the psychological constellations of masculinities and femininities? "What is a parent?" is a question that has a multitude of dimensions and permits no straightforward answer. The chapters of this book each present a different perspective; what we shall see is that there are as many answers as there are dimensions to the question. Each perspective is, of necessity, partial and contingent; what emerges is a complex picture of parents, as social, legal and psychological subjects, in an uncertain and changing world.

In this introductory chapter, we present a brief overview of the historical changes in ideas about parents and in the legal provisions which have helped to construct parental identities and practices. We discuss legal changes against a background of the social and ideological undercurrents that have lent particular meanings to law, highlighting the complex matrices of laws, discourses and practices in which parents are constructed.

As Juliet Mitchell and Jack Goody argue in Chapter 6 below, in the female-homemaker/male-breadwinner ideology which underpinned "traditional" family arrangements in the years after the Second World War, while mothers were seen as essential for children's psychological well-being, fathers were simply regarded as family providers. In the pro-natalist climate of the time (Riley, 1983), the psychoanalyst and paediatrician Donald Winnicott could state that "there is no such thing as a baby" (Winnicott, 1952) with every confidence that his readers and listeners would know what he meant. These were the days when only mothers and children were defined in relation to each other, when, indeed, one was inconceivable without the other. These were the days of what Ingleby (1974) has referred to as "desert island psychology" when the mother-infant dyad was all there was; fathers were notable, but only for their absence,[2] as indeed was the social world in which they all lived (Richards, 1986a).

---

[1] Gender has been said to be one of the main dimensions of family change. See Fox Harding (1996); Elliott (1996).

[2] For example, Winnicott's book *The Child, the Family and the Outside World*, first published in 1957, but based on earlier BBC broadcasts, was explicitly addressed to mothers. Fathers were assumed to be primarily preoccupied with the world of work outside the home. Winnicott saw fathers as playing their part in child-care primarily in terms of supporting the mother's essential "bonding" with her child. This book includes a chapter entitled "What About Father?" in which he says that "mothers can get their husbands to help in little things, and can arrange for the baby to be bathed when father can watch, and even take part if he wants to . . . One could not assume in every case that it is a good thing for father to come early into the picture" (p.113). For Winnicott, fathers were important to the extent that they were able to provide support for the mother-infant relationship, and insofar as they represented the world outside the mother-infant dyad. But he also took the view that it was the mother's responsibility to facilitate the father-child relationship: "What about

It helps to understand these ideas about parents within a broader intellectual and socio-political context. On the one hand, with the benefit of hindsight, we can interpret them as a reaction within the psychoanalytic community, against the primacy of the father in Freud; Winnicott was a member of the British Object Relations school which emphasised, not the primary importance of the Oedipus complex in the formation of psycho-sexual identity, but that of the pre-oedipal period when the mother reigned supreme. On the other hand, it is no accident, that Object Relations theory (and the remedial social practices, such as the Child Guidance movement, and much social work practice, which flowed from it), gained a popularity at a time after the Second World War, when the priorities of social policy centred unashamedly on reconstructing "the family" in a society that had been ravaged by war (Riley, 1983).[3] The pro-natalist policies of the time, whatever their intention, had the effect of bringing mothers out of the munitions factories and off the land, back into the home, the "haven in a heartless world" (Lasch, 1977) where their children needed them. In the wake of the wartime evacuation of thousands of children (see Chapter 6 below), the "maternal deprivation" thesis of psychoanalyst and ethologist John Bowlby,[4] identified children separated from their mothers as at risk of a range of personal and social problems, from "affectionless psychopathy" to "juvenile delinquency": bad mothers, it seemed, produced bad children, and social problems for us all.

These theories contained powerful prescriptions for mothering. They were supported by a range of expert interventions designed to promote a particular kind of hands-on motherhood which mothers failed to follow at pains of considerable damage to their children. Winnicott's work assisted in naturalising the scenario;[5] mothers, he said, fell naturally into a state of "primary maternal preoccupation" following the birth of their infants which, in most cases, ensured that "good enough" mothering would ensue (Winnicott, 1960).[6] Thus, we saw in the years following the Second World War, in the era of the "companionate

father? I suppose it is clear to everyone that, in normal times, it depends on what mother does about it whether father does or does not get to know his baby" (p.113). Bowlby later adopted a similar position.

[3] See also Thom (1990); Rose (1990); Urwin and Sharland (1990).

[4] Bowlby's ideas about attachment, separation and loss are published in a trilogy. See Bowlby (1971, 1975, 1981).

[5] Despite the broader appeal to biology in the ethological influences on his work, Bowlby was quite clear that attachment figures did not have to be biologically related, though an assumption that such figures would usually be birth mothers pervaded his work. In contrast to later ideas about "bonding", Bowlby himself was hardly concerned with the earliest parent-infant interactions; in this, he took quite a different view from Winnicott.

[6] In the adoption practices of the time, the blood tie was rendered unimportant, as children were given new families, quite severed from the old. In the overwhelming majority of cases, it was children of single mothers who were adopted by married heterosexual parents, a practice that was underpinned by a powerful ideology that the heterosexual nuclear family was the best forum for healthy child development. See Susan Golombok (Chapter 9 below) for further discussion of child development in the context of homosexual families.

marriage" (Finch and Summerfield, 1991)[7] and "the golden age of the nuclear family" (Goldthorpe, 1987, p.56), a powerful ideology of the centrality of mothers that supported the intentions of the government of the day to reconstruct "the family" as the cornerstone of a stable and prosperous society. This ideology positioned mothers as nurturers and emotional providers and fathers as financial providers, in a gendered breadwinner/homemaker duality. In this context, the gender-neutral term "parent" could hardly have emerged, let alone carried the range of meanings that it does today. In effect, this ideology presented a considerable obstacle both to mothers who might have wished to hatch aspirations of a life outside the home, and to fathers who wished to play a more major role in the direct care and upbringing of their children.

In this climate, "what is a parent?" would have been merely a rhetorical question, if it could have been asked at all; a parent was a mother or a father, a firmly gendered identity that both flowed from and supported the gendered practices of parenting. However, research shows quite clearly that many mothers did continue to be involved in pursuits, many of them income-generating, outside of child-care (see, for example, Roberts, 1995), fathers were not as firmly wedded to the public world of work (Wilmott and Young, 1960) as is popularly believed, and better-off parents sent their children off to boarding schools where they were routinely "deprived" of parental input for substantial periods of time.

By the 1960s, the familial ideology had begun to be challenged by the "sexual revolution" and by the second wave of feminism (see, for example, Abbott and Wallace, 1997). It is doubtful whether women at this time still took seriously the "bad mother—bad children" equation; women were moving into the paid labour force in greater numbers and, more importantly perhaps, were beginning to expect fathers to do their share in the home and in relation to child-care. The "bad mothers equals bad children" ideology was gradually superseded by the "mad mothers equals mad children" thesis of the anti-psychiatrists, most notably R. D. Laing (see Laing, 1965, 1967). He argued that the communicative "double binds", in which families habitually tied themselves, were schizophrenogenic; mental illness was no more than a comprehensible (even "rational") response to the psychological convolutions that masqueraded as ordinary family relations. Importantly, however, it was still mothers who were portrayed as central to the emotional side of family life.

This popular thesis appeared at a time when "traditional" family life had begun on an inexorable trajectory of what was to be radical change. Sociologists began to talk about the darker side of family life (see, for example, Gavron, 1966), child abuse emerged as a pressing social problem (see Kempe *et al*, 1962; Kempe and Helfer, 1968; Kempe and Kempe, 1978), and domestic violence reared its ugly head in the public arena (Pizzey, 1974). The arguments of sociologists which sought to question the "sanctity of the family" were eagerly

---

[7] The conditions for the "companionate" marriage were, of course, set down much earlier (see, for example, Stone, 1977). The role of fathers as companions for both mothers and children was arguably more prominent before the Second World War than it was afterwards.

supported by the ascendancy of feminists in the academy who lost no time in identifying the so-called "traditional" (nuclear) family as *the* source of women's oppression (see, for example, Firestone, 1970; Millett, 1971). In this climate, theories that tied mothers to children and to home and hearth inevitably came under attack, and the way was paved for the emergence of the father not, as previously, as provider or as *paterfamilias*, but instead as a loving and nurturing force to be reckoned with (see Lewis, 1986; Lewis and O'Brien, 1987).

As men as fathers followed men as obstetricians into the delivery room, by the end of the 1970s it was commonplace for fathers to be present at the births of their babies. The move was almost wholeheartedly endorsed by the feminists of the time who were anxious to assert that women's oppression in the "private" sphere could quickly be alleviated if men could be encouraged to perform a greater share of caring activities in the home. The boundaries of parenting were changing, and these changes were supported by feminist sectors of the psychoanalytic community who came up with theories that "dual parenting" was what was needed in order to guarantee the gender revolution; Nancy Chodorow (1978) and Dorothy Dinnerstein (1976), though from different perspectives, both argued that if men could become more involved in child-care, the whole edifice of social gender relations would change. Women would no longer be denigrated, individually and socially, and the goal of women's liberation would be achieved.

But these ideals proved rather more difficult to achieve in practice than might have been supposed. First, no sooner had the idea of dual parenting been mooted than it came under intense criticism from several quarters (see, for example, Tong, 1989). Some pointed out that "the family" presupposed by the dual-parenting thesis was of a particular kind: that of a western, white, middle-class, heterosexual, nuclear ideal; dual parenting, on this view, would simply have the effect of reproducing this norm as the paradigm for all families. Others argued that dual parenting, far from alleviating the oppression of women, would have the effect of exacerbating it. Elshtain (1981), for example, asked the important question of what might be lost as well as gained through the process of dual parenting. Rossi (1981) argued that dual parenting would simply be a "rearrangement" of women's problems rather than an answer to them. Raymond (1986) argued that the fact that women mother is not *the* problem, or even *a* problem; rather, it is the social organising of parenting which is the problem, and the fact that women's parenting (mothering) has been socially constructed in the context of a society informed primarily by patriarchal values. Thus, the early ideas about the involvement of fathers as carers and nurturers were intensely debated, particularly by feminist sociologists and psychologists; there was clearly some ambivalence about fathers becoming "parents" in the day-to-day practical way that mothers were.

Secondly, a further set of issues around law and policy arose in relation to the changes in parenting which were afoot in the late 1970s and early 1980s, whilst feminist critics expressed a range of ambivalences about those too. Whilst some early sociological research on parental responsibilities and activities had suggested that although gender segregation of men and women in "the family" persisted, there did seem to be some evidence of an increase in sharing of parental responsibilities. As Young and Wilmott (1957/1962) stated: "Nowadays the father as well as the mother takes a hand in the care of children" (p.28) and "The husband portrayed by previous social investigation is no longer true to life. In place of the old comes a new kind of companionship between man and woman, reflecting the rise in status of the young wife and children which is one of the great transformations of our time. There is now a nearer approach to equality between the sexes and, though each has a peculiar role, its boundaries are no longer so rigidly defined nor is it performed without consultation" (p.30).

However, much subsequent research has indicated that such changes as there have been in this kind of paternal behaviour are small (see, for example, Backett, 1982; Lewis, 1986); fathers remain peripheral as carers for children in most cases, even in dual earner families (Brannen and Moss, 1987). As Segal (1994) argues, it seems that those men who are sharing family responsibilities more equally are likely to be the men for whom a combination of factors work together to make sharing a more attractive choice. This combination of factors, however, is not present for all men, not least because of structural constraints in the workplace, the lack of social policy support (for example, paternity leave), and the continuing ideological construction of masculinity as the Other of caring and nurturing femininity.[8]

Family law has both reflected and contributed to these changes and these dilemmas. In her 1997 eighth Annual ESRC Lecture, the Right Honourable Mrs Justice Hale points to the tensions inherent in the questions of what family law can do and what it is for. She points out that family law developed in order to support traditional marriage and the "orderly descent of [a man's] family's status, property and power". But over the last one hundred and fifty years, as the institution of marriage has changed, and as family patterns, meanings and priorities have altered, family law has increasingly evolved to support a new kind of marriage, one which provides a "loving, supportive environment for the couple and their children".

But there are considerable tensions involved; in many ways the legacy of the past lives on in family law, and comes into conflict with newer expectations and requirements. There have been debates, for example, about how far family law should try to serve the interests of individuals, and how far it should address the interests of the wider family group or of the community as a whole.[9] Importantly, however, for our purposes, in the evolution of family law from its "traditional dynastic purposes" to its concern to promote "stable and functional

---

[8] On the interrelationships among social and emotional factors in relation to masculinity, see Connell (1987, 1995); Hall (1991); Mac an Ghaill (1996). On fatherhood more specifically, see Lupton and Barclay (1997).

[9] For overviews of these debates, see, for example, Freeman (1984); Fox Harding (1996); Rodger (1996).

family units" (Hale, 1997), there has been a succession of different ideas about what a "parent" is and should be that have been closely linked to a new rhetoric about children and their needs.

Importantly, in the context of these social changes, "parent" has increasingly fragmented into "social" and "biological" (or "genetic") varieties, which exist in some tension with each other, posing problems for law and policy (Deech, 1993). Andrew Bainham explores this tension in Chapter 2 below, and argues that the genetic/social divide, around which some debates about parents have polarised, is unhelpful. In a legal context, debates about the relative importance of biological versus social parenthood are something of a red herring,[10] serving only to distract us from the more pressing problems of legal definition and of the kinds of rights and responsibilities that should attach to each.

What a parent is, or should be, are questions that the law implicitly (if not explicitly) addresses. To return to the point we raised at the beginning of this chapter, these questions have been closely linked with legal constructions of the nature of children. In these complex manoeuvres, the law has not been immune from the influence of broader ideologies, such as we have been discussing so far. The fragmentation of "parents" into "social" and "biological" forms is, on closer inspection, a gendered phenomenon. It is in debates around the status and rights of fathers that the significance to be attached to biology has emerged (Neale and Smart, 1999) in a context where genetic discourses are increasingly dominant.

Improvements in the social position and status of women have been central to social, legal and ideological change in relation to "the family" and to parenting (Elliott, 1996; Fox Harding, 1996). In the 1960s, as the "second wave" of feminism emerged, many women demanded equal rights with men; it was not uncommon, at this time, for feminists to denounce "the family" as the primary locus for women's oppression and sociologists began to talk about the trauma and misery experienced by many women in their traditional roles as wife and mother (see, for example, Friedan, 1963; Gavron, 1966; Mitchell, 1966; Oakley, 1974; Brown and Harris, 1978). Some went as far as to point the finger at motherhood as the source of these discontents (see, for example, Firestone, 1970), and powerful criticisms of the work of theorists like Bowlby and Winnicott, who it seemed had "naturalised" mothers' relationships to child care, emerged (see Riley, 1983). In this context, the calls for men to become more involved in the home (and in parenting) were understandable. However, an emerging focus on the problems of child abuse and domestic violence strengthened feminist

---

[10] Similarly, Eekelaar (1994a) reminds us that the "natural" events of bearing and begetting children have always been socially interpreted. He also argues that "legal" and "biological" parenthood should always co-incide, and that the concept of "parental responsibility" should be associated with social parenthood. Almond (1994) takes issue with Eekelaar's thesis, and argues against the "fractionalisation" of the concept of "parent". She points out that social change, developments in reproductive technologies and the increasing visibility of surrogacy have resulted in tripartite divisions of fatherhood—biological, legal and social; motherhood—genetic, gestatory and commissioning; and parenthood—biological, legal, and "parental responsibility".

criticisms about the dangers of family life for women and children at the same time as they problematised the idea that a greater involvement on the part of men could address, let alone solve, the problem. The attempt, therefore, to arrive at a more gender-neutral concept and a more gender-equal practice of parenting has been beset with difficulties.

Traditionally, men and women in marriage were profoundly unequal partners, with wives (along with children) being denied status as legal persons,[11] and unable (until the 1880s) to hold property in their own names. Further, under the "dynastic" purposes of family law (Hale, 1997), it was marriage that established a father's link to his children, and there remains a presumption in law that a married man is the father of the children conceived by or born to his wife during the subsistence of the marriage. As Mavis Maclean and Martin Richards point out in Chapter 14 below, traditionally fathers had rights over the children of the marriage to the exclusion of mothers, rights which were embodied in law in the concepts of "natural guardianship" and "legal custody". Thus, although mothers were granted the right in 1839 to apply to the Court of Chancery for custody of or access to their children aged less than seven,[12] the common law would usually enforce the father's right to custody, regardless of his behaviour or the age of the child in question (Maidment, 1984).

There was, however, some degree of tension between the common law and the equitable jurisdiction in matters relating to children, with Equity more willing to base decisions on the child's own interests, except in disputes between mothers and fathers where it tended to follow the practices at common law.[13] However, as Maidment (1984) points out, it was the conceptual contribution of Equity that was of the greatest significance: the justification it developed for interfering with the father's rights was that it was in the "interests of the child". In an 1827 case (cited in Maidment, 1984, p.95) the court stated that it had "authority to control the legal rights of the father if the welfare of the infant renders its interference necessary". Thus, we see here the beginnings of the development of the modern "welfare principle" that is used to determine disputes between mothers and fathers over their children. The "welfare of the child" gradually became the legal principle that displaced the absolute rights of fathers[14].

---

[11] According to Blackstone, in his *Commentaries on the Laws of England*, in the mid-eighteenth century, the legal existence of the woman is suspended during marriage and becomes incorporated into that of the husband. This is the doctrine of coverture (see Doggett, 1992).

[12] This was based on the "tender years doctrine" as it was used in the interpretation of the Custody of Infants Act 1839.

[13] At common law, the rights of the father were absolute, whereas the equitable jurisdiction was inherently a more flexible one. However, Equity was concerned also with questions of culpability: the maxim "he who comes to equity must come with clean hands" meant that the court could refuse to exercise its discretionary powers in the event that the person making the claim was "tainted" in any way with respect to their claim. Thus adulterous mothers could not apply under the Custody of Infants Act 1839.

[14] In the early cases, the courts were prepared to interfere with paternal authority on moralistic grounds. For example, in *Shelley v Westbrooke* (1817) JAC 266, the courts took exception to a father (the poet, P.B. Shelley) who had declared himself an atheist.

After 1857, and the creation of a secular jurisdiction for divorce, the court was required to make custody orders in respect of children, but continued, in the main, to uphold the absolute rights of the father; at this stage, disputes were treated by the judges on the basis of the father's common law rights, or the mother's guilt (for example, her adultery), though there was an increasing tendency from this time to make reference to the welfare of the child (Maidment, 1984, p.95). By the time the systems of common law and Equity were merged in the 1873 Judicature Act, the attitude of the divorce courts was distinctly more child-centred; the Act provided that, in questions relating to the custody of children, the rules of equity should prevail. However, the emerging principle of the welfare of the child cannot be understood in isolation; indeed, in *Re Agar-Ellis* in 1883 both Cotton LJ and Bowen LJ made it clear that the meaning accorded to "the welfare of the child" by the court (the man-made law) depended heavily upon the law of nature (the natural law) which gave fathers automatic rights and mothers none (Maidment, 1984, pp.98–99):

> "When by birth a child is subject to a father, it is for the general interest of families, and for the general interest of children, and really for the interest of the particular infant, that the court should not except in very extreme cases, interfere with the discretion of the father but leave him to the responsibility of exercising that power which nature has given him by the birth of the child" (per Cotton LJ).[15]

> "It is not the benefit of the infant as conceived by the court, but it must be for the benefit of the infant having regard to the natural law which points out that the father knows far better as a rule what is good for his children than a court of justice can" (per Bowen LJ).[16]

The 1886 Guardianship of Infants Act, passed in response to the concerns of women's groups over the injustice of the decision in *Re Agar-Ellis*, has been interpreted as giving equal status to the conduct and wishes of mothers and fathers in custody or access disputes, but it was not until the turn of the century that serious inroads were made into the principle of fathers' overriding authority; it is important for our discussion that this development went hand-in-hand with an increasing emphasis on the welfare of children. It was not until 1925 (The Guardianship of Infants Act) that mothers and fathers were given statutory equality as parents in custody disputes,[17] thus overriding (in disputed cases) the rights of the father at common law; crucially, this statute also elevated the "welfare of the child" to the "first and paramount consideration".

The story which is implicit in this brief overview of the development of the law on parents and children is one in which formulations of the welfare principle have been used by the courts to challenge the overriding rights of married

---

[15] Re *Agar-Ellis* [1883] 24 Ch D 317.

[16] See n.15 above.

[17] This equality, however, *only* applied in relation to custody disputes; the common law rule remained, for other purposes, that the father had absolute rights over his children. This was not modified until the Guardianship Act 1973 gave full and equal parental rights to mothers and fathers during the subsistence of the marriage.

fathers and, ultimately, to give mothers equal status. However, two sub-texts of this story are also important. First, the developments in law can be seen both to support and reflect particular visions of childhood which, in turn, both reflect and support prevailing social conditions and political imperatives.[18] Secondly, and relatedly, the developments we have discussed were inextricably linked with a range of moral concerns that were addressed by philosophers, psychologists and psychoanalysts, whose work on the "normal" development of children[19] and their needs were reflected in changing judicial attitudes (Maidment, 1984).

Thus, particular constructions of children's welfare were used by the courts to undermine the principle of father-right[20] resulting, ultimately, in married mothers having equal rights with fathers over their children.[21] There are those who argue that developments that have occurred since 1973 testify to a further extension of fathers' rights (see, for example, Brophy, 1985; Smart, 1989; Smart and Sevenhuijsen, 1989; Hooper, 1994) that, with the benefit of hindsight, can be read as a "backlash" against the feminist project more generally. But such a reading begs a number of important questions relating to the changing nature of "the family", and changing ideas about parenting and child welfare. These issues have been debated, for example, in the context of ideas about the nature and status of children (see, for example, James and Prout, 1990; Brannen and O'Brien, 1995; James, Chapter 10 below), in relation to the provisions family law could make for the children of both married and unmarried parents (James and Richards (forthcoming); Pickford, Chapter 8 below), in relation to the "wishes and feelings" of children of divorce (Piper, 1999) and in the context of children's rights (Roche, 1999).

Crucially, the "best interests of the child" is a concept which has always lacked precise "content" and definition in law;[22] arguably, this is precisely its strength, because it is what enables family law to adapt and respond to social change, in retro-active or pro-active ways, and it is what enables courts to justify decisions in each particular case. However, the inherent indeterminacy of the welfare principle also permits legal decision-making to borrow from, and contribute to, prevailing ideologies about what is "good" for children which, in turn, involves more or less implicit prescriptions for what "good" parenting is or should be. These ideologies, in part, derive from (as well as contribute to) child welfare ideas in child welfare science which have been taken up by the courts as influential in determining the outcomes of cases (see Sales *et al.*, 1992; Dingwall and Eekelaar, 1986; King and Piper, 1995).

[18]   See James and Prout (1990) for discussion of the ways in which particular visions of childhood have been socially constructed in different historical and social circumstances. In relation to law, see Mason and Steadman (1997).

[19]   On the "moral" concerns of developmental psychology, see Rose (1990); Burman (1994).

[20]   It should be noted that this principle related only to fathers who were or who had been married. "Illegitimate" children were the sole responsibility of their mothers.

[21]   The Guardianship of Infants Act 1925; the Guardianship Act 1973 (see n.17 above).

[22]   This point was first made by Mnookin (1975). See also Alston (1994); Day Sclater (1998); Eekelaar (1994b); McWhinney (1997); Parker (1994); Trinder (1997). See also Jonathan Herring (Chapter 5 below).

Since the early 1970s, the time at which married mothers attained equal legal status with married fathers, research on the "effects" of divorce on children has burgeoned,[23] and now constitutes a vast literature. From the early work in which divorce was characterised in terms of "loss" to the child, through subsequent work which emphasised, not loss, but the "quality" of the child's relationships with both parents, to the most recent emphasis on the detrimental effects of parental "conflict", we can see evidence of particular constructions of "risk" and "harm" being made in this research, as well as in legal practice.[24] These constructions are important, because the discourses of risk and harm position children in particular ways; as Piper (1996) argues, children are positioned as the vulnerable "victims" of divorce. Crucially, however, this positioning of children has implications, not only for what "parents" do, but also for what they *are*.

As Kaganas (1999) points out, the "risk" to children was once (in the 1970s and early 1980s) posed in terms of "father absence" after divorce; the risk could be alleviated if the child could be ensured frequent and continuing contact with the absent father. More recently, the risks have been re-construed as greatest if the parents cannot maintain continuing and harmonious relationships with each other (see Lord Chancellor's Department, 1993, 1995). Significantly, for our purposes, there are powerful moral prescriptions implicit in these constructions of risk, prescriptions that participate in the discursive constructions of who and what "parents" are.

It may indeed be ironic that the very principle of gender-neutrality (in the 1973 Guardianship Act) that gave mothers equal rights with fathers over their children, is the same principle which, more recently, has been seen as undermining the position of mothers *vis-à-vis* their male partners (Brophy, 1985; Smart, 1989; Sevenhuijsen, 1992; Hooper, 1994). What is at stake here is a changing conception of the respective roles of mothers and fathers *as parents*, which has a particular significance in the context of the changing family patterns that characterise late-modern industrialised societies.[25] As Mavis Maclean and Martin Richards point out in Chapter 14 below, over the last thirty years or so there has been an increasing tendency for marriage and reproduction to be separated, such that a significant proportion of children are now either conceived outside of marriage or spend some time in a lone parent household. These developments have given rise to acute social anxieties, some of which have been expressed as fears about the "decline of the family" and its supposed impact on social stability more generally[26] and some of which have been manifested in attempts to mitigate the alleged detrimental consequences for children.

[23] For the most recent review of British research, see Rodgers and Pryor (1998).

[24] See Kaganas (1999).

[25] For a summary of these changing patterns, see Coote *et al.* (1994). For a discussion of these changes in the context of family policy, see Day Sclater and Piper (1999); Day Sclater (1999).

[26] See, for example, Morgan (1996) who argues that the high divorce rate in Britain threatens "civilisation" itself.

Family law has made some attempt to respond to these changes and the anxieties they have produced. Most notably in the Children Act 1989, the Child Support Act 1991 and the Family Law Act 1996, we can see evidence of a policy response which attempts to contain the most threatening effects of social change (Smart, 1997; Day Sclater and Piper, 1999). Smart argues that family law has attempted to address the issues raised by the changing nature of "the family" by introducing provisions which seek to ensure the emotional and financial commitment of fathers to their children. In this process, a new construction of fatherhood has emerged, in which fathers are positioned as necessary not only as financial providers but also as practical carers and emotional nurturers. James and Richards (1999), however, take issue with Smart on the grounds that she fails sufficiently to recognise the importance of children as social actors and that many of the arguments in these debates are made from an adult-centred perspective that fails to accord proper agency to children and continues to "marginalise" them; children, they say, need to be accorded full significance as a social group and recognised as a valid unit of analysis.

However, the new construction of fathers as performing an essential parenting role, that is implicit in these arguments, is not without its problems. As Collier (1995) argues, the legal construction of "safe" familial masculinities exists in profound tension with the recognition that "normal" masculinities have their "dangerous" aspects.[27] Family law has sought to manage this tension, according to Collier, by making a distinction between the safe "familial man" and "dangerous masculinities", where the dichotomy serves to obscure the problematic nature of masculinity *per se*; family law, he says, assumes that "being a family man" precludes any propensity towards violence.[28] Further, the "new man" ideology sits uneasily both with dominant constructions of masculinity, as the Other of caring, relational, nurturing femininity,[29] and with the continuing absence of opportunities for many men to put the new fatherhood into practice.[30]

Importantly, for our purposes, the implications for the meaning of parenting which both emerge from and support these legal changes are closely linked with broader ideologies about masculinity and femininity, motherhood and fatherhood, and childhood. Crucially, these developments have been closely paralleled by changing ideas about children's "needs". Despite the large number of research studies that have been carried out on children and divorce, the findings of the research are by no means unequivocal. This is unsurprising given the existence of a huge range of studies, from different jurisdictions, employing

---

[27] For example, domestic violence and child abuse.

[28] On the question of the relations between domestic violence and child contact arrangements, see Hester and Radford (1996). On the relations between domestic violence and child abuse, see Kelly (1994). On the relations between masculinities and violence, see Hester *et al* (1996).

[29] See n.8 above.

[30] For recent British research on fathers post-divorce, see Simpson *et al.* (1995).

different methodologies and conceptual frameworks.[31] But one common thread which runs throughout the mainstream research is that of the construction of the child as "at risk" of "harm" on divorce,[32] a construction that is reflected in family law (Piper, 1996).[33]

Importantly, for our purposes, the new construction of men as parents, both in law and in research, depends very heavily on a construction of the child as vulnerable;[34] the new paternal masculinity which Collier (1995) talks about is a presence which children need, and without it they will suffer.[35] What we can perhaps see here is a broadening of the concept of the "psychological" parent,[36] coupled with a range of new legal provisions designed to facilitate men's contribution to family life. The concept of "parental responsibility" in the Children Act 1989, however, has more wide-reaching consequences.

The Children Act 1989 was passed in a climate of widespread social anxiety about "the decline of the family",[37] often expressed as concern about the social consequences of increasing numbers of "fatherless" children.[38] One aspect of former Prime Minister John Major's "back to basics" ideology was a concern to effect a return to the "traditional" family; lone motherhood was denigrated, and a range of social problems were "blamed" on the demise of "family values".[39] In this context, new formulations of children's "needs" emerged, which family law attempted to meet; foremost was the "need" for children to have and maintain relationships with both parents, and to have parents who, even when separated, could co-operate over the arrangements for their children. A range of developments in legislation and case law sought, therefore, to facilitate effective and

---

[31] For discussion of the conceptual and methodological difficulties of such studies see Wallerstein (1991); Rodgers and Pryor (1998).

[32] As Gately and Schwebel (1991) note, most investigators have employed pathogenic or stress models in their research, which has prevented them from explaining positive outcomes. See also Hetherington (1989).

[33] As several commentators have pointed out, it is incongruous, to say the least, that the Family Law Act 1996 contains no provisions which attempt either to safeguard children's interests (Piper, 1994; Richards, 1995, 1996) or to listen to their voices (Piper, 1999) or to further their rights (Roche, 1999).

[34] This construction is reflected also in popluar culture, most notably in films that feature fathers in nurturing roles. See for example, the films *Three Men and a Baby, Three Men and a Little Lady, Mrs Doubtfire* and *Junior*. These films, on first impression, are narratives that challenge traditional parenting roles but, on closer inspection, can be seen as supporting traditional gender divisions in the nuclear family.

[35] The parallel here with Bowlby's ideas about "maternal deprivation" is obvious.

[36] The idea of the primacy of the "psychological parent" in relation to divorce found expression in the work of Goldstein, Freud and Solnit (1973). For criticisms of this work, see Richards (1986b) and Freeman (1997).

[37] Such rhetoric is, of course, not peculiar to our own age.

[38] See, for example, Dennis and Erdos (1992). For a similar argument in an American context, see Blankenhorn (1995).

[39] Whilst the current Prime Minister, Tony Blair, has avoided the most obvious pitfalls of a "back to basics" policy, the recent Government Paper *Supporting Families*, evinces the continuing power of this rhetoric. This discussion paper treads a difficult path between, on the one hand, idealising so-called traditional family structures whilst, on the other, attempting to accord some respect to the diversity of family forms in a multi-cultural and pluralistic Britain.

co-operative co-parenting relationships. Smart (1997) argues that these developments amount to "social engineering" and were an attempt on the part of the state to reinstate the "traditional" patriarchal family. Moreover, she argues, such attempts would be doomed to failure; the changes in family patterns which we have witnessed over the last thirty years or so are linked to broader political, social, economic and ideological changes which cannot simply be reversed. As Hale (1997) also argues, it is neither possible nor desirable to turn back the clock.

There is a sense in which, however, even if family law cannot facilitate any reversal in the fortunes of "the family", it nevertheless can be instrumental in managing and containing the familial consequences of social change; this is made possible by altering the dominant discourses[40] in which concepts of "parent" and "child" have meaning. The Family Law Act 1996 arguably represents one manifestation of such discursive management; in so far as it is built upon the presumption of father-involvement, and in so far as it provides procedures for facilitating co-operative co-parenting, it represents the means by which the whole concept of "family" can be broadened so as to accommodate the facts of social change. The Family Law Act facilitates the emergence of the "bi-nuclear" family (Ahrons, 1994), a "new" family for our times, in which married mothers and fathers attain the status of gender-neutral parents with automatic and inalienable "parental responsibility" to be exercised for the good of the child. What we can see here are close linkages between new concepts of "family", that address the anxieties generated by ideas about the "decline of the family"; new concepts of "parents", that address the anxieties generated by "fatherless families"; and new concepts of "children" as the vulnerable victims of "family breakdown", around which the new family form coheres (Day Sclater, 1999; Day Sclater and Piper, 1999).

As Hale (1997) reminds us, marriage is no longer essential to the legal concept of "family"; traditionally, it was through marriage that a man established his links to his children, but the increasing separation between marriage and parenthood has rendered it necessary for fathers' relationships with children to be put on a different footing. Since the Family Law Reform Act of 1987, unmarried fathers have had the opportunity to share parental responsibility with mothers (Hale, 1997). As Ros Pickford points out in Chapter 8 below, however, most do not enter into Parental Responsibility Agreements or seek Parental Responsibility Orders unless there is a dispute, and many simply assume that, as "natural" parents, they have all the rights and duties which are accorded to those who are married. Legislation to give certain categories of unmarried fathers automatic parental responsibility has recently been under discussion and its effect would be to broaden still further the concept of "father" that attracts legal status and formal recognition.

Developments in the technologies and procedures for DNA testing, used to establish paternity, have undoubtedly contributed to the new constructions of

---

[40] On the relations between discourse and social change, see Fairclough (1992).

fathers in biological rather than social terms. As Neale and Smart (1999) argue, the newly emerging model of family life, which the Family Law Act supports, is one which venerates biological kin ties and has entailed a refashioning of the legal status of biological parenthood; parenthood has begun to supersede marriage as the bedrock of "the family" and as the central mechanism for the legal regulation of domestic life. If marriage is no longer for life, then (biological) parenthood is. Biology now provides the main basis upon which claims to parental status rest.[41] The increasing availability of genetic testing for a range of inherited conditions, as well as for paternity, and the increasing visibility of the micro-structures which make up our bodies, have given added impetus to the salience of "biology" and "genetics" in relation to the question of "what is a parent?"

However, these developments exist in considerable tension with others that have broadened the concept of "parent" as a social entity. For example, the Children Act 1989 increased the circumstances in which people who are not biologically related to the child may obtain parental responsibility through Section 8 orders.[42] Law, it seems, has increasingly taken account of the role and status of "social" parents, which raises difficult questions, such as those discussed by Andrew Bainham in Chapter 2 below, about the relationships between "parent" as a legal status and the rights and responsibilities of those who exercise a range of parental functions in different circumstances. Should there be any difference in legal status between "social" and "genetic" parents? If so, on what basis should this be made, and what should be its consequences? The fragmentation of "parent" into "social" versus "natural" (biological or genetic)[43] thus raises legal dilemmas and ethical problems. These are compounded by developments in biomedical technologies that look set to confound even apparently simple decisions about the biological or genetic basis for decisions about parenthood to be made.

As Martin Johnson shows in Chapter 3, no sooner have ideas about parents begun to take on a biological hue, than developments in reproductive biotechnologies seem likely to disrupt the new certainties. For example, we now have the technological means to create children with multiple biological parents, not just two oppositely sexed ones. Whilst a recent report[44] has rejected outright human cloning for reproductive purposes, it has not set its face against cell

---

[41] However, the Human Fertilisation and Embryology Act 1990 provides for legal parenthood status even where no genetic relationship exists. See Martin Johnson (Chapter 3 below) and Stuart Bridge (Chapter 4 below).

[42] This possibility was, in practice, already present in the wardship jurisdiction of the High Court, although "parental responsibility" is a concept which emerged in relation to the Children Act.

[43] There are numerous difficulties associated purely with the terminology employed in these debates. Importantly, terms like "natural", "biological" and even "genetic" are inherently ambiguous. See Andrew Bainham (Chapter 2 below) and Martin Johnson (Chapter 3 below).

[44] See the joint report on *Cloning Issues in Reproduction, Science and Medicine* by the Human Genetics Advisory Commission and the Human Fertilisation and Embryology Authority (December 1998).

nucleus replacement techniques for the treatment of serious illness. The report recommends keeping the door open for these potential benefits, thereby extending the purposes for which embryo research can be carried out under close regulation in the United Kingdom. It is understood that the situation will be re-examined again in five years' time. There may currently be little public support for human reproductive cloning but, crucially, the technologies will continue to be developed and refined, and the potential benefits of such techniques, for example in connection with infertility, are likely to continue to provide a basis for further argument and debate. In this context, the question of "what is a parent?" will be raised in yet another new guise.

The contributors to this book tackle these difficult questions, and address their implications for law, policy and practice. The book is divided into three main parts. Part I addresses the issue of defining parenthood; here the issue of "genetic" versus "social" parenthood looms large. Andrew Bainham opens the debate with a careful exploration of the distinction between being a "parent" and possessing "parental responsibility", one that is seen to have far-reaching implications for family law. Stuart Bridge shows that, where a child is born as a result of approved assisted reproduction techniques, issues of defining who the parents are or should be, and deciding who should exercise parental responsibility, are fraught with problems that the law has hardly begun to address. Martin Johnson shows how accepted notions of "biological" or "genetic" parents are problematised by innovative biomedical technologies that offer a range of new possibilities for reproducing human life. Jonathan Herring explores the ways in which the "welfare principle" in family law can operate, in practice, to promote parents' interests; particular interpretations of the principle made by the courts also help to define who parents are and what they do. Juliet Mitchell and Jack Goody discuss how a particular vision of parenting, as gendered practice, emerged in the context of the wartime evacuation of children, and how this ideology was reflected in the work of psychologists at the time. As we have seen, the legacy of these ideas continues to structure how we think about who parents are and the contributions they make to the development of children.

Part II examines a range of contemporary issues in parenting. Ros Pickford discusses unmarried fathers, and presents the arguments for and against men in this category being given the same automatic parental responsibility as is conferred on all birth mothers. Susan Golombok considers the widely debated issue of lesbian and gay parents; increasingly we hear calls for some recognition of the diversity in family forms, but there have been widespread doubts about the "effects" on children's development of being brought up by lesbian or gay parents. Susan Golombok reports on the research that has been done, and concludes that these children fare no better and no worse than others who have heterosexual parents. Rachel Cook, in her chapter, examines the issue of "donating parenthood", and discusses a range of dilemmas raised by gamete donation and surrogacy. Loraine Gelsthorpe, discusses parents and criminal children. She traces the ascent and demise of a welfare perspective in the juvenile justice system, and considers the provisions of the Crime and Disorder Act 1998 that hold parents accountable for crimes committed by their children. Bridget Lindley looks at the vexed question of the relations between parents and the state. Public law provisions in relation to "the family" must reflect and maintain the difficult balance between parental autonomy, on the one hand, and the imperatives of child protection, on the other. There will inevitably be some tension between the two, and the principle of "partnership" in the public law provisions of the Children Act is frequently challenged as local authorities seek to protect children at risk. Allison James discusses the frequently neglected topic of what children themselves think about parents. Parenting, as usually conceived, she argues is seen as something done *to* children; it is an adult-centric concept, and its employment in law and in research studies reflects a particular view of children, as lacking in human agency and as deprived of a voice in decisions which affect their lives. Together, the chapters in this section cover a range of contemporary situations where the notion of "parent" is contested and shifting and, importantly, where its fluid meanings are closely interwoven with changing constructions of children and childhood.

In the final part on parenting and divorce, the contributors explore the social, legal and psychological issues that arise in the context of divorce. Margaret Ely, Wendy Solomou and their colleagues, drawing on data from an MRC study on healthy ageing, consider the longer term impact of divorce and remarriage on the parent-child relationship in later life. Their work confirms earlier findings that the disruptions in kinship ties on divorce have a long-term impact on patterns of social contact and support, and they discuss the interrelationships among a range of factors that lead to different outcomes. Mavis Maclean and Martin Richards address the complex issue of the changing patterns of public intervention in the relationship between parents and their children when a marriage ends. Drawing on recent empirical data, they identify tensions in policy development between the wish to affirm the responsibility of individual parents for their children and the concern to support family members through the transitions that divorce presents. They then consider the implications of their analysis for the implementation of the private law provisions of the Family Law Act 1996; they look to the future, and at the ways in which information meetings, mediation and parenting plans can best be organised to ensure that divorcing families get the support they need. Finally, Shelley Day Sclater and Candida Yates discuss how mothers and fathers negotiate the conflicting demands that divorce places upon them. Using extracts from case study data, they examine the ways in which men's and women's accounts of post-divorce parenting are gendered, and they explore the psychological constellations that are implied by the gendered interpretations which mothers and fathers make.

Together, the contributions to this book explore a range of issues raised by social and demographic change, legal reform and biotechnological advances; these developments all impact on how we think about parents, and how we see fit best to provide for the work that parents do. The chapters show the complex inter-dependencies among notions of parents, family and children; they question our taken-for-granted assumptions, and reveal the fluid and contingent nature of contemporary answers to the question "what is a parent?"

REFERENCES

Abbott, P. and Wallace, C., *An Introduction to Sociology: Feminist Perspectives* (London, Routledge, 1997).

Ahrons, C., *The Good Divorce: Keeping Your Family Together When Your Marriage Falls Apart* (London, Bloomsbury, 1994).

Almond, B., "Parenthood: social construct or fact of nature?" in D. Morgan and G. Douglas (eds.), *Constituting Families: A Study in Governance* (Stuttgart, Franz Steiner Verlag, 1994).

Alston, P., "The best interests principle: towards a reconciliation of culture and human rights" (1994) 8 *International Journal of Law and the Family* 1–25.

Backett, K. C., *Mothers and Fathers* (Basingstoke, Macmillan, 1982).

Blankenhorn, D., *Fatherless America: Confronting Our Most Urgent Social Problem* (New York, Basic Books, 1995).

Bowlby, J., *Attachment and Loss, Attachment, Volume 1* (Harmondsworth, Pelican, 1971).

Bowlby, J., *Attachment and Loss, Separation: Anxiety and Anger, Volume 2* (Harmondsworth, Pelican, 1975).

Bowlby, J., *Attachment and Loss, Loss: Sadness and Depression, Volume 3* (Harmondsworth, Pelican, 1981).

Brannen, J. and Moss, P., "Fathers in dual-earner households—through mothers' eyes" in C. Lewis and M. O'Brien (eds.), *Reassessing Fatherhood: New Observations on Fathers and the Modern Family* (London, Sage, 1987).

Brannen, J. and O'Brien, M. (eds.), *Children in Families* (London, Falmer, 1995).

Brophy, J., "Child care and the growth of power: the status of mothers in custody disputes" in J. Brophy and C. Smart (eds.), *Women in Law: Explorations in Law, Family and Sexuality* (London, RKP, 1985).

Brown, G. and Harris, T., *Social Origins of Depression* (London, Tavistock, 1978).

Burman, E., *Deconstructing Developmental Psychology* (London, Routledge, 1994).

Chodorow, N., *The Reproduction of Mothering: Psychoanalysis and the Sociology of Gender* (Berkeley, CA., University of California Press, 1978).

Collier, R., *Masculinity, Law and the Family* (London, Routledge, 1995).

Connell, R. W., *Gender and Power* (Cambridge, Polity Press, 1987).

Connell, R.W., *Masculinities* (Cambridge, Polity Press, 1995).

Coote, A., Harman, H. and Hewitt, H., "Changing patterns of family life" in J. Eekelaar and M. Maclean (eds.), *A Reader on Family Law* (Oxford, Oxford University Press, 1994).

Day Sclater, S., "Children and Divorce: Hidden Agendas?" paper presented at the Children and Social Exclusion Conference, University of Hull, March 1998.

Day Sclater, *Divorce: A Psychosocial Study* (Aldershot, Ashgate, forthcoming).

Day Sclater, S. and Piper, C., "The Family Law Act in context" in S. Day Sclater and C. Piper (eds.), *Undercurrents of Divorce* (Aldershot, Ashgate, forthcoming).

Deech, R., "The rights of fathers: social and biological concepts of parenthood" in J. Eekelaar and P. Sarcevic (eds.), *Parenthood in Modern Society: Legal and Social Issues for the Twenty-First Century* (London, Martinus Nijhoff, 1993).

Dennis, N. and Erdos, G., *Families Without Fatherhood* (London, Institute of Economic Affairs, 1992).

Dingwall, R. and Eekelaar, J., "Judgements of Solomon: psychology and family law" in M. Richards and P. Light (eds.), *Children of Social Worlds* (Cambridge, Polity, 1986).

Dinnerstein, D., *The Rocking of the Cradle and the Ruling of the World* (London, Souvenir Press, 1978).

Doggett, M.E., *Marriage, Wife-Beating and the Law in Victorian England* (London, Weidenfeld and Nicholson, 1992).

Eekelaar, J. and Sarcevic O. (eds.), *Parenthood in Modern Society: Legal and Social Issues for the Twenty-First Century* (London, Martinus Nijhoff, 1993).

Eekelaar, J. (1994a), "Parenthood, Social Engineering and Rights" in D. Morgan and G. Douglas (eds.), *Constituting Families: A Study in Governance* (Stuttgart, Franz Steiner Verlag, 1994).

Eekelaar, J. (1994b), "The interests of the child and the child's wishes: the role of dynamic self-determination" (1994) 8 *International Journal of Law and the Family* 42–61.

Elliott, F. R., *Gender, Family and Society* (Basingstoke, Macmillan, 1996).

Elshtain, J. B., *Public Man, Private Woman* (Princeton, NJ., Princeton University Press, 1981).

Fairclough, N., *Discourse and Social Change* (Cambridge, Polity Press, 1992).

Finch, J. and Summerfield, P., "Social reconstruction and the emergence of the companionate marriage" in D. Clark (ed.), *Marriage, Domestic Life and Social Change* (London, Routledge, 1991).

Firestone, S., *The Dialectic of Sex: The Case for Feminist Revolution* (New York, William Morrow, 1970).

Fox Harding, L., *Family, State and Social Policy* (Basingstoke, Macmillan, 1996).

Freeman, M. D. A. (ed.), *State, Law and the Family: Critical Perspectives* (London, Tavistock/Sweet and Maxwell, 1984).

Freeman, M. D. A., "The best interests of the child? Is it in the best interests of children?" (1997) 11 *International Journal of Law, Policy and the Family* 360–388.

Friedan, B., *The Feminine Mystique* (Harmondsworth, Penguin, 1963).

Gately, D. W. and Schwebel, A. I., "The challenge model of children's adjustment to parental divorce: explaining favourable postdivorce outcomes in children" (1991) 5 *Journal of Family Psychology* 60–81.

Gavron, H., *The Captive Wife: Conflicts of Housebound Wives* (Harmondsworth, Penguin, 1966).

Goldstein, J., Freud, A. and Solnit, A. J., *Beyond the Best Interests of the Child* (New York, Free Press, 1973).

Goldthorpe, J. E., *Family Life in Western Societies* (Cambridge, Cambridge University Press, 1987).

Hale, Dame B., "Private Lives and Public Duties: What is Family Law For?" 8th ESRC Annual Lecture, Economic and Social Research Council, Swindon, 1997.

Hall, L.A., *Hidden Anxieties: Male Sexuality, 1900–1950* (Cambridge, Polity Press, 1991).

Hester, M. and Radford, L., *Domestic Violence and Child Contact Arrangements in England and Denmark* (Bristol, The Policy Press, 1996).

Hester, M., Kelly, L. and Radford, J., *Women, Violence and Male Power* (Buckingham, Open University Press, 1996).

Hetherington, E.M., "Coping with family transitions: winners, losers and survivors" (1989) 60 *Child Development* 1–14.

Hooper, C. A., "Do families need fathers? The impact of divorce on children" in A. Mullender and R. Morley (eds.), *Children Living with Domestic Violence* (London, Whiting and Birch, 1994).

Ingleby, D., "The psychology of child psychology" in M.P.M. Richards (ed.), *The Integration of a Child into a Social World* (Cambridge, Cambridge University Press, 1974).

James, A. and Prout, A. A. (eds.), *Constructing and Reconstructing Childhood* (London, Falmer Press, 1990).

James, A. and Richards, M., "Sociological perspectives, family policy, family law and children: adult thinking and sociological tinkering" (1999) *Journal of Social Welfare and Family Law* 23–39.

Kaganas, F., "Contact, conflict and risk" in S. Day Sclater and C. Piper (eds.), *Undercurrents of Divorce* (Aldershot, Ashgate, 1999).

Kelly, L., "The interconnectedness of domestic violence and child abuse: challenges for research, policy and practice" in A. Mullender and R. Morley (eds.), *Children Living with Domestic Violence* (London, Whiting and Birch, 1994).

Kempe, C. H. and Helfer, R. E. (eds), *The Battered Child* (Chicago, University of Chicago Press, 1968).

Kempe, R. S. and Kempe, C. H., *Child Abuse* (London, Fontana, 1978).

Kempe, C. H., Silverman, F. N., Steele, B. B. *et al.*, "The battered child syndrome" (1962) 181 *Journal of the American Medical Association* 17–24.

King, M. and Piper, C., *How the Law Thinks About Children*, 2nd edn. (Aldershot, Arena, 1995).

Laing, R. D. (1960), *The Divided Self* (London, Tavistock, Harmondsworth, Pelican, 1965).

Laing, R. D., *The Politics of Experience and the Bird of Paradise* (Harmondsworth, Penguin, 1967).

Lasch, C., *Haven in Heartless World* (New York, Basic Books, 1977).

Lewis, C., *Becoming a Father* (Milton Keynes, Open University Press, 1986).

Lewis, C. and O'Brien, M. (eds.), *Reassessing Fatherhood: New Observations on Fathers and the Modern Family* (London, Sage, 1987).

Lord Chancellor's Department, *Looking to the Future: Mediation and the Ground for Divorce, A Consultation Paper* (London, HMSO, 1993).

Lord Chancellor's Department, *Looking to the Future: Mediation and the Ground for Divorce, The Government's Proposals* (London, HMSO, 1995).

Lupton, D. and Barclay, L., *Constructing Fatherhood: Discourses and Experiences* (London, Sage, 1997).

Mac an Ghaill, M., *Understanding Masculinities* (Buckingham, Open University Press, 1996).

Maidment, S., *Child Custody and Divorce* (London, Croom Helm, 1984).

Mason, J. and Steadman, B., "The significance of the conceptualisation of childhood for child protection policy" (1997) 46 *Family Matters* 31–36.

McWhinney, R., "*Parentes Meundi*—in the best interests of our children" (1997) 35 *Family and Conciliation Courts Review* 388–392.

Millett, K., *Sexual Politics* (1971, reprinted London, Virago, 1977).

Mitchell, J., *The Longest Revolution: On Feminism, Literature and Psychoanalysis* (London, Virago, 1966).

Mnookin, R., "Child custody adjudication: judicial functions in the face of indeterminacy" (1975) 39 *Law and Contemporary Problems* 226–293.

Morgan, P., "Family crisis affects us all" in C. Donnellan (ed.) *Marriage and Divorce: Issues for the Nineties* (Cambridge, Independence Educational Publishers, 1996).

Neale, B. and Smart, C., "In whose best interests? Theorising family life after separation and divorce" in S. Day Sclater and C. Piper (eds.), *Undercurrents of Divorce* (Aldershot, Ashgate, 1999).

Oakley, A., *The Sociology of Housework* (London, Martin Robertson, 1974).

Parker, S., "The best interests of the child: principles and problems" (1994) 8 *International Journal of Law and the Family* 26–41.

Piper, C., "Looking to the future for children" (1994) 6 *Journal of Child Law* 98–102.

Piper, C., "Divorce reform and the image of the child" (1996) 23 *Journal of Law and Society* 364–382.

Piper, C., "The wishes and feelings of the child" in S. Day Sclater and C. Piper (eds.), *Undercurrents of Divorce* (Aldershot, Ashgate, 1999).

Pizzey, E., *Scream Quietly or the Neighbours Will Hear* (Harmondsworth, Penguin, 1974).

Raymond, J., "Female friendship: contra Chodorow and Dinnerstein" (1986) 1 *Hypatia* 44–45.

Richards, M., "Introduction" in M. Richards and P. Light (eds.), *Children of Social Worlds* (Cambridge, Polity, 1986a).

Richards, M., "Behind the best interests of the child: an examination of the arguments of Goldstein, Freud and Solnit" (1986) *Journal of Social Welfare Law* 77–95 (1986b).

Richards, M., "But what about the children? Some reflections on the divorce White Paper" (1995) 7 *Child and Family Law Quarterly* 223–227.

Richards, M., "The socio-legal support for divorcing parents and their children" in B. Bernstein and J. Brannen (eds.), *Children, Research and Policy* (London, Taylor and Francis, 1996).

Riley, D., *War in the Nursery:Theories of the Child and Mother* (London, Virago, 1983).

Roberts, E., *Women and Families: An Oral History, 1940–1970* (Oxford, Blackwell, 1995).

Roche, J., "The politics of children's rights" in J. Brannen and M. O'Brien (eds.), *Children in Families* (London, Falmer, 1995).

Roche, J., "Children and divorce: a private affair?" in S. Day Sclater and C. Piper (eds.), *Undercurrents of Divorce* (Aldershot, Ashgate, 1999).

Rodger, J. J., *Family Life and Social Control: A Sociological Perspective* (Basingstoke, Macmillan, 1996).

Rodgers, B. and Pryor, J., *Divorce and Separation: The Outcomes for Children* (York, Joseph Rowntree Foundation, 1998).

Rose, N., *Governing the Soul* (London, Routledge, 1990).

Rossi, A., "On the reproduction of mothering: a methodological debate" (1981) 6 *Signs* 497–500.

Sales, B., Manber, R. and Rohman, L., "Social science research and child-custody deci-
    sion making" (1992) 1 *Applied and Preventive Psychology* 23–40.
Segal, L., "A feminist looks at the family" in J. Muncie, M. Wetherell, R. Dallos *et al.*
    (eds.), *Understanding the Family* (London, Sage, 1994).
Sevenhuijsen, S., "The gendered juridification of parenthood" (1992) 1 *Social and Legal
    Studies* 71–83.
Simpson, B., McCarthy, P. and Walker, J., *Being There: Fathers After Divorce*
    (Newcastle Upon Tyne, Relate Centre for Family Studies, 1995).
Smart, C., "Power and the politics of child custody" in C. Smart and S. Sevenhuijsen
    (eds.), *Child Custody and the Politics of Gender* (London, Routledge, 1989).
Smart, C., "Wishful thinking and harmful tinkering: sociological reflections on family
    policy" (1997) 26 *Journal of Social Policy* 301–321.
Smart, C. and Sevenhuijsen, S. (eds.), *Child Custody and the Politics of Gender* (London,
    Routledge, 1989).
Stanworth, M. (ed.), *Reproductive Technologies: Gender, Motherhood and Medicine*
    (Cambridge, Polity Press, 1987).
Stone, L., *The Family, Sex and Marriage in England 1500–1800* (London, Weidenfeld
    and Nicholson, 1977).
Thom, D., "Wishes, anxieties, play and gestures: child guidance in inter-war England" in
    R. Cooter (ed.), *In the Name of the Child* (London, Routledge, 1990).
Tong, R., *Feminist Thought* (London, Routledge, 1989).
Trinder, L., "Competing constructions of childhood: children's rights and children's
    wishes in divorce" (1997) 19 *Journal of Social Welfare and Family* Law 291–305.
Urwin, C. and Sharland, E., "From bodies to minds in childcare literature: advice to par-
    ents in inter-war Britain" in R. Cooter (ed.), *In the Name of the Child* (London,
    Routledge, 1990).
Wallerstein, J. S., "The long-term effects of divorce on children: a review" (1991) 30
    Journal of the American Academy of Child and Adolescent Psychiatry 349–360.
Wilmott, P. and Young, M., *Family and Class in a London Suburb* (London, Routledge
    and Kegan Paul, 1960).
Winnicott, D., "Anxieties associated with insecurity" (1952, reprinted in *Collected
    Papers: Through Pediatrics to Psychoanalysis*, London, Tavistock, 1958).
Winnicott, D., "Ego distortion in terms of the true and false self" (1960, reprinted in *The
    Maturational Process and the Facilitating Environment*, London, Hogarth Press,
    1965).
Winnicott, D., *The Child, the Family and the Outside World* (Harmondsworth, Penguin,
    1964).
Young, M. and Wilmott, P., *Family and Kinship in East London* (1957, revised edn.,
    Harmondsworth, Penguin, 1962).

Part I

Defining Parenthood

2

Parentage, Parenthood and Parental Responsibility: Subtle, Elusive Yet Important Distinctions

ANDREW BAINHAM

1. INTRODUCTION

What is a parent? Judge De Meyer, giving judgment in the European Court of Human Rights in 1997, was quite confident that he knew the answer to this question.[1] The issue was whether the United Kingdom had violated rights to family life and had discriminated against a female-to-male transsexual (X) in refusing to register him as the father of a child (Z) born to his female partner (Y) following insemination by donor sperm. In holding that the UK authorities had not breached the Convention he said that the "principles and rules are quite simple . . . It is self-evident that a person who is manifestly not the father of a child has no right to be recognised as her father". So, the implication is, we all know a father when we see one—it is the man who has the genetic link with the child—the man whose sperm brings about the child's conception. The difficulty with this view is all too apparent and several other judges in the European Court drew attention to it.[2] If X had been born a biological *male* there would have been no question that he could have been registered as the father under the status provisions of the Human Fertilisation and Embryology Act 1990. This treats as the *legal* father of a child the man who undergoes licensed treatment together with a woman who conceives with the use of donated gametes.[3] The result seems to be that to qualify as a "father" (and hence a "parent") it is not necessary to be the genetic *father* but it is necessary to start life as a biological *male*. This view of the legal position of transsexuals is open to question but is beyond the scope of the present discussion.[4]

My concern in this chapter is whether it is just possible that Judge De Meyer was right after all—that being a parent is a genetic notion and that the mistake

---

[1] *X, Y and Z v The United Kingdom* (1997) 24 EHRR 143.
[2] See particularly the dissenting judgment of Judge Foighel.
[3] 1990 Act s. 28(3).
[4] For further discussion of the implications of this decision for transsexuals see Bainham (1997).

we have made as a society is to treat or regard as *parents* many social carers of children who lack this genetic connection.

Before examining the issues it is necessary to say something about the terminology used in this chapter. Judges and legal commentators frequently use the terms *genetic parent* and *biological parent* interchangeably as if they were synonymous. There are frequent references also to the *natural parent* and the *blood tie*. All these expressions have been used to distinguish those who have a genetic connection with a child from those who do not but may be caring for that child. The latter are usually described as *social parents*. The primary thrust of this chapter is to explore the legal significance of this distinction and, in this sense, any of these expressions would do equally well. However, it must be acknowledged that there are scientifically important distinctions to be drawn between the existence of a *genetic link* and what may be thought to be the wider components of *biological parentage*. These components are analysed in depth by Martin Johnson (in Chapter 3 below). The distinction between what is *biological* and what is *genetic* may be particularly important in the context of assisted reproduction.

Distinctions may also need to be drawn between *mothers* (who will usually, but not always, satisfy all the components of *biological parentage*) and *fathers* (who will frequently, but not always, have only a *genetic* connection with a child). Since the key arguments in this chapter surround the presence or absence of a genetic link, the expression *genetic parent* is generally preferred to that of *biological* or *natural parent*. But the reader should bear in mind that many *genetic parents* will clearly be *biological parents* in the wider sense identified by Johnson. Further, in the case of mothers, the various techniques of assisted reproduction can result in the four components of biological parentage being shared by more than one woman (most obviously the genetic and gestational components). In these instances careful thought needs to be given to the legal significance which is attached to each of these distinctive contributions.

I shall explore these issues by looking at the subtleties inherent in the concepts of *parentage, parenthood* and *parental responsibility*. One of my aims is to draw attention to the incongruity between the social and legal uses of these terms. In particular I suggest that in social usage a meaningful distinction can be drawn between the ideas of *parentage* and *parenthood* which is not currently reflected in the law. Legislation does not use the term *parenthood* as such and rarely uses *parentage*,[5] preferring instead to concentrate on the concept of *being a parent*.[6] I speculate on whether there could be value in establishing separate legal concepts of *parentage* and *parenthood* as a means of recognising the distinctive

[5] Under Family Law Act 1986, s. 56 a person may apply to the court for, *inter alia*, "a declaration . . . that a person named in the application is or was his parent". Such declarations are referred to in the legislation, in the heading to the section, as "Declarations of Parentage".

[6] This is true, for example, of the Children Act 1989, the Adoption Act 1976 and the Child Support Act 1991, although under this last mentioned legislation it is possible to refer *disputes about parentage* (s. 26) to court for a *declaration of parentage* (s. 27). I am very grateful to Stuart Bridge for this insight.

interests which children have in establishing and sustaining links with genetic parents where the social parenting role is performed by someone else.

My chapter attempts to cut across the familiar debate about "genetic" versus "social" parenthood by focusing more closely on the above distinctions. It will be my contention that, with growing recognition of the child's fundamental right to knowledge of genetic origins,[7] it will be necessary to have a clear concept that gives expression to this link. Alongside this, I accept that there ought to be equally clear recognition of the significance and importance of what has been termed *social parenthood* to children and that this status must also be given proper weight in law. Increasingly the question will not be whether to *prefer* the genetic or social parent but how to accommodate *both* on the assumption that they both have distinctive contributions to make to the life of the child. In essence I shall argue that, as far as possible, the notion of *being a parent* should turn on a presumed or actual genetic connection with the child, leaving *parental responsibility* as the device for giving to *social parents* most but, crucially, not all of the status which attaches automatically to genetic parents—at least where the child is born to a married couple.[8] Thus, although it would remain perfectly usual to describe those performing the social role of parents as *social parents* they would usually not be *legal parents*. Put another way, the concept of *social parenthood* would embrace the legal powers and duties associated with *parental responsibility* and its exercise but not the wider legal status of *being a parent*.

A difficulty arises in relation to those instances in which the law has already gone beyond conferring *parental responsibility* on social parents and has indeed allowed them to become *legal parents*. This is true in both adoption and certain instances of assisted reproduction where the link between genetic and legal parenthood has been broken. It is here that I will suggest there might be some utility in separating out the concepts of *parenthood* and *parentage* in law. In short it might, in cases like adoption and assisted reproduction, be important to find two independent concepts which can, respectively, give effect to the legal status of, say, the adopters as parents and the child's interest, perhaps right, to a certain level of knowledge about and contact with the genetic parent. The former we might call *legal parenthood* and the latter *legal parentage*.

2. IS IT ALL JUST SEMANTICS?

An obvious question to pose at the outset is whether it really matters at all that someone is *called* a "parent" or not. Suppose, for example, that following

---

[7] See particularly United Nations Convention on the Rights of the Child, Article 7.

[8] Where a child is born to a married couple both will be *parents* and both will have *parental responsibility* Children Act 1989, s. 2(1)). Where the mother and father are unmarried they will both be *parents* but only the mother will, initially at least, have *parental responsibility* Children Act 1989, s. 2(2)).

divorce a mother sets up home with a man whom she may or may not marry. In due course the children come to regard this man as their father and they call him "Dad". He is regarded as the father of the children by friends and others in the community. The law cannot, and would not want to, attempt to prevent the step-father or cohabitant from being known *informally* as the parent of the children. But *formally* the position is quite different even though this may not be fully appreciated by those concerned (see Pickford, Chapter 8 below). "Dad" remains in law as merely the *social* father, in no stronger position than any other *de facto* carer of children. The *legal* father is the genetic, now divorced, father. A recent decision of the High Court brings out this distinction between *informal* and *formal* parenthood rather well.[9] A mother had, independently, changed the surname of the children without the knowledge or consent of the natural father. It was ordered that, although the mother had behaved unlawfully, the children could continue to be known informally by the new surname but the mother was prohibited from taking any steps to "cause, encourage or permit any person or body to use the new surname without the prior consent of the father or the court". In effect the continuing legal parental status of the natural father was preserved through his name when it came to official dealings with educational, medical authorities and other outsiders.

So *being a parent* is not just a matter of language but something which confers a legal status. It therefore becomes important to consider closely the precise legal significance of establishing maternity or paternity, the circumstances in which the law should confer the full status of parent and what this ought to entail and, likewise, the circumstances under which parental responsibility should be obtained and how this might differ from being a legal parent. But, before doing so, it may be helpful to compare the way in which we generally use the expressions *parentage, parenthood* and *parental responsibility* with their technical legal uses.

3. SOCIAL AND LEGAL USAGES

(a) Being a parent: parentage and parenthood

We sometimes speak of the *parentage* of children. It is quite common to find legal commentators using the expression *parentage* interchangeably with *parenthood*. This is perfectly understandable since, as noted above, the law does not distinguish between the two and legislation instead usually refers to *parents* or, occasionally, to *mothers* and *fathers*. Yet *socially*, I suggest, we tend to use them somewhat differently. If we say "X's parentage is unknown" what we are talking about is *genetic* parentage. We are not usually raising questions about who has the right to look after the child. The dictionary definition of *parentage*

---

[9] *Re PC (Change of Surname)* [1997] 2 FLR 730.

which refers to "descent from parents, lineage" seems to confirm this view. Arguably, therefore, *parentage* is an exclusively genetic idea and it may be that we have here a concept capable of giving effect to the child's alleged right or interest in genetic origins.

The notion of *parenthood* in everyday usage is more problematic and ambiguous. While many people referring to *parenthood* would immediately associate it with the status held by the child's genetic father and mother, others might well associate it with those who are acting out the *social role* of parents by looking after a child. Often the expression *parenthood* is accompanied by a prefix. We talk of *step*-parenthood, *foster*-parenthood or *adoptive* parenthood. An umbrella term often used by commentators, though not, I suggest, in wider society, is *social parenthood*. One distinction then between *parentage* and *parenthood*, at least as a matter of everyday language, may be that the former, but not the latter, is an *exclusively* genetic idea. But this is not, in my view, the only point of distinction. *Parentage*, I suggest, has a "one-off" character. It is about genetic truth, or at least a *presumed* genetic link—as in marriage. Once parentage has been established following the birth of the child we tend not to continue using the term—unless perhaps someone in the family dies and it becomes important to resurrect the question of genetic links for the purposes of succession to property[10] or, more commonly, someone is denying financial liability for child support under the Child Support Act. *Parenthood* is arguably different. It conveys an on-going status in relation to the child and, in particular, is associated with the responsibility for raising a child.

So far as the law is concerned, *being a parent* is a legal status which has traditionally been associated with a presumed or actual genetic link.[11] But adoption (introduced in England in 1926) has long represented an exception to the principle that *genetic* and *legal* parenthood should coincide. In this context it is clear to everyone that the legal, adoptive parent is not the genetic parent. Since 1990 the instances of non-genetic parenthood have increased in the context of assisted reproduction. Under the Human Fertilisation and Embryology Act 1990 there are several instances in which a person who is patently not the *genetic* parent will be treated as the *legal* parent.[12] (See Bridge, Chapter 4 below). It should also be said that artificial insemination by donor (AID) has been around for half a century and that many children born into marriages will have been presumed (wrongly) to be the genetic children of the respective husbands. These cases are however distinguishable from those under the 1990 legislation since legal parenthood still arose in the pre-1990 cases from a *presumed genetic connection*,

[10] For a particularly striking illustration see *Re Overbury (deceased)* [1955] Ch 122.

[11] Within the context of marriage there is a legal presumption that a child born to a married woman is the child of her husband. The presumption is encapsulated in the Latin maxim *Pater est quem nuptiae demonstrant*.

[12] Thus under s. 28(2) the husband of a woman who did not object to her receiving various forms of infertility treatment will be treated in law as the father. The same is true of an unmarried man under s. 28(3) where there has been a course of treatment services provided for the mother and that man together.

albeit an inaccurate one. What made the 1990 legislation so special was the willingness of Parliament to acknowledge openly the *legal parenthood* of those who lacked *genetic parentage*.

The position is complicated further in that the legal parent may, in the case of a genetic father not married to the mother, lack parenthood in the full sense, in that the law withholds from him parental responsibility. Thus it is necessary, at least from a legal perspective, to distinguish between being a parent and having parental responsibility—a subtlety which is probably not appreciated by many in society including those most directly affected (see Pickford, Chapter 8 below).

(b) Parental responsibility

If we consider how the expression *parental responsibility* might be used in society we can again observe a distinction between its social and its legal usage. Let us take the example of a young unmarried mother whose parents (the baby's grandparents) look after the baby while the mother gets on with her life—perhaps, shall we say, by going off to college. If we were to ask people generally who has "parental responsibility" for the baby in these circumstances, we could reasonably expect that some would see the grandparents as exercising it. They would be, as it were, *in loco parentis* to the child. Yet they do not have *legal* parental responsibility. Parental responsibility, in the technical legal sense, remains vested in the mother and the grandparents have only those powers and duties which other *de facto* carers possess.[13] Parental responsibility in law is not therefore just about the fact of looking after a child. But equally it is not just about being a parent either. The unmarried father is undoubtedly a parent with the status of legal parenthood but he lacks the powers and duties which go with having parental responsibility[14] (see Pickford, Chapter 8 below). Conversely many social parents succeed in obtaining parental responsibility in the legal sense but do not thereby acquire the full status of being parents and the very expression "parent" is in this context a legal misnomer.

To summarise, therefore, we can say that the social usage and perceptions of *parentage, parenthood and parental responsibility* may not always coincide with the legal significance of these concepts and that the first two (though perhaps socially distinguishable) are legally conflated in the notion of *being a parent*. If therefore we want to ask the question "what is a parent?" we need to ask further questions about whether we are seeking to establish genetic parentage, invest someone with the status of legal parent or merely give to that person the

[13] Under Children Act 1989, s. 3(5) a person who does not have parental responsibility but has care of a child may "do what is reasonable in all the circumstances of the case for the purpose of safeguarding or promoting the child's welfare".

[14] He can however acquire parental responsibility by agreement with the mother Children Act 1989, s. 4(1)(b)) or by obtaining from the court a parental responsibility order Children Act 1989, s. 4(1)(a)).

legal powers and duties which are associated with raising a child and are encapsulated in the legal concept of "parental responsibility". These are not just questions of terminology since there are real distinctions of substance between merely having genetic parentage established, being a legal parent and possessing parental responsibility.

4. WHAT IS THE LEGAL SIGNIFICANCE OF PARENTAGE, PARENTHOOD AND PARENTAL RESPONSIBILITY?

What makes the legal situation so complex is that genetic parentage, legal parenthood and parental responsibility may be split between different individuals or institutions in relation to a particular child. This is, of course, frequently not the case. Perhaps the best example is again the situation of the unmarried mother (or two married parents). Where an unmarried woman gives birth (assuming she conceived by sexual intercourse) she will be the genetic parent, the legal parent and she will possess parental responsibility. However, the genetic father, if established, will also be the legal parent but will not have parental responsibility. To take a second example, if the mother and her unmarried partner had "produced" a child together with the use of licensed donor sperm, the partner would *not* be the genetic parent (this would be the sperm donor); the partner would be the legal parent but would still not have parental responsibility. Suppose that the mother then separated from the partner and married another man with whom she successfully obtains a joint residence order. Now the former partner is still the *legal* parent but her husband, who is neither the legal nor genetic parent, shares parental responsibility with the mother by virtue of the residence order. In this last example genetic parentage, legal parenthood and parental responsibility are split between three different men. It would not be difficult to dream up more complicated situations than this (Eekelaar, 1994).

What these examples suggest is that careful thought needs to be given to the legal consequences which flow from the establishment of genetic parentage, the attribution of legal parenthood and the granting of orders which give parental responsibility. Perhaps, more importantly, there needs to be a re-evaluation of the circumstances in which it is appropriate to allocate to individuals the status which goes with these distinctive concepts.[15] Thus, for example, when it is argued that being a parent is nowadays more about the *intention* to perform the role of a parent, rather than the fact of procreation (Barton and Douglas, 1995), we need to be clear about whether we are concerned merely with the acquisition of parental responsibility or with the wider status of legal parenthood.

---

[15] There has, in particular been much debate about the legal status of step-parents which raises questions about whether they should be allowed to acquire the full legal status of parent (through adoption), parental responsibility (automatically, by agreement with the genetic parent or by court order) or whether they should merely have the legal status of other *de facto* carers.

(a) The legal significance of establishing genetic parentage

The establishment of *genetic parentage* will generally result in the attribution of *legal parenthood* with the consequences which attach to this status but, as discussed above, it will not always do so since there are instances in the context of assisted reproduction and adoption, in which the genetic parent either will not become, or will cease to be, the legal parent. Furthermore, whether or not the establishment of genetic parentage will create the *full* legal status of parenthood (inclusive of parental responsibility) will depend, in the case of the father, on the presence or absence of *marriage* to the mother.[16] Where the father, being married to the mother, acquires this full legal status of parenthood, it is not necessary to distinguish between the effects of legal parenthood and those of parental responsibility—he gets *both* since they are subsumed or conflated in the general notion of *being a parent*. Where however, he is *not* married to the mother, it is necessary to make this distinction. Hence we need to be able to separate the legal consequences of *being a parent* from those which derive from having *parental responsibility*. It is of course the case that many now argue that the unmarried father should automatically have a full parental status but this has thus far been resisted in England. (See Pickford, Chapter 8 below and on the different position taken by the Scottish Law Commission, see Scottish Law Commission (1992) and Bainham (1993)). The debate about this and other matters, such as liability for child support, largely hinges on the question of what consequences, if any, should flow from the *mere fact* of establishing genetic parentage; it might arguably be helpful to have an independent concept of *legal parentage* (as distinct from legal parenthood) as a mechanism for defining these consequences.

(b) The attribution of legal parenthood

As noted above, genetic parentage will usually trigger the legal status of parent. But we have now broken the necessary connection between the two. Legal parenthood may be attributed to social or intentional parents, as where a commissioning couple obtain a "parental order" under the Human Fertilisation and Embryology Act 1990.[17] Except in the case of the unmarried father, those who are legal parents will also have parental responsibility, but the distinction between the two concepts has an importance which goes well beyond this. This is because the legal effects which are peculiar to *parenthood* will not pass to *social parents* who get *parental responsibility*. Let me reinforce this point. Leaving aside the exceptional situation of the unmarried father, legal parent-

---

[16] Being married at the time of the child's birth here carries an extended meaning in accordance with Children Act 1989, s. 2(3) and Family Law Reform Act 1987, s. 1. The expression includes some children of void marriages, legitimated and adopted children and children who are treated as legitimate.

[17] 1990 Act, s. 30.

hood *includes within it* parental responsibility—but the reverse is not true. Parental responsibility *does not include* the wider legal effects of parenthood. This leads me to one of the most important issues for the future. In allocating parental responsibility to more and more social parents, is it necessary or desirable to go the extra mile and confer on them legal parenthood? It will be my strong contention that this is neither necessary nor desirable and that legal parenthood, with some exceptions, ought to be confined to genetic parents. This is because those legal effects, which are peculiar to parenthood, are fundamental to the genetic link and provide a basis for continuing to recognise this while parental responsibility, at the same time, can give a measure of legal security to social parents.

What are these fundamental effects of legal parenthood which do not pass with parental responsibility? The first is arguably the most important and is also the most frequently neglected. This is that legal parenthood, but not parental responsibility, makes the child a member of a family, generating for that child a legal relationship with wider kin going well beyond the parental relationship. This is expressed most concretely in the law of succession where entitlements on intestacy depend on being able to establish these kinship links. Beyond this, the social or psychological value of belonging to a particular family is a nebulous subject for lawyers and is more the terrain of the anthropologist or psychologist. What the lawyer *can* point out is that the loss of the legal status of parent will entail the loss, at least in law, of these wider relationships. Let us suppose, for example, that a mother divorces H1 and remarries H2. Both men have siblings. The mother and H2 apply to adopt the mother's children who are the genetic children of H1. If the adoption is granted, the children will lose their legal relationship with the uncles and aunts derived from H1. They will acquire new uncles and aunts from H2. If, on the other hand, a joint residence order is made rather than an adoption order, the children will retain the legal link with H1's siblings and any relationship with H2's siblings will be social rather than legal. It may be that this does not matter but it is surely a factor which should be considered before we allow too readily those who have performed a social role to become legal parents.

Other effects which arise specifically from legal parenthood are financial liability for child support,[18] the right to object or consent to adoption[19] (though this also depends on possessing parental responsibility), and the right to object to a change of the child's surname and to removal of the child from the jurisdiction,[20] the right to appoint a guardian[21] (although guardians themselves also have this right and the parent must possess parental responsibility), a presumption of

---

[18] Social Security Administration Act 1992, s. 78(b) and Child Support Act 1991, s. 1(2).

[19] Adoption Act 1976, s. 16.

[20] These rights, recognised at common law, are not lost where a residence order is made in favour of the other parent or someone else. See Children Act 1989, s. 13(1).

[21] Children Act 1989, s. 5(3).

contact where a child is in care[22] and an automatic right to go to court.[23] One might have thought that there would be an equivalent presumption of contact in the private context but decisions of the courts have cast doubt on this.[24]

Are these distinctive legal effects just anomalies, historical accidents of the piecemeal development of the law? Surely they should all now be subsumed under the central organising concept of parental responsibility? (Lowe, 1997). It is my contention that, on the contrary, they continue to serve a vital purpose in that they give expression to the continuing importance of the genetic link. What they all have in common is that they relate to fundamentals which go beyond the everyday decisions involved in upbringing. Allowing the child to be adopted severs the parental link completely (at least traditionally in English law); allowing the child to be taken permanently out of the country or changing the child's name threatens its existence, in the case of the latter perhaps only symbolically. If we are to move in the direction of giving effect to a child's right to knowledge of genetic origins we are going to need some legal means of preserving the genetic connection and it is the concept of legal parenthood which currently achieves this. As noted earlier there are limited exceptions to this principle in which some other distinctive mechanism is perhaps required, since legal and genetic parenthood have become divorced from one another.

(c) The effect of conferring parental responsibility

Parental responsibility is now a technical legal concept. It conveys a status which is held automatically by both parents where they are married and by the mother alone where the child is born out of wedlock. Yet many people who are not genetically related to children, but are looking after them, can acquire parental responsibility through court orders or, in the event of the death of a natural parent, through being privately appointed guardian by that parent (Douglas and Lowe, 1992). The most usual order will be the residence order, the effect of which is automatically to give parental responsibility to the person in whose favour it is made—but only for so long as the order lasts.[25] Orders will usually terminate when the child attains sixteen years of age.[26] Here we can see immediately one very clear distinction between being a legal parent and holding parental responsibility. The legal parent will remain a parent for life. Although many of the legal effects of parenthood will terminate when the child attains majority at eighteen, the legal family relationship of parent and child will

[22] Children Act 1989, s. 34(1)(a).
[23] Thus a parent may apply, without leave, for any "Section 8 order" under the Children Act 1989 (s. 10(4)) and this includes the unmarried father despite his lack of parental responsibility (see *M v C and Calderdale Metropolitan Borough Council* [1994] Fam. 1).
[24] See the House of Lords decision in *S v M (Access Order)* [1997] 1 FLR 980.
[25] Children Act 1989s. 12(2).
[26] Children Act 1989, s. 91.

endure for good.[27] Thus, in quite a number of countries (and formerly under the English Poor Law), adult children have legal obligations in certain circumstances to provide for the financial support of elderly parents. In contrast parental responsibility is really a sort of trusteeship over the child which is more limited and, since the Children Act 1989, will usually cease even before the child reaches majority. Under the draft Adoption Bill 1996 it would be possible for orders over children to be extended to the age of eighteen thus ensuring a continuation of parental responsibility (Department of Health and Welsh Office, 1996). But this has not been brought before Parliament.

So what exactly is *parental responsibility*? A great deal has been written on the subject and while the Scots have attempted in their 1995 legislation to define its content,[28] the English approach has been to leave things rather vague, at least on the statute book, and to presuppose some knowledge of the effects of being a parent which the courts have formulated over a long period of time at common law. But, for what it is worth, the Children Act defines *parental responsibility* as

> "all the rights, duties, powers, responsibilities and authority which by law a parent of a child has in relation to the child and his property".[29]

The definition does not tell us what these are, which is why some question its usefulness, but it is, in a broad sense, fairly clear what it is talking about. At the risk of over-simplification, the person possessing parental responsibility will have a right to look after the child (unless this has been removed by a Court order)[30] and the right and duty to take all major decisions relating to the child's upbringing including such matters as where the child is to live, which school the child should attend or what medical treatment the child should, or should not, receive.[31]

Thus, where a social parent succeeds in obtaining parental responsibility he or she will have the legal right to look after the child and to take all the everyday and important decisions about upbringing which a parent could take. But the social parent will not *become* the legal parent in the fullest sense and one obvious question for policy-makers is why the social parent might feel the need to press for full legal parenthood. Why isn't having parental responsibility

---

[27] It was largely for this reason that an adoption order was made in *Re D (A minor) (Adoption Order: Validity)* [1991] 2 FLR 66. The child here was only six days short of majority when the adoption application was made but suffered from severe mental handicap. It should also be noted that some jurisdictions still allow the adoption of adults.

[28] Children (Scotland) Act 1995, ss. 1 and 2 set out, respectively, the *responsibilities* and *rights* of parents. English law subsumes the rights of parents, insofar as they exist, in the general notion of *parental responsibility*.

[29] 1989 Act, s. 3(1).

[30] The effect of a residence order or care order could be to prevent a person with parental responsibility from having the right to look after the child.

[31] These rights or powers are not absolute (*Gillick v West Norfolk and Wisbech Area Health Authority* [1986] 1 AC 112) but they do confer a good deal of discretion with which the courts may be reluctant to interfere (see, for example, *Re T (Wardship: Medical Treatment)* [1997] 1 FLR 502).

enough in itself? Why is it, for example, that so many step-parents, following the liberalisation of divorce in 1969, sought to adopt their step-children rather than merely to acquire the equivalent of what is now parental responsibility through a joint custody (or, latterly, a residence) order with their spouses? (Houghton, 1972). At least part of the explanation must surely lie in the fact that orders that confer what is now parental responsibility are *revocable* whereas adoption (which creates full legal parenthood) is *permanent* other than in very restricted circumstances.[32] This is particularly striking in the case of the unmarried father who, having acquired parental responsibility, may subsequently have it revoked by the court. So adoption offered greater *security* to *de facto* carers like step-parents, foster-parents and others, and the wish to have this security is readily understandable. But there is more to the push for parenthood than this. It seems entirely likely that many of those raising children have a psychological need to be regarded as, or called, *parents* and here we are perhaps back to the semantic debate alluded to earlier in this chapter. For many people, perhaps especially step-parents in a reconstituted family, it is not enough to be given the powers and duties of parents—they want to *be* parents.

The policy of the law has been to restrict the circumstances, again with step-parents particularly in mind, in which the *de facto* carer should be able to go beyond acquiring parental responsibility and actually attain full legal parent-hood. I believe this policy to have been well-founded in view of what is increasingly recognised as the importance of the genetic link to the child. I turn to this in the next section. But before doing so, it should not go unnoticed that there has been some erosion of this policy and that the Children Act amended earlier provisions that were designed explicitly to discourage step-parent adoption and adoption by natural relatives (Bainham, 1990). Another point which ought to be raised here is that the concern of social parents for legal security in the process of raising a child is real and justifiable. It certainly suggests that further consideration should be given to the introduction of an *irrevocable* order, such as an irrevocable residence order or a form of *inter vivos* guardianship, which would stop short of making the social parent the legal parent but would also erase any real fear that the child could be removed from the social parent during the child's minority.

5.   IS THERE A RIGHT TO KNOWLEDGE OF GENETIC ORIGINS?

Exactly what is the value of the genetic link to children or indeed to adults in later life is not something upon which lawyers are fit to pronounce. This is surely a matter for others such as geneticists and psychologists. But it does seem to be accepted that there are perhaps two major reasons why knowledge of

---

[32] For an unsuccessful attempt to revoke an adoption order see *Re B (Adoption: Jurisdiction to Set Aside)* [1995] 2 FLR 1. For a rare successful revocation see *Re K (Adoption and Wardship)* [1997] 2 FLR 221.

genetic background is thought to be important (O'Donovan, 1998). The first relates to information about an individual's medical history in the context of the wider family, and the second stresses the psychological need of individuals to have knowledge of their background in acquiring a sense of identity. Any uncertainty over the value of the genetic link has not stopped the international community from passing an extremely widely ratified Convention which appears to acknowledge the child's fundamental right to establish connections with his or her genetic parents. Article 7(1) of the United Nations Convention on the Rights of the Child provides that:

> "The child shall be registered immediately after birth and shall have the right from birth to a name, the right to acquire a nationality and, as far as possible, the right to know and be cared for by his or her parents".

Article 8(1) reinforces the previous article by providing obligations relating to the preservation of the child's identity, family relations etc. It provides that:

> "States Parties undertake to respect the right of the child to preserve his or her identity, including nationality, name and family relations as recognised by law without unlawful interference".

It might be argued that the expression "parents" in Article 7 is wide enough to include not only genetic parents but also those performing the social role of parents. What is not in dispute is that the purpose behind Article 7 was an attempt to combat the problem of children's statelessness. Article 7, as Jane Fortin puts it, "makes it clear that states parties must provide a method whereby the child is 'labelled' or named immediately she is born and thereby linked accurately and quickly to the people who brought her into the world, her birth parents" (Fortin, 1998). It is equally clear that Article 8 was inspired by the international community's need to respond to "the abuses committed by the military regime in Argentina during which babies had been abducted from their mothers at birth, before their births could be registered and illegally given to childless couples, associated with the armed forces and police" (Fortin, 1998; see also Le Blanc, 1995; Van Bueren, 1995).

Notwithstanding this background, the Convention contains no definition of "parents" and its meaning is therefore legitimately a matter of interpretation upon which opinions may differ. It is argued here, for a number of reasons, that the expression should be interpreted in the conventional sense of genetic parents. First, the history of Articles 7 and 8 reveals that the concern of the international community was with the rights of children from the moment of birth and in relation to their birth parents. It was precisely the threat of removal of the child from the birth parents by others which was the *raison d'être* of Article 8. Secondly, we must remember that the Convention is a *legal* document. In 1989, when it was adopted, there was, for example, no legislation anywhere in the world regulating assisted reproduction which has been the engine for the re-evaluation of traditional definitions of parenthood. Leaving aside adoption, legislation worldwide has traditionally defined parenthood as genetic parenthood. The legal tie has closely followed the genetic connection. Thirdly, as noted below, the jurisprudence generated under another international Convention, the European Convention on Human Rights, again supports the notion of "family life" from birth and has confirmed that this includes the potential relationship of a child with his or her genetic father even where unmarried. Finally, as discussed below, the conventional interpretation was adopted by the Court of Appeal in the one reported decision which directly invokes Article 7. For all these reasons it is submitted that "parents" in the Convention was intended to mean genetic parents and that the onus is very firmly on those who would argue for an unconventional interpretation.

Although the United Nations Convention is not directly incorporated into English law, it does require the government to adopt a social policy that is consistent with its international obligations, and Article 7 has already had a significant, perhaps decisive, influence on the outcome of one paternity dispute which reached the Court of Appeal.[33] In that case the mother, who had both a lover and a husband who had had a vasectomy, was told robustly by Lord Justice Ward that "honesty was the best policy", that she ought not to be telling lies and that the child had the right to know the truth of his paternity and "the sooner the better". Lord Justice Ward was at pains to distinguish between the two separate rights in Article 7. For him, the fact that the genetic father was not in a position to care for the child did not detract from the child's *independent* right to know of his genetic origins. A succession of decisions by the European Court of Human Rights have also made it plain that under the European Convention there are *positive* obligations on states to foster the "family life" of children from birth and that this "family life" is not confined to relationships within marriage.[34] These decisions are also founded in part on the importance of the genetic link which generates mutual fundamental rights for both children and parents in or out of marriage.

What the lawyer can therefore say with some confidence is that there are legal obligations which mean that it will not be lawful for states to devalue or ignore the link between the child and his or her genetic parents, though the extent of these obligations, especially positive obligations to take action, remains unclear.

How far English law currently complies with these international obligations is open to doubt. Adopted adults have a legal right of access to their original birth certificates but they do not, as the law stands, have a right to be told that they are adopted nor access to their original birth certificates *during childhood*. Children born with the use of donated gametes do not have the right to be told, while children, that they were conceived in this way but there are limited rights to "non-identifying information" to establish that there is no risk of marrying someone to whom a person is closely genetically related (Maclean and Maclean,

---

[33] *Re H (Paternity: Blood Test)* [1996] 2 FLR 65.
[34] See, for example, *Johnston v Ireland* (1986) 9 EHRR 203 and *Keegan v Ireland* (1994) 18 EHRR 342.

1996). There is no general obligation to establish genetic paternity in all cases of childbirth and there is some ambivalence in the attitude of the courts to the direction of blood testing or DNA tests in the event of paternity disputes.[35] It should perhaps be said that, with the ready availability of DNA testing and the possibilities for surreptitious removal of small quantities of genetic material such as hair roots, the role of the courts may in future be somewhat pre-empted by resort to such DIY measures.

The extent to which the law does or should accommodate biological parenthood alongside social parenthood is therefore going to be the subject of ongoing debate and in the next two sections I attempt to outline two possible approaches.

6. A RADICAL APPROACH—SHOULD PARENTHOOD BE EXCLUSIVELY GENETIC?

A radical and extreme response to the emerging right of the child to knowledge of genetic origins (and perhaps the logical conclusion from the existence of such a right) would be to regard as *parents* only those who can establish the genetic relationship. We should perhaps note, in passing, that Article 7 is not simply about knowledge—it talks of the right of the child "to know *and be cared for* by his or her parents" but only "as far as possible". This would seem to imply that the Convention is concerned not merely with establishing the initial link (what I have called the *parentage* issue above), but also with the on-going status of being a parent (what I have identified with *parenthood*).

I should say immediately that I am not advocating the following approach and it is my view that there is no possibility whatever of its adoption in England. The clock simply could not be turned back in this way. But there is value in speculating on what changes would flow from a reconceptualisation of our view of legal parenthood. I emphasise that I am only talking about the *legal* status of parenthood since, as discussed above, the law has no real control over the *social* usages of the term.

What, then, would have to change if we woke up tomorrow morning with the startling news that *only* those with an established genetic link with a child would, in law, be regarded as *parents*? The first and most obvious point is that it would make no difference whatever to the situation which applies already to the majority of children. Most children born into marriages are *in fact* the genetic children of both parents. Birth registration and indeed birth within marriage are not, of course, conclusive proof of a genetic connection with the men concerned, but these events do give rise to a *presumption* that this is the case. If we wanted to be absolutely sure we would have to test everyone, including the child, in every case of childbirth but, as far as I am aware, no-one has seriously

---

[35] Contrast particularly *Re F (A minor) (Blood Tests: Parental Rights)* [1993] Fam 314 with *Re H* (n. 34 above).

proposed this. Certainly the radical approach would suggest that if anyone decided to *contest* paternity and put these presumptions in doubt, scientific tests should always be directed by the courts. This would certainly involve a change from current practice and I return to this issue in the next section. However, one point which ought not to be lost is that, in my view, legal paternity under these rules does not arise *because* of marriage or *because* of birth registration. It arises from the *presumed genetic link* which is triggered by these events. To that extent these rules are consistent with the radical thesis that parenthood is genetic.

The first real problem the radical approach would have to face is adoption. The effect of adoption under English law is what has been called a "legal transplant". The birth parents are replaced by the adoptive parents who step into their shoes. So *legal parenthood*, and not merely parental responsibility, is transferred. This form of adoption, as we know it in England, would have to go. But we should not make the mistake of believing that there is something inevitable or sacrosanct about the "transplant" model. Many civil law countries (essentially those whose legal systems derive from Roman law) have long recognised a distinction between *full adoption*, which broadly corresponds with the English version, and *simple adoption*, which does not extinguish the child's links with the wider birth family. In recent years a number of Latin American countries have reformed their adoption laws and the future of the dual system of adoption seems somewhat uncertain (Grosman, 1998; Alzate Monroy, 1998). The point is that it would not be impossible to conceive of a new kind of adoption order which gave long-term legal security to the adoptive parents but which also continued to preserve the legal link with the birth family in some way.

What about assisted reproduction? If legal parenthood were to be exclusively genetic, the anonymity of gamete donors would have to go—radical indeed, and calculated to reduce the number of volunteers, but scarcely revolutionary. Sweden has done it and Switzerland has enacted legislation which gives to the sixteen-year-old child, born of medically assisted procreation, the right to know a sperm donor's identity (Guillod, 1997). Surely surrogacy would represent a massive problem. On a closer examination perhaps the problem would not be as great as it seems at first sight. Under current legislation a commissioning couple can obtain a "parental order", the effect of which is similar to adoption in that it makes that couple the legal parents of the child and extinguishes the parental status of the surrogate mother.[36] The requirements for making such an order are themselves an interesting reflection of official ambivalence about what parenthood is, since at least one commissioning parent must have a genetic link with the child, they must be married and they must already be acting as the child's social parents. We may well speculate, in the light of this, whether it is the fact of procreation, family life within marriage or the intention to act as social parents which generates the greatest claim to legal parenthood. If legal parenthood were to be exclusively genetic, a "non-genetic" member of the

---

[36] Human Fertilisation and Embryology Act 1990, s. 30(1) provides that the effect of the order is that the child is "to be treated in law as the child of the parties to a marriage".

commissioning couple could no longer be the legal parent but this would not prevent him or her from being given parental responsibility. In the context of heterosexual unmarried cohabitation, we already have one intriguing decision which has allowed the male partner to adopt while giving the female partner only parental responsibility under a residence order.[37] Where a surrogacy arrangement breaks down, the law already arguably attaches greatest importance to the biological position since the surrogate mother, who carries the child and gives birth, will be the legal mother.[38] Cases of full surrogacy do, of course, raise questions as to whether the genetic link is to be regarded as more important than the biological contribution involved in carrying a pregnancy and giving birth.

The determination of fatherhood in cases of assisted reproduction would undoubtedly present a major problem. The attribution of legal fatherhood to the husband or partner[39] who receives licensed treatment services "together with" his wife or partner would have to be abolished. But, again, this would not necessarily involve denying that man any legal status. He too could be given parental responsibility rather than being made a parent and this would give him the legal powers and duties he would need to raise the child.

What this review perhaps reveals is that, although there would be substantial doubts about the desirability of reserving legal parenthood as an exclusively genetic concept and, although this is clearly not going to happen, it would not be impossible to achieve. It might be somewhat easier to achieve than would be commonly supposed with an intelligent use of the alternative legal notion of parental responsibility.

7. A MODERATE APPROACH—HOW CAN WE ACCOMMODATE GENETIC AND SOCIAL PARENTHOOD?

If we reject the radical approach, as now we surely must, how else might due weight be given to the genetic link alongside the very proper recognition of social parenthood? Again we perhaps need to focus on those instances in which the law separates genetic from legal parenthood by giving the legal status of parenthood to the social parent. The broad question which needs to be asked is whether the law adequately upholds the child's right to knowledge of genetic origins and preservation of that link.

What about adoption? The law and practice of adoption has already been moving slowly but surely towards a more "open" system although, as Bridget Lindley has pointed out, there are different manifestations of "openness" and the meaning of "open adoption" is not wholly clear (Lindley, 1997). Nor is the

---

[37] *Re AB (Adoption: Joint Residence)* [1996] 1 FLR 27.

[38] Human Fertilisation and Embryology Act 1990, s. 27(1). In some of these instances of course the gestational mother will not be the genetic mother.

[39] Human Fertilisation and Embryology Act 1990, ss. 28(2), (3).

precise shape of adoption reform.[40] But we do seem to have arrived at the point where we are prepared, in some circumstances, to countenance on-going contact of a limited kind with the birth family following adoption.[41] It has also been proposed that a child should have a legal right to be told that he or she has been adopted—but the question of precisely when the child should be given information, and how much, remains contentious. It is even more contentious in the case of the children of assisted reproduction, but we need to continue to ask hard questions about why adopted children are allowed access to much more information about their genetic beginnings than are these children (Freeman, 1997; Maclean and Maclean, 1996).

More, much more, needs to be done about the process of establishing genetic paternity but already there are signs that the courts are beginning to shift the balance more towards genetic truth and are less obsessed with preserving family stability. As Lord Justice Ward has put it, when deciding to direct blood tests in the "vasectomy" case, "the issue of biological parentage should be divorced from psychological parentage . . . Mr B's parental responsibility should not dent Mr H's social responsibility".[42] Thus Lord Justice Ward was of the opinion that we should not *necessarily* assume that to establish the genetic parentage of an outsider will "upset the apple cart" as far as the social family situation is concerned. The child may have interests, perhaps rights, in an *inclusive* approach which acknowledges the different but complementary roles of genetic and social parenthood. With the growing societal acceptance of social parenting, and the very great range of family arrangements in which children move in and out of different kinds of households (Maclean and Eekelaar, 1997), there may be much less stigma attached to paternity outside marriage than there used to be.

I would go further than this. We need to look more closely at the responsibility of *the state* in establishing the genetic connection. If the child does have fundamental rights, this is a matter which perhaps ought not to be left to the various adults concerned. In Scandinavia and, until recently, Germany, the state has taken on a much more active role in attempting to establish genetic paternity in *all* cases of child birth—although the *pater est* presumption is still applicable to births in wedlock (Eriksson and Saldeen, 1993). The German case is an interesting one since the state, perhaps surprisingly, has traditionally had a much more assertive function in the former West Germany than in the former German Democratic Republic (Frank, 1997, 1998). It now seems, following reunification, that the state's role will recede at least in part because the kind of investigations carried out by social welfare agencies in the West would be found unacceptable by East Germans. In France and many other civil law jurisdictions there is much greater opportunity for a man to acknowledge his paternity

---

[40] The 1996 Draft Adoptiom Bill has never been presented to Parliament and, at the time of writing, there is no indication that the Labour Government intends to make adoption reform a priority.

[41] See, for example, *Re C (A minor) (Adoption Order: Conditions)* [1988] 2 FLR 259 and *Re T (Adopted Children: Contact)* [1995] 2 FLR 792.

[42] See n. 34 above at 82.

independently and without the initial need for co-operation by the mother or a court order (Senaeve, 1993; Meulders-Klein, 1990). Compare these approaches with the stance taken in England. I think it is fair to say that the only circumstances in which the state, in the guise of the Child Support Agency, bothers to get interested in the establishment of paternity is where the mother is dependent on social security. Otherwise she is under no obligation to register the name of the father and a man believing himself to be the father has no right to acknowledge his paternity without either the mother's consent or a court order.[43] There is not so much as a whiff of any independent right of the child in all this.[44]

A final consideration might be that we should continue to scrutinise carefully the circumstances under which social parents are actually allowed to become legal parents. Top of the list here is the position of step-parents. It is a matter of regret that the strong recommendations of the Houghton Committee (Houghton, 1972) which led to provisions in the Children Act 1975 designed to discourage step-parent (and relative) adoption,[45] were first subverted by the courts[46] and then eroded by Parliament, without much discussion, in the Children Act 1989 (Bainham 1990). The vast majority of step-parents become step-parents following the divorce of their spouses. In most of these cases the divorced parent will still be on the scene and perhaps involved with the children to a greater or lesser extent. We should be vigorously defending the parental status of the divorced parent in these cases and not pretending that a step-parent is a parent. To do otherwise would be directly contrary to the philosophy of continuing parental status following divorce.[47] Neither am I personally convinced that we should even go so far as to confer parental responsibility on the step-parent—at least not routinely. I think Brenda Hale got it exactly right when she said that the step-relation is not the same as the "normal" family constituted within marriage and "perhaps we should not pretend that it is" (Hoggett, 1987, p.126). The step-relationship may, however, arise in rather different circumstances. Perhaps the mother is widowed or the relationship with the natural father broke down before the child was born. In cases like this there is a much stronger case for giving parental responsibility to the step-father or, even perhaps, parenthood through adoption. These last examples do perhaps suggest that a general distinction should be drawn between cases in which the genetic parent is known and "on the scene" from those in which he or she is either unknown or has disappeared. The case for creating a new parent for the child

[43] Births and Deaths Registration Act 1953, s. 10, as amended.

[44] The child does not, for example, have a right to require the state to disclose information about his father's whereabouts which it has obtained as a result of its investigations for the purposes of enforcing his liability to support the child financially. See *Re C (A minor) (Child Support Agency: Disclosure)* [1995] 1 FLR 201.

[45] Children Act 1975, s. 37(1), (2) and Adoption Act 1976, ss. 14(3), 15(4).

[46] *Re D (Minors) (Adoption by Step-parent)* [1980] 2 FLR 102; *Re S (A minor) (Adoption or Custodianship)* and *Re A (A minor) (Adoption: Parental Consent)* [1987] 1 WLR 153.

[47] The theory of the Children Act is very clear and is that parents remain parents despite divorce. Thus, both parental status and parental responsibility are unaffected by termination of the marriage.

to replace one which has been effectively lost is, I suggest, much stronger than where the child already has both parents intact. But this itself involves a deep philosophical question about why it is that children are apparently not entitled to more than *two* parents and sometimes have less than two.[48]

8. CONCLUSION

The great irony of the present time is that just at the moment when it has become possible to establish genetic parentage virtually conclusively it seems to matter less to do so since we are now much more accepting of social parenthood in its many manifestations. This has given rise to a good deal of debate about whether we should attach more importance to the one rather than the other. In the context of paternity disputes it has been presented as an issue of truth versus stability. Elsewhere there is much talk of genetic versus social parenthood.

A primary aim of this chapter has been to suggest that as we move into the twenty-first century we are not really going to be confronted with this polarised "either/or" dilemma. Because of the acceptance internationally of the child's fundamental rights regarding his/her genetic origins, to say nothing of domestic concerns about medical knowledge and psychological well-being, it is going to be necessary to take an *inclusive* approach. The Children Act 1989 is in fact full of inclusive ideas of partnership and the notion that children can relate to a range of adults.[49] Yet we remain stoutly resistant to the idea that a child could have more than two parents. On the other hand it is a feature of the new concept of parental responsibility that it can be shared out among a potentially unlimited range of adults. The real question in this sharing process will be who gets legal parenthood and who gets only parental responsibility, if anything. It could have been exceptionally neat and tidy to say that those with a proven genetic connection are the parents and everyone else gets parental responsibility and no more. But this is not the course we have followed in England and it is too late to change course now. Given that legal and genetic parenthood will not coincide in a number of instances, it may just be that thought needs to be given to resurrecting or creating a legal concept which could be exclusively genetic and could thereby serve the independent rights or interests of children to knowledge of origins in these cases. I tentatively put forward the idea that *parentage* might in law be distinguished from *parenthood* and be given a technical importance which would, I believe, bring it closer to its ordinary social usage.

---

[48] Under the provisions of the Human Fertilisation and Embryology Act 1990, s. 28, where no man is deemed to be the legal father the child can be "fatherless" viz. without a legal father.

[49] A principle which applies particularly to the relationship between the state and parents and which is also reflected in the provision that "a person who has parental responsibility for a child at any time shall not cease to have that responsibility solely because some other person subsequently acquires parental responsibility for the child".

REFERENCES

Bainham, A., "The privatisation of the public interest in children" (1990) 53 *Modern Law Review* 206.

Bainham, A., "Reforming Scottish children law—sense from north of the border" (1993) 5 J. *of Child Law* 3.

Bainham, A., "Sex, gender and fatherhood: does biology really matter?" (1997) 56 *Cambridge Law Journal* 512.

Barton, C. and Douglas, G., *Law and Parenthood* (London, Butterworths, 1995).

Department of Health and Welsh Office, *Adoption—A Service for Children: Adoption Bill—A Consultative Document* (London, March 1996).

Douglas, G. and Lowe, N. V., "Becoming a parent in English law" (1992) 108 *LQR* 414.

Eekelaar, J., "Parenthood, social engineering and rights" in D. Morgan and G. Douglas (eds.), *Constituting Families: A Study in Governance* (Stuttgart, Franz Steiner Verlag, 1994).

Eriksson, A. and Saldeen, A., "Parenthood and science—establishing and contesting parentage" in J. Eekelaar and P. Sarcevic (eds.), *Parenthood in Modern Society* (The Hague, Martinus Nijhoff, 1993).

Fortin, J., *Children's Rights and the Developing Law* (London, Edinburgh and Dublin, Butterworths, 1998).

Frank, R., "Germany: the need for reform in parentage law" in A. Bainham (ed.), *The International Survey of Family Law 1995* (The Hague, Martinus Nijhoff, 1997).

Frank, R., "Germany: a fundamental reform of parentage law is pending" in A. Bainham (ed.), *The International Survey of Family Law 1996* (The Hague, Martinus Nijhoff, 1998).

Freeman, M. D. A., *The Moral Status of Children* (The Hague, Martinus Nijhoff, 1997).

Grosman, C. P., "The recent reform of Argentine adoption law" in A. Bainham (ed.), *The International Survey of Family Law 1996* (The Hague, Martinus Nijhoff, 1998).

Guillod, O., "Switzerland: Choosing its own way or following others?" in A. Bainham (ed.), *The International Survey of Family Law 1995* (The Hague, Martinus Nijhoff, 1997).

Hoggett, B. M., *Parents and Children: The Law of Parental Responsibility*, 3rd edn. (London, Sweet and Maxwell, 1987).

Houghton Report, *Report of the Departmental Committee on the Adoption of Children* (Cmnd. 5107, 1972).

Le Blanc, L. J., *The Convention on the Rights of the Child* (Lincoln and London, University of Nebraska Press, 1995).

Lindley, B., "Open adoption—is the door ajar?" (1997) 9 *Child & Family Law Quarterly* 1997.

Lowe, N. V., "The meaning and allocation of parental responsibility—a common lawyer's perspective" (1997) 11 *International Journal of Law, Policy & the Family* 192.

Maclean, M. and Eekelaar, J., *The Parental Obligation* (Oxford, Hart Publishing, 1997).

Maclean, S. and Maclean, M., "Keeping secrets in assisted reproduction—the tension between donor anonymity and the need of the child for information" (1996) 8 *Child & Family Law Quarterly* 243.

Meulders-Klein, M. T., "The position of the father in European legislation" (1990) 4 *International Journal of Law & the Family* 131.

Alzate Monroy, P., "Adoption law in Colombia" in A. Bainham, (ed.), *The International Survey of Family Law 1996* (The Hague, Martinus Nijhoff, 1998).

O'Donovan, K., "Who is the father? Access to information on genetic Identity" in G. Douglas and L. Sebba (eds.), *Children's Rights and Traditional Values* (Aldershot, Ashgate, Dartmouth, 1998).

Scottish Law Commission, *Report No. 135* (1992).

Senaeve, P., "Reform of affiliation law in France and the Benelux countries" in J. Eekelaar and P. Sarcevic (eds.), *Parenthood in Modern Society* (The Hague, Martinus Nijhoff, 1993).

van Bueren, G., *The International Law on the Rights of the Child* (The Hague, Boston and London, Martinus Nijhoff, 1995).

3

A Biomedical Perspective on Parenthood

MARTIN JOHNSON*

In this chapter, the biological elements that make a parent are considered together with a discussion of their patterns of interaction and possible disassociation. How each of these elements might contribute to social and legal views of parenthood is discussed in the context of the contemporary emphasis on genetics in science and the introduction of the new Assisted Reproductive Technologies (ARTs). In particular, the United Kingdom legislation on ARTs is examined for the underlying views of parenthood that seem to be informing it. Some of the arguments and materials described are technical. The chapter therefore starts with an outline summary of the thinking that will be developed in the body of the chapter.

1. OUTLINE SUMMARY

We tend to think of people as having two parents, a mother and a father, each of whom contributes to the child's biological inheritance, and so to biological parenthood, in up to four not fully equivalent ways. This heterosexual two-parent norm is reflected in popular culture and law. What are these four biological components?

First, there is a genetic component to parenthood. We now know that biologically the production of a viable human conceptus *requires* two distinctive subsets of chromosomes, one of which *must* be derived from a woman and the other from a man. The mother's egg alone also contributes a much smaller additional and essential chromosome (<1 per cent of total genetic material) in a non-nuclear structure called a mitochondrion, whilst the father's sperm contributes a non-chromosomal structure which is, however, essential for cell survival and proliferation in the embryo. Thus, genetic parents of both sexes are required and make non-equivalent contributions to their off-spring.

• I am indebted to Joan Stevenson-Hinde for her unfailing stimulation and support, to Anne Ferguson-Smith, Joe Herbert and Martin Richards for their valuable advice, and to my colleagues in the Cambridge Socio-Legal Group for their patience, stimulation and advice.

Secondly, there is a coital component to parenthood. Since fertilisation occurs inside the body, an act of coitus or mating is required between male and female. In humans, coitus is not linked tightly to female fertility, unlike the situation in most mammals, so the act of coitus itself has taken on a meaning additional to its simple reproductive function. Moreover, although monogamous societies assume that the male partner is also the coital partner and therefore both genetic and coital father, only the female can be sure of this, unless social or legal controls on female behaviour are sufficiently strong to prevent mating outside of the pair, something that family law has traditionally tried to address.

Thirdly, there is a gestational or uterine component to parenthood, which is exclusively the province of the female. The mother provides a uterus and there is accumulating evidence that her behaviour, mental state, diet and health during pregnancy may affect enduringly the health, traits and well-being of the child that is subsequently born. The tendency to overlook this important parental contribution to the child may have over-emphasised the significance of the genetic component to parenthood.

Finally, there is a post-natal component to parenthood. Higher primates such as humans transmit not just their genes but also their culture from one generation to another. Post-natal parenthood is sometimes called "social parenthood", but since this component of parenthood has evolved it does have an important biological component to it. Moreover, the hormonal events of pregnancy, and in particular the changes that occur at birth, may have direct or indirect physiological influences on the early parental behaviour of both sexes.

The heterosexual two-parent norm deriving from biology may be circumvented in various ways, traditionally through extra-pair mating, adoption, fostering, loss of one parent or group-rearing, and latterly through the agency of the new assisted reproductive technologies, mostly based on *in-vitro* fertilisation, but also involving the donation of spermatozoa and their insemination artificially. Reproductive cloning may provide the opportunity for an embryo to have only one genetic parent in which a single woman provides all the chromosomes, including the mitochondrial chromosomes, plus the cell proliferation structure normally provided by the sperm. She may also provide the uterus and post-natal care and thus be truly uniparental in every biological sense of the word. Cloning might also provide other opportunities for unconventional genetic parenting: for example, three genetic parents (one man, one woman plus a third woman's mitochondrial chromosomes) or two women only. There is currently no possibility of one or two genetic exclusively male parents because of the requirement for a woman's mitochondrial chromosomes, but reproductive cloning of a man would result in over 99 per cent of the chromosomal material coming from the male. In addition, by combining together different embryos, each of which has a different pair of genetic parents (making so-called chimaeras), a tetra-parental genetic parenthood can be established. Thus, conventional patterns of heterosexual bi-parental genetic parenting could in principle be circumvented, even though the law only allows for a maximum of two parents. In addition, the donation of eggs, sperm or even embryos means that the treated couple may be acting as uterine and post-natal parents for children with whom they have no, or only partial, genetic parental connections. The use of IVF techniques or of artificial insemination also means that parenthood can be achieved without a coital component from the genetic parents at all; indeed the clinician intervenes in a quasi-coital role by introducing sperm or embryos into the uterus through the vagina of the woman, thereby perhaps displacing the genetic parents from their coital role. Surrogacy separates uterine parenthood from post-natal and genetic parenthood, the latter fully or partially so.

Thus modern medicine is challenging conventional notions of parenthood and making us rethink the relative significance of each biological component of parenthood. The sterile debate about the relative contributions of nature and nurture to the formation of a child's identity is relevant to this discussion about how we see parenthood and its biological basis. It is suggested that biology contributes powerfully to images of parenthood, whether these be social "stereotypes" or personal and individual "identities". Indeed, it is suggested that the pervasive, and at times misplaced, emphasis on genetics in modern culture is driving an unbalanced overly genetic view of parenthood as dominant, and that this is generating tensions for individuals trying to match their parental identities to social parental stereotypes. Finally, the legislation surrounding the regulation of assisted reproductive technologies is examined and it is concluded that such a highly genetic view of parenthood is the dominant theme driving legislation, both directly and paradoxically. Thus, legislation is confirming a view of parenthood that is fundamentally unbalanced from a biological perspective.

2. THE BIOLOGICAL BASIS OF PARENTHOOD

Four biological components to parenthood are considered: the genetic endowment contributed at fertilisation, the coital contribution, the gestational contribution, and the period of post-natal care including parturitional aspects.

(a) Genetic parenthood

(i) Sexual and asexual reproduction

Different species have evolved a bewildering variety of reproductive strategies that fall under two broad headings: asexual (uniparental including self-fertilising hermaphrodites) and sexual (biparental). Some species show the capacity to switch between asexual and sexual reproduction (so called facultative sexual reproduction). In asexual reproduction, one parent contributes a full set of genes and chromosomes to each of its offspring. These offspring do not differ genetically from their single parent or each other, or do so in a relatively minor way. With sexual reproduction, biparental mixing of genes yields a unique genetic make up for each new individual. Each parent forms a distinctive set of cells called *gametes* (eggs and spermatozoa), each of which carries half of the nuclear chromosomes of each parent cell (in humans 23 chromosomes from each). Two gametes come together at fertilisation so restoring an embryogenic cell with the full number of nuclear chromosomes (46), half derived from each parent. Most vertebrates reproduce sexually or biparentally. In mammals this sexual reproduction is obligatory: asexual reproduction naturally cannot occur (Johnson and Everitt, forthcoming).

However, biparental reproduction carries with it a heavy cost in evolutionary terms (Gould and Gould, 1997; Crow, 1994; Lyons, 1998). In mammals, the female half of the population is reproductively rate limiting and could be serviced adequately by many fewer males than the 50 per cent that make up the population. Thus, almost half of a sexually reproducing population are a redundant load on the economy. Moreover, there are energy costs in generating two distinct sexes developmentally and in bringing them together through courtship and coital behaviours. Courtship, which may involve elaborate displays and behaviours, and coition, itself involving a reduced awareness of potential predators or a hostile environment, both carry a vulnerability load. That such a high-cost reproductive strategy has survived during evolution implies that there must be compensatory advantages to sexual reproduction. These advantages are usually thought to derive from an increased genetic flexibility, the ability to eliminate adverse mutations rapidly, and/or the capacity to accumulate beneficial mutations within one individual effectively, all of which result from the reconstitution of a unique genetic make up for each new individual from two parental contributions. Asexual reproduction lacks this adaptability because it produces offspring that do not differ genetically from their single parent, or do so in a relatively minor way compared with sexually produced offspring. This capacity to generate genetic diversity offered by sexual reproduction seems to be especially important under times of environmental stress, when a wider range of genetic constitutions within a species may facilitate the survival of a subset of the species adaptively. Thus, in organisms that show facultative sexual reproduction, the switch from uniparental to biparental reproduction tends to occur under times of stress (environmental, pathogenic) whilst reversion to asexual reproduction occurs in times of environmental stability.

The obligatory nature of human (mammalian) sexual reproduction and our inability to revert to asexual reproduction is due to the fact that the genetic contributions from the mother and the father, whilst being as it were *anatomically* equivalent (equal numbers of chromosomes from each) are not *functionally* equivalent. It is now known that a subset of genes are modified epigenetically (*imprinted*) during sperm and egg formation (*gametogenesis*). An epigenetic change does not affect the actual nucleotide base composition of the genes (the "genetic code" itself), but does affect the way in which the genes in the imprinted subset are "wrapped up" in proteins. Moreover, it does so in a way that is perpetuated each time the genes are replicated during cell proliferation: it is an *inherited* epigenetic imprint. This imprinting process affects the availability for expression of these genes during embryogenic, embryonic and fetal development and, indeed, adult life. Thus, the imprinted genes may never be expressed, or may be expressed in reduced amounts or at different times from the non-imprinted genes. Sexual reproduction is obligatory because the subset of genes which is modified epigentically during egg formation (*oogenesis*) is different from the subset modified during sperm formation (*spermatogenesis*): so-called *parental specific imprinting* of genes. Thus, in order to have the complete set of functional genes required for full development, a conceptus *must* receive one set from mother and one set from father. Two sets from father or two sets from mother (both of which can be achieved experimentally) results in failure of the conceptus to complete development: spontaneous abortion (Bartolomei and Tilghman, 1997). It is not clear why (or more strictly in evolutionary terms, how) mammals have evolved this strategy, although some believe that it may have resulted from the unique requirement for an extended period of intra-uterine growth in mammals. However, the *effect* of differential parental imprinting is to fix us as obligate sexual biparental reproducers. We have no choice in the matter other than through the agency of nuclear transfer (*reproductive cloning*).

(ii) The numerology of genetic parenthood

Reproductive cloning by nuclear transfer involves taking a nucleus (46 chromosomes) from a differentiated embryonic, fetal or adult cell and placing it in an egg from which the nucleus has been removed (*enucleated*: Willmut *et al.*, 1997). That egg is then activated to develop as a conceptus. The genes can evidently be reprogrammed, presumably retaining their parentally imprinted status although this has not yet been demonstrated directly, so that they then can direct the full programme of development for a new individual. The nuclear chromosomal set would thus be identical to that in the man or woman providing the nucleus. The person so formed would not however necessarily be genetically completely identical to that man or woman. This is because we also inherit from our mothers, but *not* from our fathers, another set of replicating chromosomes essential for development in addition to the set of 23 maternal nuclear chromosomes. Thus, our mitochondria, responsible for generation of cellular energy, are all received exclusively from the mother via the egg (Frank and Hurst, 1996: Zeviani and Antozzi, 1997). Within each mitochondrion is a small subset of genes on a mitochondrial chromosome. The expression of these genes contributes to mitochondrial replication and function. Thus, a truly uniparental genetic parent would require that the technique of nuclear transfer involved one woman providing both the somatic nucleus and the enucleated egg: she would then have both nuclear and mitochondrial genes identical to those in the cloned conceptus so formed. Uniparental reproductive cloning of this kind would remove the requirement for males. It would, however, reduce the genetic flexibility that biparental sexual reproduction brings to humankind.

Biparental genetic parenthood by reproductive cloning has been suggested as appropriate in specific circumstances. For example, a sterile man lacking any germ cells whatsoever might provide a nucleus with a full set of 46 chromosomes from one of his body cells and his partner might provide an enucleated egg with its mitochondria and their chromosomes, and so both would thereby contribute a genetic component. Alternatively, use of nuclear transfer might provide a genetic input from two women partners. Thus, one partner might provide a somatic (46 nuclear chromosomes) nucleus whilst her partner provided an enucleated egg (mitochondrial chromosomes). In both these cases, there are two genetic parents arrived at by novel routes. Finally, cloning could give rise to triple genetic parentage if instead of using transfer of a nucleus containing 46 nuclear chromosomes, an enucleated egg with its distinct set of mitochondrial genes received only the nuclear maternal set of 23 chromosomes from another egg. This might be done, for example, in rare cases of mitochondrially-diseased mothers (Zeviani and Antozzi, 1997) so that the nuclear genes were from the mother but the mitochondrial genes were from an unaffected egg donor. At fertilisation the spermatozoon would bring in 23 more chromosomes, and so the offspring would technically gain three genetic parents: maternal nuclear chromosomes, paternal nuclear chromosomes, and donor mitochondrial chromosomes. Under current legislation, reproductive cloning by nuclear transfer is illegal in the United Kingdom (Johnson, 1997b).

Triple genetic parenthood is not, however, the upper limit. It has been known for many years in mice that if two early conceptuses, each formed from two distinct sets of parents, are aggregated together to give one single conceptus, it is capable of developing to give rise to a single individual, a so-called chimaera (Graham and Wareing, 1976; Pedersen, 1986). This chimaeric individual would be genetically tetra-parental. In principle, this approach can be applied to three, four or more aggregated conceptuses, with a corresponding multiplication of genetic parenthood, although practical problems start to arise when doing this, which reduces the number of parents reliably achievable.

Thus, the numerology of genetic parenthood is complex. The law recognises a maximum of two parents, and generally has done so on the basis of presumed genetic paternity (see Bainham, Chapter 2 above). However, on a genetic basis alone biology and modern medicine can generate conceptuses with more than two genetic parents. When other biological contributions to parenthood are considered, the plurality of potential parents increases further, although of course under law some of these situations may be covered if not by parentage then by parental responsibility (see Bainham, Chapter 2 above).

Before leaving genetic parenthood there are two further complications that need addressing, this time at the cellular stage. First, an organelle called the centrosome, which controls how the cells of the conceptus and adult divide and proliferate, is derived in humans from the father via the spermatozoon. The centrosome does not have any associated DNA (genes), and thus it is not a genetic component. However, the centrosome does replicate and distribute during cycles of cell proliferation, and it does so (usually) in parallel with the nuclear chromosomes. Moreover, without this paternal centrosome, embryonic cell division and proliferation does not occur and pregnancy fails (Simerly *et al.*, 1995). Presumably in cloning by nuclear transfer, the somatic cell provides the required centrosome. Secondly, the egg brings to the conceptus not simply its chromosomes, both nuclear and mitochondrial, but a full set of cytoplasmic organelles other than a centrosome plus reservoirs of messenger RNA and protein that are essential for the early development of the conceptus up to at least the time of implantation (Johnson and Everitt, forthcoming). Thus, at coitus two parents contribute not just a full set of functional and replicating nuclear (mother and father) and mitochondrial (mother) genes, but also a functional extra-chromosomal centrosome (father) and other cell organelles (mother). Fertilisation is not simply the coming together of the nuclear chromosomes: non-chromosomal features are critical for survival of the conceptus.

(b) Coital (or conjugal) parenthood

In mammals, fertilisation is internal and requires an act of coition in which the male gametes are deposited in the female. In most species, this occurs only when females are both ovulating and in a receptive state: both conditions controlled by the same hormones. The process of coition is preceded by a variable period of courtship and partner selection, which may include ritualistic and affective elements. Coition itself may be accompanied by the experience and expression of intense emotions of a variety of types. Monkeys, great apes and humans differ from most other mammals in that female receptivity has become relatively independent of hormonal control and so females will mate at times other than when fertile. In consequence, coital interactions can take on an increasingly social or pleasurable role as opposed to a primarily reproductive role (Johnson and Everitt, forthcoming).

There is no agreement as to the origins of this evolutionary development. In primates, an extended period of parental care is necessary post-natally to raise offspring to the reproductive age and there is a longer and more complex social learning programme for infants. This is particularly demanding for the female who has a limited supply of eggs to fertilise, carry to parturition and breast-feed, and so invests heavily in fostering close supportive relationships. It is possible that there have been evolutionary benefits to the females and her offspring in having the male remain with a female to provide care, social learning and protection. In contrast, the uncoupling of female fertility and receptivity poses a potential problem for the father, since it seems to tie up his time patrolling fertile females to prevent access of other males, when his own genetic interest encourages him to mate with as many other females as possible. Perhaps a male has also derived compensatory benefits himself from staying near a continually receptive female, so as to favour the survival of his young during their long period of learning and also to gain regular sexual, social and affective gratification. However, only the female can be sure of her parenthood and evolutionarily she wants both the best set of paternal genes around and the best paternal care available, whether or not these are provided by the same male. Indeed there is evidence from chimpanzees (Gagneux *et al.*, 1997), comparable to more detailed studies in monogamous bird pairs (Sutherland and Reynolds, 1995), that covert extra-pair or -clan mating and pregnancy by females does occur, resulting in different genetic and care-giving fathers.

Thus, seen from an evolutionary perspective, male and female genetic parental interests differ. From this biological perspective, it is understandable that human social codes, institutions and laws with messages comparable to the genetic interests of each parent have developed around coition: a permissive set for men and a restrictive set for women, with the coital relationship restricted and sanctified by marriage. The evidence from genetic testing programmes of the extent to which there is full concordance of genetic and accepted family fatherhood in traditional European populations is uncertain (Macintyre and Sooman, 1991). Modern social and medical practice increasingly divorces genetic paternity from other types of biological paternity (see below). However, from both genetic and cultural perspectives, the coital act of itself might be considered to play a contributory role in establishing parenthood, particularly for fathers whose confidence in their genetic paternity may be linked intimately with their belief, correct or erroneous, about the relationship between coitus and genetic transmission. The perception of mothers may also be influenced by such beliefs, although the impact they have on her views about parenthood may perhaps be rather different.

In this context, assisted reproductive technologies (ARTs) involve the intervention of the medical team in the process. Thus, *in-vitro* fertilisation (IVF) could be viewed as either reducing coital parenthood to zero, or making the process multi-parental by incorporating the doctor and the medical team in the concept of parent. Indeed, during fertility treatment it is not unusual for the doctor to talk of "giving the couple a baby", which encapsulates linguistically his coital role, nor for him to be pictured beaming with "his" test-tube babies. Is the doctor (usually male) achieving a surrogate coital multi-fatherhood in this way and how do the couple in treatment incorporate him in their own parental identities? More potently perhaps, where donor insemination is offered to couples in which the male partner either has no gametes or has gametes that are defective in some way, the doctor actively inserts the donor semen into the vagina on behalf of the male partner. In this situation, there are discordances between genetic, coital and post-natal fatherhood. The implications for the view of parenthood by each gender in the partnership are likely to be different. In this context it is of interest that where use of artificial insemination is involved, couples may engage, or be encouraged to engage, in coition at or around the time of insemination so as to offer a chance, however small, of fertilisation occurring naturally. This element of uncertainty about potential or actual genetic paternity may also allow a perception of coital parenthood to be retained and the coital paternity of the doctor reduced. It would be of interest to explore this idea directly.

(c) Gestational (uterine) parenthood

We are the rare survivors of a profligate reproductive process. In humans, a successful act of fertilisation probably results in a baby being born in less than 5 to 10 per cent of cases. Whilst many, perhaps most, of these losses are due to defects in the conceptus, others may be due to deficiencies in the uterine environment itself. This type of loss represents the extreme end of a spectrum of uterine effects on the developing embryo/fetus through which gestational parenthood is exerted. These uterine losses may be influenced by environmental exposure and behaviours (conscious or otherwise) of the carrying mother, factors which also may influence, via uterine effects, the development of the minority of conceptions that do survive to term. Thus, there are clearly demonstrated effects of maternal life-style (smoking, alcohol and drug-taking) during pregnancy on birth weights and fetal well being (Johnson and Everitt, forthcoming). More controversially, maternal nutrition during pregnancy has been claimed to affect enduringly the health status of the offspring during later adult life, influencing susceptibility to, for example, cardio-vascular disease and non-insulin dependent diabetes mellitus (Barker, 1994, 1997; Paneth and Susser, 1995; Paneth *et al.*, 1996). Maternal prenatal stress and psychosocial state can influence the patterns of hormone levels in pregnancy (Wadhwa *et al.*, 1996) and are correlated with altered pregnancy outcome and neonatal experience (Sandman *et al.*, 1994; Lederman, 1995). Materno-fetal stress in animals and humans is associated in infants with enduring changes to the hypothalamic-pituitary-adrenal axis of the offspring, attentional deficits, hyper-anxiety and disturbed social behaviour (Weinstock, 1997), and may contribute to the development of vulnerability to schizophrenia, especially in boy infants (van Os and Selten, 1998). IQ is correlated with birth weight and may be lowered after maternal exposure to alchohol, drug consumption, lead or smoking or raised with dietary supplementation (Churchill, 1965; Rush *et al.*, 1980; Streissguth *et al.*, 1989; Lynn and Hattori, 1990; Reinsich *et al.*, 1995; Baghurst *et al.*, 1992; Olds *et al.*, 1994). It is reasonably clear that the experiences of the mother during pregnancy can have enduring effects on her offspring and thus represent an important parental contribution to them.

The intervention of ARTs may complicate this process further since, during very early "pregnancy" at least, the test tube or culture dish is the uterine equivalent or surrogate. There is clear evidence that the patterns of metabolism and gene expression of the conceptus *in vitro* differ from those *in vivo*: the conceptus adapts to its changed environment (Johnson and Nasr-Esfahani, 1994). These adaptations may have enduring effects. For example, in farm animals *in-vitro* conceptuses produce larger offspring when reimplanted *in utero* (Walker *et al.*, 1996). It is not clear why this should be, but there is evidence that gene expression patterns may change during or as result of *in vitro* culture (Vernet *et al.*, 1993; Sasaki *et al.*, 1995), perhaps in part through effects on the pattern of parental epigenetic imprinting (Romer *et al.*, 1997).

The biology of the gestational component of parenthood, and its potential impact directly on the developing fetus and indirectly on maternal parental behaviour and so on post-natal components of parenthood (see next section), has been relatively under-explored compared with genetic and post-natal parenting. We simply do not yet know whether, for example, uterine influences on each member of a monozygotic twin pregnancy differ significantly, and if so how this might influence the interpretation of studies on twins separated at birth.

We do know that twinning incidence falls between the first trimester and birth, estimates varying widely but probably being of the order of 20 to 50 per cent (Landy *et al.*, 1986; Seound *et al.*, 1992). Monozygotic twins are also frequently of very different birth weights. Since differential loss and growth do occur, differential effects of the uterine environment on traits might also be highly significant.

Comparative modelling studies on IQ in twins (mono- and di-zygotic which share the same uterine environment) and in siblings from different gestations (which do not) have suggested a large maternal (uterine) effect of around 20 per cent for twins and 5 per cent for siblings of IQ covariance with a corresponding reduction in the contribution of heritability to under 50 per cent (Devlin *et al.*, 1997). Failure to acknowledge an important influence of gestational parenthood on traits and attributes might lead us to ascribe erroneously more weight to genetic parenthood than is appropriate. Moreover, there is evidence that the experiences of pregnancy can interact with post-natal parental behaviour, further emphasising the potential importance of gestational parenthood.

(d) Post-natal parenthood including parturitional aspects

Reproduction is essential for the propagation of the species and a reductionist evolutionary view would be that parents are simply vehicles for genes. However, in humans and higher primates the efficient transmission of the genes has evolved into a very complex and sophisticated process in which a post-natal period of lactational nutrition, extended parental care and acculturation plays an essential and influential role. Thus, higher primates transmit not just their genetic inheritance from one generation to the next, but also their culture (linguistic, social, religious, economic, scientific etc). This cultural inheritance also evolves, thereby playing a key role in the survival, or demise, of the community and species. The parenthood involved in the post-natal care of young is often called "social", which could convey the impression that it is non-biological. Since prolonged post-natal care, and probably many of the parental and child behaviours observed during it (Hinde, 1987), form an intrinsic part of our evolved biology, this distinction is questionable and could lead to a devaluation of physiological aspects of post-natal parenting. This is not to claim post-natal care exclusively or even primarily for biology (Strathern, 1993), but to emphasise the point that biology has something important to say about this phase of parenthood.

There are suggestive links between gestational and post-natal parenting that seem to transcend cultures. The hormonal changes at parturition seem to set the context for maternal care-giving and thus for future mother-child interactions. Maternal attitudes, psycho-physiology and behaviour may be influenced by hormonal changes during pregnancy so that even mothers with initially negative attitudes towards being pregnant generally develop more positive attitudes by about five months and fetal movements. The increasing concentrations of a number of steroids including oestrogens, progesterone and the opioids may be involved, although how is not clear (Corter and Fleming, 1995). In addition, the abrupt fall in all hormone levels except prolactin occurring around parturition, may influence parental behaviour and so contribute a physiologically driven component to the development of a parental identity. Cortisol is particularly implicated, being high in pregnancy, peaking at parturition and then declining over the first week post-partum. Cortisol release is associated with high affect (Corter and Fleming, 1995). Oxytocin, also associated with parturition, is implicated in the initiation of parental bonding and behaviours in many mammalian species, although the evidence relating to our own species remains circumstantial (Anderson-Hunt and Dennerstein, 1995; Nissen *et al.*, 1995; Carter and Altemus, 1997). During the post-partum period, 40 to 80 per cent of women experience mood changes, the intensity of which is thought to arise from endocrine change and the valence of which to be situational. There is also correlative evidence consistent with cortisol changes facilitating early maternal responsiveness to sensory cues from infants including their odours. Interestingly, when some fathers of post-partum babies are compared with mothers, their cortisol patterns also show changes in the same direction but to a lesser extent (and their androgens fall), both probably stress induced, and these changes are also correlated with a greater sensitivity to the infant sensory cues than is shown by non-parental controls. However, fathers do not sustain and develop this responsiveness in the ways that women do as the time from birth elapses (reviewed in Corter and Fleming, 1995). If the endocrine changes at parturition are indeed facilitatory, the briefest duration between parturition and extended contact with the infant would be expected to facilitate various aspects of early maternal behaviour. Claims that this is indeed the case (Klaus and Kennel, 1976) have been questioned (Richards, 1984, 1992). Whilst none of these endocrine changes are likely to be essential for effective maternal function, they may have the potential to contribute and thus may constitute part of the parental identity forming experience.

The parent-infant bond then develops through patterns of mutual interaction from these early post-natal events, and parental experience becomes an important factor in determining how rapidly these patterns develop. There is an extensive literature on post-natal care patterns and child development stimulated and dominated in large measure by the work of Bowlby and his colleagues on attachment (1973, 1980, 1982; Ainsworth *et al.*, 1978). The focus of this work has been very much from the child's perspective and how patterns of mothering might affect child development and attachment patterns, and what these might mean for the child's patterns of behaviour in later life, including their parenting abilities (Hinde and Stevenson-Hinde, 1991). There has been a tendency to infer that patterns of parenting are simply reciprocal to the attachment needs of the child, but this inference assumes that the interests of the parent and child will always be concordant. There is evidence from observation on patterns of parent-child interactions that this is not so, and the assumption is intuitively unlikely (Solomon and George, 1996). There are clearly likely to be circumstances in which abandonment or death of the child may be in the best interest of the inclusive fitness of the parents, for example where not to let the child go would threaten the survival or well-being of siblings or parents themselves. This stark choice is being faced by increasing numbers of parents (for embryonic, fetal or post-natal stages) as the range and reliability of genetic testing increases and the capacity of medicine to keep premature and/or afflicted babies and infants alive improves. The unbalanced emphasis of research on the child's perspective and on the long-term consequences for the child of post-natal parenting patterns may in part explain the undue weight given to the child's concerns in recent legislation (see Herring, Chapter 5 below). The immediate needs and concerns of the parents themselves are important considerations, not only for the parents themselves but also because to frustrate or ignore them is unlikely to be of advantage to the developing infant (Richards, 1992). More work is needed to address how parenting patterns affect and reflect the parents' needs and to determine where there is conflict with the child's needs and how best to manage this.

3. INTERACTION AND/OR DISSOCIATION OF THE BIOLOGICAL COMPONENTS OF PARENTHOOD

Parenthood is an amorphous concept with roots in biology but the social construction of which changes with time, culture and the status of the observer (Strathern, 1993). It thus resembles in some ways gender and sexuality. Borrowing and adapting some terminology from the study of these examples, individuals might therefore be considered to have a view of a society's *parental stereotypes*: what it means in that society to be a parent, a socially constructed view measurable by social surveys. Individuals might also be thought to have, or to develop a *parental identity:* the internal conceptual state of what being a parent means for that individual, measurable through tests of attitude, affect, beliefs, and, via its expression, as behaviours by observation. The concepts of stereotype and identity seem to be potentially useful, not least because they may help frame approaches to research, but also because they may in themselves offer some helpful insights into the conflicting views about parenthood that seem current with the advent of the new Assisted Reproductive Technologies (ARTs). For example, just as there may be conflict between the *perceived and experienced* sexual or gender stereotype and the *felt* sexual or gender identity, so parental identity may conform with or react against the parental stereotype and result in behaviours regarded as more or less acceptable socially and personally (Edwards, 1993; Hirsch, 1993). Low congruence between stereotype and identity may create internal and external tensions. For example, Richards (1992) has pointed out how unrealistic expectations about parental bonding in the post-partum period might prove stressful for some parents of premature babies or for mothers who have had difficult deliveries, and so who are not able to live up to the stereotype. They may thus start parenthood with a diminished or impaired sense of parental identity. The use of ARTs might induce the same responses by removing genetic, coital or gestational components of parenthood selectively. Breaking down parenthood into stereotype and identity might also make it easier to analyse, since it separates the social view from the individual view and simplifies the framing of questions about each and their relationship. It also refocuses on parents, shifting the balance of interest away from overemphasis on simply the child's needs.

There do seem to have been recent changes in the parental stereotype in Western European culture. Thus, until quite recently, the four biological components of parenthood discussed in detail above were implicitly assumed, socially and legally, to be concordant and to involve just two parents (Table 3.1). Overt acknowledgement of deviation from this pattern could be labelled "abnormal" and be hidden or punished, or could in limited ways be socially acceptable. Thus for women, the option of uniparental post-natal motherhood might be imposed or, less acceptably until recently in our society, chosen. Prior to the advent and use of the assisted reproductive technologies (ARTs), some uncoupling of post-natal parenthood from the other three could occur to a greater or lesser extent acceptably, if not always "normally", via adoption, fostering, wet nursing, step-parenting and forms of extended family systems (see Mitchell and Goody, Chapter 6 below). For fathers, the possibilities for uncoupling were greater, but social and legal sanctions were used to reduce these and in practice it was assumed in the absence of evidence to the contrary that the birth of a child to a married couple represented the outcome of fully concordant parenthood for each. Moreover, given the legally enforced stability of family relationships and the size of families, the four biological components of parenthood were also largely congruent with extended kinship patterns.

Table 3.1: Summary of concordance relationships for the four classes of parenthood for females (F) and males (M) for different patterns of unassisted reproduction approaches.

Reproductive approach (Total no. Parents)	Type of Parent						
	Female				Male		
	genetic	coital	gestational	post-natal	genetic	coital	post-natal
Unassisted (2)	A	A	A	A	Z	Z	Z
Adoption (4)	A	A	A	B	Z	Z	Y
Fostering (2–4)	A	A	A	B/A	Z	Z	Y/Z
Step father (3)	A	A	A	A	Z	Z	Y
Step mother (3)	A	A	A	B	Z	Z	Z
Single mother(1)	A	A	A	A	0	0	0

* Where all columns record A for female and Z for male, the same female/male member of the "couple" undergoing treatment provides all four components of parenthood. Different letters each denote a "parent" additional to the primary couple. A 0 means no parent of this category.

More recently, family planning, social mobility, and the relaxation of social attitudes to extra-marital sex, divorce, single parenting, and sexual experimentation mean that (i) fully concordant biological parenthood is no longer immediately assumed, and (ii) kinship influences have changed or weakened. The advent of ART has probably contributed to the reduced concordance and placed stresses on established notions of kinship (Table 3.2). Comparison of the two tables shows that ART has provided a change which is both quantitative and qualitative. Whilst both Tables provide examples of incomplete parenthood and oligoparenthood, Table 3.2 contains more possibilities for both categories. In addition, ART has provided a new category of partial or mixed parenthood for women through surrogacy and donation. Reproductive cloning by nuclear transfer, were it to be allowed, would expand this range further. It is arguable that the advent of ART and its application has accelerated and expanded the range of socially acceptable variation in non-assisted parenthood, such as gay and lesbian parenting, post-mortem parenting, parenting by peri- and post-menopausal women etc, and in so doing is radically transforming the parental stereotype. ART has certainly reinforced the dominance of the biological components of the parental stereotype at the expense of other social or cultural components of kinship (Strathern, 1993).

It may not only be medical technology that has had this effect. The scientific discourse about genetics, especially filtered through the media, has also changed over the same period. In Western culture generally, the scientific debates

Table 3.2: Summary of concordance relationships for the four classes of parenthood for females (F) and males (M) for some types of assisted reproductive technologies.

ART (Total no. parents)	Type of Parent						
	Female				Male		
	genetic	coital	gestational	post-natal	genetic	coital	post-natal
Unassisted (2)	A	A	A	A	Z	Z	Z
IVF/GIFT/ICSI (2–3[a])	A	0/A[a]	A	A	Z	0/Y[a]	Z
HI (2–3[a])	A	0/A[a]	A	A	Z	0/Y[a]	Z
DI (3–4[a])	A	0/A[a]	A	A	Z	0/Y[a]	X
Egg donation +IVF (3–4[a])	A	0/B[a]	B	B	Z	0/Y[a]	Z
Embryo donation (4–5[a])	A	0/B[a]	B	B	Z	0/Y[a]	X
Partial surrogacy (3)	A	0	A	B	Z	0	Z
Host/full surrogacy (3)	A	0	B	A	Z	0	Z
Embryo donation [b] full surrogacy (5)	A	0	B	C	Z	0	Y
Cloning of male (3–5)	A[c]	0/B[a]	B	0/B/C (if surrogate used)	Z	0/Y[a]	Z
Cloning of female (2)	A plus B[d]	0/A[b] or B[a]	A[b] or B	A[b] or B	0	0	0

* Where all columns record A for female and Z for male, the same female/male member of the "couple" undergoing treatment provides all four components of parenthood. Different letters each denote a "parent" additional to the primary couple. 0 means no parent of this category. IVF = in vitro fertilisation; GIFT = gamete intra-fallopian transfer; ICSI = intracytoplasmic sperm injection; HI = artificial insemination by husband; DI = artificial insemination by donor; partial surrogacy = the surrogate supplies the egg and the commissioning male provides the sperm; host/full surrogacy = the commissioning couple provides the embryo.

[a] If doctor perceived as coital partner.

[b] If cloning self.

[c] Mitochondrial genes; if donor of enucleated egg also provides the uterus then A[c] = B.

[d] Mitochondrial genes unless enucleated egg is from same woman providing nuclear chromosomes, in which case A = B[d].

occasioned by the nature/nurture conflict turned decisively away from genetic influence towards environmental (largely seen as post-natal rather than gestational influence) in the pre- and post-war periods. The eugenic views of the first half of this century, deriving from the coalescence of Mendelian genetics with the discovery of chromosomes, was rejected, in part due to the aversive experience of certain sorts of eugenics in action but also because of the widely published developmental studies of Bowlby and others. The critical role of parents, especially mothers (see Mitchell and Goody, Chapter 6 below) in bringing up their children was emphasised at the expense of genetic factors. More recently, with the emphasis on the human genome project, the pendulum has swung back towards genes, perhaps too violently.

A large body of work has attempted to assess the relative contributions of the different components of parenthood to the establishment of an individual's physical, behavioural and psychological development. Usually these focus on genetic versus environmental (which lumps post-natal, gestational and coital biological aspects together with social and environmental factors such as disease, experience, etc.). These studies use intra-familial comparisons and especially comparisons between mono- and dizygotic twins, between adopted and non-adopted siblings, and between differently adopted monozygotic twins (Plomin *et al.*, 1997). A measure of heritability is produced which is simply a quantitative description of that part of the phenotypic variation within a population that can, under the specific circumstances of the study, be ascribed to a genetic influence. The heritability in most studies of complex behaviours tends to be less than 50% (Plomin *et al.*, 1997) which means that non-genetic factors account for more of the variability in phenotype.

It is important to emphasise that abuse of measures of heritability risks oversimplistic reductionist conclusions. Our cultural inheritance is the accumulated product of our collective social experience, winnowed through the more recent specific experiences of ourselves as children. That cultural inheritance is itself to a large extent conditioned and limited by our individual and species genetic make-up. Attempts to separate out the two discretely into components may be fundamentally misguided. Cultural and genetically-based inheritances interact in ways that may not be linear or simply additive (Hinde, 1987). For example, the activities of nerves (neurones) in the developing and adult nervous system condition the patterns of inter-neuronal contacts and the circuitry that develops. The activities themselves can depend upon the environment experienced. Exposure to certain environments can affect the hard-wiring of the brain so that some circuits are lost and others are developed (e.g. Breedlove, 1997; Pantev *et al.*, 1998; Fregnac, 1998). Some of these exposures may be gestational whilst others are post-natal. Thus although the basic wiring pattern is almost certainly laid down according to genetic specifications, this process may simply provide the substrate on which environmental, including gestational and cultural, experiences can work to determine the final structural and functional wiring patterns achieved.

Moreover, most of the behavioural traits studied are complex e.g. intelligence, aggression, sexuality, criminality, depression etc. The more complex the trait, the more difficult is a precise and uniformly applied definition of the trait, and this is problematic when making claims of associations with particular genetic make-ups. Each trait is also made up of a number of components: at its simplest sensory, cognitive, affective and motor components. A genetic effect on the basic wiring circuitry of motor performance will therefore be likely to be associated significantly with the way in which a particular trait develops and is expressed, and may indeed limit or change the way in which learning and experience can modulate the trait. This effect is quite different from saying that there is a gene causing the trait (as in gay gene, aggression gene, dyslexic gene). In general, clean separation of genetic and environmental components may not be achievable in a way that is meaningful. Thus, when the heritability of a trait is described as being 45 per cent, it does not explain how the genes contribute 45 per cent of the trait or at what level or through what sorts of interactive processes. Neither does it mean that the answers to each of these questions are the same for different individuals or different populations under different conditions: it is an averaging statement about a particular population within which variety exists.

However, the simplistic press reporting of genes "for" gayness, cognitive ability, dyslexia or schizophrenia is likely to encourage the belief that complex behaviours are genetically "caused" and therefore programmed (Johnson, 1997a). To the lay person, this reported strong emphasis of genetic influences on complex behaviours can easily coalesce with common sense observations of the sort "he behaves just like his dad" to produce a view that genes are the basis for the behaviours and thus constitute the most important biological component of parenthood.

It should not surprise us that the quantitative genetics of complex traits is misunderstood by journalists and by the general public, because Richards (1996) has shown that the much simpler concepts of Mendelian genetics are not understood even by couples with experience of genetic counselling. Despite their exposure to specific genetic education, their beliefs about how genetic information is inherited is based on their experience of kinship patterns, rather than their knowledge of genetics. The fact that public beliefs may not be accurate, does not of course mean that they are not powerful. It is difficult to believe that the greater public exposure to genetics has not increased the perceived significance of genetics as a contributor to parental stereotype and identity. Data on this supposition and, if it is sustained, on how the exposure to genetics has been interpreted would be interesting, and might help future efforts at education as well as informing on parental stereotypes and identities.

Given the complexity of biological influences on particular outcomes , and given the mis-use or mis-interpretation of the developing knowledge about both biology and its manipulation in pursuit of parenthood, popular culture and the law itself are unlikely to be immune from distortion. Parental sterotypes, parental identities and the law as it relates to parents are likely to reflect the emphases emerging from biological research. In the next section, aspects of recent legislation in this area are examined for evidence on this point.

4. VIEWS OF PARENTHOOD AND THE HUMAN FERTILISATION AND EMBRYOLOGY ACT

The roles of ART and indeed of the new genetics in influencing the concept of parental stereotype are to some extent codified in the Human Fertilisation and Embryology Act 1990 and in the regularly revised code of practice issued by the Human Fertilisation and Embryology Authority (HFEA), which administers the Act. I wish to consider four areas of this Act which illustrate how the relative contributions of the four biological components of parenthood to the parental stereotype have been used.

(a) The status of the embryo

The events leading up to the HFE Act were driven primarily by concern about the status of the human embryo *in vitro* (Mulkay, 1997). The whole tone of the discussion accepted explicitly or implicitly that the establishment of the genetic make-up of the conceptus at fertilisation was critical. Some argued directly for this change of status to be reflected in law by full protection from fertilisation onwards. Others argued that whilst the genetic make-up was indeed established at fertilisation, it was not until later (14 days or the primitive streak stage) that genetic expression had occurred and the unique *individual* genetic identity of a viable conceptus was established. It was agreed by all that from fertilisation onwards the conceptus deserved special *respect*. Parliament accepted the latter of the two propositions. However, the fundamental assumption underlying both arguments was that genetic identity was paramount. Following from this, gametes were given protection under the law only to the extent that they are to be used as "genetic material" in producing a conceptus, despite the biological fact that gametes bring a great deal more that is essential to the conceptus than their genes (see Johnson, 1989 and earlier for discussion). Not surprisingly, therefore, the emphasis in the Act is on the control of creation, storage and use of this genetic material before and after fertilisation. The genetic inheritance, removed from the body and stored and manipulated in the public domain, seems to be treated like the inheritance of other commodities with issues of parental ownership, consent and obligation clarified. The genetic nature of parenthood is emphasised by much of the Act.

(b) Gamete and embryo donation

Of the various ARTs, donor insemination (DI) has been established for longest, but its status has changed only recently. Children produced by DI were regarded as illegitimate, reflecting a genetic view of paternity, until the Family Law Reform Act of 1987, and this situation was clarified further in 1990 with the passage of the Human Fertilisation and Embryology Act. Egg and embryo donation are more recent. On this subject, therefore, the Act appears to change gear noisily, in that it allows the child born from donation to be registered on the birth certificate as the child of the couple being treated, as long as both parents consent to this. The genetic parenthood of the child is ignored and the gestational and post-natal parentages are paramount. This part of the Act appears to shift away from the otherwise predominantly genetic view of parenthood. However, it is hedged with provisions that reflect the dominant role of the genetics of parenthood elsewhere in the Act. Thus, there is an overemphatic and almost systematic denial of genetic parenthood in the provisions that prevent children so born from identifying their genetic origin or even from obtaining useful information for sharing with their gestational/post-natal parents. Indeed, the level of openness within these families appears to be very limited, a situation implicitly encouraged by the law (Kovacs *et al.*, 1993; Lui *et al.*, 1995). These provisions seem to be there largely for the benefit of donors (genetic parents), and not for the benefit of the children (Maclean and Maclean, 1996). I suggest that they reflect the predominance and potency of genetic parenthood and the obligations it brings, and are trying to offer legal protection to donors at the expense of children. Given the dominant role of genetics in our current thinking, it will be interesting to see whether this provision of the Act withstands legal challenge by children born of donation who wish to gain access to information about their genetic origins held on a register by a government body but denied to them. The incorporation of the European Convention on Human Rights into English law, together with the growing trend in international law to recognise the right of the child to knowledge of biological/genetic origins, makes such a challenge more likely (see also Bainham, Chapter 2 above). It may also be that some donors, far from feeling protected, may come to challenge their inability to gain access to the identities of their genetic children. I have a general feeling that the law, in effectively denying genetic parenthood after donation, is not chiming with current social thinking and values of parenthood, and certainly within the Act itself is internally very confused on this issue.

(c) Surrogacy

Surrogacy is a minor concern of the HFE Act (section 30), but is also regulated via the Surrogacy Arrangements Act 1985. The whole issue of the regulation of surrogacy has recently been the subject of a review and a public consultation for the Department of Health. The current legislation also appears at first sight to contradict the strong emphasis on genetic parenthood seen elsewhere in the legislation on ARTs, in that the surrogate mother has legal claim to maternity of any child born, whether or not she has contributed genetic material to its conception. The commissioning couple, even if the child is wholly related to them genetically, has no legally enforceable claim to the child without the full consent of the surrogate mother. Thus, gestational parenthood has primacy over genetic parenthood. Given the overemphasis on genetic material and the control of its use elsewhere in the legislation, this paradoxical situation is resolvable by reference back to the tone of the Warnock Report (1984), which expressed a very negative and discouraging view of surrogacy, although a minority report was slightly less hostile. The legislation, which cannot be said to be encouraging of the practice, reflects this view. Couples are almost challenged by the law not to risk entering unenforceable surrogacy agreements by giving them little or no control over their own genetic material. Thus, even the surrogacy legislation seems to be driven by a largely genetic view of parenthood.

(d) The welfare of the child

One condition of licences issued by the HFEA for provision of treatment services is that:

> "a woman shall not be provided with treatment services unless account has been taken of the welfare of any child who may be born as a result of the treatment (including the need of that child for a father), and of any other child who may be affected by the birth" (section 13(5)).

This condition applies only to centres with a treatment licence (i.e. for IVF, DI, egg or embryo donation using IVF or GIFT). Once it applies, however, it covers *any* of the services these centres offer to assist conception or pregnancy whether or not these services require a licence under the Act. The HFEA is not prescriptive about how this condition is applied. It does, however, require the licensed centres to have clear written procedures for assessing the welfare of the child. It also gives advice in its Code of Practice about the sort of considerations that centres might take into account and notes the importance of a stable and supportive environment for a child.

Implicit in making any assessment of the welfare of a child to be born of ART is an idea of what a good (or at the very least a bad) parent is (Douglas, 1993). Since the clinician is required to undertake this assessment, the clinician's view of parental stereotypes is likely to be influential. Not surprisingly, there is evidence that licensed centres have considerable difficulty in applying this condition (Price, 1993; Lieberman *et al.*, 1994), notably in respect of parental age, death, absence, gender and sexuality, HIV status, ability to pay, and cancer or other health status including genetic disease. Moreover, there is wide variation in the procedures by which the condition is formally applied and in the criteria used in applying it (Patel and Johnson, 1998).

It is interesting to compare the wording in the HFE Act with that in the Children Act 1989, in which the child's welfare is described as being "paramount" rather than "taken account of", especially since the Children Act covers the future life of the child including adulthood. Empirically, one might think it arguable that where there is only a virtual or imaginary child (and indeed parents), the quality of consideration given to the child's interests should be higher not lower. Thus, the outcome of the consideration might be an act of child creation and so is susceptible of being avoided: not options open with existing children where actions must be remedial rather than preventative. Moreover, given the primary involvement of the clinician (therapeutically and often financially too) for her/his patients (the potential parents), the potential child could be considered to deserve if anything a stronger voice simply by virtue of its physical absence. This point is all the more acute when the agent(s) of operation of the conditions are considered. Thus, for the Children Act, the independent agents of Social Services and the courts are involved, whereas for the child to be born of ART there *is* only the doctor plus such colleagues and ethical committees as s/he may choose to consult: the final decision is however the doctor's alone. This is a considerable burden on someone for whom dispassion is difficult and who may have a direct interest in the outcome of the consideration. Finally, it can be argued that the potential for conflict of interests between child and parent is likely to be more painful where the child already exists than where it does not, and that therefore in principle as well as in practice a lower threshold should operate with existing children: hence perhaps the presumption (and evidently the practice: Herring, Chapter 5 below) that only *in extremis* will the Children Act be invoked. All of these points seem to argue for a higher hurdle in the HFE Act than the Children Act, the reverse of the current situation.

I am not arguing that the HFE Act *should* impose a higher threshold but pointing out an apparent inconsistency. Perhaps the reason for it arises from a stronger, or at least more immediate, comparison: namely that the establishment of non-ART mediated pregnancies has no threshold at all. However, there is a practical point. Given the difficulty that clinicians have in applying the HFE Act, could the experience of the Children Act give them guidance? In particular, could the criteria accepted by Social Services and/or the courts for separating existing children from parents be summarised for clinicians to apply to the HFE Act? There is no case law that I am aware of concerning the application of section 13(5) of the HFE Act, although a judicial review (*R v Ethical Committee of St Mary's Hospital Manchester*, 26 October 1987) did consider that grounds for refusing to allow a couple to foster or adopt could reasonably be applied to a refusal to treat by IVF. In the Diane Blood case, the main issues turned on consent and (eventually) free trade. The "need of the child for a father" was addressed in evidence by expert witnesses and Mrs Blood herself, but these were not matters considered material to the judgement. It is also not clear how section 13(5) of the HFE Act sits with the European Convention on Human Rights (Chapter 5 below). Again, perhaps the confusion and difficulties posed by this part of the Act derive from the strong emphasis elsewhere on "genetic material" as the most important component of parenthood. This provision sits rather uneasily within the Act and, as indicated above, is proving problematic for practitioners to implement.

5. CONCLUSION

Biology does not give an answer to the question: what is a parent? That question goes beyond biology to a conceptual level, which, I have argued, is itself a hybrid of social stereotype and individual identity. Biology can inform about how different components of the process of reproductive parenting might influence the child produced and so the ways in which the significance of each component might be viewed for parenthood or by parents. Biomedical science through its technology and its discourse has also undoubtedly influenced parental stereotypes and identities, and the law relating to parents. In preparing this chapter, I was surprised at how little emphasis there has been on the parental view in studies on early child development, and at how this may have affected social and legislative programmes. I was also surprised to find little research on how people think of parents and why, what really influences them, and how they integrate what science is saying into their own parental stereotypes and identities. As a result, there is more conjecture than I would have liked in trying to relate biomedical knowledge and understanding to the more complex social and legal question: what is a parent?

REFERENCES

Anderson-Hunt, M. and Dennerstein, L., "Oxytocin and female sexuality" (1995) 40 *Gynecol-Obstet Invest.* 217–21.

Ainsworth, M. D., Blehar, M. C., Waters, E. *et al.*, *Patterns of Attachment* (Erlbaum, Hillsdale, New Jersey, Erlbaum, 1978).

Baghurst, P. A., *et al.*, "Environmental exposure to lead and children's intelligence at the age of seven years" (1992) 327 *N. Eng. J. Med.* 1279–1284.

Barker, D. J. P., *Mothers, Babies and Disease in Later Life* (London, BMJ Publishing Group, 1994).

Barker, D. J. P., "The fetal origins of coronary heart disease" (1997) 422 *Acta Paediatrica*, Supplement 78–82.

Bartolomei, M. S. and Tilghman, S. M., "Genomic imprinting in mammals" (1997) 31 *Annual Review of Genetics* 493–525.

Bowlby, J., *Attachment and Loss Volume 1*, 2nd edn. (London, Hogarth, 1982).

Bowlby, J., *Attachment and Loss Volume 2* (London, Hogarth, 1973).

Bowlby, J., *Attachment and Loss Volume 3* (London, Hogarth, 1980).

Breedlove, S. M., "Sex on the brain" (1997) 389 *Nature* 801.

Carter, C. S. and Altemus, M., "Integrative functions of lactational hormones in social behaviour and stress management" (1997) 807 *Ann. N.Y. Acad. Sci.* 164–74.

Churchill, J. A., "The relationship between intelligence and birth weight in twins" (1965) 15 *Neurology* 341–347.

Corter, C. M. and Fleming, A. S., "Psychobiology of Maternal Behavior in Human Beings" in M. H. Bornstein (ed.), *Handbook of Parenting, Volume 2* (Bornstein, Mahwah, New Jersey, Lawrence Erlbaum Associates 1995).

Crow, J. F., "Advantages of sexual reproduction" (1994) 15 *Developmental Genetics* 205–213.

Devlin, B., Daniels, M. and Roeder, K., "The heritability of IQ" (1997) 388 *Nature* 468–471.

Douglas, G., "Assisted reproduction and the welfare of the child" (1993) 5 *Current Legal Problems* 53–74.

Edwards, J., "Explicit connections: ethnographic enquiry in north-west England" in J. Edwards *et al.* (eds.), *Technologies of Procreation* (Manchester, Manchester University Press, 1993), 42–66.

Frank, S. A. and Hurst, L. D., "Mitochondria and male disease" (1996) 383 *Nature* 224.

Fregnac, Y., "Homeostasis or synaptic plasticity"? (1998) 391 *Nature* 845–846.

Gagneux, P., Woodruff, D. S. and Boesch, C., "Furtive mating in female chimpanzees" (1997) 387 *Nature* 358–359.

Gould, J. L. and Gould, C. G., *Sexual Selection* (New York, W.H. Freeman, 1997).

Graham, C. F. and Wareing, P. F., *The Developmental Biology of Plants and Animals* (Oxford, Blackwell Science, 1976).

Hinde, R. A., *Individuals, Relationships and Culture: Links between Ethology and the Social Sciences* (Cambridge, Cambridge University Press, 1987).

Hinde, R. A. and Stevenson-Hinde, J., "Perspectives on attachment" in C. Murray Parkes, J. Stevenson-Hinde and P. Marris (eds.), *Attachment Across the Life Cycle* (London, Routledge, 1991).

Hirsch, E., "Negotiated limits: interviews in south-east England" in J. Edwards *et al.* (eds.), *Technologies of Procreation* (Manchester, Manchester University Press, 1993).

Johnson, M. H., "Did I begin"? (1989) 9 *New Scientist* (December), 39–42.

Johnson, M. H., "Genetics, the free market and reproductive medicine" (1997) 12 *Human Reprod.* 408–410.

Johnson, M. H., "Cloning humans"? (1997) 19 *BioEssays* 737–739.

Johnson, M. H. and Everitt, B. J., *Essential Reproduction*, 5th edn. (Oxford, Blackwell Science, forthcoming).

Johnson, M. H. and Nasr-Esfahani, M. H., "Radical solutions and cultural problems" (1994) 16 *BioEssays* 31–38.

Klaus, M. H. and Kennell, J. H., *Parent-Child Bonding* (St Louis, Mosby, 1976).

Kovacs, G. T., Mushin, D., Kane, H. *et al.*, "A controlled study of the psychosocial development of children conceived following insemination with donor semen" (1993) 8 *Human Reproduction* 788–790.

Landy, H. J., Weiner, S., Corson, S. L. *et al.*, "The vanishing twin: ultrasonographic assessment of fetal disappearance in the first trimester" (1986) *Am. J. Obstet. Gynecol.* 14–19.

Lederman, R. P., "Relationship of anxiety, stress, and psychosocial development to reproductive health" (1995) 21 *Behavioral Medicine* 101–112.

Lieberman, B. A., Matson, P. L. and Hamer, F., "The UK Human Fertilisation and Embryology Act 1990—how well is it functioning?" (1994) 9 *Human Reproduction* 1779–1782.

Lui, S. C., Weaver, S. M., Robinson, J. *et al.*, "A survey of semen donor attitudes" (1995) 10 *Human Reproduction* 234–238.

Lynn, R. and Hattori, K., "The heritability of intelligence in Japan" (1990) 20 *Behav. Genetics* 545–546.

Lyons, E. J., "Sex and synergism" (1998) 390 *Nature* 19–20.

Macintyre, S. and Sooman, A., "Non-paternity and prenatal genetic screening" *The Lancet* 869–871.

Maclean, S. and Maclean, M., "Keeping secrets in assisted reproduction—the tension between donor anonymity and the need of the child for information" (1996) 8 *Child and Family Law Quarterly* 243–251.

Mulkay, M., *The Embryo Research Debate* (Cambridge, Cambridge University Press, 1997).

Nissen, E., Lilja, G., Widstrom, A. M. *et al.*, "Elevation of oxytocin levels early post partum in women" (1995) 74 *Acta-Obstet-Gynecol-Scand.* 530–3.

Olds, D. L., Henderson, C. R. and Tatelbaum, R., "Intelligence impairment in children of women who smoke cigarettes during pregnancy" (1994) 93 *Pediatrics* 221–227.

Paneth, N., Ahmed, F. and Stein, D. S., "Early nutritional origins of hypertension: a hypothesis still lacking support" (1996) 14 *J. Hypertension* S121–129.

Paneth, N. and Susser, M., "Early origin of coronary heart disease (the 'Barker hypothesis')" (1995) 310 *British Medical Journal* 411–412.

Pantev, C., Oostenveld, R., Engelien, A. *et al.*, "Increased auditory cortical representation in musicians" (1998) 392 *Nature* 811–814.

Patel, J. C. and Johnson, M. H., "A survey of the effectiveness of the assessment of the welfare of the child in UK in-vitro fertilisation units" (1998) 13 *Human Reproduction* 766–770.

Pedersen, R. A., "Potency, lineage, and allocation in preimplantation mouse embryos" in J. Rossant and R. A. Pedersen (eds.), *Experimental Approaches to Mammalian Embryonic Development* (Cambridge, Cambridge University Press, 1986).

Plomin, R., DeFries, J. C., McClearn, G. E. *et al.*, *Behavioral Genetics*, 3rd edn. (New York, W.H. Freeman and Co., 1997).

Price, F., "Beyond expectation: clinical practices and clinical concerns" in J. Edwards *et al.* (eds.), *Technologies of Procreation* (Manchester, Manchester University Press, 1993).

Reinsich, J., Sanders, S. A., Mortensen, E. L. *et al.*, "In utero exposure to phenobarbital and intelligence defects in adult men" (1995) 274 *J. Am. Med. Assoc.* 1518–1525.

Richards, M. P. M., "The myth of bonding" in J.A. Macfarlane (ed.), *Progress in Child Health, Volume 1.* (London, Churchill Livingstone, 1984) pp. 113–120.

Richards, M. P. M., "Psychological aspects of neonatal care" in N.R.C. Roberton (ed.). *Textbook of Neonatology*, 2nd. edn. (London, Churchill Livingstone, 1992).

Richards, M. P. M., "Lay and professional knowledge of genetics and inheritance" (1996) 5 *Public Understanding of Science* 217–230.

Romer, I., Reik, W., Dean, W. *et al.*, "Epigenetic inheritance in the mouse" (1997) 7 *Current Biology* 277–280.

Rush, D., Stein, Z., Susser, M. *et al.* (eds.), *Diet in Pregnancy: A Randomised Controlled Trial of Nutritional Supplements* (New York, Lis, 1980).

Sandman, C. A., Wadhwa, P. D., Dunkelschetter, C. *et al.*, "Psychobiological influences of stress and HPA regulation on the human fetus and infant birth outcomes" (1994) 739 *Annals of the New York Academy of Sciences* 198–210.

Sasaki, H., Ferguson-Smith, A. C., Shum, A. S. *et al.*, "Temporal and spatial regulation of *H19* imprinting in normal and uniparental mouse embryos" (1995) 121 *Development* 4195–4202.

Seound, M. A. F., Toner, J. P., Kruithoff C. *et al.*, "Outcome of twin, triplet and quadruplet in vitro fertilization pregnancies: the Norfolk experience" (1992) 57 *Fertil. Steril.* 825–834.

Simerly, C., Wu, G., Ord, T. *et al.*, "The paternal inheritance of the centrosome, the cells microtubule-organising centre, in humans, and the implications for infertility" (1995) 1 *Nature Medicine* 47–52.

Solomon, J. and George, C., "Defining the caregiving system: towards a theory of caregiving" (1996) 17 *Infant Mental Health Journal* 183–197.

Strathern, M., "A question of context" in J. Edwards *et al.* (eds.), *Technologies of Procreation* (Manchester, Manchester University Press, 1993).

Streissguth, A. P., Barr, H. M., Sampson, P. D. *et al.*, "I.Q. at age 4 in relation to maternal alchohol and smoking during pregnancy" (1989) 25 *Dev. Psychol.* 3–11.

Sutherland, W. J. and Reynolds, J. D., "Honesty in sexual selection" (1995) 375 *Nature* 280–281.

van Os, J. and Selten, J. P., "Prenatal exposure to maternal stress and subsequent schizophrenia—the May 1940 invasion of The Netherlands" (1998) 172 *British Journal of Psychiatry* 324–326.

Vernet, M., Cavard, C., Zider, A. *et al.*, "*In vitro* manipulation of early mouse embryos induces HIV1-LTR*lacZ* transgene expression" (1993) 119 *Development* 1293–1300.

Wadhwa, P. D., Dunkelschetter, C., Chiczdemet, A. *et al.*, "Prenatal psychosocial factors and the neuroendocrine axis in human-pregnancy" (1996) 58 *Psychosomatic Medicine* 432–446.

Walker, S. K., Hartwich, K. M. and Seamark, R. F., "The production of unusually large offspring following embryo manipulation: concepts and challenges" (1996) 45 *Theriogenology* 111–120.

Warnock Report, *Report of the Committee of Enquiry into Human Fertilisation and Embryology* (Cmnd. 9314, London, HMSO, 1984).

Weinstock, M., "Does prenatal stress impair coping and regulation of hypothalamic-pituitary-adrenal axis"? (1997) 21 *Neuroscience and Biobehavioral Reviews* 1–10.

Willmut, I., Schneike, A. E., McWhir, J. *et al.*, "Viable offspring derived from fetal and adult mammalian cells" (1997) 385 *Nature* 810–813.

Zeviani, M. and Antozzi, C., "Mitochondrial disorders" (1997) 3 *Molecular Human Reproduction* 133–148.

4

Assisted Reproduction and the Legal Definition of Parentage

STUART BRIDGE

The revolution in the assisted reproduction technologies has caused particular problems for both lawyers and social scientists, in identifying the legal relationships, and in assessing the social consequences, which flow from the circumstances of conception. Various jurisdictions have taken different views of the effect of the use of the new techniques, but the United Kingdom position has been particularly interesting, and will provide the focus to this chapter. The Warnock Report, published in 1984, was one of the first major contributions to the moral debate surrounding assisted reproduction, and its recommendations led the United Kingdom Parliament to provide a regulatory system for fertility clinics which was both highly innovative and highly influential. The statutory creation of the Human Fertilisation and Embryology Authority, charged with the duty of licensing fertility treatments, research on and storage of gametes and embryos, and maintaining and enforcing a code of practice for clinics, has promoted the discussion of vital issues in this area of continuing change. This chapter concentrates on the attribution of parentage to children born as a result of assisted reproduction techniques, and the problems which the legislation has attempted to solve. In doing so, it is essential that we begin by considering the role of parentage as a legal concept.

1. THE STATUS OF PARENTAGE

Parentage comprises a status of great legal significance.[1] This has been most evident in recent years in the context of the English law of child support, which firmly imposes liability for maintaining children on their parents,[2] and which has resulted in many cases being litigated where men have sought to deny their parental status in an attempt to escape the financial consequences. Indeed, it can

---

[1] A status has been judicially defined as "the condition of belonging to a class in society to which the law ascribes peculiar rights and duties, capacities and incapacities" (*The Ampthill Peerage* [1977] AC 547, 577, per Lord Simon of Glaisdale, describing the status of legitimacy).

[2] Child Support Act 1991, s.1 (see also s.54: " 'parent', in relation to any child, means any person who is in law the mother or father of the child").

be argued that in the context of liability to maintain others within the family, the status of parentage has now assumed a greater importance than that of marriage. The unyielding formula of the Child Support Acts gives parents little leeway and has had a massive impact on the application of discretion between spouses on their divorce. But parentage has other important consequences too. The law of succession confers entitlement on intestacy on issue of the deceased, and claims for family provision from an estate can be made where an applicant is the child of the deceased.[3] Where the parent's death is tortiously caused, the child, as a dependant may bring a claim for damages against the tortfeasor.[4] Thus, the question "Who is my parent?" is a vital one.

It is important that a clear line is drawn between parentage and parental responsibility ("all the rights, duties, powers, responsibilities and authority which by law a parent has in relation to the child and his property").[5] Where a person is a parent of a child, the relationship is accurately described as one of parentage. Parentage may or may not lead to the imposition of parental responsibility on the parent. Parental responsibility is automatically conferred on the parent who is the child's mother. Parental responsibility is, at the time of writing, automatically conferred on the father only where he is married to the mother at the time of the birth, or where they marry subsequently,[6] although the Government has proposed that unmarried fathers should obtain parental responsibility automatically where the father has signed the birth register jointly with the mother, and where his name appears on the child's birth certificate.[7] Save for this major exception, a father who does not marry the mother of the child can only obtain parental responsibility by court order to that effect, by written agreement with the mother, or where a residence order is made in his favour.[8] Parental responsibility may also be conferred on persons who are not themselves parents of the child in question. Thus, where a residence order is made in favour of a non-parent, that person will obtain parental responsibility for the child for the duration of the order.[9]

Andrew Bainham argues in Chapter 2 above for the recognition and support of *parenthood*, as the continuing relationship between the parent and the child, the "on-going status", which is particularly associated with the responsibility for raising the child. He presents a convincing case for parenthood as a useful shorthand expression for the state of continuing parental responsibility. But as persons who have parental responsibility in respect of children may or may not be their parents, and as many parents do not have parental responsibility at all,

[3] Administration of Estates Act 1925, s.46, as amended; Inheritance (Provision for Family and Dependants) Act 1975, s.1(1)(c).

[4] Fatal Accidents Act 1976, s.1(3)(c).

[5] Children Act 1989, s.3.

[6] Children Act 1989, s.2.

[7] Statement by Geoff Hoon, Parliamentary Secretary at the Lord Chancellor's Department at Conference of Tavistock Marital Studies Institute, 2 July 1998.

[8] Children Act 1989, ss.4, 12(1).

[9] Children Act 1989, s.12(2), although subject to certain limitations: see further s.12(3).

parenthood is clearly very different from parentage. Whenever the United Kingdom Parliament and the English judges have had to consider whether the legal status of parent and child exists, the term "parentage" has been used.[10] In an attempt to preserve some consistency of terminology, the female and male parental status will be referred to here as "maternity" and "paternity" respectively (rather than the possibly confusing "motherhood" and "fatherhood").

The parentage question may be asked at any stage in the life of the child. In most cases, it will arise during minority (at present, it is most frequently litigated where child support is the issue), but succession law may require consideration of parentage much later. In this chapter, we shall focus on the question "Who are the parents?" as at the date the child is born. Not only does this facilitate analysis, and allow concentration on the problems caused by advances in techniques of medically assisted reproduction, it also enables us to distinguish the conferment of parental status which is effected by an adoption order. This is not to belittle the legal significance of adoption. It is accepted that adoption does create, for all legal purposes, a relationship of parent and child, and it can be definitively stated that where an adoption has taken place the issue of parentage would thereafter be determined in favour of the adoptive parent in all cases. But chronologically and legally, parentage at birth remains of the first importance. Indeed, adoption requires in most cases the consent of the parents (who have parental responsibility),[11] and save in the unlikely instance of a child who has been adopted previously, this will mean the mother, and quite possibly the father, of the child at the date of the child's birth.

2. MATERNITY: GENETIC OR GESTATIONAL?

Until 1978, and the birth of Louise Brown, the first IVF baby, maternity was, to coin Lord Simon of Glaisdale's phrase in the celebrated *Ampthill Peerage* case, "proved demonstrably by parturition". The genetic mother was the gestational mother and was the legal mother. Nothing else was biologically possible, or therefore legally necessary. But *in vitro* fertilisation gave rise to the possibility that the woman who gave birth to a child was not genetically related to her offspring. A woman may have an embryo created from a donated egg, and the sperm of her husband or partner, or donated sperm, implanted into her uterus. Alternatively, in surrogate cases, a woman may agree to the implantation in her uterus of an embryo created from another woman's egg, on the understanding that the resulting child will be the child of the commissioning parents, and will be given to and cared for by them. While making use of the same medical technology, the two cases are very different. In the former, the basic arrangement is that

---

[10] See, for example, Child Support Act 1991, ss.26, 27.
[11] Adoption Act 1976, s.16. The definition of parent is to be found in Adoption Act 1976, s.72. The unmarried father who has not obtained parental responsibility is not required to agree to the adoption of his child.

the gestational mother should bring up the child, and indeed assume maternity; the egg donor, whilst genetically related to the child, has no desire to assume any caring role, still less any legal liability.[12] In the latter case, the parties' initial intentions, which may be expressed in a formal contractual agreement, are that the gestational mother shall give the child up to the genetic mother, who shall care for and be legally responsible for the resulting child.

The Warnock Report considered that in allocating maternity the dominant factor was the need for certainty, such that the risk of a child being born without a mother who was ready and able to care for them was minimised (Warnock, 1984, paras. 6.6–6.8). It felt that the donation of an egg for transfer to another woman should be treated as absolute, and that the donor should in consequence have no rights or duties with regard to the resulting child. This should be the case whether the arrangement was by way of licensed treatment using donor eggs, or by way of a surrogacy agreement. Although the effect would run counter to the intentions of the parties to a surrogacy agreement, this would in itself be consistent with the disapproval of surrogacy elsewhere explicit in the Report.[13] Should commissioning parents wish to "enforce" the surrogacy agreement, they could do so through the adoption procedure. Section 27(1) of the Human Fertilisation and Embryology Act 1990 (which applies whether the woman was in the United Kingdom or elsewhere at the time of the placing in her of the embryo or the sperm and eggs) accordingly provides:

> "The woman who is carrying or has carried a child as a result of the placing in her of an embryo or of sperm and eggs, and no other woman, is to be treated as the mother of the child".

In somewhat stark contrast to the paternity provisions contained in the same Act,[14] section 27 is simple, clear and straightforward, and has not given rise to difficulties of interpretation. Where no medical intervention has taken place, or there has been nothing more than artificial insemination, the mother will inevitably be the woman who gives birth: the fact of parturition remains conclusive evidence of maternity. The sop to surrogacy agreements is to be found in section 30, which gives the courts jurisdiction to make "parental orders" in favour of gamete donors. Application must be made within six months of the birth, and a list of statutory conditions must be satisfied. Parental orders, which provide a fast track adoption procedure, whereby the normal waiting periods are waived,[15] can only be made where the applicants are respectively husband

---

[12] In egg or embryo donation cases, we shall refer to the woman whose egg is fertilised *in vitro* as the "genetic mother", and the woman who carries the child to term as the "gestational mother". The phrase "biological mother", which is sometimes encountered, is ambiguous. There is some evidence that egg donors do wish to know (amongst other things) whether their donation has resulted in a child being born: see Price and Cook (1995).

[13] *Ibid.*, paras. 8.17–8.20.

[14] Considered below.

[15] As the commissioning parents are not "parents" of the child, an adoption order could not be made until the child is at least 12 months old, and has lived with them (or one of them) for 12 months: Adoption Act 1976, s.13(2).

and wife, and the gametes of one or both have been used to bring about the creation of the embryo. The home of the child must, at the time of the application, be with the applicants, and the father (if there is one) and the woman who has carried the child must have freely and unconditionally agreed to the order "with full understanding of what is involved," in the woman's case more than six weeks after the birth. If applicants are unable to satisfy the onerous conditions of section 30, they may nevertheless seek leave to apply for a residence order under the Children Act 1989,[16] as a first step on the long road towards obtaining an adoption order from the court.

However, the underlying assumption that surrogacy should be discouraged in all cases is now being questioned. In October 1998, a Review, commissioned by United Kingdom Health Ministers, of the current arrangements for payments in and regulation of surrogacy cases, was presented to Parliament (Cm 4068, Review team: Professors Margaret Brazier, Alistair Campbell and Susan Golombok). Taking its lead from recent statements of opinion within the medical profession (see Surrogacy Review, para. 1.6), the Review acknowledges a wider social acceptance of surrogacy in the years since Warnock, and identifies the crucial issue as the level of state intervention necessary to protect the interests of the various parties. The surrogacy legislation which followed (but did not in all respects implement) Warnock is criticised for resting on "no coherent basis of policy", and the Review advocates the control of payments to surrogate mothers and the state regulation of surrogacy by the United Kingdom health departments. The allocation of maternity is not given any specific treatment (indeed it is outside the remit of the Review), but certain reforms to the current scheme of parental orders are proposed to ensure compliance with the other reforms and with the new Code of Practice.[17]

The vesting of maternity in the gestational, rather than the genetic, mother, is to be found in both France and Germany as well as the United Kingdom.[18] Indeed, the disapproval of surrogacy receives even stronger backing in France, where the courts have refused to sanction adoption of the child born as a result of a surrogacy agreement by the commissioning parents. But the courts in California have viewed the matter somewhat differently. The leading case is *Johnson v Calvert*.[19] Mark and Crispina Calvert, a married couple, desired to have a child, but Crispina, although able to produce eggs, had undergone a hysterectomy and could not conceive and carry a child. The Calverts signed a written contract of surrogacy with Anna Johnson providing that an embryo created by the sperm of Mark and the egg of Crispina would be implanted in Anna, that she would carry the child to term, and that on birth the child would be taken

---

[16] Section 10.
[17] The revised parental order would not authorise the judge to approve otherwise impermissible payments to the surrogate. Use of an unregistered surrogacy agency would be in breach of the Code of Practice.
[18] See generally on other European jurisdictions Neilsen (1996).
[19] (1993) 5 Cal. 4 th 84; 851 P.2d 776.

into the Calverts' home as their child. Anna agreed to relinquish all parental rights in the child, and in return she was paid $10,000 in instalments. Relations between the parties deteriorated. When the child was born, Anna refused to hand her over, although blood tests indicated that Mark and Crispina were the genetic parents. Litigation ensued. Faced with a dispute between the genetic mother, Crispina, and the gestational mother, Anna, the majority of the Supreme Court considered that as both women had presented acceptable proof of maternity, resolution was to be made by reference to the parties' respective intentions:

"They [sc. Mark and Crispina] affirmatively intended the birth of the child, and took the steps necessary to effect in vitro fertilisation. But for their acted-on intention, the child would not exist. Anna agreed to facilitate the procreation of Mark's and Crispina's child. The parties' aim was to bring Mark's and Crispina's child into the world, not for Mark and Crispina to donate a zygote to Anna. Crispina from the outset intended to be the child's mother. Although the gestative function Anna performed was necessary to bring about the child's birth, it is safe to say that Anna would not have been given the opportunity to gestate or deliver the child had she, prior to implantation of the zygote, manifested her own intent to be the child's mother".

The court concluded that Crispina, who "intended to bring about the birth of a child that she intended to raise as her own" was the natural mother under Californian law, and so reached a decision which was diametrically opposite to the legal consequences of a surrogacy agreement in the United Kingdom. There, the child would be the child of Anna, as the gestational mother, by reason of section 27 of the Human Fertilisation and Embryology Act 1990. Any attempt by Mark and Crispina to assume parental status for the child would have to be by resort to adoption proceedings, as Anna's opposition to any transfer would bode ill for the success of an application for a parental order under section 30 of the 1990 Act.

The English law is therefore clear and pragmatic. The mother of the child is the woman who gives birth, the gestational mother, not the genetic mother. Unlike California, the intentions of the parties to a surrogacy arrangement carry no weight in answering the question of parentage at the date of the birth. It may be open to the genetic mother to seek to establish a parental relationship with the child by resort to adoption proceedings or section 30 of the 1990 Act, but in the absence of such application, the gestational mother will remain the parent of the child.

3. PATERNITY: CONSENTING HUSBANDS AND PARTICIPATING PARTNERS

Paternity has always given rise to greater problems of proof than maternity. In the context of draconian child support laws based upon genetics, the quality of evidence has never been so important. In recent years, at the prompting of what is now scientifically possible, the law has shifted perceptibly away from presumptions to proof.

(a) Man married to gestational mother

The English common law, on which many American states have based their principles, has traditionally relied upon, or at least hidden behind, assumptions of marital propriety, in particular that a child born to a married woman is presumed to be the child of her husband ("the presumption of paternity"). This is no more than a presumption of evidence; thus, as scientific advances have provided significantly better proof of paternity, it has been steadily undermined, with potential for prejudice to the child. Thus where a man is (or has been) married, and a child has been born to his wife following treatment with donated sperm, it is now possible to establish, by DNA testing, that he is not the genetic father of the child, and thereby to deny liability to maintain on separation from the child's mother. This occurred in *Re M (Child Support Act) (Parentage)* [1997] 2 FLR 90. Children conceived as a result of artificial insemination with donated sperm were born, in 1981 and 1986 respectively, to a woman who was at the time married to Mr M. Following their divorce, in the course of which Mr M admitted that he had treated the children as "children of the family",[20] the Child Support Agency claimed that Mr M was liable to maintain the children as their "parent" under the Child Support Act 1991. Bracewell J rejected the Agency's claim. Mr M had to be either the "biological" father of the children or to have become their father by operation of law. The fact that the husband had consented to his wife's fertility treatment was of no legal significance. He was not their parent for the purposes of the child support legislation.[21]

Re M would have been decided differently had the children been born after the coming into force of the Family Law Reform Act 1987. The Warnock Report proposed that where a married man had consented to his wife's fertility treatment using donated sperm, he should be treated in law as the father. Despite Parliamentary opposition, the Family Law Reform Act 1987 gave legislative effect to this proposal, and it is now contained in section 28(2) of the Human Fertilisation and Embryology Act 1990:

> "If—
>
>   (a) at the time of the placing in her of the embryo or the sperm and eggs or of her insemination, the woman was a party to a marriage, and
>
>   (b) the creation of the embryo carried by her was not brought about with the sperm of the other party to the marriage, then, subject to subsection (5) below,[22] the other

---

[20] He was therefore liable to the jurisdiction of Part II of the Matrimonial Causes Act 1973, and also the Children Act 1989, s.15, Sch. 1.

[21] Although not a parent, Mr M would be entitled to apply for a contact order under the Children Act 1989, s.10(5)(a).

[22] Section 28(2) does not apply to any child who, by virtue of the rules of common law, is treated as the legitimate child of the parties to a marriage or to any child to the extent that the child is treated by virtue of adoption as not being the child of any person other than the adopter(s).

party to the marriage shall be treated as the father of the child unless it is shown that he did not consent to the placing in her of the embryo or the sperm and eggs or to her insemination (as the case may be)".

This provision is not self-standing, and it must be considered in the context of existing common law. Thus, the presumption of paternity still applies. Where the parties are married, and the wife gives birth to a child following artificial insemination or IVF, the husband will be presumed to be the father. If the husband attempts to rebut this presumption by resort to DNA tests, he will nevertheless remain the father as a matter of law unless he can prove (and the burden will be on him) that he did not consent to his wife's treatment. This will in many cases be difficult, as, where a licensed fertility centre is involved, it must comply with the HFEA Code of Practice. The Code stipulates:[23]

> "If a married woman is being treated with donated sperm, centres should explain the position and ask her whether her husband consents to the treatment. If he does, the centre should take all practicable steps to obtain his written consent. If the woman does not know, or he does not consent, centres should, if she agrees, take all practicable steps to ascertain the position and (if this is the case) obtain written evidence that he does not consent".

Not only is the test of spousal consent both workable and fair, it also appears reasonable to apply a presumption of consent, requiring the husband to prove that he did not consent to the treatment of his wife. This legal position has also held sway in much of the USA. In the recent Jaycee B litigation[24] a married couple, John and Luanne Buzzanca, entered an agreement with a surrogate whereby an embryo, genetically unrelated to either of them, would be implanted in the surrogate, and she would then carry and give birth to the child on their behalf. Prior to the birth of the resulting child, Jaycee, the Buzzancas split up, and Luanne, to whom Jaycee was handed over, sought financial support from her estranged husband. The Californian Court of Appeal applied a presumption akin to that of paternity. As both husband and wife had initiated and consented to the medical procedure which resulted in Jaycee's birth to the surrogate, they would both be deemed to be her parents. Giving effect to the parties' intentions at the time of the agreement, John was the father of the child, and was liable to support her financially.

(b) Men who are not married to the gestational mother

The vesting of paternity in men who are not married to the woman being treated is a far more complex and difficult area. Men donating sperm to licensed fertility centres are protected by statute in the United Kingdom. The need to protect the identity of donors, and thereby ensure that supplies of sperm continue, is

---

[23] Para. 5.7.
[24] (1998) 61 Cal. App. 4th 1410.

thought to require donation to have no legal consequences for the donor, and so there is blanket immunity from parental status for sperm donors, provided that the sperm is to be used for the purposes of "licensed treatment services".[25] "Do-it-yourself" insemination, where a man informally provides sperm without any medical intervention, is not covered by the statute, and there are potentially serious consequences for such donors.[26] However, in cases of "physician assisted" artificial insemination, or *in vitro* fertilisation using donated sperm, there is a significant risk that "fatherless" children will be born. There is no bar on single women receiving fertility treatment, although licensed centres, in making the decision to treat, are required to consider the welfare of any resulting child, and to take account of the need of that child for a father.[27]

A question which arises is the extent to which a male partner of an unmarried woman might be vested with paternity for the child born as a result of her treatment. It is a question which was not considered in the Warnock Report, but the Human Fertilisation and Embryology Act 1990 makes an attempt to find a father for such a child. By section 28(3):

"If no man is treated, by virtue of sub-section (2) above, as the father of the child but—
   (a) the embryo or the sperm and eggs were placed in the woman, or she was artificially inseminated, in the course of treatment services provided for her and a man together by a person to whom a licence applies, and
   (b) the creation of the embryo carried by her was not brought about with the sperm of that man, then, subject to subsection (5) below, that man shall be treated as the father of the child".

This is a unique provision. It comprises the one instance in English law of paternity being vested, from the moment of birth, in a man who is neither genetically related to the child nor married to the mother. But there are clear difficulties in its practical application. Instead of asking the obvious question whether the man consents to the treatment of his partner, the provision requires the court to consider whether the "treatment services" were provided for the woman and man together. "Treatment services" are elsewhere defined as "medical, surgical or obstetric services provided to the public or a section of the public for the purpose of assisting women to carry children". The problem to which section 28(3) gives rise can be simply stated. If the embryo is not brought about by the sperm of the male partner, how can it be said that the man is any meaningful sense being provided with treatment services? Johnson J outlined the resulting conundrum in *Re Q (Parental Order)* [1996] 1 FLR 369:

---

[25] Human Fertilisation and Embryology Act 1990, Sch.3, para.5.
[26] See the Californian case of *Jhordan C v Mary K* 179 Cal. App. 3d. 386, where a man who had donated sperm personally to the mother for home insemination purposes was held to be the father of the resulting child. California has a similar provision to that in the United Kingdom denying the paternity of a man who has provided sperm to a licensed physician for use in artificial insemination of a woman other than the donor's wife (Civil Code, para. 7005, subd. (d)).
[27] Human Fertilisation and Embryology Act 1990, s.13(5). See further Douglas (1993).

"It seems plain to me that the section envisages a situation in which the man involved himself received medical treatment, although as presently advised I am not sure what treatment is envisaged since the subsection refers to a man whose sperm was not used in the procedure".

The receipt of treatment services together has been interpreted more liberally in other cases. For example, in *Re B (Parentage)* [1996] 2 FLR 15, the mother was inseminated with the sperm of Mr B (to whom she was not married) in December 1991, as a result of which twins were born to her. This was not a decision on section 28(3), but on a similarly worded provision elsewhere in the 1990 Act.[28] The mother alleged that she and Mr B were involved in a sexual relationship, and argued that Mr B had donated sperm with the intention of making her pregnant. Although Mr B had not given a written consent to the use of his sperm, this was not necessary, as she and Mr B were being "treated together" by the fertility centre. Bracewell J found that, against a background of discussions between the hospital and both parents, Mr B's attendance at the hospital to give sperm indicated that this was a clear case of a joint enterprise. They had been receiving treatment services "together", and Mr B was accordingly the parent of the twins. However, this was a relatively straightforward finding of fact. As provider of the sperm, Mr B was of course the genetic father of the children.

In *R v Human Fertilisation and Embryology Authority, ex parte Blood*,[29] Sir Stephen Brown P considered whether Mr and Mrs Blood were "receiving treatment services together" such that a written consent by Mr Blood to the storage and use of his sperm was not necessary. While they had been trying to conceive in the course of their sexual relationship prior to the sudden onset of meningitis, they had not at any time sought medical services to further their objectives. In context, Mrs Blood's request that sperm be taken from her comatose husband by electro-ejaculation could not be construed as the couple "receiving treatment services together". Storage and use of Mr Blood's sperm was therefore unlawful.[30]

In these two cases, neither of which directly concerned section 28(3), and in both of which the sperm of the male partner had been used, the courts applied a test of joint enterprise, or course of conduct, asking whether the couple had set out to instigate the woman's pregnancy. The test was satisfied in *Re B*, but not in *ex parte Blood*. A similar analysis was adopted in the most important English decision to date on parentage and assisted reproduction, *U v W (Attorney*

---

[28] By Human Fertilisation and Embryology Act 1990, Sch. 3, para. 5(1), a person's gametes must not be used for the purposes of treatment services unless there is an effective (written) consent by that person to their being used. However, by para. 5(3), para. 5(1) does not apply to the use of a person's gametes for the purpose of that person, *or that person and another together*, receiving treatment services.

[29] [1996] 3 WLR 1176. The Court of Appeal agreed with this aspect of Sir Stephen's judgment: *ibid.*, [1997] 2 WLR 806.

[30] It should be noted that children born to Mrs Blood as a result of her insemination with the sperm of her late husband would be as a matter of law fatherless: see Human Fertilisation and Embryology Act 1990, s.28(6)(b).

General Intervening) [1997] 2 FLR 282. It is of particular interest in that section 28(3) is directly involved, as the gametes were not those of the partner but were those of an anonymous donor.

At the commencement of their affair in March 1990, Mr W was aged 47 (and married to Mrs W), and Miss U was aged 30 (and unmarried). Mr W separated from his wife, and went to live with Miss U in November of that year. For significant spells during the ensuing three and a half years, Mr W and Miss U lived together, although they were not cohabiting throughout all of that time. Miss U wanted a child, and they jointly attended a fertility centre, but attempts to effect *in vitro* fertilisation using Mr W's sperm (which was of poor quality) were not successful. The strains of the processes told on them—they separated briefly in 1993—but in April 1994, having exhausted, so they felt, the possibilities in the United Kingdom, they attended a clinic in Rome under the direction of Dr A. They clearly hoped that he would be able to assist them in having a child whose genetic father was Mr W. Eggs were taken from Miss U, and attempts were made to inject them both with Mr W's sperm and with donated sperm. Twelve embryos resulted, eleven of which had been fertilised by the donor sperm. They were then advised that multiple implantation of embryos would considerably increase the chance of pregnancy occurring. Mr W and Miss U faced a dilemma. Did they wish to maximise the chances of a successful outcome, and run the very considerable risk of producing a child whose genetic father was not Mr W, or was the genetic link so important to them that they would only proceed if they could be assured that the child would be genetically related to Mr W? Miss U and Mr W considered the dilemma jointly, and they decided (and, the judge found, this was a joint decision) that Miss U would receive the donor embryos as well as that created from Mr W's sperm. They returned to the clinic, and both signed a declaration (which was in Italian, but was accurately translated to them before they signed it) in which they each acknowledged, and undertook not to disclaim subsequently, the maternity and paternity of any resulting child.

Mr W returned to England because of the demands of his work. Miss U remained at the clinic. She was told that Mr W's embryo had died, and she had six donor embryos placed within her. On her return to England, her relationship with Mr W broke up. In due course, Miss U gave birth to twins. Tests confirmed that she was the genetic mother, but that Mr W was not genetically related. In subsequent legal proceedings, Miss U sought a declaration that Mr W was as a matter of law the father of the children, and therefore liable to maintain them under the Child Support Act 1991.

In *U v W*, Wilson J began by attempting to interpret section 28(3), in particular whether Miss U and Mr W had been provided with treatment services together. What had to be proved was that, in the provision of treatment services with the donated sperm, the doctor was "responding to a request for that form of treatment made by the woman and the man as a couple". It was not required that the man had consented to become the father of the prospective child, or to be legally responsible for him. Applying these principles to the facts, the judge was able to say that the treatment services were being provided for Miss U and Mr W together. They had, as Mr W had admitted, a long history of joint treatment in the United Kingdom prior to their visit to the Italian clinic. While it was possible that the treatment could cease to be "joint" once donated sperm was used, that would require Mr W to disassociate himself from the move into that form of treatment. Having taken time to consider, Mr W had supported Miss U in the decision which was made, and they had both signed the declaration in the clinic. All other things being equal, the creation of embryos by donor sperm, and their implantation in Miss U, was treatment in which Mr W had participated, and he would therefore be deemed in law to be the father of the resulting children. But all other things were not equal. The treatment did not take place in the United Kingdom, where the HFEA has power to license clinics, but in Italy, where it has not. Thus, section 28(3), which has effect only where the centre is one to which a licence applies, did not assist Miss U to establish the non-genetic paternity of Mr W. There followed an ambitious but ultimately unsuccessful attempt by Miss U's lawyers to invoke EU law to confer paternity on Mr W.

Mr W may well have been fortunate, but he was not made aware of the full legal implications of participation in the treatment. As the Italian clinic was operating outside the jurisdiction of the HFEA, the paternity position was not explained as fully as the HFEA Code of Practice now requires.[31] The Code makes a valiant attempt to make sense out of the statute. Paragraph 5.8 provides:

> "If a woman is being treated together with a male partner, using donated sperm, and she is unmarried or judicially separated or her husband does not consent to the treatment, her male partner will be the legal father of any resulting child. Centres should explain this to them both and record at each appointment whether the man was present. Centres should try and obtain the written acknowledgement of the man both that they are being treated together and that donated sperm is to be used".

One wonders whether centres are sometimes faced with puzzled partners who ask, quite genuinely, who is being treated. It will come as some surprise to the woman undergoing unpleasant, painful, and physically invasive medical examinations and procedures that treatment is joint. The partner is not a patient, after all. The model form of acknowledgement proposed by the HFEA is a necessary and well-intentioned attempt to provide further clarification:

> "I am not married to [the patient] . . . but I acknowledge that she and I are being treated together and that I will become the legal father of any resulting child".

Section 28 of the Human Fertilisation and Embryology Act 1990 does not apply where the sperm used in the treatment is that of the husband or partner. In such cases, the genetic link between the male provider of the gametes and the resulting child will usually lead to paternity.[32] This has a certain logic. Where a child

---

[31] The Code was commended in this respect in *U v W* as being "drafted with enviable clarity".

[32] It is always open to the man to argue that he was not being treated jointly with his wife or partner, and did not consent to the use of his gametes in this way: see *Re B (Parentage)*, above, for an

is conceived as a result of sexual intercourse, the law is founded on the principle that the male party to the act is the father of the child. The impracticability of positive proof in the vast majority of cases leads to a reliance, where the child is born to a married mother, on the presumption of the paternity of her husband. The man, by his voluntary participation in intercourse, is deemed to accept the consequences flowing from it, including liability for any resulting child. Although contraceptive precautions may have been taken, he has assumed a risk by his consent to the potentially procreative act. The same logic can be applied to medically assisted reproduction. Where a man consents to his wife undergoing *in vitro* fertilisation, or artificial insemination using donated sperm, the existence of a continuing marital relationship should be a sufficient and rational basis on which to infer an assumption of liability (or even parental responsibility) for any resulting child. It is perfectly fair and just to expect a husband who does not wish to accept liability to refuse to consent to his wife's treatment.

The test of consent is applied by section 28(2) of the Human Fertilisation and Embryology Act 1990 where the parties are married, the wife is undergoing treatment, and the husband's sperm is not being used. It remains open for the husband to argue that he did not in fact consent to his wife's treatment, and that he should not therefore be the father of a child with whom he has no genetic link, and whose procreation he did not support. Consent is attractive from a pragmatic point of view as well. It enables centres, following the guidance of the HFEA, to ask direct and pertinent questions of the husband, and thereby to establish clearly whether the child will have a father as a matter of law.

But where the woman being treated is not married, it is much more difficult to make any assumptions—either about the nature of her relationship with any partner she might have (and who may or may not attend the clinic with her) or about her or their intentions with respect to any resulting child. They may have lived together for many years, have been trying unsuccessfully to start a family, and have a relationship which is for all practical purposes indistinguishable from marriage. They may not live together, but have a sporadic sexual relationship. They may have no sexual relationship at all—the man may be a friend who has taken on a supportive role and wishes to ensure that the woman is cared for during her treatment and her pregnancy. To ask such a variety of couples whether they are receiving the treatment services together is, in truth, an impossible question, as Johnson J intimated in *Re Q (Parental Order)*.[33] However one looks at it, the man is not being treated. His sperm is not being used. At best, it can be said that the infertility of the parties' relationship is being treated. Yet their intentions are in fact being analysed in the particular circumstances of each case—whether they have made a joint request for treatment, and whether they jointly intend to bear and bring up any child which might result

example of such an argument. However, where the man has jointly attended at the clinic with his wife or partner, and provided sperm, it will be easy to draw the inference (as Bracewell J did in *Re B (Parentage)*, that they were being treated jointly.

[33] See above.

from the treatment being effected. This is not what the statute says, but it is how it has been judicially interpreted.

In summary, the current legal principles which govern the vesting of parentage in men following the successful application of assisted reproduction techniques on their partners are flawed, inconsistent, and difficult to operate. Would it be better to have a principle which is more direct and immediate? An obvious contender is the consent of the male partner to the treatment of the woman, which would lead to a satisfying consistency with the test contained in section 28(2). Satisfying, but not satisfactory. The existence of the marital relationship makes an assumption that the parties wish to have children a relatively safe one—and the husband can in any case deny that he consented. Where a man merely attends a clinic with a woman to whom he is not married, giving her no more than emotional support, he would, if asked, be likely to say that he consents to her treatment, but will not think anything of it, save perhaps that it is a peculiar question to ask of him. Outside the context of a marital relationship, consent to the treatment of the woman does not necessarily carry the same inferences, and it is unlikely to work as well. It would be possible to define, as many statutes now do, cohabitants, and provide that cohabitants should be deemed to consent to the treatment with donated sperm, subject to the contrary being proved. But again it places a heavy burden of detective work on the centre which may have better things to do. What is needed is a simple workable formula.

Barton and Douglas, in their important book *Law and Parenthood*, have contended that "the extent to which legal recognition is given to a person's intention or desire to be regarded as a parent, and to fulfil the functions of a parent, has increased over time, so that it is now the *primary* test of legal parentage" (Barton and Douglas, 1995). They refer to the work of the two leading supporters of intention-based criteria for parentage, Professors Shultz and Hill.[34] Both of these commentators deal specifically with the impact of assisted reproduction techniques on orthodox methods for the establishment of parentage, and give particular attention to the problems posed by surrogacy arrangements. There is no doubt that the arguments lucidly articulated by these American professors influenced the Supreme Court of California in *Johnson v. Calvert*. But, as we have seen, an English court, applying legal principles in a jurisdiction which denies the enforceability of surrogacy contracts by force of statute, would inevitably have come to the opposite conclusion on similar facts. And even in California, the limitations of *Johnson v. Calvert* have been recognised. The deference paid there to parental intent was not apparent when a later court had to determine whether a woman who had been artificially inseminated with the sperm of a married man pursuant to a surrogacy agreement was as a matter of law the mother of the resulting child. In *Moschetta v Moschetta*[35], the Court of Appeal held that the surrogate was the only mother of the child. The father's

---

[34] Shultz (1990); Hill (1991). For a recent detailed study of the respective advantages of parental intent and interests of the child as tests for parentage in the USA, see Dolgin (1997).

[35] (1994) 25 Cal. App. 4th 1218.

wife had no genetic or gestational link with the child, and the court would refuse to enforce the surrogacy agreement. Thus in a "traditional" surrogacy case, where the child is created from the egg of the surrogate mother, there was no resort to the parties' intentions. That was only necessary where a gestational surrogacy had occurred, and it was necessary "to break the tie" occasioned by the claims of the two biological mothers. Professor Hill had himself drawn a similar line:

> "Intentionality acts as a trump for the intended parents when conflicting claims are made by parties who have contributed biologically to the creation of the child. Intentionality, however, is not the only way to acquire parental status. Where no party has intended to create a child, as in the case of an unplanned child, there are no intentional parents. Thus the claims of the biological parents would take precedence".[36]

The truth is that English law does not take an entrenched view, even in surrogacy cases. The paramount consideration will be, inevitably, the welfare of the resulting child. It is important to have a point of departure, an imposition of maternity, applied by statute to the gestational mother, but there remains plenty of scope, conferred by the miriad statutory judicial powers, to transfer the parental status to commissioning parents or others. In exercising such powers, the court would not be seeking to enforce the surrogacy arrangement, but determining, by consideration of the individual circumstances of the case, where the welfare of the child lies.

We have seen that the attribution of paternity to partners of women undergoing fertility treatment with donated sperm is fraught with difficulty. Where the partner is married to the woman, consent is a sensible and workable test. Where the partner is not married, the test currently applied, namely participation in the treatment, is proving an elusive and difficult concept. Perhaps here there is room to move along the lines suggested by Professors Hill and Shultz. In *Johnson v Calvert*, Panelli J asked whether a person seeking parentage following gestational surrogacy intended to bring about the birth of a child that he or she intended to raise as their own. This question is attractive. It is direct, and it is to the point. Moreover, it strongly implies, in a case where the answer is positive, an assumption of responsibility for the child which would dovetail neatly with the child support liability which the man would as a result incur. It is a question which can be asked directly of the man, and the man can be expected to understand. It is not far removed from the question ultimately asked by Wilson J in *U v W* as he struggled to come to terms with the opacity of the legislative provisions.

Professor Shultz elucidated a valuable message for legislators in this area when she argued that:

> "[I]ntentional arrangements that arise out of reproductive technology offer the opportunity for a constructive experiment. In considering such an experiment, it should be

---

[36] Likewise, Shultz (1990, p.323) sees parental intent as providing a presumption of legal parenthood within the context of artificial reproductive techniques.

borne in mind that existing status-based parental responsibility has hardly been a model of success, particularly as regards divorced or unwed fathers' obligations to children. A narrow experiment with chosen rather than imposed responsibility could hardly come off worse than the dismal realities of abdication and non-compliance that now confront us".[37]

Reproductive technology arrangements are based upon an intention to procreate which is powerful and unambiguous. A woman who undergoes IVF does so with a desire to conceive, and any partner (whether or not the donor of the sperm being used) must hold a view as to whether they wish to be the parent of any resulting child. In the interests of openness and accountability, the partner should be informed, before treatment commences, of the legal and financial consequences of being a parent, and then asked whether this is a status which they seek to obtain. To ask whether the partner intends to register as the father of the child, and thereby incur parental responsibility, would be both reasonable and fair, as by signing the certificate, the man will be accepting his status as father of the child, and the rights, responsibilities, and obligations which that status accords. In short, positive answers to direct questions are preferable to the current uncertainty of joint enterprise. This is not an area where parentage should be imposed by default, but by an assumption of responsibility which is both fully informed and freely given.

REFERENCES

Barton, C. and Douglas, G., *Law and Parenthood* (London, Butterworths, 1995).
Dolgin, J., *Defining the Family: Law, Technology and Reproduction in an Uneasy Age* (New York, New York University Press, 1997).
Douglas, G., "Assisted reproduction and the welfare of the child" (1993) *Current Legal Problems* 53.
Hill, J., "What does it mean to be a 'parent'? The claims of biology as the basis for parental rights" (1991) 66 *New York University Law Review* 353.
Neilsen, L., "Legal consensus and divergence in Europe in the area of assisted conception—room for harmonisation?" in D. Evans (ed.), *Creating the Child—The Ethics, Law and Practice of Assisted Procreation* (Martinus Nijhoff, The Hague, 1996).
Price, F. and Cook, R., "The donor, the recipient and the child-human egg donation in UK licensed centres" (1995) 7 *Child and Family Law Quarterly* 145.
Shultz, M., "Reproductive technology and intent-based parenthood: an opportunity for gender neutrality" (1990) *Wisconsin Law Review* 297.
Surrogacy Review, *Surrogacy: Review for Health Ministers of Current Arrangements for Payments and Regulation* (Cm 4068, London, HMSO, 1998).
Warnock Report, *Report of the Committee of Inquiry into Human Fertilisation and Embryology* (Cmnd. 9314, London, HMSO, 1984).

---

[37] Shultz (1990, p. 396).

5

The Welfare Principle and the Rights of Parents

JONATHAN HERRING

Parenthood demands enormous sacrifices. But there is not a parent in the country who always places their child's interests before their own—inevitably and quite rightly family relationships involve "give and take". In many families the children's interests are pre-eminent, but on some occasions fairness and practicality demand that the interests of a child must be subordinated to those of the parents or other family members.[1] By contrast, the basis of the law in England and Wales[2] relating to children is section 1 of the Children Act 1989 which states that whenever the courts are required to make decisions concerning the upbringing of a child "the child's welfare shall be the court's paramount consideration". This is commonly known as the welfare principle.[3] It has been interpreted by the courts to mean that the interests of children shall prevail over those of their parents. So the court could make an order for the purpose of promoting a child's welfare, however great the sacrifice demanded of the parents or other members of the family, and even if the benefit to the child would be minimal. Indeed court orders requiring that a parent does not move from a particular geographical area,[4] or that the parent's new partner does not stay overnight in the family home are in theory available, and have been obtained in other jurisdictions.[5]

And that is the topic of this chapter: to consider the extent to which the courts are and should be entitled to make orders that infringe the rights of parents and others in order to pursue the welfare of a child. How can we reconcile the

---

[1] Indeed our society as a whole does not make children's interests a priority in, for example, economic policy.

[2] The welfare principle is a central part of the law relating to children in many countries. See Article 3 of the United Nations Convention on the Rights of the Child, although the interests of the child are to be a "primary" consideration rather than "paramount". There is, of course, great difficulty in many cases in ascertaining what would promote a child's welfare.

[3] There are *dicta* in the House of Lords stating that parents are to exercise their powers in respect of children in order to promote the child's welfare (Lord Fraser in *Gillick v West Norfolk and Wisbech Area Health Authority* [1986] AC 112 at 170D–E).

[4] Courts have on occasions refused to give leave to a parent wishing to take children out of the jurisdiction e.g. *Re K (A Minor) (Removal from Jurisdiction)* [1992] 2 FLR 98; *Re T (Removal from Jurisdiction)* [1996] 2 FLR 352.

[5] e.g. *Parrillo v Parrillo* 554 A 2d 1043 (1989), a case heard in the Rhode Island Supreme Court, USA.

welfare principle's centrality to the law with the realisation that doing so may require sacrifices of parents that could be unjust or impractical? I will first consider some of the decided cases where the courts have had to balance the interests of the child and parents. Despite the existence of the welfare principle the courts have given weight to the interests of parents and I will attempt to demonstrate the various means by which they have done so. I will then consider whether it would be better to abandon or explicitly limit the application of the welfare principle but conclude that what is required is an understanding of welfare that recognises the importance to a child of relationships based on justice and equality, rather than the current individualised conception of welfare. Before approaching these issues it is necessary to outline briefly the law relating to parents and children.

1. PARENTS' DUTIES AND RIGHTS IN LAW[6]

The law emphasises the responsibilities of parents rather than their rights. Mothers and some fathers[7] are given "parental responsibility" by the law.[8] This is defined as "all the rights, duties, powers, responsibilities and authority which by law a parent of a child has in relation to the child and his property".[9] The "rights" mentioned in this definition of parental responsibility have been held by Lord Fraser in the House of Lords to exist solely for the purpose of promoting the welfare of the child.[10] It is far from clear when these legal parental rights are of practical importance,[11] but it is generally thought that they are most significant when third parties interact with children. For example, only a person with parental responsibility can give effective consent to a doctor to carry out an operation on a child lawfully. It should also be stressed that the nature of parents' legal rights change as the child grows up.[12] A person who does not have parental responsibility but has care of a child (for example a babysitter) may still "do what is reasonable in all the circumstances of the case for the purpose of safeguarding or promoting the child's welfare".[13]

Alexander McCall Smith (1990) has usefully divided parental rights into parent-centred and child-centred rights. The child-centred rights are given to a

---

[6] For a detailed discussion of the law see Bainham (1998). For empirical research on relationships between children and parents after their separation see, for example, Maclean and Eekelaar (1997).

[7] Those fathers who are married to the mother and those who have been awarded parental responsibility under Children Act 1989, s.4.

[8] It is possible for non-parents to apply to the court for a residence order which if granted would award parental responsibility to the applicant: Children Act 1989, s.12(2).

[9] Children Act 1989, s.3(1).

[10] *Gillick v West Norfolk and Wisbech Area Health Authority* [1986] AC 112 at 170D–E.

[11] Contrast Children (Scotland) Act 1995, s. 1 which is a little more explicit. It should also be noted that parents cannot sue in tort for interference of their parental rights: *F v Wirral Metropolitan Borough Council* [1991] Fam 69.

[12] *Gillick v West Norfolk and Wisbech Area Health Authority* [1986] AC 112.

[13] Children Act 1989, s.3(5).

parent to ensure that the child receives at least the minimum care expected in our society. Hence the right (and indeed duty) to clothe, feed and provide for the child. The parent-centred rights are given to a parent in respect of those issues over which there is no particular state-approved view, for example what kind of religious education a child should receive from his or her parents. There are benefits to the state from these parent-centred rights. They help the state avoid having to take a controversially interventionist stance over a topic for which there is no agreed societal response. They also encourage a culturally diverse society. In addition to these parental rights parents also have rights as individuals. It is the clash between this third category of parents' rights and the interests of children with which this chapter is particularly concerned.

Mention must briefly be made of the rights of children, a topic of increasing interest amongst commentators, but only acknowledged to a limited extent by the law. For present purposes it is convenient to accept the classification of children's rights as set out by John Eekelaar (1986). He recognises a child as having three categories of interests: "basic interests" (the essential requirements for the nurturing of the child); "developmental interests" (those interests necessary to enable the child to examine and develop his or her potential as a person); and "autonomy interests" (enabling the child to choose a course of action for him or herself). Eekelaar suggests that the autonomy interests must yield to basic or developmental interests if they are in conflict. This version of children's rights could be seen as consistent with the welfare principle.[14] Basic and developmental interests are clearly in line with the welfare principle. Autonomy interests can be brought in line with the welfare approach if it is accepted that the child's welfare can be furthered by allowing children to learn by their mistakes. I will be returning briefly to children's rights later, but the main focus of this chapter is the conflict between parental interests and the welfare principle.

The present core meaning of the welfare principle[15] is usually said to be contained in the speech of Lord McDermott in *J v. C*,[16] who stated:

> "it seems to me that [the welfare principle] must mean more than that the child's welfare is to be treated as the top item in a list of items relevant to the matter in question. I think [it] connote[s] a process whereby when all the relevant facts, relationships, claims and wishes of parents, risks, choices and other cases are taken into account and weighed, the course to be followed will be that which is most in the interest of the child's welfare as that term has now to be understood. That is the first consideration because it is of first importance and the paramount consideration because it rules on or determines the course to be followed".

This seems clearly to place the interests of children always above the interests of parents. Hence it is regularly stated in the case law that the interests of parents

---

[14] Although many argue that the welfare principle creates an image of children as weak and in need of protection which militates against recognition of children's autonomy "rights".

[15] With the checklist of factors listed in Children Act 1989, s.1(3).

[16] [1970] AC 668 at 711. Approved by House of Lords in *Re KD (A Minor) (Ward: Termination of Access)* [1988] AC 806.

are only relevant in a case involving the upbringing of children in so far as they affect the welfare of the child.[17] Welfare is understood in a wide sense and includes emotional, physical and moral welfare. It also includes considering the child's welfare into the future, including adulthood.[18] However, as I hope to demonstrate below, the courts have adopted a rather narrow approach to welfare, considering the welfare of the child as an isolated individual rather than as a person living within a community. This has created difficulties for the courts in accommodating the interests of parents, but they have found various ways of doing so. I will now consider these.

2. HOW THE COURTS HAVE DEALT WITH TENSIONS BETWEEN THE WELFARE PRINCIPLE AND PARENTS' RIGHTS

I will concentrate on four ways in which the law has been able to place weight on parents' interests despite the dominance of the welfare principle.

(a) Non-enforcement of the welfare principle

It is very noticeable that the legal supervision of parents' care for and nurturing of their children is limited. There is no overt attempt by the state to "police" parenting and to ensure that families are promoting the child's welfare.[19] It is interesting to contrast the law's attitude to day-care and child-minding with that of parenting. Day-care centres and child-minders need to be registered with a local authority and are subject to careful regulation and inspection to ensure the protection of the child's welfare.[20] There is no such formal surveillance with parental care.[21]

Generally, a court may become involved with the upbringing of children in three situations. The first is where the child is suffering harm to such an extent and in such circumstances that it is appropriate for the state to intervene to protect the child, for example by taking the child into care or instituting criminal proceedings against a parent.[22] Here the dispute is essentially a state–parent dispute and the aim of the proceedings is to ascertain whether the child needs state protection. The second is where there is a dispute between two adults, normally

---

[17] See, for example, *Re B (Contact: Stepfather's Opposition)* [1997] 2 FLR 579 at 585B.

[18] *Re B (A Minor) (Wardship: Sterilisation)* [1988] AC 199.

[19] Although see for example Donzelot (1980).

[20] Children Act 1989, Part X and Sch. 9. See Department of Health (1991).

[21] Although some professionals that are involved with children (e.g. teachers, health visitors) have guidelines about notification of evidence of unacceptable parental behaviour. See also Home Office (1998).

[22] Even then the courts have limited control over how a child in care is treated. See, for example, *Re T (A Minor) (Care Order)* [1994] 2 FLR 423.

the parents, over the upbringing of a child.[23] Here the role of the courts is to resolve what is usually a parent–parent dispute. The third is where a child brings proceedings against his or her parents. This is rare. Apart from these three situations the law generally does not interfere directly with the standard of parenting children.[24]

In a state–parent dispute the state is generally only entitled to intervene if the child has suffered or is likely to suffer significant harm.[25] In the absence of such harm state intervention is not permitted, even if it would promote the child's welfare. In those cases where there is no significant harm the welfare principle is promoted by the court in parent–parent cases.[26] However the fact that there is a parent–parent dispute does not necessarily indicate that the child is in particular need of court intervention but rather it simply indicates a need to resolve a dispute between adults (Bainham, 1990). Indeed those cases where parents or relatives are in dispute are often instances where there is in fact no order that can be made positively in the interests of the child and the court has to make an order which is least harmful to the child. Further the Court of Appeal has stated that the courts should not be used to resolve disputes concerning "day-to-day" issues.[27] So court enforcement of the welfare principle in private households is very limited (Freeman, 1997).

(b) Protection of parents' rights while using the welfare principle

There are various ways in which the courts have managed to place significant weight on the interests of parents in the process of applying the welfare principle. I am not necessarily criticising the results in these cases but seeking to demonstrate that the use of the welfare principle by the courts at present tends to disguise what is often the real issue—a clash between the interests of parents and the interests of children. The disguises can take various forms. I will consider three.[28]

(a) The first is by merging the interests of parents and children. It is natural that a judge will see a close link between the interests of parents and children. A child cared for by a miserable parent is likely to suffer more than one being cared for by a content parent. But there is always a danger that a court, when considering the welfare of the child, might confuse the welfare of the child with that of the parents.[29]

[23] Although it could be, for example, the grandmother who brings the matter before the court: *Re W (Contact: Application by Grandparent)* [1997] 1 FLR 793.

[24] Although there are some restrictions relating to education. See, for example, Education Act 1996, s.7.

[25] Children Act 1989, s.31.

[26] Children Act 1989, s.8(1) describes the orders that are available.

[27] *Re P (A Minor) (Parental Responsibility Order)* [1994] 1 FLR 578.

[28] The case law referred to will only be a selection from that available.

[29] As the Court of Appeal has acknowledged in, for example, *Re O (Contact: Imposition of Conditions)* [1995] 2 FLR 124.

In a recent case, *Re T*,[30] the Court of Appeal considered what should happen to a seriously ill young child who required a liver transplant. The child had already suffered some unsuccessful surgery and the parents decided not to authorise further surgery. The issue was brought before the court by the doctors. The unanimous medical opinion was that the prognosis for the child if the operation were to go ahead was good but that without the treatment the child would die. However the court decided the operation should not go ahead as it would not promote the child's interests. The Court of Appeal closely identified the interests of the child with those of the mother. It was argued that were the operation to be successful the child would require long-term care by the parents. If the parents were not willing to provide the care the child would suffer greatly and it was decided that this was not in the child's best interests:

> "She [the mother] will have to comply with the court order, return to this country and present the child to one of the hospitals. She will have to arrange to remain in this country for the foreseeable future. If [the father] does not come she will have to manage unaided. How will the mother cope? Can her professionalism overcome her view that her son should not be subjected to this distressing procedure? Will she break down?"[31]

Butler Sloss LJ went on to say:

> "The mother and this child are one for the purpose of this unusual case and the decision of the court to consent to the operation jointly affects the mother and son and so also affects the father. The welfare of the child depends upon his mother".[32]

By so closely identifying the child's interests with those of the mother the court was able to give weight to the mother's interests while appearing to adhere to the welfare principle.[33]

Another example of this is *Re Y*.[34] The case involved a mentally handicapped adult, but would seem to be applicable to children as the principle used in such cases is whether the treatment is in the patient's welfare. In *Re Y* permission was sought and granted to remove bone marrow from Y to give to her sister. It was stated by Connell J that the operation would be in Y's interests because the bone marrow might save the sister's life and this would prolong the life of the mother who was very close to Y. There were fears that were the sister to die the mother's life expectancy would diminish and this would be contrary to Y's best interests.[35]

---

[30] *Re T (A Minor) (Wardship: Medical Treatment)* [1997] 1 FLR 502.

[31] At 511H.

[32] At 510G.

[33] Contrast *Re C (Medical Treatment)* [1998] 1 FLR 384 where the court approved the doctors' decision not to provide treatment for a severely ill child, despite the parents' request for treatment.

[34] Re *(Mental Incapacity: Bone Marrow Transplant)* [1997] 2 WLR 556.

[35] Other examples could be cases involving disputes between parents over whether a child should be removed from the jurisdiction where a parent with a residence order will be granted permission to leave if the proposals are reasonable—*Re H (Application to Remove from Jurisdiction)* [1998] 1 FLR 848.

There are two significant concerns with the merging of the interests of parents and children. First it can mean that interests of children are not given sufficient weight. *Re T* is particularly concerning. No doubt the demands placed on the parents if the surgery were ordered would be immense and it might be improper to compel the parents to suffer this sacrifice. However the court seems to have placed insufficient weight on the possibility of the parents requesting that the child be cared for by the local authority or foster parents.

A second danger is that the courts' approach hides the real issues.[36] For example, in *Re Y* merely focusing on the indirect benefit of improving the mother's well-being and so improving Y's welfare seems an unduly narrow way of looking at the issues involved. It was of crucial importance that the bone marrow transplant might save the sister's life. Surely the case would have been quite different if, say, the sister required some bone for cosmetic surgery, even if such a donation might improve Y's relationship with her mother.[37]

(b) The second form of covert recognition of parents' interests using the welfare principle is by means of using various "presumptions" or "well known facts of nature". For example Lord Templeman's dicta are often quoted:

> "the best person to bring up a child is the natural parent. It matters not whether the parent is wise or foolish, rich or poor, educated or illiterate, provided the child's moral and physical health are not endangered".[38]

Similarly there is the assumption that mothers are better than fathers at the task of caring for young children,[39] and an assumption that it is in a child's interests that she maintains contact with both parents.[40] All these assumptions can be viewed as protecting parental rights in that they emphasise interests highly valued by parents. For example, is it really true that wealth is not relevant when deciding the best place of residence for a child or is this really a presumption used to ensure there is fairness between adults?

(c) The third way that the welfare principle can be manipulated is by the court expressing the child's interests in terms as perceived by an adult or a lawyer rather than a child. For example, in *Re F*[41] a father sought a specific issue order that his twin children aged eleven be interviewed by his solicitor to consider whether or not they should be called to give evidence at the father's trial on charges of assault occasioning actual bodily harm and indecent assault against

---

[36] Cf. Montgomery (1989).

[37] Another example of where children and parents interests are conflated could be where there is genetic screening of young children in order to determine whether any further children of the parents will carry a genetic disorder.

[38] *Re KD (A Minor) (Ward: Termination of Access)* [1988] AC 806 at 812 per Lord Templeman. Approved and applied in *Re M (Child's upbringing)* [1996] 2 FLR 441.

[39] This is not however a legal presumption: *Re A (Children: 1959 United Nations Declaration)* [1998] 1 FLR 356; *Brixley v Lynas* [1996] 2 FLR 499 (a House of Lords decision on appeal from Scotland).

[40] *A v L (Contact)* [1998] 1 FLR 361; although this is not an irrebutable presumption: *Re B (Contact: Domestic Violence)* [1998] 2 FLR 171. See also Family Law Act 1996, s.1(c)(iii), s.11(4)(c).

[41] *Re F (Specific Issue: Children Interview)* [1995] 1 FLR 819.

the mother. The Court of Appeal granted the order arguing that it would be in the children's interests that their father should have the opportunity of a fair trial.[42] Although this was a criminal trial, in effect it was a dispute between the children's mother and their father. Pitching the children into the centre of this dispute and requiring them to give evidence seems undesirable. How crucial the fairness of the trial was *to the children* is debatable.

Another example is the law concerning changes to a child's surname. This is described by the courts as "a profound issue".[43] Whether to change a child's name is one of the few questions which a lone parent with parental responsibility cannot decide on their own and it requires the consent of both parents, or else a decision of the court.[44] It might be questioned whether changing a name is a more profound issue than, say, determining when and how a child can be educated; the latter is a decision that a lone parent with parental responsibility can make. It appears that the law here is using a perception of the child's welfare to promote interests important to adults.

(c) Limiting the application of the welfare principle by acknowledging parents' rights

In the previous section I have looked at the way in which the courts have applied the welfare principle but in so doing have disguised the real issues and have protected parents' interests. In this section I will consider cases where the courts have held that they ought not to make the requested order, even though it would promote the child's welfare, explicitly because to do so would infringe parents' rights. This is either on the basis that such orders were not contemplated by the Children Act 1989 or that such orders could be obtained from another statute and the safeguards in those statutes should not be circumvented. I will consider one example but there are several.[45]

In *Re E*[46] the Court of Appeal considered an application for an order that the children reside with the mother on condition that she remained in London, unless the non-resident father consented in writing. Although the Court accepted that it had the power to make such an order:

> "a general imposition of conditions on residence orders was clearly not contemplated by Parliament and where the parent is entirely suitable and the court intends to make a residence order in favour of that parent, a condition of residence is in my view an

---

[42] Quite why the trial would be unfair if the child did not give evidence is unclear.

[43] *Dawson v Wearmouth* [1997] 2 FLR 629.

[44] *Re C (Change of Surname)* [1998] 2 FLR 656.

[45] Other examples include *Re D (Residence: Imposition of Conditions)* [1996] 2 FLR 281; *Re D (Prohibited Steps Order)* [1996] 2 FLR 273; *Re M (Minors) (Disclosure of Evidence)* [1994] 1 FLR 760; *D v N (Contact Order: Conditions)* [1997] 2 FLR 797; *B v B (Residence Order: Restricting Applications)* [1997] 1 FLR 139.

[46] *Re E Residence: Imposition of Conditions* [1997] FLR 638.

unwarranted imposition upon the legal right of the person to choose where he/she will live within the UK or with whom".[47]

So it seems here that despite the fact that the condition might promote the children's interests, it was not imposed out of concern to protect the parent's right to choose where she lived. Quite how placing such weight on this right is consistent with the welfare principle was not explained.[48]

(d) Cases where the welfare principle has been said not to apply

An alternative way that the law has been able to protect parents' interests is to hold that the welfare principle does not apply, although the interests of the child may still be an important consideration. Such circumstances have included divorce; domestic violence; financial redistribution of property on divorce; secure accommodation orders;[49] disclosure of evidence;[50] adoption;[51] medical experiments (Mclean, 1991); anonymity for sperm donors (Bainham, 1989); and blood tests.[52] The welfare principle does not apply in these cases either because it is decreed by statute or because the issue has been said by the courts to be not directly related to the upbringing of children, and so section 1 of the Children Act 1989 does not apply. Two points should be made about this list (which is not exhaustive by any means). First, the list does not necessarily reflect those issues where there is a low level of children's interests: for example, the result of a domestic violence application is of fundamental importance to a child. Indeed it is tempting to see these cases as cases where the *parents'* interests are of particular importance. Secondly, by taking a strict reading of "children's upbringing" the courts have used what can be highly artificial distinctions. For example, there have been a series of cases involving a parent seeking an order concerning publicity about their child. The leading case is *Re Z*,[53] which stated that the law distinguishes two situations. The first is where the publicity directly concerns the child (for example, a case where a disabled child was to be filmed while receiving specialised treatment). In this case the matter "is with regard to the child's upbringing" and so the welfare principle does apply. The second is where the publicity only indirectly concerns a child (e.g. where a television programme is to be made about her parents), in which case the welfare principle does not apply. In such cases the Court of Appeal in *Re H*[54] suggests "the important

---

[47] At 642.

[48] Cf. Hansard (HL), 16 March 1989, col. 346.

[49] *Re M (Secure Accommodation Order)* [1995] 1 FLR 418.

[50] *Re L (Minors) (Police Investigation: Privilege)* [1997] AC 16.

[51] Adoption Act 1976, s.6.

[52] *S v S; W v Official Solicitor* [1972] AC 24.

[53] *Re Z (A Minor) (Freedom of Publication)* [1996] 1 FLR 191. The other important recent cases include: *Re H (Minors) (Injunction: Public Interest)* [1994] 1 FLR 519; *Mrs R v Central Independent Television PLC* [1994] 2 FLR 151.

[54] *Re H (Minors) (Injunction: Public Interest)* [1994] FLR 519.

question in this appeal is whether the respondent's and the media's freedom to publish matters of public interest outweigh the risk of harm to the children".

This distinction between publicity relating directly and indirectly to the child seems dubious as it reflects neither the level of harm to the child nor the amount of the public interest, although it is comprehensible as an attempt to balance the rights of parents and children.

The law also produces arbitrary results when a case involves two children. In such cases the child whose welfare is paramount is the child who is named in the application before the court as the subject of the proceedings. This is so even though it may be a matter of chance precisely what form the proceedings take.[55]

3. WHEN ENFORCING THE WELFARE PRINCIPLE DOES INFRINGE A PARENT'S INTERESTS

There are, of course, many cases where the welfare principle is used to require parents to act contrary to their wishes in a way that promotes the child's welfare. But it is rare for the courts to make orders that infringe the rights a parent has as an individual. By far the most common circumstance where this does occur is in relation to contact between children and the non-resident parent after the breakdown of a relationship.[56] A court order may, for example, require the resident parent to facilitate contact between the other parent and the child.[57] The clash is between the interests of a child in keeping contact with a parent with whom she is no longer living and the interests of the parent with a residence order for whom a contact order may infringe their freedom to choose whom to meet. The case law in dealing with this tension places great weight on the "right of the child to contact". It requires the court to decide whether the resident parent's objections are justifiable. If the objections are not justified, it is simply "implacable hostility", and contact will be ordered despite the objections of the resident parent.[58] The one exception to this is where the contact would cause such "major emotional harm",[59] to the resident parent, that the child would be harmed. Although such cases can be seen as cases where the interests of the resident parent are sub-ordinated to the interests of the child, it is also possible to see these cases as examples of where the welfare principle is used to prefer the interests of one parent (the non-resident parent) over the interests of another (the resident parent).

---

[55] *Birmingham City Council v H (No.3)* [1994] 1 FLR 224; *Re T and E (Proceedings: Conflicting Interests)* [1995] 1 FLR 581; *Re S (Contact: Application by Sibling)* [1998] 2 FLR 897.

[56] Prohibited step and specific issues orders usually only conflict with the interests of a parent in exercising their rights qua parent rather than their rights as an individual.

[57] Such as reading letters to a child (e.g. *Re O (Contact: Imposition of Conditions)* [1995] 2 FLR 124) or taking a child to visit a father in prison (cf. *Re P (Contact: Discretion)* [1998] 2 FLR 969).

[58] *Re D (Contact: Reasons for Refusal)* [1997] 2 FLR 98; but see *Re H (Contact: Domestic Violence)* [1998] 2 FLR 47.

[59] *Re D (A Minor) (Contact: Mother's Hostility)* [1993] 2 FLR 1 at 7G per Waite LJ.

4. ALTERNATIVE APPROACHES

I have attempted to demonstrate above that although the welfare principle is central to the law relating to children, the courts have still found ways of protecting parental interests. There is no monitoring of parents to ensure the welfare of children is promoted day to day. Where the courts are involved and the welfare principle does apply the judiciary have found ways of placing weight on the interests of parents. The present law is unsatisfactory. It is not that the results in the cases are necessarily wrong but rather that the use of the welfare principle hides the real issues involved. Also, the courts have had to use strained reasoning to avoid applying the welfare principle as they have understood it, because to do so might produce unfairness to parents.

So how should the law deal with these cases which involve clashes between the interests of children, mothers and fathers?[60] I will examine three possible approaches. The first is to abandon the welfare principle and instead openly balance the interests of different parties. The second is to use the welfare principle but understand that there is a limit to the principle and that those orders which infringe "fundamental rights" of a parent are not permitted. The third is to re-examine the welfare principle and consider whether a better understanding of the welfare principle can be utilised. It is this third approach which I will suggest is the most appropriate.

(a) Abandoning the welfare principle

The increasing uneasiness with the welfare principle is revealed by Lord Nicholls's *dictum* in the House of Lords that "the paramountcy principle must not be permitted to become a loose cannon destroying all else around it".[61] The criticisms of the welfare principle are well known. Some commentators deny its practicality: the court lacks the time, objectivity, evidence and foresight with which to make the necessary prediction of a child's future. Even if the court could make the necessary predictions there is doubt whether it could determine which alternative would promote the child's welfare. One response is that the judge should refer to the relevant standards of the community, if these can be ascertained. Even if the judge is able to find an "accepted standard" he or she may simply be perpetuating the inequality in society by enforcing that standard. For example, Helen Reece (1996) in discussing cases involving homosexual parents has recently argued that:

> "the child's need to be protected from teasing has led, not just to the subordination of, but to the total negation of, a far more important and socially significant value, the equal right of lesbian and gay men to be parents".

[60] This can be seen as a clash between an approach based on rights or based on utility. See Parker (1992).

[61] *Re L (minors) (Police Investigation: Privilege)* [1997] AC 16 at 33B.

While not everyone will agree with this balance it highlights the potential dangers of relying on community standards (see also Golombok, Chapter 9 below). A slightly different argument is that the welfare principle is unduly narrow in not being able to incorporate such concepts as children's rights of autonomy or privacy.

Other objections are concerned with the way that the welfare principle operates in practice. As Frances Olsen (1992) has argued, "legal protection of children can be and has been used as a basis for controlling women". Others have argued that the welfare principle's lack of predictability generates and encourages disputes (Schneider, 1989). Some commentators have suggested that the welfare principle is essentially a rhetorical or political device and perhaps not to be taken too literally. Hence it has been suggested that "overstating the importance of [a] child's welfare prevents parents, judges and legislators from systematically undervaluing it" (Altman, 1997).

In the face of such criticism the welfare test has shown surprising durability. The real reason behind the durability of the test is the absence of an alternative. Space prevents a full discussion of the criticisms of the welfare principle but I will focus on the particular criticism which is most relevant to this chapter: can the welfare principle be justified given its lack of emphasis on the interests of adults?

Helen Reece (1996) has argued:

> "the paramountcy principle must be abandoned and replaced within a framework which recognises that the child is merely one participant in a process in which the interest of all the participants count".

The difficulty with this approach is the lack of protection for children. The strength of the welfare principle is that it focuses the court's attention on the person whose voice may be the quietest both literally and metaphorically and who has the least control over whether the issue arrives before the court or in which way it does. The child may also be the person with whom the court is least able to empathise. As we have seen from the case law we do not at present have a problem with the interests of children being given excessive weight at the expense of the interests of adults. Indeed it is interesting that despite Helen Reece's attack on the welfare principle in English law there is a notable shortage of cases in her article where she feels the interests of parents were not adequately protected. She focuses on the rare cases of homosexual parents. As we have seen, the courts have in fact put weight on the interests of parents despite the welfare principle. The courts have also shown willingness to value wider principles, for example, free speech. The lack of protection of parents' interests does not require the abandonment of the welfare principle, but there is a need for the welfare principle to be better understood in order to prevent the court's reasoning becoming so strained.

(b) Protecting parent's fundamental rights

A second approach would be to state that orders infringing certain rights of parents are not available. For example orders limiting a parent's right to live where or with whom they choose; restricting a parent's religious practices; or infringing on a right of free speech, could be impermissible. There could be a specific reference to the rights referred to in the Human Rights Act 1998. An example of such an approach has been promoted by Andrew Bainham (1994) who has suggested that it is necessary to distinguish between the "primary" and "secondary" rights of parents and children. He suggests:

> "in some cases the primary interest would be the child's while in others it would be the parents' interests. The more fundamental the interest in question, and the more serious the consequences of failing to uphold it, the more likely it would be that *that* interest would be regarded as the primary interest".[62]

It may then be necessary to require parents (or children) to sacrifice a secondary interest to promote a primary interest.[63] There are two particular difficulties with this approach. First, the test requires the court to perceive the situation as a battle between parents' and children's interests. As will be seen below this is an unnecessarily individualistic approach. Secondly, the welfare principle has carried enormous political significance, not least as a central plank of the United Nations Convention on the Rights of Children. To limit its application explicitly would seem unacceptable; it is better to reconceptualise it.

(c) Reconceptualising the welfare principle

The conception of the welfare principle adopted by the courts is often too narrowly individualist and focuses on a self-centred approach to welfare. A broader version of the welfare principle could allow consideration of the parent's interests. There are two elements to the argument for pursuing a wider understanding of the welfare principle. The first is that it is part of growing up for a child to learn to sacrifice as well as claim benefits. Families, and society in general, are based on mutual co-operation and support. So it is important to encourage a child to adopt, to a limited extent, the virtue of altruism and an awareness of social obligation.[64] It needs to be stressed that it is a very limited altruism that is being sought. Children should only be expected to be altruistic to the extent of not demanding from parents excessive sacrifices in return for minor benefits.

The second element of this approach is that the child's welfare involves ensuring that the child's relationships with the other family members are fair and just

---

[62] At 173.

[63] It is not clear how Bainham would deal with the problem where two primary interests clash.

[64] *Re B (A Minor) (Wardship: Sterilisation)* [1988] AC 199 made it clear that in considering a child's welfare the long-term consequences into adulthood can be considered.

(Bartlett, 1988). A relationship based on unacceptable demands on a parent is not furthering a child's welfare. As the preamble to the United Nations Convention on the Rights of Children states:

> "the child, for the full and harmonizing development of his or her personality, should grow up in a family environment, in an atmosphere of happiness, love and understanding".

It is in the child's welfare to be brought up in a family whose members respect each other and so, on occasion, sacrifices may be required from the child. An analogy could be drawn by asking whether it would be to our benefit to have a personal slave to perform all our menial tasks for us. From a narrow perception one may say that to have such a slave would promote our welfare, although I imagine that most people would not accept that achieving ease and comfort in this way would be to a person's emotional, moral and general welfare (as well as, of course, being an infringement on the slave's rights). Of course parenthood is not slavery(!), but the point is that conceptions of welfare should take into account the kind of sacrifice demanded of parents to obtain benefits for the children.

The effect of this approach is to move away from conceiving the problem as a clash between children and parents and in terms of weighing two conflicting interests, and towards seeing it rather as deciding what is a proper parent-child relationship. The child's welfare is promoted when he or she lives in a fair and just relationship with each parent. Understood in this way, the welfare principle can protect children while properly taking into account parents' rights.

The argument can also operate where a child's welfare may require a sacrifice for the obtaining of some greater social good. This view has been recognised by Ward LJ:

> "although the welfare of the children is paramount in the sense that it rules upon and determines the course to be followed, that does not mean that when this is the test, the freedom of publication is not to be weighed in the scales at all. Of course it is. It is one of the relevant facts, choices and other circumstances which a reasonable person would take into account. We do not live in a vacuum and our choices have to be made for ourselves as well as for our children in the realisation that we sometimes have to sacrifice self for the greater good of social order".[65]

This understanding of welfare has five particular advantages. First, it is more in accord with practice in many families. As noted at the very start of this chapter most family dynamics involve "give and take" and do not consider exclusively the child's interests. Secondly, it is in accord with what most of us would have wished when we were being brought up. I suspect that most adults would not have wanted their parents to have been obliged to make extraordinary sacrifices to pursue a minor increase in their welfare, but would have expected a fair level of sacrifice by the parents.[66] Thirdly, this approach enables a court to

---

[65] *Re Z (A Minor) (Freedom of Publication)* [1996] 1 FLR 191 at 212G.
[66] Cf. Rawls (1972).

consider explicitly the interests of all family members while still adhering to the welfare principle. This is what is done already, but covertly. Fourthly, this approach enables the interests of adolescents to be better understood. As a child becomes older the relationship with his or her parents changes, but in complex ways. It no longer becomes necessary for the parents to determine the child's own interests—the child can determine this for him or herself. Similarly, the demands that a child can make on a parent can lessen. Andrew Bainham (1993) refers to the "democratic model of decision making", which usefully captures the sense of co-operation within families focused upon by this approach to welfare. Fifthly, by focusing on a child's relationships this may encourage the law to develop ways in which a child's voice may be heard more effectively in proceedings.

It might be helpful to consider briefly how some of the cases we discussed earlier might be perceived with such an understanding of the welfare approach. Take *Re Y* where it will be recalled that the issue was whether it was in the welfare of Y to donate bone marrow to a sibling. The decision of the court was that it was in Y's interest as the bone marrow transplant would potentially save the life of the sibling and this would improve the health and happiness of the mother, and as she was central to Y's well-being this would benefit Y. I mentioned earlier that this argument is rather artificial. Under the suggested understanding of the welfare principle Y's welfare would not be limited to simply a consideration of her own physical well-being but also a decision on whether this was a just exchange for her as a member of this family. This recognises the benefit to individuals of co-operation within communities, of giving and taking. I suspect the answer would be the same as that reached by the court. But in the variation on cosmetic surgery suggested above the court may well feel this was too small a gain for such a sacrifice. This approach it is submitted better raises the real issues for the court than the individualistic understanding of the welfare principle used by the court in *Re Y*.

Consider also *Re E*[67] where it will be recalled that the issue was whether an order should be made requiring a mother to stay in London so that the contact between the child and father could be retained. Here the court simply stated that in most cases the parent's right to choose where to live overrode any interests of the child. It is submitted that the proper question is whether ordering the mother to stay in London would be part of a just and fair relationship between the child and the mother or whether it would create an abusive relationship where the sacrifices to the mother would be too great compared to the benefit to the child. A child brought up in such a one-sided relationship would not be benefited.

Recall also those cases involving publicity and children. As said earlier a rather artificial distinction is drawn between those cases where the publicity relates to the upbringing of the children (in which cases the child's welfare is paramount) and those where it does not (where the child's welfare has to be

---

[67] *Re E (Residence: Imposition of Conditions)* [1997] 2 FLR 638.

taken into account but is not paramount). Again I suggest that this can be dealt with simply under a broader understanding of the welfare concept. As a member of society a child can expect to make some sacrifices for the general good, to benefit society. Learning respect for others and for the values that society holds dear are an important part of the education and development of a child. Experiencing sacrifices, if those sacrifices are appropriate and fair to the child, is in the child's welfare. The question is whether a child's welfare will benefit from being brought up in a society that requires such sacrifices.

5. CONCLUSION

This chapter has considered the legal regulation of parenthood and, in particular, whether the interests of parents should be taken into account when using the welfare principle. The courts have used a rather individualised conception of welfare. This has caused difficulties in cases where the interests of children and parents clash. It has been argued that the courts have in fact found ways of protecting parents' interests despite the prominence of the welfare principle. However in so doing it has been necessary to manipulate or circumvent their narrow view of the welfare principle and thereby disguised the real issues at play.

It has been suggested this need not be so. A full understanding of the welfare principle should include ensuring that the relationship between the parent and child is a fair and just one, with respect of each individual's rights. A child's welfare will be best promoted by being brought up by parents in a family and community based on appropriate mutual co-operation and respect. With this broader understanding of the welfare principle we have no need to seek to undermine or avoid its application and it can take a legitimate and effective pride of place in the law relating to children.

REFERENCES

Altman, S., "Should child custody rules be fair?" (1997) 325 *Journal of Family Law* 354.
Bainham, A., "When is a parent not a parent? Reflections on the unmarried father and his child in English law" (1989) *International Journal of Law and the Family* 208.
Bainham, A., "The privatisation of the public interest in children" (1990) 53 *Modern Law Review* 206.
Bainham, A., "Growing up in Britain: adolescence in the post-Gillick era" in J. Eekelaar and P. Sarcevic (eds.), *Parenthood in Modern Society* (Netherlands, Kluwer, 1993).
Bainham, A., "Non-intervention and judicial paternalism" in P. Birks (ed.), *Frontiers of Liability* (Oxford, Oxford University Press, 1994).
Bainham, A., *Children: The Modern Law*, 2nd edn. (Bristol, Family Law, 1998).
Bartlett, K., "Re-expressing parenthood" (1988) 98 *Yale Law Journal* 293.
Department of Health, *The Children Act Guidance and Regulations*, Volume 2 (London, HMSO, 1991).

Donzelot, J., *The Policing of Families* (London, Hutchinson, 1980).

Eekelaar, J., "The emergence of children's rights" (1986) 6 *Oxford Journal of Legal Studies* 161.

Freeman, M., "The best interests of the child? Is the best interests of the child in the best interests of children?" (1997) *International Journal of Law and Family* 36.

Home Office, *Consultation Paper, Supporting Families* (London, HMSO, 1998).

Maclean, M. and Eekelaar, J., *The Parental Obligation* (Oxford, Hart Publishing, 1997).

McCall Smith, A., "Is anything left of parental rights?" in E. Sutherland and A. McCall Smith (eds.), *Family Rights. Family Law and Medical Ethics* (Edinburgh, Edinburgh University Press, 1990).

McLean, J., "Medical experimentation with children" (1991) 9 *International Journal of Family Law* 173.

Montgomerty, J., "Rhetoric and welfare" (1989) 9 *Oxford Journal of Legal Studies* 397.

Olsen, F., "Children's rights: some feminist approaches to the United Nations Convention on the Rights of the Child" (1992) *International Journal of Law and the Family* 192.

Parker, S., "Rights and utility in Anglo-Australian family law" (1992) 55 *Modern Law Review* 311.

Rawls, J. A., *A Theory of Justice* (Cambridge, Massachusetts, Harvard University Press, 1972).

Reece, H., "The paramountcy principle: consensus or construct?" (1996) 49 *Current Legal Problems* 267.

Schneider, C., "Discretion, rules, and law: child custody and the UDMA's best interest standard" (1989) *Michigan Law Review* 2215.

6

Family or Familiarity?

JULIET MITCHELL and JACK GOODY

"I miss hidings from my Dad when I get into trouble"
(evacuée boy aged fourteen) (Bowlby, 1951, p.79)

Editorial Introduction

This chapter offers an historical perspective on the question of "what is a parent?". Contemporary debates on changing family patterns reflect an underlying deep concern with parenting. In the years since the Second World War, we have witnessed an increasing separation of marriage and parenthood such that, as Maclean and Richards argue in Chapter 14 below, marriage is fast being replaced by parenthood as the basis for "family". In this climate, considerable tensions exist between, on the one hand, a desire to quell widespread social anxieties occasioned by declining marriage rates and high divorce rates (which, for some, amount to nothing less than a "decline of the family") and, on the other hand, the necessity of acknowledging the realities of social and cultural change, and the need to regard difference and diversity in more positive ways. These tensions appear, for example, at the heart of the recent Government consultation paper Supporting Families. *These debates form the context in which two contradictory, but interdependent, images have acquired meaning and significance: the ideal of the "cornflake packet" nuclear family is shaped and sustained by its opposite, that of the family fragmented into single mothers and absent or "deadbeat" dads.*

The "traditional" gendered arrangement of expressive mother-at-home and instrumental father-at-work (Parsons and Bales, 1955) has been increasingly challenged by newer gender-neutral concepts of parents in dual-earner families. The new ideal to strive for has been enshrined in law, for example, in the concept of "parental responsibility" in the Children Act 1989. This image of gender-neutral parents is created and sustained in demands that mothers should work in the paid labour force and in the hope that fathers will care for and nurture children. The realities of family life and the vicissitudes of parenting for most people remain, however, several steps removed from any such ideal. On the contrary, mothers' and fathers' parenting practices continue, in the main, to be gendered activities. The negative imagery of single mothers and absent fathers itself sustains implicit ideas about the desirability of polarisation along gender lines in the nuclear family ideal.

This chapter explores the historical origins of these current ambivalences and ambiguities around parenting. The construction of denigrated single mums and deadbeat dads is located within the drive to produce the ideal family, as a guarantor of social stability and cohesion, in the years after the Second World War. The analysis is based on an examination of the psychological and psychoanalytic literature of the time, and policy reports, based on studies of evacuee children. The authors show how this literature produced gendered images of mothers as carers and fathers as financial providers, the legacy of which continues to inform current debates. The literature effectively sidelined fathers from a moral, ethical, educational and caring role whilst it placed mothers at the centre stage of their children's development. These gendered images sit uncomfortably with contemporary ideas of parents as gender-neutral beings. The matricentred scenario that we identify has a history that goes back at least to the rise of the notion of "moral motherhood" in the last decades of the nineteenth century (Seccombe, 1993), and that it gathered new impetus from the input of psychoanalysis and the creation of what the authors call "psychological motherhood" during and after the Second World War.

The authors re-examine the psychological material and the psychoanalytically-based thinking that apparently established the overwhelming significance of the mother for child development. They offer a new reading of the evidence, and argue that evacuee children were "deprived" of "familiarity" as much as they were deprived of mother and "family". In this context, answers to the question of "what is a parent?" can be seen as inextricably linked to broader historical, social and political conditions. They conclude that, as new family policies are formulated in the context of specific socio-economic practices and their ideological counterparts, we might be wise to re-think the significance we have tended to accord to individual parents' effects on children's lives, to the exclusion of broader influences and phenomena.

That wars affect family life is obvious. Karl Marx notoriously proposed that wars gave us a prognosis of future social patterns—as regards the Second World War and future family constellations he may well have been right. But academic discussions of the subject have made less grandiose claims, tending instead to concentrate upon the death of parents (especially the father), the problems of widows and orphans, and, a somewhat larger issue, the changes, apparently temporary but having more permanent implications, in the division of labour. In France adoption was re-introduced, after some fifteen hundred years, as the result of the increasing number of orphans created by the First World War. In England, although many social changes took place before 1914, the war assisted the women's movement in achieving increased participation for women in the national economy and the final stages of achieving the vote. Losses in war confirmed the pre-war emphasis on government provisions for pensions and care.

The mass "world" wars of this century led to the destruction and dispersal of families as well as to an emphasis on the mother-child tie. However if we look at the family in the dominant groups in the West after the "world" wars we can see that at the end of the First World War there was a move to draw together the bonds of "the family", but always within the context of the alterations in social relations which the War had helped bring about.

There was a similar tendency in Britain after the Second World War, but one that took a special practical and theoretical form, associated above all with the name of the psychoanalyst John Bowlby. That approach attributed a number of psychological and social ills to "maternal deprivation", to the absence of maternal care when mother and child were separated in the early years. The thesis received widespread attention as a result of a report Bowlby was asked to write for the World Health Organisation (Bowlby, 1951) arising out of the decision of the United Nations in 1948 to study the needs of homeless children. Children "deprived of a normal home life" are seen as "a source of social infection as real and serious as are the carriers of diphtheria and typhoid" (p.157). "Home life" was given a narrow interpretation: "mother-love in infancy and childhood is as important for mental health as are vitamins and proteins for physical health" (p.158).

The report argued that the solution to this problem of mental hygiene lay in the proper training of a social worker (female); if she did not have "a good understanding of unconscious motivation she would be powerless to deal with many an unmarried mother, many a home which is in danger of breaking up, and many a case of conflict between parent and child" (p.157) Bowlby's words undoubtedly have a dated approach in his references to the "break up of families and the shunting of illegitimates" (p.157), but his message can still be heard in today's references to single mothers.

Part of the "break-up" of families, caused by the War, was brought about by the absence of men at the front, but little research effort seems to have been directed at this feature, presumably because the mother-small child relationship remained intact as even with evacuation small children and infants—as would seem to be a world-historical pattern—went with their mothers. What did get a lot of attention was the "break-up" of families (the separation of children from both parents) as a result of the large-scale movement of school children from the towns to country areas because of the fear of the bombing of urban centres.

The "evacuation" was a massive social undertaking, voluntarily carried out in September 1939 in the first days of the Second World War. It affected 47 per cent of the country's school children who went with their teachers, and a large number of mothers and younger children who went together (Padley and Cole, 1940). The total amounted to seven hundred and fifty thousand schoolchildren, five hundred and forty two thousand mothers with young children, twelve thousand expectant mothers and seventy-seven thousand other persons, all of whom were transported from cities to the countryside or to smaller towns. Not all stayed long in their foster homes. Of the mothers and young children, around 87 per cent had gone home by January 1940; for the return of unaccompanied school children, the figure was 43 per cent.

About three thousand evacuated to Cambridge from the boroughs of Tottenham and Islington subsequently formed the basis of a study organised by

Susan Isaacs, who was Head of the Department of Child Development at the Institute of Education and had been Head of the Malting House School in Newnham. She was also an eminent psychoanalyst and fellow of the British Psychological Society. Isaacs was assisted by a number of others, including John Bowlby of the Tavistock Clinic, the psychoanalyst Melanie Klein and R.H. Thouless of the County Department of Psychology who later edited a book on survey methods in the social sciences. The group was advised by a distinguished committee including the sociologist Maurice Ginsberg from the London School of Economics, Carr-Saunders also of the LSE and F.C. Bartlett, Professor of Psychology at Cambridge, who had been a pupil of the important psychologist-anthropologist W.H.R. Rivers.

Of the reasons for the high rates of return to potentially dangerous situations (the bombing of London's East End did not in fact begin until the summer of 1940), the most prominent given was the "crucial importance of family ties and of the feelings of parents and children towards and about each other" (Isaacs, 1941, p.7). This was evident in the "anxiety and loneliness of the parents, the homesickness or worry of children" (p.7). "The feeling of family unity and the intense resistance to its being broken up" (p.8) was apparent in the reasons parents gave for not wishing to send their children away in the first place. That view was reinforced by the situation following the bombing of London's East End where:

> "this need to keep the family together and to cling to familiar home surroundings may override even the worst dangers. Among the simple and the poor, where there is no wealth, no pride of status or of possessions, love for the members of one's own family and joy in their bodily presence alone make life worth living" (p.9).

The importance of the family among "the poor" also emerged from the stories of teachers and pupils in which the "chief source of difficulty was the break in family life, the parting with loved ones and the securities [of] home" (p.9).[1]

The wartime evacuation of children was a case of temporary mass fostering. Note that it did not affect young children, who were evacuated with their mothers; there no maternal separation occurred (see Oakley, 1996). Fostering, the provision of substitute parents, did of course occur in peacetime; Isaacs comments that in pre-war Britain some forty thousand children were boarded out in private families, some because of what were considered "problem families", (now of "difficult homes"), others because of "broken" ones.[2] Temporary separations occurred in many others, for example, in the earlier custom of frequent

---

[1] This was a "discovery". Isaacs was critical and self-critical of the extent to which the prime movers of the evacuation plan had discounted family feeling among the poor, assuming that the improved conditions and mostly improved status of life among families in Cambridge would simply bring gratitude.

[2] Isaacs, 1941, p.13: "In Great Britain some 40,000 children at least are boarded every year in private families. About ten years' ordinary experience in the placing of children had been condensed into one week of evacuation. Surely something could be learned from this. Many countries are far in advance of Great Britain in this kind of knowledge".

initial separation of the new-born child from the mother in hospital and of hospitalised sick children. In Britain, it was during and after the Second World War that the practice of separating sick children from their mothers in hospital was questioned and gradually changed.

In the case of the evacuation to Cambridge, the move was relatively successful. Most children were well received and were happy with their billets. Dissatisfaction with the fostering arrangement was highest among adolescent children, not among the younger group. Many, especially among the latter, made a happy accommodation with their substitute families and parental visits were sometimes complicated by this relationship; "the affection which children began to show for their foster parents was sometimes hard for their own parents to bear" (Isaacs, 1941, p.49). Class factors were also present; less well-adapted children were more frequent among the poorer, Islington, sample. Beveridge reported that in England "a family still remains the greatest single cause of poverty".[3] Adaptation did not seem to be related to the frequency of parental visits.[4] The negative effects of moving to a new home were partly alleviated if brothers and sisters went together, emphasising the importance of continuing family ties, but of the sibling rather than the parental relationship.

Like Melanie Klein, Bowlby was involved in the study carried out by Isaacs and references to the enquiry were made in his path-breaking report to the World Health Organization entitled *Maternal Care and Mental Health* (1951). This was the report that had resulted from a decision of the United Nations to make a study of homeless children "that are orphaned or separated from their families for other reasons and need care in foster homes, institutions or other types of group care".

The work that Bowlby summarised related to "a continuous relationship with a nurturant figure during . . . the early years" (1951, p.52). Bowlby suggested that mothers should want to be with their infants twenty-four hours a day. He stressed the mother's satisfaction as well as the child's needs. In fact, the earlier chapters of his report focused on the period from six to twelve months as being the one where most crucial care was needed to avoid the development of a psychopathic personality. In very different ways, both Melanie Klein and Donald Winnicott were also emphasising the importance of these earliest months for "good" or "bad" psychic development. The failure of such a mother-infant relationship may be described as "maternal deprivation" and the word "mother" was frequently used in Bowlby's report. But mother substitutes did in fact seem to be accepted as adequate (except for example in Levy's work quoted by Bowlby on the failure of substitute mothers to satisfy the needs of early life). Who then were these mother substitutes? They included adoptive parents, providing the adoption was early. The work by Powdermaker *et al* also discussed

---

[3] Cited by Bowlby, 1951, p.90.

[4] Isaacs, 1941, p.60. Though it was related to the way in which the fostering family treated the child—according to Isaac's interpretation of the data there was distress if children were regarded not as part of the family but as servants.

by Bowlby referred to the absence of a "family tie". However even for children from "bad" homes, foster parents can rarely replace "natural" parents (Bowlby, 1951, p.69), and those "parents" are most often identified with the mother; "at least his parents have cared for him after a fashion all his life, and not until someone else has shown herself equally or more dependable can he trust her" (pp.72–73).

Not only were "parents" often reduced to the "mother" but there is a slippage between the "mother" and the "family" or the child's "natural home group" where "normal home life" is to be found. Indeed "one of the principal purposes of the family is the preservation of the art of parenthood" (p.69). What is excluded is some but not all "institutional care" (p.40) and especially the movement of young children from one environment to another (p.44).[5] No specific mention is made here of grandmothers, step-mothers or other nurturant figures, so that inferences and conclusions concerning the break-up of families and the loss or absence of the "maternal role" (as distinct from the mother) seem quite out of place. But Bowlby does call for research into the reasons why relatives are unable to act as substitutes (p.154), embodying a view of parenthood which few outside the urban middle class of north western Europe would accept.

Can men (as well as other women) play a maternal role? Little mention is made in the report of fathers, except for the general apology for their omission in Chapter 1. They support their wives economically and emotionally; no mention is made of direct father-child relationships in gross contrast to earlier Freudian theory:

> "In the young child's eyes father plays second fiddle and his value increases only as the child's vulnerability to deprivation decreases. Nevertheless, as the illegitimate child knows, fathers have their uses even in infancy. In what follows, therefore, while continual reference will be made to the mother-child relation, little [i.e. nothing] will be said of the father-child relation, his value as the economic and emotional support of the mother will be assumed" (Bowlby, 1951, p.13).

A truly remarkable absence of clinical or theoretical work relating to fathers followed. Whether or not there is evidence of the mother's overwhelming importance from clinical work in psychoanalysis is a difficult question to answer. It is important that Bowlby turned not to clinical cases but to ethology to support his conclusions.

Certainly the matricentric focus encourages a tendency to neglect the possible positive role of other carers in infancy that Bowlby rather tendentiously characterises as "mother-substitutes and others" (and even the mother-substitutes are not "natural").[6] This marginalising of other figures in the infant's environment makes the universal claims seem very ethnocentric. Even for later childhood the argument tends to continue to stress the mother's role at the expense of the father's.

---

[5] In an appendix Bowlby discusses the differences in Rorschach response between institution children and others (Loosli-usteri in Geneva in the late 1920s and Goldfarbs in New York in the 1950s.)

The attachments of the child, certainly in the Isaacs' study (1941), are more varied, especially from the children's own reports. In the first place there was a high degree of satisfaction with the foster homes: only just over 8 per cent were unsatisfactory. What children most missed in their new environments were, it is true, most commonly "parents and relatives" (p.67) but other items came high on the list such as friends, home and home activities. When they did miss family, the comments quoted by Isaacs show more missing siblings (seven) than mother (one plus one) or father (three). This acknowledgement of the absence of the father is striking. One girl missed her father most of all "as there is no man in (the) billet", while a fourteen year-old boy missed getting "hidings from my dad when I get into trouble" (p.79). At least on the surface (which is all we have) maternal deprivation seems to play little part in the lives of these older and temporary foster children. One might posit that maternal affection is taken for granted as the child apparently sees the absence of other members of the family as being more important.

As we have seen, when during the first year of the War there was no bombing, many children returned to London. The reasons might be financial, or the parents' dissatisfaction with the foster home, but the dominant reason was:

"family ties, showing themselves either in the anxiety or loneliness of one or both parents without their children, or in the homesickness or persistent desire of the child himself to return home" (Isaacs, 1941, p.120).

However, the trained interviewers got the strong impression that the description of the child's homesickness was a reflection of the parent's loneliness. In other words, the problem lay not so much with deprivation on the part of the child, but of loneliness on the part of parents or mothers left single. The children appear to have minded less than the adults and even when they missed home, their statements show that it was not so much the parents that they missed, but their siblings, their house, their playthings and their physical environment. In other words, familiarity as much as family.

Bowlby, however, interprets the results in his own framework. Reports on evacuated children between five and sixteen make it clear, he claims, that the children suffered deprivation and were "not yet emotionally self-supporting". "Teachers reported that homesickness was prevalent and power of concentration on schoolwork declined" (Bowlby, 1951, p.28). But reading the reports makes it clear that that is only part of the story. These sources also reported improvements in health and personal appearance, better relations with teachers and peers, a widening of interests and a tremendous increase in self-reliance (Isaacs, 1941). This omission of the positive suggests that the negative aspects must be seen within the total context, which includes not simply the mother, not just the family, but the familiar activities and surroundings as well. It also points to a high degree of ideological interference with the assessment of the research results.

Essentially Bowlby sees the problems raised by family life as capable of being treated if economic, social and medical difficulties were understood and acted upon. This treatment would be the end (or reduction) of "illegitimacy, neglect, maladjustment, and desertion", as well as other forms of family failure as not being "unavoidable social evils" (1951, p.75) but capable of being combated and, in a sense "cured". Bowlby argues that if they are not cured, even a bad family is the best home for a child, thereby raising questions that are highly topical since the Cleveland affair and the contemporary preoccupation with abuse. But, despite all efforts, these features of health and socio-economic welfare have become more, not less, important. We have to see the psychological aspects of the family as embedded within socio-economic conditions and subject to long-term changes of which "illegitimacy" and family break-up, that is, increasing non-marriage and "demariage", are fundamental trends associated with the avoidance of the ties of formal marriage and the desire to choose and change partners that marks contemporary domestic life.

What light, if any, does evidence from other cultures shed on the question? Bowlby's discussion of maternal deprivation refers exclusively to Western societies. But in other cultures observers with psychological interests have stressed the importance of parenting; that is, of the largely maternal role in initial care of infants and the need for both father and mother figures in childhood. But the biological base of these social roles is by no means universally found. In some matrilineal societies the mother's brother gives some of the support that fathers give elsewhere; in any case that role is split. In some polygynous societies, father's wives may share the tasks of child-care and sometimes of nursing. In childhood in West Africa, fostering by distant kin is common and is not seen as a second best to parental care, indeed in some cases it is preferred; many successful men and women in the society will have been through an experience which is held to have some of the advantages of a boarding school education (E. Goody, 1982). In medieval times in Europe upper-class families sent their own sons out as squires to learn of service in other families. In many cultures— including the southern states of America—childless wealthier kin would take in a child from poorer, larger families.

With high mortality among adults as well as children, with frequently high rates of divorce and separation in many simpler societies, the culture has to be prepared for mother-substitutes who are not seen as marking low status categories nor as associated with maternal deprivation. Indeed when alternatives are so frequent and so accepted, would it be correct to speak of maternal deprivation at all? Such considerations led Parsons and Bales (1955) to treat family relationships as a sub-set of ones within small groups that required instrumental (mainly male) and expressive (mainly female) leadership. The value of this approach is questionable but it does avoid some of the over-specific assumptions derived from the study of the Western family. However, that study remains ethnocentric overall.

Do studies of other cultures also bear upon the question of familiarity as distinct from family? Certainly, if the family is interpreted in a narrow sense. Most observers of these societies place emphasis on the household and the organisation of domestic groups in preference to the family *per se* and both the notions of household and *domus* stress place as well as the people who use it as a base. In other words one values the presence or regrets the absence of the familiar rather than specifically the family, at least of a nuclear kind.

What bearing does an analysis of the psychosocial studies of Susan Isaacs and John Bowlby have on the socio-legal aspects of contemporary parenting? Those writers were part of a shift from the male-oriented discussions of family relations in much of the earlier psychoanalytic literature, to a female-oriented one embedded in the work of Melanie Klein, Anna Freud, Sandor Ferenczi, Alice and Michael Balint, Donald Winnicott and others that started in the years immediately after the First World War and that came to prominence following the Second World War. But there was also a further shift, not of gender but of generation, that both reflected and influenced the perception of intra-familial relations. The concept of maternal deprivation, for example, concentrated attention on the needs of children rather than those of parents, a focus that became embodied in Parliamentary decisions and formalised in statutes. Such an approach tended to disregard the fact that all rights (whether sanctioned legally or not) require corresponding responsibilities and duties on the part of others (Hohfeld, 1923); and that, in any case, the household (not necessarily the "family") is a socio-economic group subject to certain constraints that affect parent-child relationships, for example, whether the return on labour (or indeed the absence of employment) allows the parent or prospective parent to provide for a child. In this case the obligations of care and support may not be held to fall either on the parent or on the state (in the manner currently embodied in Western practice and theory), but on other actors in the wider community, ranging from more distant kin (as for example in Central America and Mediterranean countries) or on local groups of one kind and another (as effectively within many states even now and certainly in earlier times). These responsibilities cannot be exclusively located at the level of the individual (or couple) nor yet of the nation state and therefore may well lie outside the sphere of the law *sensu strictu*.

Although today's idiom is very different from Bowlby's (far less so than from Isaacs') there is, despite all appearances, a direct continuation of ideas about what constitutes the right family and what provides for the needs of an infant and child in order for it to become a psychically healthy adult. The recognition of multiple forms of coupling may be progressive but there is a continuing ideological emphasis on mother-as-carer and father-as-financial-provider that fixes the centrality of nuclear parenting, even where that is absent as a social reality. The nature of these roles are changing but so too is parenting itself, which is increasingly practised in single terms or with step-parents, while the state, the school and other agencies take over aspects of parenting; that is what welfare is about. The child-centred approach clearly remedied many wrongs but at the expense of bonding the child only to "good" or "bad" parents, not to being a member of a wider community or kin network.

A child from a large but poor Guatamalan-Belizean family was taken in by more prosperous, childless cousins. Two other siblings lived with their grandparents. After a highly successful period, she started to misbehave. After tolerating the misbehaviour for some while, the substitute father took the child aside and explained that though they loved her, liked her living with them and would pay for her schooling and future, if she continued her misbehaviour they would have to ask her to go back to her "nuclear" family (a family with which she had continued to maintain close contact). The effect was instantaneous, the child became a happy and enormously successful carer of the new baby and bright and responsible around her foster home.[6]

There is considerable evidence for the importance of mother-infancy interaction. We are not arguing against this. We are pointing to the fact that an important part of the research on which the argument was based does not lead in that direction. Attitudes to today's lone mother must be read in conjunction with the creation of the story of the "nursing couple".

Serious deprivation of any kind probably has a deleterious effect, with maternal deprivation no less, and possibly more, than most. The studies of evacuée children offer us a more complex picture of the home, as more than the sum of the nuclear parents. Parents are never simply the 'biological" ones (as Bowlby assumes). They include step-parents, godparents, adoptive parents as well as grandparents (for all of whom we retain the title). These all represent intimate relationships with the child. However, for the latter the family often includes not only persons but the environment and objects that surround them. If one set of ties are disturbed, it becomes more essential to maintain the others and hence to widen the whole notion of parents in a psycho-social sense. Susan Isaacs commented that the boy who said he "missed" his father's hidings was using "miss" in a different sense than the questionnaire had intended. Probably he was—he was emphasising the importance of familiarity over the family. This is something we need to consider as we change family legislation in the context of socioeconomic practices and their ideological counterparts.

REFERENCES

Bowlby, J., *Maternal Care and Mental Health* (Geneva, World Health Organisation, 1951).
Flügel, J. L., *The Psychoanalytic Study of the Family* (London, International Psychoanalytical Press, 1921).
Goody, E., *Parenthood and Social Reproduction; Fostering and Occupational Roles in West Africa* (Cambridge, Cambridge University Press, 1982).
Hohfeld, W. N., *Fundamental Legal Conceptions* (New Haven, Yale University Press, 1923).

[6] See *Mansfield Park* and *Jane Eyre* for a more problematic account of respectively family fostering and family adoption.

Isaacs, S. *et al* (ed.)., *The Cambridge Evacuation Survey* (London, Methuen, 1941).

Middlemore, M. P., *The Nursing Couple* (London, Hamish Hamilton, 1941).

Oakley, A., *Man and Wife: Richard and Kay Titmuss: My Parents' Early Years* (London, Harper Collins, 1996).

Padley, R. and Cole, M., *Evacuation Survey, a Report to the Fabian Society* (London, Routledge, 1940).

Parsons, T. and Bales, R. F., *Family, Socialization and Interaction Process* (Glencoe, The Free Press, Ill, 1955).

Seccombe, W., *Weathering the Storm: Working-Class Families from the Industrial Revolution to the Fertility Decline* (London, Verso, 1993).

Part II

New Issues in Contemporary Parenting

7

Donating Parenthood: Perspectives on Parenthood from Surrogacy and Gamete Donation

RACHEL COOK

"Mrs White, when the children were asked to share a love story, your son said he grew in your sister's tummy and she gave birth to him. He sounds confused. Perhaps you'd better talk to him."
Note from a Sunday School teacher, from McDaniel (1994, p.307)

"So when my son went to school on Monday morning, and the teacher asked how everyone's weekend went, he said 'My Mom had twins'. And she said, 'Oh, what did she name them?' He said, 'I don't know—they weren't hers' "
Comment from a surrogate mother, from Smith (1998)

1. INTRODUCTION

All societies have methods for the acquisition or transfer of parental status from one individual or set of individuals to another. Whilst adoption would be a familiar example, there are other formal and informal strategies, including gamete donation, surrogacy and gynegamy (where an infertile woman "marries" another woman, her male partner acting as genitor, but not father, to ensuing children; for example, Robertson (1991)). Viewed from this perspective, gamete donation and surrogate motherhood are not unusual. However, there is considerable evidence that both surrogacy and gamete donation are seen as unacceptable—or only acceptable as a "reproductive option of last resort" (BMA, 1996). Within Western culture, surrogate mothers,[1] gamete donors and recipients have been stigmatised. They have been represented as abnormal in their behaviour and pathological or psychopathic in their desires (for example,

---

[1] The term *surrogate mother* is used in this chapter because it is recognisable and familiar. Use of the term is not intended to imply that it is accurate or impartial; nor is it intended to reflect a particular approach to the concept of motherhood. The difficulties associated with the terms in use in this area, and the ways in which the terms may be used, have been addressed by Morgan (1990) and Tangri and Kahn (1993) amongst others.

see Shenfield (1994); Schmukler and Aigen (1989); Feversham Committee (1960); Gerstel (1963)). Surrogacy in particular has engendered fierce debate over ethical issues, with its connotations of baby-selling, its alleged parallel with prostitution, and the potential for exploitation of women and commodification of children (for example, Page (1985); Rothman (1989); Arditti (1987); Kornegay (1990); Erin and Harris (1991); Van Niekerk and Van Zyl (1995)). Surrogacy is prohibited in the majority of European countries either by legislation, government regulations, or ethics committees. Israel and the United Kingdom are the two exceptions.[2] A major moral concern in relation to these types of family formation is the fragmentation of parenthood. This fragmentation is more explicit in surrogacy than any other reproductive option: it separates social motherhood from gestation and genetics. This chapter reviews aspects of these fragments of parenthood from the perspectives offered by surrogacy and gamete donation (see Table 7.1).

2. GAMETE DONATION

The use of donated semen as a solution to infertility was first documented over 100 years ago (Small and Turskoy, 1985). In the United Kingdom, donor insemination (DI) has been used in the treatment of infertility since the 1930s (Pfeffer, 1993). It is now widely practised and portrayed in the medical literature as an acceptable solution to the problem of untreatable male infertility. Around one thousand, five hundred live births a year result from treatment using donated sperm.[3]

Donated sperm is chiefly required for heterosexual couples in which the male partner has no sperm (azoospermia), few sperm (oligospermia), sperm abnormalities, potentially mutagenic alterations in his sperm (for example, due to chemotherapy) or ejaculatory dysfunction (Barratt and Cooke, 1993). It is commonly used when a vasectomy reversal has been unsuccessful and more rarely when the male partner is a carrier for a genetic disorder. It may also be used to enable single heterosexual and lesbian women to have children. Donated semen is mainly utilised in procedures where semen is introduced into a woman's vagina (donor insemination: DI) or uterus (inter-uterine insemination: IUI) in the hope that a pregnancy will result. It may also be used in combination with other assisted methods of conception such as *in vitro* fertilisation (IVF) or as part of surrogacy procedures. Most "treatment" using donated semen takes place in licensed centres, but clearly private transactions can and do take place, with a woman or couple finding their own sperm donor. In addition, a situation

---

[2] Although in the United Kingdom the Surrogacy Arrangements Act 1985 prohibits payments to surrogate mothers, other than expenses, it does not prohibit surrogacy (Morgan, 1986); Israel permits only full or gestational surrogacy (Schenker, 1997).

[3] Although this number (a) does not include private arrangements and (b) may be in decline (HFEA 1994; HFEA 1997).

Table 7.1: Genetic, Gestational and Social Elements of Parenthood

	Motherhood	
Social ✓	*Genetic*	
Gestational ✓	✓ IVF with own eggs "Natural" mother*	✗ IVF with donated eggs
✗	Intended mother (full)	Intended mother (partial) IVF with donated embryos
Social ✗	*Genetic*	
Gestational ✓	✓ Surrogate mother (partial) Surrogate mother (natural)*	✗ Surrogate mother (full)
✗	Egg donor	–

	Fatherhood	
	Genetic	
Social ✓	✓ "Natural" father* IVF father Intended father*	✗ DI father "Natural" father
✗	Sperm donor*	–

* Potential sexual parents

where a woman has sex with a man other than her (infertile) partner in order to become pregnant could be defined as "donor insemination" (and parallels partial-natural surrogacy).[4]

In contrast with the long history of semen donation, the donation of oocytes (eggs) only became possible with the development of IVF techniques. The first successful pregnancy using a donated egg was reported in the early 1980s (Lutjen *et al.*, 1984). The extent of treatment services using donated eggs is much smaller than that of donated semen, with around seventy births each year.

---

[4] For example, Danesh-Meyer *et al.* (1993) describe a case in which, reportedly, frustration with the lack of success of DI led a woman to decide upon asking a work colleague to inseminate her "naturally", in addition to the treatment.

Donated eggs are mainly used for heterosexual couples in which the female partner cannot produce eggs of her own (due to ovarian failure or premature menopause), or has failed to respond to ovarian stimulation for IVF. In addition, they may be used when there is high risk of genetic disease (Leeton *et al.*, 1984). The donated eggs are used in IVF or similar procedures, with embryos transferred to the recipient woman.

3. SURROGACY

Surrogacy is not a single route to parenthood (Erin and Harris, 1991). The term covers a number of practices that vary in detail, but essentially involve a woman (the surrogate mother) initiating and carrying a pregnancy with the intention of giving the child[5] at birth to be raised by others (the intended parents or commissioning couple). Although there are numerous possibilities for genetic and social relationships within the practice of surrogacy, there are two fundamental types. In the case of *full surrogacy* (also termed host motherhood and gestational surrogacy), *in vitro* fertilisation and embryo transfer (IVF-ET) allow the surrogate mother to carry a child which is derived from the sperm and egg of the intended parents; the surrogate mother has no genetic relationship with the child. In *partial surrogacy* (also described as straight or genetic surrogacy), the surrogate mother's egg is fertilised by the intended father's sperm. We can further divide partial surrogacy into that achieved by artificial insemination, assumed to be the more common practice, and partial-natural surrogacy, achieved by sexual intercourse between intended father and surrogate mother.[6]

Full surrogacy gives both parents a genetic relationship with the child, whereas in partial surrogacy the intended father and the surrogate mother are the child's genetic parents. In both cases the surrogate mother carries and delivers the child i.e. performs tasks which normally enable us to identify a person as a mother. It is important to note that there are more constraints on participation in full surrogacy. As it requires the use of IVF procedures it must be carried out at a licensed infertility centre and is subject to the Human Fertilisation and Embryology Authority (HFEA) Code of Practice.

Surrogate motherhood is not a new phenomenon, and evidence from a variety of sources indicates a growing increase in the number of surrogacy arrangements in Britain (British Medical Association, 1996). This may in part be due to increasing acceptability of surrogacy amongst the medical profession. The British Medical Association recommendations on surrogacy altered dramati-

---

[5] There seems to be no short and wholly satisfactory term to describe people conceived as a result of gamete donation or surrogacy; as many commentators have pointed out, these are not perpetual children. I have tended to use offspring although it seems to me insufficiently human a term.

[6] See, for example *Re Adoption Application (Payment for Adoption)* [1987] 2 FLR 291: where the intended father and the surrogate mother "had sexual intercourse on a few occasions . . . It was physical congress with the sole purpose of procreating a child".

cally between 1987—when they stated that doctors should not be involved in surrogacy—and 1990—when they envisaged surrogacy as a treatment to be considered only when no other alternatives are available (British Medical Association, 1987; 1990). The precise numbers of surrogacy arrangements cannot be determined however, as surrogacy is currently unmonitored in the United Kingdom. The recent Department of Health Report on Surrogacy recommends that statistics on surrogacy should be collected in order to provide better information on its incidence (Brazier *et al.*, 1998). This recommendation is yet to be implemented. However, both donor insemination and surrogacy can be performed without medical intervention as entirely personal arrangements and they are therefore "not susceptible to regulation" (Zipper and Sevenhuijsen, 1987).

4. POTENTIAL PARENTS: WHO PARTICIPATES?

Neither gamete donation nor surrogacy is a simple method of family formation and those who participate are likely to be highly selected individuals. As well as the influences on decision-making for participants at an individual level, there are other factors affecting the composition of this population. Attitudes of the general public to techniques of family formation will influence who participates. Thus there are likely to be personality differences between those prepared to perform a behaviour when it is perceived as socially beneficial and valuable, and those who are prepared to perform the same behaviour when it is not generally acceptable and is potentially stigmatising. The former appears to occur with semen donation, where sperm donors tend to be outgoing, assertive, extroverted, independent and adventurous (Nicholas and Tyler, 1983; Handelsman *et al.*, 1985; Fidell and Marik, 1989).

Legislation plays a part in the selection of prospective parents in gamete donation and full surrogacy. Legislation concerning assisted conception in the United Kingdom tends to support the view espoused in the Warnock Report (1984) that "as a general rule it is better for children to be born into a two-parent family, with both mother and father". The Human Fertilisation and Embryology Act 1990 states that the HFEA will give:

"guidance for those providing treatment services about the account to be taken of the welfare of children who may be born as a result of treatment services (including a child's need for a father), and of other children who may be affected by such births".

Thus the HFEA Code of Practice says that treatment services cannot be provided unless account is taken of "the need of (a) child for a father" (HFEA, 1993). This becomes rather nonsensical when "father" is subsequently defined in the Act as a man married to the mother or receiving treatment with the mother.[7] It has been suggested that the Government's intention was to restrict

[7] Presumably the wording also permits the conclusion that children do not need fathers.

the provision of treatment to certain types of women or couples (Morgan and Lee, 1991).

Clinics and their ethics committees may also have criteria for the acceptance or rejection of participants, whether explicit or not. There is no public information on suitability criteria which are in use, although within gamete donation, numerous criteria for exclusion of potential recipients have been identified. These include a history of child abuse, having children from a current or previous relationship, severe or life-threatening illness, the age of the mother (and occasionally the father), a poor chance of success, infertility which "is perceived by others to be a consequence of earlier life-style choices" (such as prostitution), being fertile (excepting fertile couples with genetic disorder, or fertile individuals with an infertile partner), sexual orientation or marital status, previous psychiatric history, poor understanding of or commitment to the procedure, or a history of marital conflict or violence (Stewart *et al.*, 1982; Knoppers and LeBris, 1991; Daniels and Taylor, 1993). These criteria are rarely explicitly stated. Determination of who is suitable to be a parent can therefore depend upon subjective assessments of parenting ability of those with different family structures or from different socio-economic backgrounds.

Prospective parents are unlikely to be subject to *formal* screening of a social or psychological nature in the United Kingdom, although this is commonplace in the USA. Those in favour of screening in assisted reproduction argue from the basis that individuals wishing to adopt are subject to a stringent screening process; conversely, those against point out that individuals who conceive naturally are subject to no such process. The issue of psycho-social screening gained prominence in the United Kingdom with the implementation of the Human Fertilisation and Embryology Act 1990 which requires clinics to take account of the "welfare" of children when providing this treatment service (this applies to existing children of participant adults as well as the prospective child). Clinicians might therefore be considered to be evading their responsibility to the potential offspring if some psychological evaluation of prospective parents is not carried out. A major obstacle, however, to the adoption of screening is the absence of validation of criteria for assessment of individuals as suitable parents (Kerr and Rogers (1975); Rosenkvist (1982); Stewart *et al.* (1982); Sparks and Hamilton (1991)). Humphrey *et al.* (1991) argue for a distinction between vetting and screening in this context. They propose that whilst the vetting which is usually applied to prospective adoptive parents would be inappropriate, couples applying for DI should be able to satisfy basic criteria regarding the quality and stability of their relationship and their psychological adjustment to their infertility. They argue that this kind of approach might at least enable unsuitable couples to withdraw.

Couples may choose partial surrogacy for many reasons, but adopting this unregulated route can avoid any kind of selection criteria that may be in operation, other than those of the surrogacy support agency and the individuals involved. We might expect therefore that partial surrogacy participants would be a more diverse population, but this is speculation as there are no data on the prevalence of either option or the characteristics of participants.

Legislation does not specify who is suitable to become a surrogate mother or gamete donor. However, the HFEA Code of Practice directs clinics to consider an individual's suitability before accepting them as a donor. The factors that should be taken particular account of include "the attitude of the donor towards the donation" (HFEA, 1993) but there are no guidelines on what sort of attitudes would be considered appropriate, leaving interpretation open to individual clinics. One study reports that the attitude of the potential donor to the donation leads to the rejection of 10 per cent (or fewer) of men in 35 per cent of United Kingdom semen donation programmes. However, there is no information on what sorts of attitudes lead to rejection. Similarly, although a comparable proportion of prospective donors is reported to be rejected because of personality difficulties, this seems unlikely to be the result of systematic personality assessment (Golombok and Cook, 1994).

Psycho-social screening of the adult participants who do *not* intend to become parents does not appear to have been widely adopted in the United Kingdom although again it is commonplace in the USA. In one survey, 78 per cent of American egg donor programmes required some form of psychological screening (such as interviews, personality assessment or other tests) and most had criteria for the rejection of donors (Mechanick Braverman, 1993). As with physical screening, there is little consistency between programmes or consensus on the purpose of screening (Bustillo *et al.*, 1984; Sauer *et al.*, 1989). Psychological screening might have a number of aims: it may be used to predict compliance, to identify psychological disorder in the donor, to evaluate the donor's motivations, to assess the donor's expectations about donation and how realistic these are, to assess the donor's ability to cope with the procedures, to exclude those who might be harmed by participating (for example, because of current life stressors), and to ascertain that the donor was not coerced into donating either by financial need or pressure from others (Schover *et al.*, 1991; Raoul-Duval *et al.*, 1992). In essence therefore, psychological screening is performed to safeguard the donor's well-being, because of the risks to which he or she is exposed.[8]

Both assisted reproduction using donated gametes and surrogacy permit people who might not otherwise have become parents to do so. In theory they allow a greater number of potential candidates for the role of parent or greater flexibility in the concept of "parent". Yet there are practical constraints and cultural prescriptions about the appropriate type and number of parents. For example, the BMA (1996) states that it is "preferable for a surrogacy arrangement to involve two parents who together intend to raise the child" if only for

---

[8] It is interesting to note that generally female donors appear to be subject to greater psychological assessment than male donors. This may reflect concerns about the exploitation of egg donors or the increased risks to which they are exposed; or it may just be a reflection of different policies between clinics and countries.

the practical reasons that parental orders can only be applied for if the applicants are married and adoption "favours those in stable heterosexual relationships". In reality, practice probably reflects the parental prescriptions and therefore endorses, rather than challenges, existing notions of the family. Having said this, we should note two things. First, we know very little about the practice of surrogacy or about private arrangements using donated gametes, so it is possible that there are situations in which there is more flexibility over parental roles, of which we are not aware. Both partial surrogacy and DIY-DI could be techniques enabling "unfit" women to have children.[9] Secondly, we do not know anything about the level of consistency between overt behaviour and internal emotion and cognition. It is therefore possible that surrogate mothers accept the transfer of parental responsibility to others whilst simultaneously retaining a concept of themselves as the "real" mothers.

5. THE GENETIC RELATIONSHIP AND IMBALANCE
IN GENETIC RELATEDNESS

One of the features of sexual reproduction is that each parent makes a genetic contribution to the child. Adoption retains this balance as neither parent makes a genetic contribution. Couples may choose adoption rather than techniques involving donated gametes because they wish to maintain this balance. Full surrogacy enables both intended parents to have a genetic relationship with their child; partial surrogacy and gamete donation, however, do not. The importance of a genetic connection with their children for many parents is not in doubt, if we consider preferences indicated by couples in all kinds of circumstances— those who are fertile, infertile or carriers of recessive disorder (Snowdon and Green, 1994; Snowdon and Green, 1997).

Concern has been expressed in relation to DI in particular that the imbalance in the genetic relatedness of parent to child which arises when this method of conception is used might have consequences for the relationship between the parents, and between the parents and their child (See, for example, Warnock Report (1984); Humphrey and Humphrey (1988)). The social father might, for example, feel resentful of his tentative relationship with his child, or feel that the child is not "really" his, and this might be reflected in his behaviour towards his partner and child. That this imbalance may also be psychologically significant in surrogacy is suggested by the fact that, in the USA, few couples take up the usual contractual option of a paternity test once the child is born. Ragoné (1994) proposes that retaining some doubt about the child's paternity may help to redress the genetic imbalance.

---

[9] For example, Zipper and Sevenhuijsen (1987) suggest that surrogacy can be used, like self-insemination, as a self-help technique to enable women, who would otherwise be deemed unsuitable, to have children.

Studies of adopted children and children conceived using DI or IVF suggest that this concern may be unjustified.[10] A genetic relationship is not essential for good social parenting or the satisfactory social and emotional development of children, and a parental imbalance in genetic relatedness appears to have no major effects, detrimental or otherwise (Golombok *et al.*, 1995). Equally, a genetic relationship between parent and child provides no guarantee of ability to rear children (Schuker, 1987). The desire for genetic relatedness may stem from reasons for becoming a parent—such as the wish to transmit valued physical or personality characteristics of the self to future generations—or more generally serve as evidence for the individual's claim to be the parent in circumstances where this is in doubt. However, this desire in potential parents will not necessarily correspond with subsequent parental behaviour; we cannot assume that because a potential parent would prefer a genetically related child, then the subsequent experience of being a parent of an unrelated child will be deficient in some way. The experience of having a child who is not genetically related may directly or indirectly affect the parent's preference. Thus the parent may come to acknowledge that they were mistaken about the need for genetic relatedness. Less directly, they might re-evaluate their perception of the importance of genetic connections in the light of their behaviour, i.e. they perceive that they have had a child who is not genetically related to them, therefore they conclude that, after all, they do not attach great importance to genetic connections (as might be proposed by self-perception theory: see Bem (1972)).

Current understanding of the psychological ramifications of surrogacy depends upon inference from studies of assisted conception and on this basis we might tentatively conclude that negative effects are unlikely to arise from the genetic imbalance. However, there are several reasons why we should be cautious in doing so.

First, there are important differences between surrogacy and treatment using donated gametes. With the latter the donor/genetic parent is usually anonymous.[11] With surrogacy, the person contributing the genetic material (or in the case of full surrogacy, lending her gestational capabilities) is usually known and present, rather than anonymous and absent. This might have effects which are psychologically beneficial. For example, the surrogate mother might provide information about the child's origins helpful to the establishment of identity. However, there might be other more detrimental effects. It might be confusing for the child and a painful intrusion upon the relationship of the intended parents.

Secondly, caution should be exercised because in studies of families using assisted conception, the response rate amongst those with children conceived using donated gametes tends to be lower than that for other types of families.

---

[10] The relative newness of treatment using donated eggs means that there is little evidence from studies of children conceived in this way.

[11] Note that this is the case if DI is carried out in a clinic but not where personal arrangements are made.

We might easily argue therefore that those families which encounter difficulties as a result of the method of conception of their offspring have simply not been studied.

Thirdly, there may be no effect of an imbalance in genetic relatedness in donor insemination because social fathers do not accept this imbalance: they may believe that they *are* the genetic father (see, for example, Snowden *et al.* (1983)). A child conceived after a woman has DI treatment does not necessarily result from this treatment. A woman may have unprotected sexual intercourse around the time she undergoes DI and when she subsequently conceives, the paternity of the child is uncertain.[12] In one study, 41 per cent of couples reported having sexual intercourse after donor insemination and suggested that the social father could be the genetic father (Klock and Maier, 1991). There is some evidence to suggest that a very small proportion—perhaps 1 to 2 per cent—of children conceived during DI treatment may in fact be the result of sexual intercourse. Amuzu *et al.* (1990) note that 8.4 per cent of their sample of couples who had conceived after DI had a subsequent natural conception (see also Robinson *et al.*, 1991). Of course, this does not mean that the social father is necessarily also the genetic father: two of these arose when the male partner had no live sperm. However, they also report that 6.6 per cent of their study group thought that the social father was the genetic father, and in one family a minor "physical variation" in both child, social father and some of his other direct relatives appeared to confirm this. Retention of uncertainty about the child's genitor may occur, as suggested by Ragoné (1994), as an attempt to partially redress the genetic imbalance. Psychological uncertainty is not a comfortable state and, at least in the case of DI, it is possible that it is retained as a justification for non-disclosure of the child's origins, on the basis that if the social father *might be* the genetic father, then it would be inappropriate to inform the child that he is not (Klock and Maier, 1991; Cook *et al.*, 1995). The converse of this is not generally expressed by DI parents: that if the social father *might not be* the genetic father, then it would be inappropriate to permit the child to assume that he is. Parents might be using a coping strategy of denial to deal with their impossible situation (which adoptive parents also have to confront) of "Accept this child as your own; now tell the child they are not your own" (Walby and Symons, 1990).

With full surrogacy, the use of IVF creates considerable certainty about the genetic relationships between parents and child. This certainty is absent in partial surrogacy where the genetic father may be either the intended father, the surrogate mother's partner, or someone else.

---

[12] It used to be fairly common practice for clinicians to mix the donor's semen with the husband's; the HFEA Code of Practice advises clinicians that they should not treat a woman with gametes from more than one man at the same time. However, this would not prevent clinicians from advising a patient to have sexual intercourse around the time of insemination.

6. THE SEXUAL RELATIONSHIP AND "TEST TUBE ADULTERY"

The use of assisted conception techniques tends to eliminate the sexual aspect of becoming a parent (Tangri and Kahn, 1993). However, we cannot assume that because sexual intercourse does not lead directly to the child's conception, that sex is not relevant to that conception. Generally speaking, it has been suggested that "the physician treating an infertile couple is unavoidably imbued with the power to impregnate" (McDaniel *et al.*, 1990). In addition, most techniques entail a reduction of involvement of the usual sexual partner, for example, male contribution in donor insemination. Fears have been expressed that this reduction in physical involvement might be paralleled by a reduction in emotional involvement in the process (Golombok *et al.*, 1990) and several authors comment on the practice of encouraging participation of the male partner by getting him to do the insemination (Mazzola and Stangel, 1984; Klock and Maier, 1991). There is as yet no research demonstrating a foundation for this concern.

This reduction in involvement by one sexual partner implies the replacement of their contribution or involvement by someone else. This intrusion of an "outsider" into the couple's relationship appears to carry implications of unfaithfulness or adultery.[13] Research into the motivations and perceptions of semen donors suggests that the concept of insemination may be inextricably linked with sexual behaviour. Novaes (1989) proposes that the "image of semen donation may be sexual", the "donation" entailing the insemination of a woman with sperm obtained by masturbation from a stranger. Similarly, the motives of semen donors may be viewed with suspicion and many men who are willing to donate blood are ambivalent about donating semen, perceiving it as illegitimate sexual behaviour, expecting their partner's disapproval (Novaes, 1989; Haimes, 1993). Hirsch's (1993) interviews with married couples in England similarly found perceptions of sperm donation as unfaithfulness in a married man, and artificial insemination as "test tube adultery"; he suggests that semen cannot be isolated from social and or sexual relationships.

In DI, the association between sperm donor and female recipient can be rendered harmless by the anonymity and secrecy which currently operate. However the association between the intended father and the surrogate mother can be regarded as ambiguous (Blyth, 1994). In partial-natural surrogacy, conception is achieved by sexual intercourse between the intended father and surrogate mother. Intended parents may resort to this method when insemination is unsuccessful, but little is known about the extent of this type of surrogacy. It is assumed that partial surrogacy does not normally involve sexual intercourse, but it has nevertheless been portrayed as adulterous.

Additionally, it has been suggested that the surrogate mother is the *real* mother (Morgan, 1990); if she is a surrogate, then she is a surrogate *wife* for the

---

[13] Note this does not appear to occur in relation to egg donation, where the donation is from one woman (or her ovaries) to another.

intended father. This ambiguity may make relationships between the three adults (four, if we include the surrogate mother's partner) difficult. The birth of the child establishes a spouse-like relationship between the surrogate mother and the intended father which may lead the intended mother to feel excluded (Ragoné, 1994). These difficulties might be exacerbated when the surrogate mother is a close friend or family member: Harrison (1990) describes cases where relationships have been "ruined". On the other hand, Leeton *et al.* (1988) suggest that "altruistic" surrogacy with a close friend or relative "possibly represents the most acceptable form of surrogate pregnancy, with minimal potential complications". Probably the best that can be said about this statement is that it is optimistic and naïve, taking little account, for example, of the threat to existing relationships which family surrogacy arrangements might pose.

The whole concept of "altruistic" surrogacy is a difficult one. For example, the Brazier Report (1998) recommends the implementation of strategies to prevent surrogacy arrangements from being entered into for financial benefit. This is not consistent with the current United Kingdom approach to sperm donation, where it is fairly clear that men are induced to become donors for money (see Cook and Golombok, 1995). Whilst there are obvious ethical issues here, it also begs the question: if not for money, then why? The literature both on donors' and surrogates' motivations tends to represent motivations dichotomously: money versus altruism. Yet stating that donors are altruistic (i.e. are not paid) does not provide any explanation of their behaviour. Nor is there any evidence that would help us discern the "best" motivations for donation, for example, in terms of psychological outcome for donors. Some of the inherent difficulties are acknowledged in the legislation of many European countries which do not permit donation by family members or friends because of the potential complications and ambiguity over subsequent relationships (Schenker, 1997).

There are also inconsistencies in the approach to egg and sperm donation which arise not just from the different procedures, but may be derived from different public perceptions of appropriate gender role behaviour. For example, clinical guidelines encourage the use of anonymous semen donors, and state that practitioners have declined to carry out inseminations with known or related sperm donors. In contrast, the use of known oocyte donors is accepted, because of "pragmatic considerations" (American Fertility Society, 1993). Demand always exceeds the supply of eggs, as the majority of potential egg donors withdraw at an early stage (Horne *et al.*, 1993). Thus egg donors may be recruited from friends or relatives of the recipient; known donors may donate either to move the recipient up the waiting list, or directly to their friend or relative (Raoul-Duval *et al.*, 1992). Whilst the shortage of donated eggs has led to the acceptance of known oocyte donors, a similar solution has not been proposed to ease the shortage of sperm donors. Such differences are not only reflected in practice guidelines for donation, but also in attitudes of practitioners and the general public: egg donation between sisters is seen as acceptable whilst sperm donation between brothers is regarded as inappropriate (Lessor *et al*, 1990).

7. THE GESTATIONAL RELATIONSHIP AND UTERINE INFLUENCE

There is individual variation in the perception of the importance of genetics and genetic relationships. It is not unreasonable to assume similar variation in perception of the importance of gestation for the development of relationships between parents, particularly the gestating parent and child. Given a theoretical "choice" between the two, some people prefer genetics and some gestation (Thornton *et al.*, 1994). For most people, however, it is unlikely to be a matter of choice. This type of research tells us that individuals differ in their preferences, but it is impossible to judge the importance of these preferences in terms of real-life decision-making or in terms of the consequences for parent-child relationships.

The period of gestation is generally seen by psychologists as important for the development of bonding between mother and child (Raphael-Leff, 1993). Pre-natal feelings of attachment have been found to be strongly associated with feelings about the baby after delivery (Reading *et al.*, 1984, Reading *et al.*, 1989). Thus it is assumed that a surrogate mother who develops strong attachment during pregnancy is likely to find it particularly difficult to relinquish the child. In a controlled study, Fischer and Gillman (1991) found that surrogate mothers indeed showed less attachment to the foetus and different experiences of pregnancy when compared with non-surrogate mothers. On the other hand, women's feelings of attachment to the baby they are carrying generally increase over pregnancy (Reading, 1983). Reame (1989) found that six out of the eight surrogate mothers studied had come to love the baby by the ninth month of gestation.

In some American states, trusting that emotions can be regulated by the law, enforceable surrogacy contracts often include provision that the surrogate mother should not form any emotional attachment to the child (Harrison, 1990). An absence of emotional attachment is not likely to be in the interests of the child, however, if it prevents the surrogate mother from adopting healthy behaviours, or avoiding risky ones. It has been suggested that the successful surrogate may need to dissociate from her body or from reality (Chesler, 1990). Similarly, Harrison suggests that she requires the ability to perceive the baby as belonging to someone else, and "for the women who are unsuccessful surrogates, *it is the fantasy that the baby is not theirs* that breaks down". This is a fantasy which Mary Beth Whitehead in the famous "Baby M" case was unable to sustain: "It wasn't until the day I delivered her that I finally understood that I wasn't giving Betsy Stern her baby. I was giving her *my* baby" (cited in Rowland, 1992, p.187).

It is not clear whether the ability to perceive a baby as someone else's requires a special set of circumstances or a special kind of "mother". It has been commented that "the most difficult aspect of treatment by IVF surrogacy is in fact the extreme care with which the host needs to be selected by the genetic couple"

(Brinsden and Rainsbury, 1992). In a sense, this is unarguable. However, selection with care cannot take place unless there are established criteria for selection which can tell us what kind of women under what kind of circumstances can act as surrogate mothers. At present, no such criteria exist.

If gestation is normally regarded as significant for the development of attachment to the forthcoming baby then we need to consider not only the consequences of gestation for the surrogate mother but also the consequences of the absence of gestation for the intended mother. In the United Kingdom, surrogacy contracts are unenforceable at law. The experience of intended parents is therefore characterised by lack of control and uncertainty, both about the process of the arrangement, and the outcome. Potentially, this may lead to difficulties or delay in the establishment of a relationship with the baby, lower self-esteem and self-efficacy in relation to feelings about being a parent, and a more stressful experience of parenting. IVF mothers initially tend to rate their children as more difficult, and have lower self-esteem and self-efficacy as mothers (Gibson *et al.*, 1996). The existence or extent of these difficulties may depend upon the coping strategies used by the intended parents, for example, to foster the belief that the baby is "really" theirs. It is clear however that a gestational relationship is not a necessary condition for motherhood: adoptive mothers lack this initial relationship with their children without negative consequences. Intended mothers and fathers have in fact more opportunity for the development of a relationship with their baby during gestation (albeit rather one-sided) than do adoptive parents. If we recognise adoptive mothers as mothers, there is no reason why we should not regard intended mothers as "real" mothers also.

A further important issue in the gestational element of parenthood is that of uterine influence. The distinction between full and partial surrogacy is sometimes drawn on the basis that the gestational surrogate mother is just a vessel in which another woman's baby is being carried, or an incubator (see, for example, Rowland, 1992). There is now considerable evidence that the health status and behaviour of the gestating mother have important influences on the wellbeing of the foetus she carries, both in the short and longer-term (Godfrey *et al.*, 1994). In this sense, the surrogate mother is likely to have a lasting impact on the child she carries.

8. THE SOCIAL PARENT AND THE CONCEPT OF PROCREATIVE INTENT

Individuals who have a biogenetic or social relationship with a child may have a legitimate claim to be a parent of that child. In addition, an individual can become a candidate for parenthood by virtue of their relationship with a person who has a more legitimate claim to be a parent. This is most commonly seen in situations where men are identified as fathers as a result of their relationship with the mother of a child. Recipients of donated gametes and intended parents must minimise the biogenetic aspects of parenthood, to strengthen the claim of the prospective parent who lacks this relationship (Ragoné, 1994). In the case of surrogacy however, this is somewhat contradictory. Surrogacy as a method of family formation does in fact *emphasise* the genetic relationship, but between *father* and child. Significance however is placed on social parenthood as a combination of motivation, intention, involvement and nurturance.

The intended mother therefore can have a unique role as the instigator of the pregnancy. Conception is "ordered" or "commissioned" by the intended parents, who are motivated (it is assumed) by usual parental motivations such as the need for adult status and identity, the opportunity for the development of affectionate and intimate relationships, and the need for expansion of the "self" (Hoffman *et al.*, 1978; Bell *et al.*, 1985; Woollett, 1991). Achieving parenthood removes the stigma of infertility (Miall, 1986); it is perhaps ironic that the method itself is stigmatised. Alongside this, the surrogate mother's intention is clear although her motivations may not be. Whilst there is increasing research interest in surrogacy, few studies have made more than a superficial examination of surrogate mothers' motivations. A major concern is that surrogate mothers may be motivated by financial gain (see, for example, Brazier Report (1998)); it is this that raises the spectres of baby-selling and prostitution. What information there is suggests that whilst financial gain can be a motive, women usually report that there are a number of factors behind the decision, including financial need, a high value placed on children and parenthood, great sympathy with childless people, easy and enjoyable experience of pregnancy and childbirth, desire to re-experience these without the responsibility of rearing the child, desire for enhanced self-esteem or self-worth, need to overcome health problems, and attempts to resolve feelings associated with previous reproductive losses (Franks (1981); Parker (1983); Reame and Parker (1983); Einwohner (1989); MacPhee and Forest (1990); Fischer and Gillman (1991); Blyth (1994)). We do not know the extent to which stated motivations are a reflection of social influences and perceptions of what the "right" motivations should be. Nor do we know the extent to which they result from experiences—that is, how stated motivations are influenced by the experience of surrogacy. Finally, we cannot judge the extent to which becoming a surrogate mother fulfils these expectations in the longer term.

Initially it is the intention of all adults in a surrogacy arrangement that the intended parents become the social parents. Whilst it is this intention which engenders surrogacy, it is also what appears to be problematic about it. In contrast with adoption, where the pregnancy appears unintentional, the surrogate mother may be represented as becoming pregnant with the intention of abandoning "her" child (see, for example, Shenfield (1994)) or surrogacy represented as encouraging the "evil of maternal abandonment" (Schmukler and Aigen, 1989). This has consequences for the surrogate mother: her behaviour as represented in this way, is not consonant with being a good mother. This generalises to concerns about her own children. For example, it is speculated that her children will feel abandonment anxiety and may be susceptible to depressive reactions of the type shown when children lose siblings under other circumstances (Steadman and McCloskey, 1987).

The emphasis on social parenthood also necessitates involvement on the part of the intended parents. Material from surrogacy support agencies focuses on the necessity of intended parents' involvement, both with the surrogate mother and with the pregnancy (COTS, unpublished). It is suggested that this involvement can simultaneously provide much-needed social support for the surrogate mother as well as a continued reminder of the identity of the "real" parents (Fischer and Gillman, 1991; Blyth, 1994). Thus the involvement of the intended parents is increased whilst the detachment of the surrogate mother is encouraged. The latter parallels the concept of detachment of the sperm donor, where donors may be recruited specifically because they demonstrate detachment and show no interest in the outcome of their donation (Rowland, 1983) and formal and informal rules (legislation, clinic policies) discourage involvement.

The final element shoring up the claim to parenthood of the intended parents is nurturance. Intended parents and surrogate mothers emphasise this aspect of parenthood above genetic and gestational elements (Ragoné, 1994). Comparison with adoption again informs us that the other elements may be valued, but are indeed unnecessary. It is clear that from a psychological perspective neither the genetic, sexual or gestational elements are necessary for successful parenting. However, to state the obvious, this does not imply that the absence of these elements in the presence of intention to procreate and parent will necessarily lead to successful parenting.

REFERENCES

Achilles, R., "Protection from what? The secret life of donor insemination" (1993) 12 *Politics and the Life Sciences* 171–179.

American Fertility Society, "Guidelines for gamete donation" (1993) 59 *Fertility & Sterility* Supplement 1, 1S–9S.

Amuzu, B., Laxova, R. and Shapiro, S., "Pregnancy outcome, health of children, and family adjustment after donor insemination" (1990) 75 *Obstetrics & Gynaecology* 899–905.

Arditti, R., "The Surrogacy business" (1987) *Social Policy* (Fall), 42–46.

Barratt, C. L. R. and Cooke, I. D., *Donor Insemination* (Cambridge, Cambridge University Press, 1993).

Bell, S. J., Bancroft, J. and Philip, A., "Motivation for parenthood: a factor analytic study of attitudes towards having children" (1985) 16 *Journal of Comparative Family Studies* 111–119.

Bem, D. J., "Self-perception theory" in L. Berkowitz (ed.), *Advances in Experimental Social Psychology, Volume 6* (New York, Academic Press, 1972).

Blyth, E., " 'I wanted to be interesting. I wanted to be able to say "I've done something interesting with my life" ': interviews with surrogate mothers in Britain" (1994) 12 *Journal of Reproductive and Infant Psychology* 189–198.

Brazier, M., Campbell, A. and Golombok, S., *Surrogacy. Review for Health Ministers of Current Arrangements for Payments and Regulations. Report of the Review Team* (Cm 4068, London, HMSO, 1998).

Brinsden, P. R., "IVF Surrogacy" in P. R. Brinsden and P. A. Rainsbury (eds.), *A Textbook of In Vitro Fertilisation and Assisted Conception* (London, Parthenon Publishing, 1992).

British Medical Association, *Surrogate Motherhood. Report of the Board of Science and Education* (London, BMA, 1987).

British Medical Association, *Surrogacy: Ethical Considerations. Report of the Working Party on Human Infertility Services* (London, BMA, 1990).

British Medical Association, *Changing Conceptions of Motherhood. The Practice of Surrogacy in Britain* (London, BMA, 1996).

Bustillo, M. I., Buster, J. E., Cohen, S. W. *et al.*, "Nonsurgical ovum transfer as a treatment in infertile women" (1984) 251 *Journal of the American Medical Association* 1171–1173.

Chesler, P., *Sacred Bond* (London, Virago Press, 1990).

Cook R. and Golombok, S., "A survey of semen donation. Phase II—the view of the donors" (1995) 10 *Human Reproduction* 951–959.

Cook, R., Golombok, S., Bish, A. *et al.*, "Disclosure of donor insemination: parental attitudes" (1995) 65 *American Journal of Orthopsychiatry* 549–559.

COTS (Childlessness Overcome Through Surrogacy) *Information Booklet*, unpublished.

Danesh-Meyer, H. V., Gillett, W. R. and Daniels, K. R., "Withdrawal from a donor insemination programme" (1993) 33 *Australian & New Zealand Journal of Obstetrics & Gynaecology* 187–190.

Daniels, K. R. and Taylor, K., "Secrecy and openness in donor insemination" (1993) 12 *Politics and the Life Sciences* 155–170.

Einwohner, J., "Who becomes a surrogate: Personality characteristics", in J. Offerman-Zuckerberg (ed.), *Gender in Transition: A New Frontier* (New York, Plenum Publishing Corporation, 1989).

Erin, C. A. and Harris, J., "Surrogacy" in (1991) 5 *Bailliere's Clinical Obstetrics & Gynaecology* 611–635.

Feversham Committee, *Report of the Departmental Committee on Human Artificial Insemination* (London, HMSO, 1960).

Fidell, L. S. and Marik, J., "Paternity by proxy: artificial insemination with donor sperm" in J. Offerman-Zuckerberg (ed.), *Gender in Transition. A New Frontier* (New York, Plenum Publishing Corporation, 1989).

Fischer, S. and Gillman, I., "Surrogate motherhood: attachment, attitudes and social support" (1991) 54 *Psychiatry* 13–20.

Franks, D., "Psychiatric evaluation of women in a surrogate mother program" (1981) 138 *American Journal of Psychiatry* 1378–1379.

Gerstel, G., "A psychoanalytic view of AID" (1963) 17 *American Journal of Psychotherapy* 64–77.

Gibson, F. L., Ungerer, J. A., Saunders, D. M., *et al.*, "Psychosocial adjustment, child behaviour and quality of attachment relationship, at 1 year post partum for mothers conceiving through IVF", paper presented at the American Society for Reproductive Medicine Conference, November, Boston, Mass., USA, November, 1996.

Godfrey, K. M., Forrester, T., Barker, D. J. *et al.*, "Maternal nutritional status in pregnancy and blood pressure in childhood" (1994) 101 *British Journal of Obstetrics & Gynaecology* 398–403.

138   *Rachel Cook*

Golombok, S., Bhanji, F., Rutherford, T. *et al.*, "Psychological development of children conceived by in vitro fertilisation: A pilot study" (1990) 8 *Journal of Reproductive and Infant Psychology* 37–43.

Golombok, S. and Cook, R., "A survey of semen donation. Phase I—the view of UK licensed centres" (1994) 9 *Human Reproduction* 882–888.

Golombok, S., Cook, R., Bish, A. *et al.*, "Families created by the new reproductive technologies: quality of parenting and social and emotional development of the children" (1995) 64 *Child Development* 285–298.

Haimes, E., "Secrecy and openness in donor insemination: a sociological comment on Daniels & Taylor" (1993) 12 *Politics and the Life Sciences* 178–179.

Handelsman, D. J., Dunn, S. M., Conway, A. J. *et al.*, "Psychological and attitudinal profiles in donors for artificial insemination" (1985) 43 *Fertility & Sterility* 95–101.

Harrison, M., "Psychological ramifications of "surrogate" motherhood" in N. L. Stotland (ed.), *Psychiatric Aspects of Reproductive Technology* (Washington, American Psychiatric Press, 1990).

Hirsch, E., "Negotiated limits: Interviews in south-east England" in J. Edwards, S. Franklin, E. Hirsch, *et al.* (eds.), *Technologies of Procreation. Kinship in the Age of Assisted Conception* (Manchester, Manchester University Press, 1993).

Hoffman, L. W., Thornton, A. and Marris, J. D., "The value of children to parents in the United States" (1978) 1 *Journal of Population* 91–131.

Horne, G., Hughes, S. M., Matson, P. L. *et al.*, "The recruitment of oocyte donors" (1993) 100 *British Journal of Obstetrics & Gynaecology* 877–878.

Human Fertilisation and Embryology Authority, Code of Practice (London, HFEA, 1993).

Human Fertilisation and Embryology Authority, *Annual Report* (London, HFEA,1994).

Human Fertilisation and Embryology Authority, *Annual Report* (London, HFEA, 1997).

Humphrey, M. and Humphrey, H., "Parenthood by donor insemination" in *Families with a Difference: Varieties of Surrogate Parenthood* (London, Routledge, 1988).

Humphrey, M., Humphrey, H. and Ainsworth-Smith, I., "Screening couples for parenthood by donor insemination" (1991) 32 *Social Science and Medicine* 273–278.

Kerr, M. G. and Rogers, C., "Donor insemination" (1975) 1 *Journal of Medical Ethics* 30–33.

Klock, S. C. and Maier, D., "Psychological factors related to donor insemination" (1991) 56 *Fertility & Sterility* 489–495.

Knoppers, B. M. and LeBris, S., "Recent advances in medically assisted conception: legal, ethical and social issues" (1991) 17 *American Journal of Law and Medicine* 329–361.

Kornegay, R. J., "Is commercial surrogacy baby-selling?" (1990) 7 *Journal of Applied Philosophy* 45–50.

Leeton, J., King, C. and Harman, J., "Sister-sister in vitro fertilization surrogate pregnancy with donor sperm: the case for surrogate gestational pregnancy" (1988) 5 *Journal of In Vitro Fertilization and Embryo Transfer* 245–248.

Leeton, J., Trounson, A. and Wood, C., "Use of donor oocytes and embryos in the management of human infertility" (1984) 24 *Australian and New Zealand Journal of Obstetrics & Gynaecology* 265–270.

Lessor, R., Reitz, K., Balmaceda, J. *et al.*, "A survey of public attitudes toward oocyte donation between sisters" (1990) 5 *Human Reproduction* 889–892.

Lutjen, P., Trounson, A., Leeton, J. *et al.*, "The establishment and maintenance of pregnancy using *in vitro* fertilisation and embryo donation in a patient with ovarian failure" (1984) 207 *Nature* 174–176.

MacPhee, D. and Forest, K., "Surrogacy: programme comparisons and policy implications" (1990) 4 *International Journal of Law and the Family* 308–317.

Mazzola, P. and Stangel, J., "Artificial insemination performed by husband" (1984) 41 *Fertility & Sterility* 654.

McDaniel, S. H., "Within-family reproductive technologies as a solution to childlessness due to infertility: psychological issues and interventions" (1994) 1 *Journal of Clinical Psychology in Medical Settings* 301–307.

McDaniel, S. H., Hepworth, J. and Doherty, W. J., *Medical Family Therapy. A Biopsychosocial Approach to Families with Health Problems* (New York, Basic Books, 1990).

Mechanick Braverman, A. M., "Survey results on the current practice of ovum donation" (1993) 59 *Fertility & Sterility* 1216–1220.

Miall, C. E., "Perception of informal sanctioning and the stigma of involuntary childlessness" (1986) 6 *Deviant Behaviour* 383–403.

Morgan, D., "Who to be or not to be: the surrogacy story" (1986) 49 *The Modern Law Review* 358–368.

Morgan, D., "Surrogacy: An Introductory Essay" in R. G. Lee and D. Morgan (eds.), *Birthrights. Law and Ethics at the Beginning of Life* (London, Routledge, 1990).

Morgan, D. and Lee, R. G., *Blackstone's Guide to the Human Fertilisation and Embryology Act 1990. Abortion, Embryo Research, the New Law* (London, Blackstone Press, 1991).

Nicholas, M. K. and Tyler, J. P. P., "Characteristics, attitudes and personalities of AI donors" (1983) 2 *Clinical Reproduction and Fertility* 47–54.

Novaes, S. B., "Giving, receiving, repaying: Gamete donors and donor policies in reproductive medicine" (1989) 5 *International Journal of Technological Assessment in Health Care* 352–355.

Page, E., "Donation, surrogacy and adoption" (1985) 2 *Journal of Applied Philosophy* 161–172.

Parker, P. J., "Motivations of surrogate mothers: initial findings" (1983) 140 *American Journal of Psychiatry* 117–118.

Pfeffer, N., *The Stork & The Syringe. A Political History of Reproductive Medicine* (Cambridge, Polity Press, 1993).

Ragoné, H., *Surrogate Motherhood. Conception in the Heart* (Oxford, Westview Press, 1994).

Raoul-Duval, A., Letur-Konirsch, H. and Frydman, R., "Anonymous oocyte donation: a psychological study of recipients, donors and children" (1992) 7 *Human Reproduction* 51–54.

Raphael-Leff, J., *Psychological Processes in Childbearing* (London, Chapman Hall, 1993).

Reading, A., *Psychological Aspects of Pregnancy* (New York, Longman, 1983).

Reading, A. E., Chang, L. C. and Kerin, J. F., "Attitudes and anxiety levels in women conceiving through in vitro fertilization and gamete intra-fallopian transfer" (1989) 52 *Fertility & Sterility* 95–99.

Reading, A. E., Cox, D. N., Sledmere, C. M. *et al.*, "Psychological changes over the course of pregnancy: a study of attitudes towards the fetus/neonate" (1984) 3 *Health Psychology* 211–221.

Reame, N. E., "Maternal adaptation and postpartum responses to a surrogate pregnancy", abstracts of the 9th International Congress of Psychosomatic Obstetrics &

Gynaecology (1989) 10 *Journal of Psychosomatic Obstetrics & Gynaecology* Supplement 1.

Reame, N. and Parker, P., "Surrogate pregnancy: clinical features of 44 cases" (1983) 162 *American Journal of Obstetrics & Gynaecology* 1220–1225.

Robertson, A. F., *Beyond the Family. The Social Organization of Human Reproduction* (Cambridge, Polity Press, 1991).

Robinson, J. N., Forman, R. G., Clark, A. M. *et al.*, "Attitudes of donors and recipients to gamete donation" (1991) 6 *Human Reproduction* 307–309.

Rosenkvist, H., "Donor insemination" (1981) 28 *Danish Medical Bulletin* 133–148.

Rothman, B. K., "On surrogacy: constructing social policy" in J. Offerman-Zuckerberg (ed.), *Gender in Transition. A New Frontier* (New York, Plenum Publishing Corporation, 1989).

Rowland, R., "Attitudes and opinions of donors on an artificial insemination by donor (AID) programme" (1983) 2 *Clinical Reproduction and Fertility* 249–259.

Rowland, R., *Living Laboratories. Women and Reproductive Technology* (London, Lime Tree, 1992).

Sauer, M. V., Francis-Hernandez, M., Paulson, R. J. *et al.*, "Establishment of a non-anonymous donor oocyte program" (1989) 52 *Fertility & Sterility* 433–436.

Schenker, J. G., "Assisted reproduction practice in Europe: legal and ethical aspects" (1997) 3 *Human Reproduction Update* 173–184.

Schmukler, I. and Aigen, B. P., "The terror of surrogate motherhood" in J. Offerman-Zuckerberg (ed.), *Gender in Transition. A New Frontier* (New York, Plenum Publishing Corporation, 1989).

Schover, L., Collins, R. L., Quigley, M. M. *et al.*, "Psychological follow-up of women evaluated as oocyte donors" (1991) 6 *Human Reproduction* 1487–1491.

Schuker, E., "Psychological effects of the new reproductive technologies" (1987) 13 *Women & Health* 141–147.

Shenfield, F., "Filiation in assisted reproduction: potential conflicts and legal implications" (1994) 9 *Human Reproduction* 1348–1354.

Small, E. C. and Turskoy, R. N., "A view of artificial insemination" (1985) 12 *Advances in Psychosomatic Medicine* 105–123.

Smith, S., *The Fertility Race, Part 4: Surrogate Motherhood* (1998), http://news.mpr.org/features/199711/20smiths_fertility/part4/sidebar1.shtml

Snowden, R., Mitchell, G. D. and Snowden, E. M., *Artificial Reproduction: A Social Investigation* (London, George Allen & Unwin, 1983).

Snowdon, C. and Green, J. M., *New Reproductive Technologies: Attitudes and Experiences of Carriers of Recessive Disorders* (Cambridge, Centre for Family Research, University of Cambridge, 1994).

Snowdon, C. and Green, J. M., "Preimplantation diagnosis and other reproductive options: attitudes of male and female carriers of recessive disorders" (1997) 10 *Human Reproduction* 101–110.

Sparks, C. H. and Hamilton, J. A., "Psychological issues related to alternative insemination" (1991) 22 *Professional Psychology: Research and Practice* 308–314.

Steadman, J. H. and McCloskey, G. T., "The prospect of surrogate mothering: clinical concerns" (1987) 32 *Canadian Journal of Psychiatry* 545–550.

Stewart, C. R., Daniels, K. R. and Boulnois, J. D. H., "The development of a psychosocial approach to artificial insemination of donor sperm" (1982) 95 *New Zealand Medical Journal* 853–856.

Tangri, S. S. and Kahn, J. R., "Ethical issues in the new reproductive technologies: perspectives from feminism and the psychology profession" (1993) 24 *Professional Psychology: Research and Practice* 271–280.

Thornton, J. G., McNamara, H. M. and Montague, I. A., "Would you rather be a 'birth' or a 'genetic' mother? If so, how much?" (1994) 20 *Journal of Medical Ethics* 87–92.

Van Niekerk, A. and Van Zyl, L., "The ethics of surrogacy—women's reproductive labor" (1995) 21 *Journal of Medical Ethics* 345–349.

Walby, C. and Symons, B., *Who Am I? Identity, Adoption and Human Fertiliation* (London, British Agencies for Adoption & Fostering, 1990).

Warnock Report, *Report of the Committee of Inquiry into Human Fertilisation and Embryology* (Cmnd. 9314, London, HMSO, 1984).

Woollett, A., "Having children: accounts of childless women and women with reproductive problems" in A. Phoenix, A. Woollett and E. Lloyd (eds.), *Motherhood. Meanings, Practices and Ideologies* (London, Sage Publications, 1991).

Zipper, J. and Sevenhuijsen, S., "Surrogacy: feminist notions of motherhood reconsidered" in M. Stanworth (ed.), *Reproductive Technologies: Gender, Motherhood and Medicine* (Cambridge, Polity Press, 1987).

8

Unmarried Fathers and the Law

ROS PICKFORD*

1. HISTORICAL RELEVANCE OF MARRIAGE TO FATHERHOOD

Law has played an important part in our construction of fatherhood. The unavailability, until very recently, of a means of proving factual paternity has been a crucial factor in how men have been identified as fathers and, thus, in the social identity of fathers. In our culture, for many centuries, ideas about father-hood have been permeated by the concept of legitimacy;[1] the legal presumption that the children born to a man's wife are rightfully both his responsibility and his heirs. Historically, the correlative of this has been that children fathered out-side marriage were legally fatherless,[2] with only tenuous claims to support from their putative fathers,[3] and socially stigmatised as illegitimate. Marriage has in the past, therefore, been a key element in our understanding of what it means to be a father.

2. DECLINE IN THE POPULARITY OF MARRIAGE

However, although this century has seen, in the 1950s and 1960s what has been argued to be the highpoint of marriage (Clark, 1991), it is nonetheless the case that marriage has, over the last three decades, been in sharp decline even for couples starting a family. Twenty-five years ago it was very unusual for a cou-ple not to marry before the birth of their child. In 1971, births outside marriage accounted for only 8 per cent of all live births and fewer than half of these were registered by the father as well as the mother. In 1996, 36 per cent of all births were outside marriage and four-fifths of these were registered by both parents. Currently, then, 28 per cent of all children are being born to unmarried parents

* The research described in this chapter was funded by the Joseph Rowntree Foundation. All opinions expressed are those of the author.

[1] See Goody (1983) for a description of the role of the church and canon law.

[2] Indeed until the late nineteenth century non-marital children were *"filius nullius"* (nobody's child) although under the Poor Law the responsibility for the upkeep of such children fell to the dis-trict responsible for the mother.

[3] For a history of affiliation proceedings whereby a man could be required to make a financial contribution for a child of whom the courts declared him to be the father see Laslett (1980).

who register the birth together.[4] Three-quarters of these couples give the same
address on the birth certificate and so may be supposed to be living together. At
least one in five children, therefore, is being born to an unmarried couple cohabiting as a family.

3. PRESENT LAW ON FATHERHOOD

As a result of changes in the law relating to illegitimacy, intended to remove the
stigma from illegitimate children (Law Commission, 1982)[5], a non-marital
father is now defined in law as a parent[6] for most purposes, for example in relation to child support obligations and inheritance of property. However, the status of illegitimacy has not been abolished altogether.[7] An important distinction
continues to exist as far as the legal powers of parents are concerned. Only a
person with "parental responsibility"[8] (PR) has the right to make decisions
about a child's upbringing. All mothers, whether married or unmarried, get PR
automatically.[9] All married fathers also have PR automatically, but unmarried
fathers do not.[10] As far as fathers are concerned, therefore, the effect of the current law is that all fathers, both married and unmarried, automatically have the
liabilities associated with parenthood, such as the duty to support the child
financially.[11] However, unlike a married father, an unmarried father, even when
he is living with his child in a family unit, will not automatically have any
parental powers.[12] He will not, for example, be entitled to make decisions such
as where the child shall live or go to school, or to give consent for the child to
have medical treatment. Furthermore, he will have not have a legal right to care
for his child if the mother dies, and his consent will not be required before the
child can be adopted.[13]

The Law Commisssion canvassed the possibility of removing the distinction
between the legal status of married and unmarried fathers in the course of its

---

[4] A further 8 per cent are born to unmarried mothers who register the birth without the baby's
father: (1998) *Social Trends* 28.

[5] At paras. 4.44–4.51.

[6] Family Law Reform Act 1987, s.2(3).

[7] An important exception is that a child cannot inherit British nationality from his father if his
parents are unmarried.

[8] Children Act 1989, s.3(1), defines parental responsibility as "all the rights, duties, powers,
responsibilities and authority which by law a parent has in relation to the child and his property".
However, in spite of the legal definition encompassing both powers and duties, "parental responsibility" is, in fact, concerned only with "parental powers " or "parental rights", since all parents have
the duties associated with being a parent, but only those with parental responsibility have any powers in relation to the child.

[9] Children Act 1989, ss.2(1) and 2(2)(a).

[10] Children Act 1989, ss.2(1) and 2(2)(b). Unmarried fathers can acquire PR either by making a
formal legal agreement with the mother (PRA) or by applying to a court for an order (PRO) under
Children Act 1989, s.4.

[11] Child Support Act 1991, s.1(1) and s.54.

[12] For a full discussion see Bainham (1989).

[13] Adoption Act 1976, s.72.

reviews of family law during the 1980s, in view of the increasing numbers of fathers living with their children in quasi-marital situations. However, it was considered that there were still good reasons why some unmarried fathers should not be entitled to parental responsibility,[14] and that the task of distinguishing between the "meritorious" and "unmeritorious" unmarried father was too complex for legislative solution.[15] Instead, the Law Commission proposed that parents in agreement about the father's meritoriousness should be able to confer PR on him by registering their agreement with a court (PRA), and where the parents could not agree, that a father should be able to apply to a court for an order confering PR (PRO).[16] However, PRAs and PROs have been little used since their introduction in 1990. For example, in 1996 there were 232,663 births to unmarried parents but only 3,000 agreements and 5,587 orders.

4. THE ROLE OF THE LAW IN CURRENT CONSTRUCTIONS OF FATHERHOOD

In the course of recent research (Pickford, 1999), the author attempted to investigate the part that the law currently plays in the construction of fatherhood, and in particular how the difference in legal status between married and unmarried fathers is understood by them. The first step was to find out what fathers knew about the law regarding their legal status. This was investigated through a postal questionnaire sent to random samples of fathers taken from Birth Registers, some of whom had been identified as unmarried at the time they registered the birth of their child, and some who were married.[17] The questionnaire consisted of a series of "vignettes" about the life of a couple with a young child. It asked respondents to say what they thought the legal position of the father in various situations would be, and if this would be affected by whether he was married to the mother or not. The results of the survey showed that four out of five fathers, whether married or unmarried, were aware that all fathers are financially liable for the support of their children. However, the replies also revealed that three-quarters of these same fathers were unaware that there was a difference in legal status between married and unmarried fathers, and that unmarried fathers did not have PR. In the course of interviews,[18] the reason for this became clear. It emerged that relatively few fathers had what could be defined as "knowledge" about the law, because few had had any reason to obtain information about it. The majority of replies had been based on what fathers believed to be the case, in other words, on their "assumptions" about the law. The basic assumption which underlay these fathers' answers was that

[14] See Law Commission (1988), 172 para 2.17 *et seq.*
[15] See Law Commission (1982), 118 para 4.28 *et seq.*
[16] Children Act 1989, s.4.
[17] The response rate was 25 per cent. 154 replies were received.
[18] Interviews were conducted with approximately half of those who returned questionnaires, in total 75. In addition a further 65 fathers who were contacted through the courts were also interviewed.

marriage is not a relevant criterion for distinguishing fathers in terms of their legal rights, at any rate where the parents are bringing up the child together.

The research attempted to investigate what reasons men had for the assumptions they made about the law. It emerged that fathers had ideas about their legal situation which derived from cultural beliefs such as in the existence of "common-law" marriage, or from their experience of other areas of law such as child support. Some appeared not to recognise themselves in the term "unmarried fathers", thinking of themselves as, for example, "common-law husbands". Because of this, even where they came across information about the law on unmarried fathers, they did not necessarily realise it applied to them.

A frequently mentioned reason was that men believed that the law treated married and unmarried couples in largely the same way, and this was often connected with a belief in the existence of "common-law marriage". For some the basis for this belief was that they had experienced situations, such as claiming benefits, where cohabiting couples were in the same legal position as married couples:

> "Well you know, marriage really sort of, I mean I get the same, I get the tax relief on Lucy, get the same kind of benefits, that we would if we were married or not, but then it's a legal thing isn't it. I mean it is law."

Others were under the impression that cohabitants were treated the same as a married couple once they had lived together for a qualirying period. As with the benefits situation, there was some basis in fact for this type of belief, which made the situation in relation to PR all the more confusing for these fathers:[19]

> "Isn't there something like if me and Laura live together for so many years then she's considered my common law wife?"

These views were connected to the fact that almost all fathers said that they did not perceive any distinction between their own family's lifestyle and circumstances and that of a married couple, and for this reason they had not anticipated that any distinction would exist in law:

> "I would base it on that except [for] a marriage certificate, I'm basically living a married kind of life. You know the full family life."

Some mentioned the fact that all fathers are required to support their children financially as the basis for their belief that all fathers had the same legal status. As has already been noted, four out of five men correctly thought that there was no difference between a married and an unmarried father with regards to financial liability for a child. Many mentioned the existence of the Child Support Agency in this connection, and it was this awareness which led them to suppose that the legal situation of married and unmarried fathers was the same in all material respects:

---

[19] There are a number of instances where after a qualifying period of two years an unmarried couple will be treated in the same way as a married couple, for instance under the Inheritance (Provision for Family and Dependants) Act 1975.

"So much is now, so much more is heard about about the, er, what's it called? The agency which collects money, Child Support Agency, the, the fact that you are now so much more regarded as the father . . . Purely for the purposes of getting the child support money back so, there's a, you know, you think that the other side of the coin must be true."

Even where they did not specifically refer to legal child support obligations, a related idea which many fathers expressed was that of taking responsibility for the child's care:

"As long as I look after her and live with her to the best of my ability, you know, I can't see what difference that makes. I think I should really, I should have as much right as anybody."

All the unmarried fathers interviewed knew that there was a legal requirement to register the birth of a baby, and indeed it was the only legal formality that they were aware of in connection with the birth. This led some of them to believe that having registered as the father of the child, this gave them legal status as the child's parent:

"I didn't think there was any difference. I thought like if the child's yours and you sign the birth certificate and everything and I thought that yeah at the end of the day it's your child."

Another reason which fathers gave was their belief that fathers and mothers would have equal rights

"I think it should be quite simply, if the father's a father or the mother's a mother, then responsibilities and . . . and everything should be the same. It should be the same."

Many believed they would have rights simply because they were in fact their child's father. The term "natural" father was the one which was most often used by fathers

" 'Cos I honestly thought that as a natural father you had the same rights."

The sentiments of all these fathers were summed up most succinctly by one man who when asked how he believed he had acquired legal status as a father he replied:

"I established my rights as a father by fathering them."

5. FATHERS' VIEWS OF THE CONNECTION BETWEEN MARRIAGE AND
STARTING A FAMILY

To explore the extent to which marriage was seen as related to fatherhood, men were asked about their views of marriage. Both married and unmarried men frequently mentioned reasons connected with their children in this context. Over half the married men mentioned their children as a reason why they married: "I wouldn't want to have children without being married, no, no . . . I wouldn't have liked to have brought anybody into the world without marriage really." However, it should be noted that almost as many said starting a family was definitely not a consideration in their decision to marry. Of those who did say that it was very important to them personally to be married before starting a family, four mentioned concern about their lack of legal status if they hadn't married, but most were unaware of this factor. Nonetheless, most of these married fathers did not think it was necessary for everyone to marry before having children:

> "I wouldn't say that it, you know, before people had children they should be married, I mean I really don't think the two things, well they're connected obviously but then they shouldn't be connected to say 'right you've got to be married before you have children', I mean I don't really think it's, I won't say it's not relevant but it's, it's not as important."

Almost 50 per cent of the unmarried men also discussed marriage in connection with their children. They tended to talk about not wanting the child to experience prejudice because they were illegitimate. However, this was often done with great ambivalence; fathers didn't want to think that prejudice existed but were not absolutely sure that it did not:

> "So as far as we're concerned a piece of paper don't mean anything. As far as bringing up a child is concerned, it just is nothing. Nothing whatsoever. Nothing. It doesn't matter one little bit. Especially in this day and age, when so many couples aren't married. It's not a big thing. When they go to school, that's the only thing we've said, you know, that would perhaps make us now get married."

Evidence from this study is consistent with demographic analysis that at present for most couples cohabitation is a stepping stone to marriage (Kiernan and Estaugh, 1993). Where this occurs the father automatically acquires the legal status of a married father. However, it is clear that some will not make this transition, even where the relationship continues, either because of strong objection to marrying or because couples have other priorities. A considerable proportion of respondents fell into these two categories. Marriage was viewed as discredited or irrelevant by some who seemed unlikely, therefore, ever to marry. The majority thought they might marry in the future but many of these were very apathetic about marriage and it appeared likely that it might be some considerable time before it was sufficiently high on their list of priorities to take place and indeed that this might never happen. Amongst those who had married, some had strong views as to the importance of marriage to society, but most did not. The majority felt it was important to them personally, but that it was not important that others did not wish to marry. About a third felt it was not even particularly important to themselves. Individuals who had previous experience of marriage and divorce were to be found amongst those who had remarried, those who were now against marriage, and those who were currently indifferent. All the evidence is that the power of marriage as a cultural norm has waned both in relation to whether people choose to enter into it and whether they choose, having entered, to remain. In view of this, it was clear that many of the men interviewed would be spending a considerable portion if not the entire childhood of their children as unmarried fathers.

6. FATHERS' VIEWS OF THE LAW ON PARENTAL RESPONSIBILITY

Reactions of unmarried fathers who found out about their lack of PR as a result of being informed by the interviewer varied but almost all expressed great surprise, and many were annoyed or angry:

> "Yeah I'm obviously gob smacked over it. Obviously I'm sitting here in a family unit but you wouldn't envisage that."

> "The law might think that, but most fathers I think, would disagree with that. There's obviously gonna be some fathers that would quite happily not accept their parental responsibility, but I would imagine the majority of unmarried fathers would, and I think a lot of 'em if they understood the full implications, of not being married, would be quite shocked really."

> "I think in doing it this way, well it takes the piss really. You don't, nobody knows, I mean that's the first I've heard of it. Now nobody's going to know are they, who the hell knows? It's terrible. My reaction is not very nice actually, and a bit insulted actually. Yes that's what I'd say, insulted."

> "Surprised and frightened really. I mean obviously it wouldn't affect you I mean, but you never know do you? It seems very harsh."

Some appeared bewildered by the information and found it quite difficult to understand the import of what was being told to them. One father who already had a child from a previous married relationship was particularly puzzled:

> "In all but the marriage certificate, everything is the same, financial outlay, emotional commitment, everything is exactly the same, a married father doesn't look after a child any more expertly."

Some fathers seemed unsure as to whether they wanted to contemplate the issue as one which had relevance for them:

> "Yeah, but it's so like, everyday things I mean obviously when everything's rosy you agree on things and everything goes that way but could come a point where you say no, and obviously Debbie says yes and then you both dig your heels in and she says 'well I'm gunna do it anyway' and you find out you haven't got a say and it's quite worrying."

However, even those who felt that because their relationship was secure they had no particular concerns about their legal status *vis-à-vis* their partners, were disconcerted by the information about their lack of rights in more everyday contexts, such as being unable to give medical consent. For example, one father's initial response to hearing about unmarried fathers' status was to say:

"It's something I've never really given a lot of thought to, to be honest. I suppose in my situation, we're happy, and we get on well and you know, it's not something I'd really think about."

He became quite agitated, however, when asked how he would feel if he was told he could not give permission for his child's medical treatment:

"I would be rather annoyed. To put it politely."

The issue of medical consent aroused strong feelings of anger in several fathers, and some had experienced problems. One father who had two children with health problems, had experience of difficulties with medical consent at two different hospitals; his local hospital, and also another fifty miles away where he had gone to stay with the younger child who was an in-patient:

A: "That's another reason why I think the law should change."
Q: "Because you're not strictly speaking supposed to give permission for their treatment?"
A: "Yeah that's right. Now one of them's got heart problems. He's got a pacemaker and this and that. That's the youngest one. Last year . . . I had to go up L [hospital] with him while the mother stayed here in P. I had to go up to L for a week and a bit. You know he's going to have his pacemaker changed, but when it come down to it, the first question they ask me is, was I married? and I said Well, no then they said to me I can't sign for it. Which is ridiculous, because I was there. The mother wasn't. They had to ring up, call up the mother to come down, right, you know, so that she can sign, right. Even though I'm the father like and you know I've been there all week. You know what I mean? . . . Harry, my other boy. He has problems with his ears you know and he was gonna have an operation [at P hospital]. You see what happened was I took him up there, the mother met me up there, right. But anything that was said was said to the mother. It was sort of like 'Miss Y' that's her name, 'Can you come with us, we'll talk to you'. And you know, I thought what about me? . . . It's degrading. You know, that's another reason why I believe the law should change. I mean fair enough if it was probably a life or death situation then they probably wouldn't. But any other detail like this or a small operation or whatever, if I'm there and they can't locate the mother, what the hell am I supposed to do?"

Six of the fathers in the study had sole care of their child, either because the mother was dead or ill, or because she had abandoned the child. These fathers tended to exhibit exasperation that although they cared for the child, and in some cases had been doing so for years, they were now obliged to apply for the legal right to do so. This father was typical:

A: "I must admit I did think I would have had more rights. But as I went up to my solicitors again and they explained the situation they again said that I had no rights until it goes to the court."
Q: "So how did you feel when they said that?"
A: "Gutted naturally. Because I believe, myself, right that it's about time the law was changed. There must be a lot of other blokes out there like me, right, who probably got the children but they're the ones who have to keep going uphill to make it legal."

Another father, whose children had been abused and finally abandoned by their mother, was annoyed at being unable to give consent for treatment for a medical condition caused by the mother's abuse, until he had gone through the court process to acquire PR:

> "I mean, Chloe, I've had her in hospital for several weeks through malnutrition, which was caused by her mother. Yet, if she had to have an operation, she couldn't have one unless her mother signed for it . . . When she first went they said to me, she's got malnutrition but if there is any reason why we have to operate, we need her mother here to sign. Although that was her mother's fault she had it, and that was proven."

As well as these feelings of exasperation, most of these fathers also felt great anxiety at the precariousness of their own and their children's position. This man described how he felt while he was waiting for the court to give him PR:

> A: "Yeah, at the time, she could say, OK, no I want to stop this and I want the children back, you know and whatever."
> Q: "Yes, was that a worry?"
> A: "Yes, that's why, that's why I went for the order. Yes, cos she could turn up at the door at any time and just say well I want the children back, she could come with a police officer at any moment and just walk out, you know she could just take 'em like, and I can't do anything about it."

Several fathers said that they felt that their sense of their own worth as a father had been undermined by the discovery:

> "Totally outrageous. Making somebody who's married erm, me not being married makes me an unworthy parent. I can't look after my own child?"

> "Well I think, I think, it devalues fatherhood, you know, it, it's taking away some of my role of being her father. Just because the fact that I haven't, you know, I haven't signed a bit of paper."

Many of the fathers in this group thought that that the law was simply out of date:

> "I feel it's a bit patronising from the law point of view that obviously times now are different, things are not like this. There are many people in our situation are not married. Why should there [be] really any difference?"

Some talked about their feelings of "disappointment" with the law:

> "I was disappointed with the system not being able to acknowledge people in a relationship that's exactly in every single way the same as a married couple like next door, if not better in some ways, or, you know, but still being a couple but being penalised for that."

Others said that the law was often not sensible or logical, and sometimes even absurd:

> "It's a very strange way for a law to be set up in that way, to be married to give you rights, you know, irrespective of you're the father of the child, you should have

rights to that child irrespective of whether you're married or not. It's absolutely ridiculous."

Often fathers expressed their dissatisfaction in terms of unfairness or injustice. This was often in connection with the issue of child support which raised very strong feelings in many respondents, irrespective of whether they had been personally affected by it themselves. They tended to feel strongly that fathers should have rights if they were expected to bear responsibilities. Some expressed the view that they would refuse to fulfil support obligations if they were refused rights:

"Equality and justice and those two just literally don't come into it for unmarried fathers."

7. FATHERS' VIEWS ON PARENTAL RESPONSIBILITY AGREEMENTS (PRA)

Very few of the fathers interviewed already knew about the possibility of making a PRA. All were told about the availability of them and some said they would probably look into the possibility of making one, although how many actually did was not possible to follow up. Others, however felt that making a PRA would not be appropriate for various reasons. A common view was that inertia was likely to be the main impediment to the widespread use of the PRA in its current form:

"Cos I think your average person as I say doesn't know about it anyway, but even when he does get to know about it, he wouldn't really be bothered to go to that extreme to sort it out just on the off chance that something could happen one day."

Several men, however, expressed serious unease with the current system. One objection raised by some men to the PRA procedure, was that to have to raise the subject with their partner was not something they felt comfortable about doing, that it might be seen as implying lack of trust, and as focusing on the possibility of the breakdown of the relationship. For example, one father, who had known about PRAs for some time and was in a very insecure relationship, said:

"But it just seems that, that I mean it's all very well, it's all very good but it seems rather cold blooded and cold hearted to me, it sort of shows a lack of faith in yourself and your relationship if you have to go to court in order to, even though you, it's probably a very simple sort of thing and you just go, it's just in and out and it's over in five minutes or so."

Another father who also knew about the availability of PRAs already but whose relationship appeared to be much more secure, took a similar view:

"It's been brought up in conversation, but I've never considered going to a solicitors, I think that shows a lot of insecurity in a relationship."

The strongest feelings were aroused in those whose objection was that the current law creates a structural imbalance of power between the parents, which as well as being in itself unjust might also potentially be damaging to the relationship. Many of the men interviewed were concerned about the importance of equality within relationships and often these men did not think it appropriate that PR for fathers should depend on consent, when it did not for mothers. This father, who had tried to make a PRA, described the difficulty he felt about approaching the mother:

> "It, well it was difficult, yeah, I tell you why it was difficult, it was difficult because I had to basically approach her from the point of view that it was something I was requesting, almost as a favour, and although she didn't have any theoretical objections to it, she was suspicious of the motives."

8. SHOULD THE LAW BE CHANGED?

The Lord Chancellor's Department has recently issued a consultation paper on whether the law regarding unmarried fathers should be changed (Lord Chancellor's Department, 1998). Almost all the unmarried fathers interviewed were dissatisfied with the current law and thought it should be changed. Overwhelmingly, the feeling expressed was that marriage was irrelevant to whether fathers were deserving of legal status:

> "Being married or not married shouldn't really make a difference, no. Because I think it's so popular nowadays for people to live together and whatever and not to be married that it hardly seems any point."

9. LINKING PR AND JOINT REGISTRATION

One possibility under consideration is that PR should be conferred automatically on all fathers who register a birth jointly with the mother. On the basis of this research there appears to be nothing to suggest that more *fathers* would be deterred from registering if this conferred PR on them. Most believed that in effect it already did so. Most also knew if a man does not register as the father it does not necessarily affect whether he might be found to be the father and made liable for child support. Presumably those who believe that it does, and are worried about this, already don't register. Whether more *mothers* would refuse to allow fathers to register if it conferred PR is not known. However, the impression gleaned about them through fathers suggests that many also believe that when a father registers he gains parental status by doing so, and would be quite happy, therefore, if this was actually the case. Most of the men in the study who did not know about their lack of status assumed that their partners were equally unaware.[20] It was not apparent, therefore, that there are significant

---

[20] In two cases the mother had apparently been aware and the father had only found this out when a dispute arose.

numbers of women who at present allow the father to register knowing that it does not give PR, and would cease to do so if registration became the qualifying criterion, but the possibility cannot be excluded. McRae's study (1993) found widespread ignorance of the law amongst cohabiting mothers, although the incidence was apparently not as high as amongst the fathers in this study. However, the possibility of joint registrations being reduced for this reason is an argument against having joint registration as the sole determining factor for PR.[21]

10. COHABITATION AT THE TIME OF THE BIRTH

An alternative suggestion made in the consultation paper is that PR should be conferred on those fathers who cohabit at the time of the birth.[22] This does not appear from the data in this study to be satisfactory. A number of couples who were not cohabiting at the time of birth were cohabiting by the time they were interviewed, usually because of initial housing problems. There was also some incidence of fathers giving incorrect information regarding addresses to registrars, which would give rise to evidential problems.

11. AUTOMATIC PR FOR ALL UNMARRIED FATHERS

Another question is whether all unmarried fathers should automatically acquire PR.[23] There appear to be serious practical difficulties in conferring PR automatically on all fathers without some formalities. Perhaps the most important difficulty would appear to be one of identification. All married fathers appear on the birth certificate and are therefore identified, but not all unmarried ones do so. To have a situation where all unmarried fathers automatically had PR without some form of identification would seem to be impracticable and in effect meaningless. Furthermore, a mother has to have the possibility of refuting a claim to paternity on the grounds that it is false, if for no other reason. It is difficult to see how this could be achieved without some kind of investigative procedure.

12. "UNMERITORIOUS" FATHERS

Objections to extending PR for unmarried fathers have, in the past, focused on the issue of the difficulty of distinguishing the "meritorious" from the "unmeri-

---

[21] See below, "PR for fathers who do not jointly register".
[22] This is the position in the law in New Zealand.
[23] This was favoured by the Scottish Law Commission in its 1992 report. However, it was not adopted and Scottish law is currently the same as English law.

torious" (Law Commission, 1982).[24] Men who become fathers as a result of "transient"[25] relationships have been considered to fall into the "unmeritorious" category. Some of the respondents who had not been jointly registered as the father fell into this category and felt very strongly that they should not be regarded any differently from the mother on this account, particularly since the Child Support Agency would not so regard them. Some respondents did take the view that there was no point in conferring PR on men who did not want to be involved with their child. However, it has to be considered whether identifying these individuals would be practicable, and might not involve more cost and more litigation than might be incurred in giving PR to men who were unlikely ever to want to use it, and who could in any event be controlled by the courts if necessary. It is not in any case a principle which is applied to divorced or separated fathers many of whom also fail to keep in touch with their children. A large minority of respondents were also uneasy about men who were violent or rapists[26] having PR, but most agreed that this could just as easily apply to married men who are not at present excluded for this reason.[27] The existence of any exceptions does carry with it the risk of increased litigation. The disadvantages of having exceptions might far outweigh any justification in terms of numbers affected, as the Scottish Law Commission (1992) accepted.

13. PR FOR FATHERS WHO DO NOT JOINTLY REGISTER

In view of the possible reduction in joint registrations if this is introduced as the critierion for PR, there is a strong argument for having a simple court procedure to allow non-consensual declarations of paternity where the birth is not jointly registered, with paternity being awarded on genetic proof.[28] Current procedures, particularly for fathers, are widely acknowledged to be convoluted and unsatisfactory and a simplified procedure is under consideration.[29] Once paternity has been established, there appear few arguments for limiting the acquisition of PR. In practice unless a father has day-to-day care of a child, he has little opportunity to exercise PR actively without regulation by court order. The residual rights under PR are in essence simply rights to express a view, since they may all be overridden by court order. However, the right to be heard can be an important one. For example, currently, as has been noted,[30] an unmarried father

---

[24] See n.5 above.

[25] See Lord Chancellor's Department (1998).

[26] Again the English Law Commission was concerned about this aspect (Law Commission 1982 and 1988). The Scottish Law Commission (1992) took a different view, having heard evidence that very few children are born as the result of rapes outside marriage (at para. 2.47).

[27] Remedies for women who are victims of violence are available to both married and unmarried women under Part IV of the Family Law Act 1996.

[28] Subject to the provisions of the Human Fertilisation and Embryology Act 1990.

[29] See Lord Chancellor's Department (1998).

[30] See n.13 above.

without PR has no legal standing to take part in adoption proceedings in relation to his child.

14. IDENTIFICATION OF FATHERS

Consideration should perhaps be given to whether it would be in the interest of children and in the public interest generally that the father should be identified on the birth certificate in all possible cases. At present, approximately 8 per cent of all birth certificates (22 per cent of unmarried births) do not reveal the identity of the father (51,000 in 1996) (*Social Trends*, 1998). This may be the result of refusal by the father to be identified, refusal by the mother to allow the father to be identified, or factual uncertainty as to the identity of the father. What proportion of these are fathers wanting involvement with their children is not known. Some of the men in this study were in that situation. A proportion of these fathers will subsequently be identified through child support procedures (although a mother may still refuse to name the father on certain grounds), but the finding does not at present have any legal consequences outside the child support process. Some will also be identified through court proceedings or PR Agreements, in which cases the birth certificate can then be amended. There is, however, no positive duty to declare or to discover the identity of the father in the case of every birth.[31] The passing of the Child Support Act 1991 marked an ideological shift in the perception of the public interest in fathers taking responsibility for their children. The previous maintenance system embodied a much higher tolerance of personal choice, for both mothers and fathers, as to whether fathers were required to support their children. The current legislation (with some exceptions in the area of reproductive technology) is based on a much stronger conception of the link between genetic parenthood and financial responsibility,[32] but this has not been reflected in the adoption of a more systematised approach to the identification of fathers generally. From the child's point of view, the identity of the father may be important to their own sense of identity in later life and should arguably therefore be concealed in as few cases as possible. In adoption it has been accepted in legislation that children, once they reach eighteen, have the right to access information about their origins. However, it is currently the case that mothers and fathers may choose to conceal this information from their child, if they wish, in the case of unmarried births. It is difficult to see, from the child's perspective, the justification for such an anomaly.

---

[31] In Sweden, for example, the law operates on the basis of there being a public interest in identifying and ascribing paternity in the case of all births unless this proves to be not practicably possible, and an investigative procedure takes place in the case of all unmarried births.

[32] Although there is still some scope for mothers to refuse to identify fathers for example, where violence is feared (Child Support Act 1991, s.46).

15. CONCLUSION

The law is obliged all the time to evolve to meet new situations. The Law Commission in its report on illegitimacy recognised that family law must keep pace with social change (Law Commission, 1982). It is clear that the law relating to unmarried fathers has not. The Lord Chancellor's Department consultation document (Lord Chancellor's Department, 1998) canvasses various possible changes in the law. Other jurisdictions have different approaches to this issue and some of these are discussed in the consultation. However, what emerges from this study is that it does seem important that if changes are made they should be culturally relevant so far as possible to the majority. The recent experience of the introduction of PRAs and their lack of use suggests that there is little to be achieved by inventing procedures or importing solutions which have been adopted by other jurisdictions if these have no resonance within the lived experiences of those people to whom they are intend to apply.

The data from this research suggest that the current law on unmarried fathers is very much out of step with society's ideas about fatherhood. The focus on marriage as a defining criterion of fatherhood has no resonance amongst most fathers, even those who have chosen to marry. Furthermore, the procedure for conferring PR on unmarried fathers, introduced in 1990 to meet this difficulty, is seriously defective and unlikely ever to be very successful. There is a widespread lack of knowledge about unmarried fathers' legal status, but it is doubtful whether this could be entirely overcome through provision of information, because this particular aspect of the law is at odds with many areas of the law such as benefits legislation, with which people are familiar, and this makes it difficult for them to grasp. Practical considerations, such as fathers' inability to consent to medical treatment, provide another strong argument for change. It cannot be in the interests of children that these kinds of legal disabilities exist for thousands of parents with everyday care of their children. Perhaps even more importantly there are also serious objections in principle to the current system, which is seen as unfair. There was a widespread belief amongst respondents that married and unmarried fathers should generally be treated the same. This research suggests that what is important for the successful operation of the law, particularly in areas such as the family, is that the law should correspond with what most people think it should be, unless there are very compelling reasons why it should not. The change in the law most likely to overcome all these difficulties is for PR to accrue automatically to all fathers who register jointly. This would affect approximately one in four births currently. If both parents are prepared to recognise the fact of the man's paternity, it appears in itself a strong argument for such a change, and it would also accord with the views of most people. For those fathers who continue to participate successfully in their child's life, it avoids all the possible inconveniences and disabilities that lack of PR can involve. However, in order to minimise the risk that some mothers might then unreasonably withhold permission for joint registration, it might be advisable that there should also be a method of acquiring PR through a court process on proof of parentage. There seem to be no very convincing reasons against wider acquisition of PR by unmarried fathers, since if a father is, or becomes, unsuitable in some way, the exercise of PR can be limited in the same way as can that of a married father.

The Government in its recent consultation document *Supporting Families* (Home Office, 1998), states its belief that "strong and stable families provide the best basis for raising children", and wishes to find policies which can support families in their task. However, although it accepts that it is not possible "to put the clock back" as far as the decline in support for marriage goes, it nevertheless wishes to promote marriage as the preferred child-rearing unit. It is not possible to favour one particular family form without undermining others. The way the current law on unmarried fathers operates illustrates this very clearly, as this research shows. The unmarried fathers interviewed felt the law devalues their role as fathers solely because they are not married. The distinction between married and unmarried fathers was seen as invalid and unfair. The legal distinction between mothers and unmarried fathers was also seen as unfair and even potentially destabilising of the parental relationship. From a policy perspective this does not seem to offer support to these parental relationships and arguably works to undermine the objective of promoting a sense of involvement and responsibility amongst these fathers. This cannot be in the best interests of their children, and runs counter to the ethos present in the Children Act 1989 and the child support legislation of fostering parenting as a lifelong commitment and responsibility. It is important that policy-makers should not be afraid to face up to the implications of the fact that it is now clear that marriage has become increasingly irrelevant for the majority of people in our society and that it can no longer play a role in our construction of fatherhood.

REFERENCES

Bainham, A., "When is a parent not a parent: reflections on the unmarried father and his child in English Law" (1989) 3(2) *International Journal of Law and the Family* 208–239.

Clark, D. (ed.), *Marriage, Domestic Life and Social Change: Writings for Jacqueline Burgoyne (1944–88)* (London, Routledge, 1991).

Goody, J., *The Development of the Family and Marriage in Europe* (Cambridge, Cambridge University Press, 1983).

Home Office, *Supporting Families* (London, HMSO, 1998).

Kiernan, K. and Estaugh, V., *Cohabitation, Extra-Marital Childbearing and Social Policy* (London, Family Policy Studies Centre, 1993).

Laslett, P., Oosterveen, K. and Smith, R. M. (eds.), *Bastardy and Its Comparative History* (London, Edward Arnold for the Cambridge Group for the History of Population & Social Structure, 1980).

Law Commission, *Illegitimacy* (London, HMSO, 1982).

Law Commission, *Review of Child Law: Guardianship and Custody* (London, HMSO, 1988).

Lord Chancellor's Department Consultation Paper, *The Law on Parental Responsibility for Unmarried Fathers* (London, HMSO, 1998).

McRae, S., *Cohabiting Mothers* (London, Policy Studies Institute, 1993).

Pickford, R., *Fathers, Marriage and the Law* (London, Family Policy Studies Centre (for the Joseph Rowntree Foundation, 1999).

Scottish Law Commission, *Report on Family Law* (London, HMSO, 1992).

Social Trends (28, ONS, 1998).

9

Lesbian Mother Families

SUSAN GOLOMBOK

Public awareness of lesbian mother families dates back to the 1970s when previously married lesbian women began to fight for custody of their children when they divorced. At that time lesbian mothers were losing custody of their children on the grounds that it would not be in the child's best interests to grow up in a lesbian family. In particular, it was argued that the children would be teased and ostracised by their peers and would develop emotional and behavioural problems as a result, and also that they would show atypical gender development i.e. that boys would be less masculine in their identity and behaviour, and girls less feminine, than their counterparts from heterosexual homes (Kleber, *et al.*, 1986; Editors of the Harvard Law Review, 1990; Green, 1992). While the likelihood of a lesbian mother retaining custody through a residence order is higher today than it was in the 1970s, and there has been a marked decrease in the number of contested cases, lesbian mothers who go to court may still be denied residence with their own birth children because of their sexual orientation. For a detailed discussion of how the law regards lesbian mothers, and of changes in the courts' attitudes towards lesbian mothers from the 1970s to the present time, see Barlow *et al.* (1999).

Researchers of the psychological development of children raised in lesbian families have attempted to determine whether there is any empirical support for these assumptions by examining the areas of child development that have been the focus of concern in cases of disputed residence—children's socio-emotional and gender development. In this chapter each of these areas will be examined, first with a discussion of background issues followed by the presentation of empirical findings.

1. GENDER DEVELOPMENT

In all that has been said and written about lesbian families, greatest attention has been paid to the consequences for children's gender development of being raised by a lesbian mother. In investigations of gender development, a distinction is generally made between gender identity, gender role, and sexual orientation. Gender identity is a person's concept of themselves as male or female; gender role includes the behaviours and attitudes which are considered to be appropriate for males and females in a particular culture; and sexual orientation refers to a person's sexual attraction towards partners of the other gender (heterosexual sexual orientation) or the same gender (lesbian or gay sexual orientation). Whether or not children of lesbian mothers will differ from children brought up by heterosexual single mothers with respect to these different aspects of gender development will depend upon the extent to which it is possible for parents to influence the gender development of their children. In so far as gender development is biologically determined, the way in which parents raise their children should make little difference, and for this reason biological explanations will not be discussed here. The three major psychological theories—psychoanalytic, social learning and cognitive developmental—vary according to the psychological processes which are believed to be operative, and also in the role ascribed to parents. Each of these theories will be examined in terms of their explanations of the processes involved in gender development, particularly with respect to what they tell us about the mechanisms, if any, through which parents may play a role.

Psychoanalytic theorists believe that relationships with parents early in childhood are central to the development of gender identity, gender role, and sexual orientation in adult life. According to traditional psychoanalytic theory, gender development is rooted in the phallic stage of psychosexual development which occurs at about five years of age (Freud, 1905/1953; 1920/1955; 1933; Socarides, 1978). It is in order to resolve the Oedipal conflict (i.e. the conflict between sexual desire for the mother and fear of castration by the father) that boys are believed to shift their identification from the mother to the father and take on his male characteristics. The mechanisms involved in female identification are rather different and less clearly described. The resolution of the Oedipal conflict in girls is believed to be driven by penis envy, and involves transferring identification from the father back to the mother and adopting a female role.

For psychoanalytic theorists, the acquisition of non-traditional gender roles, and the development of a lesbian or gay sexual orientation, are often viewed as negative outcomes resulting from the unsuccessful resolution of the Oedipal conflict. It is believed that boys who fail to identify with their father, and girls who fail to identify with their mother, at the completion of the Oedipal period are more likely to identify as gay or lesbian respectively when they grow up.

So what can we predict from psychoanalytic theory about the consequences for gender development of being raised by a lesbian mother? Traditional psychoanalytic theorists, stressing the importance of the presence of heterosexual parents for the successful resolution of the Oedipal conflict, would expect that the lack of a father figure, together with the mother's atypical female role, would influence the gender development of children brought up in lesbian families. Specifically, it has been argued by expert witnesses in courts of law that boys will not identify with the male role and will therefore be less masculine in childhood and more likely to be gay in adulthood, and that girls will identify with a mother who does not conform to the traditional female role and will thus be less feminine in childhood and more likely to identify as lesbian when they grow up. More contemporary psychoanalytic theorists have also focused on the separate roles of mothers and fathers in the gender development of their children (Chodorow, 1978; Dinnerstein, 1976), again leading to the expectation that children raised in the absence of a father with one, or two, lesbian mothers may be less likely to show sex-typed behaviour in childhood and more likely to adopt a lesbian or gay sexual orientation in adult life.

From the perspective of classic social learning theory, which has focused on the development of childhood sex-typed behaviour rather than on adult sexual orientation, the two processes which are important for children's gender development are the differential reinforcement of boys and girls, and the modelling of others of the same sex as themselves, particularly the same sex parent (Mischel, 1966; Mischel, 1970; Bandura, 1977). There is much empirical evidence to suggest that parents of pre-school children do treat their sons and daughters differently, although the extent to which they are producing sex-typed behaviour, rather than simply responding to pre-existing differences between boys and girls, remains unknown (Maccoby and Jacklin, 1974; Lytton and Romney, 1991).

With respect to modelling, the idea that children acquire sex-typed behaviour by directly imitating same sex parents is now thought to be rather simplistic, and a modified version of social learning theory has been proposed (Perry and Bussey, 1979; Bussey and Bandura, 1984; Bandura, 1986). It seems that children learn which behaviours are considered to be appropriate for males and which for females by observing many men and women and boys and girls, and by noticing which behaviours are performed frequently by females and rarely by males, and *vice versa*. Children then use these abstractions of sex-appropriate behaviour as models for their own imitative performance. Thus, children observe a wide variety of role models in their daily life, not just their parents, and tend to imitate those whom they consider to be typical of their sex. Friends, in particular, appear to be important role models; school age boys and girls show a strong preference for same sex peers (Maccoby, 1988). But it is gender stereotypes, rather than specific individuals, that seem to be most influential in the acquisition of sex-typed behaviour. Gender stereotypes are pervasive in our society and children are aware of these stereotypes from as early as two years of age (Martin, 1991; Signorella, *et al.*, 1993; Stern and Karraker, 1989).

Thus, from a social learning theory perspective, it could be expected that different patterns of reinforcement may be operating in lesbian than in heterosexual families such that young people in lesbian families would be less likely to be discouraged from engaging in non-conventional sex-typed behaviour, or from embarking upon lesbian or gay relationships. Whereas contemporary social learning theorists are less likely than classical social learning theorists to emphasise the importance of the same-sex parent as a role model, it could be argued that by virtue of their non-traditional family, the sons and daughters of lesbian mothers may hold less rigid stereotypes about what constitutes acceptable male and female behaviour than their peers in heterosexual families. They may be more open to non-conventional gender role behaviour, or to their own involvement in lesbian or gay relationships. It is important to remember, however, that social learning theorists believe that individuals other than parents are also important role models and reinforcers of sex-typed behaviour for the child.

Like social learning theorists, cognitive developmental theorists have focused on the development of childhood gender identity and role rather than on adult sexual orientation. For cognitive developmental theorists, the role of parents in this respect is a minor one. A central tenet of this approach is that children play an active part in their own development; they seek out for themselves information about gender and socialise themselves as male or female. Parents are viewed as simply one source of gender-related information. Early studies of cognitive-developmental processes focused on children's developing understanding of the concept of gender (Kohlberg, 1966; Stagnor and Ruble, 1987). Basic gender identity is established at about two to three years of age. By this age, children know that they are male or female, and can correctly label other people as male or female as well. It is not until they reach the stage of gender stability a year or two later, however, that they realise that gender is stable across time. Gender constancy, the understanding that gender is a characteristic which does not change, is the final stage in the development of the gender concept and is reached at about five or six years of age.

More recently, gender schema theorists have examined the way in which children organise knowledge about gender (Martin, 1991; Martin, 1989; Martin and Halverson, 1981). Gender schemas refer to organised bodies of knowledge about gender, and are functionally similar to gender stereotypes. Gender schemas influence the way in which we perceive and remember information about the world around us so that we pay greater attention to, and are more likely to remember, information that is in line with our gender schemas than opposing information. From as early as two to three years, soon after they begin to label themselves and others consistently as male or female, children organise information according to gender. If told that a person is male or female, children will make gender-related predictions about that person's behaviour (Martin, 1989; Martin et al., 1990), and children as young as five years have been shown to have a better memory for events that fit with gender stereotypes than those that do not (Liben and Signorella, 1980; Signorella and Liben, 1984; Martin and Halverson, 1983).

Cognitive developmental theorists place even less emphasis than contemporary social learning theorists on the role of parents in the gender development of their children. According to this theory, children integrate information about sexual identity from their wider social environment, actively constructing for themselves what it means to be male or female. It would not be predicted that children raised by lesbian mothers would differ in this process from children in heterosexual families. Cognitive developmental theorists, like social learning theorists, have focused on childhood sex-typed behaviour rather than on adult sexual orientation. To the extent that cognitive processes are contributing to the adoption of a heterosexual or homosexual orientation, it would seem that young people seek out information in their social world which is in line with their emerging sexual orientation, and they come to value and identify with those characteristics which are consistent with their view of themselves as heterosexual, lesbian or gay.

Social constructionist theories start from the premise that sexual feelings are not essential qualities that the individual is born with or that are socialised by childhood experiences (Kitzinger, 1987; Simon and Gagnon, 1987; Tiefer, 1987). What these approaches have in common is an emphasis on the individual's active role, guided by his or her culture, in structuring reality and creating sexual meanings for particular acts. Sexual identity is considered to be constructed throughout the lifespan; the individual first becomes aware of cultural scenarios for sexual encounters and then develops internal fantasies associated with sexual arousal (intrapsychic scripts) and interpersonal scripts for orchestrating specific sexual acts (Gagnon, 1990; Simon and Gagnon, 1987). Identification with significant others is believed to be important for enabling an individual either to neutralise a lesbian or gay potential, or to construct a lesbian or gay identity. For example, heterosexual parents may respond negatively to what they perceive as children's same-gender sexual activity (Gagnon, 1977). Plummer (1975) suggested that awareness of others who identify as homosexual validates feelings of same-gender attraction that might otherwise go unnoticed or be denied. From a social constructionist perspective, therefore, children raised in lesbian families would be expected to be more likely than children in heterosexual families to adopt a lesbian or gay identity themselves as a result of their exposure to lesbian lifestyles, and often to gay lifestyles as well.

2. SOCIO-EMOTIONAL DEVELOPMENT

The assumption that children of lesbian mothers may be more likely to experience emotional and behavioural problems than children of heterosexual parents stems from the finding that some childhood family experiences have been found to carry an increased risk of psychiatric disorder. Of particular relevance to children of lesbian mothers are parental divorce, being raised by a single parent and absence of father.

On average, children in single parent families do less well than those in two-parent households in terms of both psychological adjustment and academic achievement (Ferri, 1976; McLanahan and Sandefur, 1994). They are also less likely to go on to higher education and more likely to leave home and become parents themselves at an early age. But it is not simply being raised by a single parent that leads to these outcomes. Children in single parent families are more likely to suffer economic hardship, and many will have been exposed to the conflict, distress and family disruption that is commonly associated with their parents' separation or divorce.

Experiencing their parents' separation or divorce can be extremely upsetting for children, and in the years following separation they are more likely to develop psychological problems than children in intact families (Amato and Keith, 1991; Hetherington, 1988, 1989; Hetherington, *et al.*, 1982, 1985; Rodgers and Pryor, 1998). Boys, in particular, can become aggressive and difficult to manage both at home and at school. Various explanations have been given for the rise in children's emotional and behavioural difficulties at this time including reduced family income and the mother's distress which may reduce her ability to look after her children. But the single most important factor leading to problems for children appears to be hostility between the parents before, and around the time of, the divorce (Amato, 1993).

When intense marital conflict continues after the divorce it can have a more harmful effect than when it occurs in intact families (Hetherington, 1988, 1989). Wallerstein and Kelly (1980) also found that children with difficulties are those whose parents remain in conflict after the divorce, and concluded that whether or not children's problems diminish is a function of whether or not divorce improves parental relationships. The quality of children's relationships with their parents is also an important determinant of psychological adjustment. Children who have good post-divorce relationships with their parents are less likely to suffer negative effects (Hetherington, 1988; Hess and Camara, 1979). It is these factors that accompany single parenthood, rather than single parenthood itself, that appear to be largely responsible for the disadvantages experienced by children in one-parent homes.

The transition from a single mother family to a step-family can also be difficult for children. In their follow-up study of young children whose parents divorced, Vuchinich, *et al.*, (1991) found that after the early stages of remarriage, boys in step-families had fewer problems than boys in non-remarried families. If the step-father was supportive, they developed a good relationship with him. However, girls had more difficulties with family relations and adjustment than girls whose mothers had not remarried, and continued to reject their step-father however hard he tried to develop a positive relationship. A later study looked at the effects of moving into a step-family on children who were approaching adolescence at the time their mother remarried (Hetherington and Clingempeel, 1992). It was found that the behaviour of these older children was often disruptive and demanding, and their relationship with their step-father was characterised by hostility on the part of the child and, after many unsuccessful attempts to form a positive relationship, disengagement on the part of the step-father. Although it is more common for children to live with step-fathers than step-mothers, Pasley and Ihinger-Tallman (1987) concluded from their review of the area that children generally experience more difficulties in step-mother families.

One question that is often posed regarding single mother families is whether the negative consequences for children result from the absence of a father in particular or the absence of a second parent from the home. This is a difficult question to answer as the two coincide making it difficult to conclude whether it is one, or the other, or both that make the difference for the child. Factors such as parental conflict and financial hardship are clearly linked to the father but we cannot say whether it is the lack or loss of a parent in general, or of a male parent in particular, that is associated with the difficulties faced by children in single mother homes.

Studies of two-parent families show that fathers spend much less time with their children than mothers, but it seems that this matters less than what they do when they are with them. The more that fathers are actively involved in parenting, the better the outcome for children's social and emotional development, and fathers appear to be particularly valued by their children as playmates (Parke, 1996; Lamb, 1997). But it does not seem to be their maleness that matters. If their gender was important we would expect children without fathers, and children with highly involved fathers, to differ in terms of their masculinity and femininity from children in traditional two-parent families. There is no evidence that this is the case. Girls in such families are no less feminine, and boys no less masculine, in their identity and behaviour than children who grow up in more traditional homes, and children of highly involved fathers hold less conventional attitudes about male and female roles (Stevenson and Black, 1988; Radin, 1994). Instead, it seems that fathers have a positive effect on their children's development in the same way as mothers do. Fathers who are affectionate to their children, who are sensitive to their needs, and who respond appropriately to their emotions, are more likely than distant fathers to have well-adjusted children (Lamb, 1997). So it appears that it is their role as an additional parent, not as a male parent, that is beneficial to the child.

Single parenthood, parental divorce and father absence are not *directly* related to rearing in a lesbian family. The expectation that being raised in a lesbian family would, in itself, increase the likelihood of psychiatric disorder in children arises from the assumption that the children would be teased about their parent's sexual orientation and ostracised by their peers. The concern is that this situation would be deeply upsetting to children, and that it would have a negative effect on their ability to form and maintain friendships. There is wide agreement in the psychological literature that satisfactory relationships with peers are important for positive social and emotional development (Kupersmidt *et al.*, 1990; Dunn and McGuire, 1992).

It has also been suggested that lesbian women would not be effective parents. In order to address this question, it is first necessary to consider what aspects of parenting matter most for children's psychological adjustment. It is well established that children's social and emotional development is fostered within the context of parent-child relationships (Maccoby, 1992; Darling and Steinberg, 1993), and by far the most accepted and comprehensive explanation of the processes involved in the development of parent-child relationships comes from attachment theory put forward by Bowlby (Bowlby, 1969, 1973, 1980) and

Ainsworth (Ainsworth, 1972, 1982; Ainsworth *et al.*, 1978). According to this theory, interactions between the parent and the child form the basis of attachment relationships, and the type of attachment that an infant develops, i.e. secure or insecure, largely depends upon the quality of interaction between the parent and the child such that parents of securely attached infants are responsive and sensitive to their infant's needs (Ainsworth, 1979). Recent research provides empirical evidence in support of this view (Grossmann *et al.*, 1985; Smith and Pederson, 1988; Pederson *et al.*, 1990; Isabella and Belsky, 1991; Izard *et al.*, 1991). For example, it has been demonstrated that secure attachments in infancy are fostered by synchronous interactions in which mothers are responsive to their infant's vocalisations and distress signals (Isabella *et al.*, 1989).

Studies have traditionally focused on the development of attachment in infancy. However, in recent years attention has turned to the examination of attachment relationships in the pre-school and school-age years. As a result, interest has grown in representational aspects of attachment. Through their early experiences with attachment figures, children are believed to form internal representations of their attachment relationships (Bowlby, 1969, 1973, 1980). Bowlby refers to these internal representations as "internal working models". According to Bowlby, the child's internal working model of an attachment figure, for example as available and responsive in the case of securely attached children or as unavailable and unresponsive in the case of insecurely attached children, will influence the child's expectations of, and behaviour towards, that person. The child's internal working models of attachment relationships are also believed to influence the child's internal representation of the self. Thus a child who represents attachment figures as responsive and emotionally available is likely to hold an internal model of the self as loveable, whereas a child with internal models of attachment figures as unresponsive and unavailable is likely to represent the self as unworthy of being loved. The child's internal representations of attachment figures and of the self are believed to have a profound influence on the individual's relationships with others in childhood and in adult life. There is growing empirical evidence in support of Bowlby's view that individuals form internal models of their attachment relationships (for example, Main *et al.*, 1985; Bretherton and Waters, 1985). It has also been demonstrated that a connection exists between working models of attachment figures and the working model of the self (Cassidy, 1988).

Aspects of parent-child relationships other than security of attachment have also been shown to shape children's development, the most widely studied of which is parental style (Baumrind, 1989). Baumrind has demonstrated that an authoritative style of parenting i.e. a combination of warmth and discipline (as opposed to an extremely authoritarian or an extremely free-and-easy parenting style) has the most positive outcomes for children's psychological development, with children of authoritative parents the most likely to be self-reliant, socially responsible and co-operative. It is important to remember, however, that parental style may, to some extent at least, be a product of the child's personality. After all, it is a much easier undertaking to adopt an authoritative style with a co-operative child than with a child who tends to be aggressive or defiant. In addition, factors other than parental style such as shared feelings and connectedness of communication are thought to be important aspects of children's relationships with their parents (Dunn, 1993).

It is not just the quality of parents' relationships with their children but also the quality of their relationship with each other that influences children's psychological well-being. Recent research has pointed to a link between marital conflict and the development of psychological problems in children, most commonly the development of antisocial behaviour and conduct problems particularly among boys (Emery, 1988; Cummings and Davies, 1994; Grych and Fincham, 1990). Although the mechanisms through which parental conflict results in psychological difficulties for children are not fully understood, there are thought to be both direct effects resulting from the child's repeated exposure to hostility between the parents (Cummings and Cummings, 1988; Harold and Conger, 1997) and indirect effects resulting from the poorer quality of parenting of mothers and fathers who are locked in conflict with each other (Fauber and Long, 1991).

An association also exists between parents' psychological well-being and the psychological well-being of their children such that children whose parents have psychological problems are more at risk for psychological problems themselves. For example, there is growing evidence that a mother's depression produces an increased risk of difficulties for her child with recent research pointing to a link between post-natal depression, the mother's lack of responsiveness to her infant, and the infant's insecure attachment to the mother (Murray, 1992).

From the above discussion it appears that several aspects of parenting are related to children's psychological well-being; sensitive responding, emotional availability, and a combination of warmth and control are associated with positive outcomes whereas marital conflict and parental psychiatric disorder can have a negative effect. Although it is impossible to predict just which children will experience difficulties, not least because some children show remarkable resilience in the face of multiple adversities (Rutter, 1985; Zimmerman and Arunkumar, 1994), there is substantial empirical evidence that these factors play a part in influencing the course of children's social, emotional and identity development. In considering the psychological development of children in lesbian mother families we should therefore examine whether these families deviate from the traditional family unit in ways that are likely to have a negative impact upon the aspects of parenting that matter most for children's psychological well-being. In so far as such parents do not differ with respect to quality of parenting, difficulties would not necessarily be expected for the child.

3. STUDIES OF LESBIAN MOTHER FAMILIES

The early investigations of lesbian mother families adopted a similar design in that they compared children in lesbian mother families with children raised in families headed by a single heterosexual mother (for reviews see Falk, 1989; Patterson, 1992). The rationale for the choice of single heterosexual mothers as a comparison group was that the two types of family were alike in that the children were being raised by women without the presence of a father, but differed in the sexual orientation of the mother. This allowed the effects of the mothers' sexual orientation on children's development to be examined without the confound of the presence of a father in the family home. As most of the children in these investigations had been born into a heterosexual marriage, the sons and daughters from the two types of family also shared the experience of parental separation or divorce.

Our United Kingdom study focused on the two areas of child development that had been the focus of concern in child custody cases; children's gender development and their psychological well-being (Golombok *et al.*, 1983). Data were obtained through in-depth standardised interviews with the mothers and their children, and the mothers and the children's teachers also completed standardised questionnaires. We found that all of the boys and girls in the two family types had a secure gender identity as male or female respectively. There was no evidence of gender identity confusion for any of the children studied, i.e. none of the children wished to be the other sex, or consistently engaged in cross-gender behaviour. In terms of gender role, no differences were found between children in lesbian and heterosexual families, for either boys or girls, in the extent to which they showed behaviour that was typical of their sex. Daughters of lesbian mothers were no less feminine, and the sons no less masculine, than the daughters and sons of heterosexual mothers.

With respect to the children's psychological well-being, children in lesbian families were no more likely to experience psychological disorder than children of single heterosexual mothers as assessed by a child psychiatrist who was unaware of the type of family to which the child belonged. Teacher's ratings of the children's emotional and behavioural problems at school also failed to differentiate children from the two family types, a finding which provided important validation for the mothers' reports. In addition, the children from the two family types did not differ with respect to the quality of their friendships, and children of lesbian mothers were no more likely than children of heterosexual mothers to be teased or bullied by peers. So from this study of children with an average age of ten to eleven years, it seemed that growing up in a lesbian family did not have an adverse effect on their social, emotional or gender development, compared with growing up with a single heterosexual mothers. Similar findings have been reported by other researchers who have studied samples with diverse geographic and demographic characteristics (Kirkpatrick *et al.*, 1981; Green *et al.,* 1986; Hoeffer, 1981; Huggins, 1989). Regarding the parenting ability of the mothers themselves, it has also been demonstrated that lesbian mothers are just as child-oriented (Pagelow, 1980; Miller *et al.,*1981; Kirkpatrick, 1987), just as warm and responsive to their children (Golombok *et al.,* 1983) and just as nurturant and confident (Mucklow and Phelan, 1979) as heterosexual mothers.

A difficulty with these investigations was that only school-age children were studied, and it has been argued that "sleeper effects" may exist such that children raised in lesbian households may experience difficulties in emotional wellbeing and in intimate relationships when they grow up. It has also been suggested that children from lesbian homes will be more likely than those from heterosexual backgrounds to adopt a lesbian or gay sexual orientation in adulthood, an outcome that is often considered undesirable by courts of law.

In order to address these questions, we followed up the children first seen in 1976/77 by Golombok *et al.* (1983) fourteen years later when their average age was 23.5 years (Tasker and Golombok, 1995; Golombok and Tasker, 1996; Tasker and Golombok, 1997). We were able to contact twenty-five young adults from lesbian families and twenty-one young adults from single heterosexual families, representing 62 per cent of the original sample. The follow-up participants did not differ from the non-participants with respect to age, sex or social class. Although the sample size was small, the advantage of the study was that the majority of children were recruited to the investigation before they reached adolescence, and so the results were not confounded by the knowledge of their sexual orientation in adult life. Each young adult took part in a standardised interview designed to assess four key areas of their lives: (i) family relationships, (ii) peer relationships, (iii) psychological adjustment, and (iv) sexual orientation. By the time of the follow-up, all but one of the original group of single heterosexual mothers had at least one new male partner who lived in the household. Similarly, all but one of the lesbian mothers had a female partner who lived in the family home. Therefore, the young adults from both types of family could report on their experience of step-family relationships. In terms of the quality of their current relationship with both their mother and their father, young adults from lesbian backgrounds did not differ from their counterparts from heterosexual homes.

However, young adults who had been brought up in a lesbian household described their relationship with their mother's partner significantly more positively than those who had been raised by a heterosexual mother and her new male partner. This difference was found both for their recollections of their relationship with their mother's partner during adolescence, and for their current feelings toward their mother's partner. So it seems that children from lesbian homes had been able to forge closer relationships with their mother's new female partner than had children from heterosexual households with their mother's new male partner. Detailed examination of the interview data suggested that children from lesbian households could more easily accept a stepparent in their family than could children from heterosexual households because she was not necessarily seen as a direct competitor to their absent father. She was more likely to be viewed as an additional parent than as a replacement parent.

With respect to peer relationships, data were obtained on the proportion of young adults in each group who reported having been teased or bullied during adolescence. Young adults from lesbian families were no more likely to report teasing by peers in general, than those from heterosexual single-parent homes. But with respect to teasing about their own sexuality, there was a tendency for those from lesbian families to be more likely to recall having been teased about being gay or lesbian themselves, although those from lesbian families may simply have been more sensitive to casual remarks from peers, and more likely to recollect incidents that had been quickly forgotten by their counterparts from heterosexual homes. Interestingly, those who were most negative about their experiences of growing up in a lesbian family, and who were most likely to have been teased by peers, tended to come from working class backgrounds and to live in a social environment that was generally hostile towards homosexuality (Tasker and Golombok, 1997). It seems, therefore, that the social context of the lesbian mother family is an important predictor of the experiences of the child.

The findings relating to psychological well-being show that children raised by lesbian mothers continue to function well in adulthood and do not experience long-term detrimental effects arising from their early upbringing. No differences between young adults from lesbian and heterosexual homes were found for anxiety level or depression as assessed by standard questionnaire measures, and their scores fell within the normal range. In addition, those from lesbian families were no more likely to have sought professional help for anxiety, depression or stress.

With respect to sexual orientation, three aspects were studied: (i) whether or not the person had experienced same-gender sexual attraction, (ii) whether or not the person had experienced same-gender sexual relationships, and (iii) sexual identity, i.e. whether the person identified themself as heterosexual, bisexual, lesbian or gay. In terms of sexual attraction, there was no statistically significant difference between adults raised in lesbian families and their peers from single-mother heterosexual households in the proportion who reported sexual attraction to someone of the same gender. Nine children of lesbian mothers (six daughters and three sons) and four children of heterosexual mothers (two daughters and two sons) reported same-gender attraction.

Regarding actual involvement in same-gender sexual relationships, there was a significant difference between groups such that young adults raised by lesbian mothers were more likely to have had a sexual relationship with someone of the same gender than young adults raised by heterosexual mothers. None of the children from heterosexual families had experienced a lesbian or gay relationship. In contrast, six children (one son and five daughters) from lesbian families had become involved in one or more sexual relationships with a partner of the same gender.

However, in terms of sexual identity, the large majority of young adults with lesbian mothers identified as heterosexual. Only two young women from lesbian families identified as lesbian compared with none from heterosexual families. This group difference did not reach statistical significance. So the commonly held assumption that lesbian mothers will have lesbian daughters and gay sons was not supported by the findings of the study. The large majority of children who grew up in lesbian families (92 per cent) identified as heterosexual in adulthood. It is, of course, possible that participants were reluctant to admit a same-gender sexual identity. However, such under-reporting seems more likely among men and women from heterosexual homes, since young adults from lesbian families appeared to be more comfortable in discussing gay and lesbian issues in general.

A limitation of these investigations of lesbian families is that the children were conceived within the context of a heterosexual relationship and spent their early life in a heterosexual family. To the extent that *early* family experiences are important determinants of later social, emotional and gender development, we cannot generalise from the conclusions of the studies discussed above to children raised by lesbian mothers from birth. It could be argued, for example, that any influence of lesbian mothering on gender development would occur before age three, as basic gender identity and gender role behaviour are established by this age.

However, a growing number of lesbian women are becoming parents after coming out as lesbian, and studies of children raised by lesbian mothers from birth are now beginning to be reported. These studies are of particular interest because they allow an investigation of the influence of the mothers' sexual orientation on children who are raised in lesbian families with no father present right from the start. While some women embark upon motherhood alone, many couples plan a family together and share the parenting role (Patterson, 1992). Pregnancy is sometimes achieved through heterosexual intercourse, but more commonly donor insemination is chosen as the method of conception. Some women prefer to attend a clinic in order to use semen from an anonymous donor. However, many donor insemination clinics refuse to accept lesbian women, even when they are allowed in law to do so, and a growing number of women are choosing self-insemination instead. Self-insemination is also the preferred method of conception for women who wish to conceive without the involvement of the medical profession. In this case, the donor may be a friend, a relative or an acquaintance of the biological mother or her partner, and may or may not remain in contact with the family as the child grows up (Saffron, 1994; Martin, 1993).

In our United Kingdom study (Golombok *et al.*, 1997), we compared thirty lesbian mother families with forty one, two-parent heterosexual families using standardised interview and questionnaire measures of the quality of parenting and the socio-emotional development of the child. Similarly, Brewaeys *et al.* (1997) studied thirty lesbian mother families in comparison with sixty-eight heterosexual two-parent families in Belgium. In the USA, Flaks *et al.* (1995) compared fifteen lesbian families with fifteen heterosexual families, and Chan *et al.* (1998) studied fifty-five families headed by lesbian and twenty-five families headed by heterosexual parents. Unlike the lesbian women of the earlier studies who had their children while married, all of the mothers in these new investigations planned their family after coming out.

Although the children investigated in the above studies are still quite young (most were in their early school years when the investigations were conducted), taking the findings together, the evidence so far suggests that they do not differ from their peers in two-parent heterosexual families in terms of gender development. It seems, therefore, that the presence of a father is not necessary for the development of sex-typed behaviour for either boys or girls, and that the mother's lesbian identity, in itself, does not have a direct effect on the gender role behaviour of her daughters or sons. The children were not cut off from men, however, and many had a close relationship with one or more of the mothers' male friends. In terms of socio-emotional development, the children appear to be functioning well; there is no evidence of raised levels of emotional or behavioural problems among children raised in a lesbian mother family from the outset. It is possibly of relevance that, unlike the majority of children in studies of father absence, almost all of those in the present investigation lived in an intact two-parent family with a good relationship between the parents, and had not experienced family disruption as a result of parental separation or divorce. The most significant finding to emerge so far from the studies of planned lesbian families is that co-mothers in two-parent lesbian families are more involved with their children than are fathers in two-parent heterosexual families.

Recent research on lesbian mother families has moved away from the investigation of the effects on children to studies of how such families function, particularly with respect to the division of labour both inside and outside the home. In the USA (Patterson, 1995; Chan *et al.* (1998) and the United Kingdom (Dunne, 1997) it has been shown that lesbian mother families are characterised by a relatively equal division of paid employment, unpaid household tasks and child-care activities. Chan *et al.* (1998) also examined the effects of parental division of labour on the psychological well-being of the child. Parental satisfaction with the arrangements, rather than actual levels of labour, was found to be associated with better adjustment among children in lesbian mother homes.

4. CONCLUSION

Studying lesbian mother families allows us to address theoretical questions about the relative importance for children's psychological adjustment of family structure on one hand, and the quality of family relationships on the other, as well as interactions between them. Comparisons between children in lesbian and heterosexual families also address questions such as the importance for children of having a parent of each sex, or of simply having two parents irrespective of their sex. What the findings appear to suggest is that whether their mother is lesbian or heterosexual may matter less for children's psychological adjustment than warm and supportive relationships with their parents and a harmonious family environment. There are also important practical implications of this research with respect to informing courts of law and social policy-makers concerned with issues such as adoption, fostering and access to assisted reproduction about what actually happens to children raised in lesbian mother homes.

REFERENCES

Ainsworth, M., "Attachment and dependency: a comparison" in J. L. Gewirtz (ed.), *Attachment and Dependency* (Washington, DC, Winston, 1972).

Ainsworth, M., "Attachment as related to mother-infant interaction" in J. Rosenblatt, R. Hinde, C. Beer *et al.* (eds.), *Advances in the Study of Behavior* (Orlando, FL Academic Press, 1979).

Ainsworth, M., "Attachment: retrospect and prospect" in C. M. Parkes and J. Stevenson Hinde (eds.), *The Place of Attachment in Human Behavior* (New York, Basic Books, 1982).

Ainsworth, M., Bleher, M., Waters, E. *et al.*, *Patterns of Attachment: A Psychological Study of The Strange Situation* (Hillsdale, NJ, Erlbaum, 1978).

Amato, P., "Children's adjustment to divorce: Theories, hypotheses, and empirical support" (1993) 55 *Journal of Marriage and the Family* 23–38.

Amato, P. R. and Keith, B., "Parental divorce and the well-being of children: A meta-analysis" (1991) 110 *Psychological Bulletin* 26–46.

Bandura, A., *Social Learning Theory* (Englewood Cliffs, NJ, Prentice Hall, 1977).

Bandura, A., *Social Foundations of Thought and Action: A Social Cognitive Theory* (Englewood Cliffs, NJ, Prentice Hall, 1986).

Baumrind, D., "Rearing competent children" in W. Damon (ed.), *Child Development Today and Tomorrow* (San Fransisco, Jossey-Bass, 1989).

Bowlby, J., *Attachment and Loss. Volume 1. Attachment* (London, Hogarth Press, 1969).

Bowlby, J., *Attachment and Loss. Volume 2. Separation* (London: Hogarth Press, 1973).

Bowlby, J., *Attachment and Loss. Volume 3. Loss* (London, Hogarth Press, 1980).

Bretherton, I. and Waters, E. (eds.), *Growing Points of Attachment Theory and Research. Monographs of the Society for Research in Child Development, Volume 50* (1985).

Brewaeys, A., Ponjaert, I., van Hall, E. *et al.*, "Donor insemination: child development and family functioning in lesbian mother families" (1997) 12(6) *Human Reproduction* 1349–1359.

Bussey, K., and Bandura, A., "Influence of gender constancy and social power on sex-linked modeling" (1984) 47 *Journal of Personality and Social Psychology* 1292–1302.

Barlow, A., Bowley, M., Butler, G., *et al.*, *Family Matters. Advising Gay and Lesbian Clients: A Guide for Lawyers* (London, Butterworths, 1999).

Cassidy, J., "Child-mother attachment and the self in six-year-olds" (1988) 59 *Child Development* 121–134.

Chan, R. W., Brooks, R. C., Raboy, B. *et al.*, "Division of labor among lesbian and heterosexual parents: Associations with children's adjustment" (1998) 12 *Journal of Family Psychology* 402–419.

Chan, R. W., Raboy, B. and Patterson, C. J., "Psychosocial adjustment among children conceived via donor insemination by lesbian and heterosexual mothers" (1988) 69(2) *Child Development* 443–457.

Chodorow, N., *The Reproduction of Mothering: Psychoanalysis and the Sociology of Gender* (Berkeley, University of California Press, 1978).

Cummings, E. M. and Cummings, J. L., "A process-orientated approach to children's coping with adults' angry behavior" (1988) 8 *Developmental Review* 296–321.

Cummings, E. M. and Davies, P., *Children and Marital Conflict* (New York, Guilford, 1994).

Darling, N. and Steinberg, L., "Parenting style as context: An integrative model" (1993) 118 *Psychological Bulletin* 487–496.

Dinnerstein, D., *The Mermaid and the Minotaur: Sexual Arrangements and Human Malaise* (New York, Harper & Row, 1976).

Dunn, J., *Young Children's Close Relationships: Beyond Attachment* (Newbury Park, CA, Sage, 1993).

Dunn, J. and McGuire, S., "Sibling and peer relationships in childhood" (1991) 33(1) *Journal of Child Psychology & Psychiatry* 67–105.

Dunne, G. A., *Lesbian Lifestyles: Women's Work and the Politics of Sexuality* (London, MacMillan, 1997).

Editors of the Harvard Law Review, *Sexual Orientation and the Law* (Cambridge, Ma, Harvard University Press, 1990).

Emery, R. E., *Marriage, Adjustment and Children's Adjustment* (Newbury Park, CA, Sage, 1988).

Falk, P. J., "Lesbian mothers: Psychosocial assumptions in family law" (1989) 44 *American Psychologist* 941–947.

Fauber, R. L. and Long, N., "Children in context: The role of the family in child psychotherapy" (1991) 59 *Journal of Consulting and Clinical Psychology* 813–820.

Ferri, E., *Growing Up in a One Parent Family* (Slough, NFER, 1976).

Flaks, D. K., Ficher, I., Masterpasqua, F. *et al.*, "Lesbians choosing motherhood: A comparative study of lesbian and heterosexual parents and their children" (1995) 31 *Developmental Psychology* 105–114.

Freud, S., *Three Essays on the Theory of Sexuality, Volume 7* (London, Hogarth Press, 1905/1953).

Freud, S., *Beyond the Pleasure Principle, Volume 18* (London, Hogarth Press, 1920/1955).

Freud, S., *Psychology of Women: New Introductory Lectures on Psychoanalysis* (London, Hogarth Press, 1933).

Gagnon, J. H., *Human Sexuality* (Glenview, IL, Scott, Foresman, 1977).

Gagnon, J. H., "Gender preference in erotic relations: The Kinsey scale and sexual scripts" in D. P. McWhirter, S. A. Sanders and J. M. Reinisch (eds.), *Homosexuality/Heterosexuality: Concepts of Sexual Orientation* (Oxford, Oxford University Press, 1990).

Golombok, S., Spencer, A. and Rutter, M., "Children in lesbian and single-parent households: Psychosexual and psychiatric appraisal" (1983) 24 *Journal of Child Psychology & Psychiatry* 551–572.

Golombok, S. and Tasker, F., "Do parents influence the sexual orientation of their children? Findings from a longitudinal study of lesbian families" (1996) 32(1) *Developmental Psychology* 3–11.

Golombok, S., Tasker, F., Murray C., "Children raised in fatherless families from infancy: Family relationships and the socioemotional development of children of lesbian and single heterosexual mothers" (1997) 38(7) *Journal of Child Psychology and Psychiatry* 783–792.

Green, R., *Sexual Science and the Law* (Cambridge, MA, Harvard University Press, 1992).

Green, R., Mandel, J. B., Hotvedt, M. E. *et al.*, "Lesbian mothers and their children: A comparison with solo parent heterosexual mothers and their children" (1986) 15 *Archives of Sexual Behavior* 167–184.

Grossmann, K. E., Grossmann, K., Spangler, G. *et al.*, "Maternal sensitivity in northern Germany" in I. B E. Waters (ed.), *Growing Points of Attachment Theory and Research. Monographs of the Society for Research in Child Development, Volume 50* (1985).

Grych, J. H. and Fincham, F. D., "Marital conflict and children's adjustment: A cognitive contextual framework" (1990) 108 *Psychological Bulletin* 267–290.

Harold, G. T. and Conger, R. D., "Marital conflict and adolescent distress: The role of adolescent awareness" (1997) 68(2) *Child Development* 333–350.

Hess, R. D. and Camara, K. A., "Post-divorce relationships as mediating factors in the consequences of divorce for children" (1979) 35 *Journal of Social Issues* 79–96.

Hetherington, E. M., "Parents, children and siblings six years after divorce" in R. H. J. Stevenson-Hinde (ed.), *Relationships Within Families* (Cambridge, Cambridge University Press, 1988).

Hetherington, E. M., "Coping with family transitions: Winners, losers, and survivors" (1989) 60 *Child Development* 1–14.

Hetherington, E. M. and Clingempeel, W. G., *Coping with marital transitions. Monographs of the Society for Research in Child Development, Volume 57* (1992).

Hetherington, E. M., Cox, M. and Cox, R., "Effects of divorce on parents and children" in M. E. Lamb (ed.), *Nontraditional Families: Parenting and Child Development* (Hillsdale, NJ, Erlbaum,1982).

Hetherington, E. M., Cox, M. and Cox, R., "Long-term effects of divorce and remarriage on the adjustment of children" (1985) 24 *Journal of the American Academy of Psychology* 518–530.

Hoeffer, B., "Children's acquisition of sex-role behavior in lesbian mother families" (1981) 51 *American Journal of Orthopsychiatry* 536–544.

Huggins, S. L., "A comparative study of self-esteem of adolescent children of divorced lesbian mothers and divorced heterosexual mothers" in F. Bozett (ed.), *Homosexuality and the Family* (New York, Harrington Park Press, 1989).

Isabella, R. A. and Belsky, J., "Interactional synchrony and the origins of infant-mother attachment: A replication study" (1991) 62 *Child Development* 373–384.

Isabella, R. A., Belsky, J. and von Eye, A., "The origins of infant-mother attachment: An examination of interactional synchrony during the infant's first year" (1989) 25 *Developmental Psychology* 12–21.

Izard, C. E., Heynes, O. M., Chisholm, G. *et al.*, "Emotional determinants of infant-mother attachment" (1991) 62 *Child Development* 906–917.

Kirkpatrick, M., "Clinical implications of lesbian mother studies" (1987) 13 *Journal of Homosexuality* 201–211.

Kirkpatrick, M., Smith, C. and Roy, R., "Lesbian mothers and their children: A comparative survey" (1981) 51 *American Journal of Orthopsychiatry* 545–551.

Kitzinger, C., *The Social Construction of Lesbianism* (London, Sage, 1987).

Kleber, D. J., Howell, R. J. and Tibbits-Kleber, A. L., "The impact of parental homosexuality in child custody cases: A review of the literature" (1986) 14(1) *Bulletin of the American Academy of Psychiatry & Law* 81–87.

Kohlberg, L., "A cognitive-developmental analysis of children's sex-role concepts and attitudes" in E. E. Maccoby (ed.), *The Development of Sex Differences* (Stanford, CA, Stanford University Press, 1966).

Kupersmidt, J. B., Coie, J. D. and Dodge, K. A., "The role of poor peer relationships in the development of disorder" in S. R. Asher and J. D. Coie (eds.), *Peer Rejection in Childhood* (Cambridge: Cambridge University Press, 1990).

Lamb, M. (ed.), *The Role of the Father in Child Development*, 3rd edn. (New York, John Wiley & Sons, 1997).

Liben, L. S. and Signorella, M. L., "Gender-related schemata and constructive memory in children" (1980) 51 *Child Development* 111–118.

Lytton, H. and Romney, D. M., "Parents' differential socialization of boys and girls: A meta-analysis" (1991) 109 *Psychological Bulletin* 267–296.

Maccoby, E. E., "Gender as a social category" (1988) 24 *Developmental Psychology* 755–765.

Macccoby, E. E., "The role of parents in the socialization of children" (1992) 28 *Developmental Psychology* 1006–1017.

Maccoby, E. E. and Jacklin, C. N., *The Psychology of Sex Differences* (Stanford, CA, Stanford University Press, 1974).

Main, M., Kaplan, N. and Cassidy, J., "Security in infancy, childhood, and adulthood: A move to the level of representation" in I. W. Bretherton and E. Waters (eds.), *Growing Points in Attachment Theory and Research,Volume 50* (1985), 209 (1–2), pp. 66–104.

Martin, A., *The Lesbian and Gay Parenting Handbook* (New York, Harper Collins, 1993).

Martin, C. L., "Children's use of gender-related information in making social judgements" (1989) 25 *Developmental Psychology* 80–88.

Martin, C. L., "The role of cognition in understanding gender effects" in H. Reese (ed.), *Advances in Child Development and Behavior, Volume 23* (New York, Academic Press, 1991), pp. 113–164.

Martin, C. L. and Halverson, C., "A schematic processing model of sex typing and stereotyping in children" (1981) 52 *Child Development* 1119–1134.

Martin, C. L. and Halverson, C., "Gender constancy: A methodological and theoretical analysis" (1983) 9 *Sex Roles* 775–790.

Martin, C. L., Wood, C. H. and Little, J. K., "The development of gender stereotype components" (1990) 61 *Child Development* 1891–1904.

McLanahan, S. S. and Sandefur, *Growing Up With A Single Parent: What Hurts, What Helps* (Cambridge, Ma, Harvard University Press, 1994).

Miller, J. A., Jacobsen, R. B. and Bigner, J. J., "The child's home environment for lesbian vs. heterosexual mothers: A neglected area of research" (1981) 7 *Journal of Homosexuality* 49–56.

Mischel, W., "A social learning view of sex differences in behavior" in E. E. Maccoby (ed.), *The Development of Sex Differences* (Stanford, Ca, Stanford University Press, 1966).

Mischel, W., "Sex-typing and socialization" in P. Mussen (ed.), *Carmichael's Manual of Child Psychology* (New York, Wiley, 1970).

Mucklow, B. M. and Phelan, G. K., "Lesbian and traditional mothers' responses to child behavior and self-concept" (1979) 44 *Psychological Reports* 880–882.

Murray, L., "The impact of post-natal depression on mother-infant relations and infant development" (1992) 33 *Journal of Child Psychology & Psychiatry* 543–561.

Pagelow, M. D., "Heterosexual and lesbian single mothers: A comparison of problems, coping and solutions" (1980) 5 *Journal of Homosexuality* 198–204.

Parke, R. D., *Fatherhood* (Cambridge, Ma, Harvard University Press, 1996).

Pasley, K. and Ihinger-Tallman, M., "The evolution of a field of investigation: Issues and concerns" in K. Pasley and M. Ihinger-Tallman (eds.), *Remarriage and Stepparenting: Current Research and Theory* (New York, Guilford Press, 1987).

Patterson, C. J., "Children of Lesbian and Gay Parents" (1992) 63 *Child Development* 1025–1042.

Patterson, C. J., " Families of the lesbian baby boom: Parents' division of labor and children's adjustment" (1995) 31 *Developmental Psychology* 115–123.

Pederson, D. R., Moran, G., Sitko, C. *et al.*, "Maternal sensitivity and the security of infant-mother attachment: A Q-sort study" (1990) 61 *Child Development* 1974–1983.

Perry, D. G. and Bussey, K., "The social learning theory of sex difference: Imitation is alive and well" (1979) 37 *Journal of Personality & Social Psychology* 1699–1712.

Plummer, K., *Sexual Stigma: An Interactionist Account* (London, Routledge, 1975).

Radin, N., "Primary caregiving fathers in intact families" in A. E. Gottfried and A. W. Gottfried (eds.), *Redefining Families* (New York, Plenum, 1994).

Rodgers, B. and Pryor, J., *Divorce and Separation. The Outcome for Children* (York, Joseph Rowntree Foundation, 1998).

Rutter, M., "Resilience in the face of adversity: Protective factors and resistance to psychiatric disorder" (1985) 147 *British Journal of Psychiatry* 596–611.

Saffron, L., *Challenging Conceptions* (London, Cassell, 1994).

Signorella, M. L., Bigler, R. S. and Liben, L. S., " Developmental differences in children's gender schemata about others: A meta-analytic review" (1993) 13 *Developmental Review* 106–126.

Signorella, M. L. and Liben, L. S., "Recall and reconstruction of gender-related pictures: Effects of attitude, task difficulty and age" (1984) 55 *Child Development* 393–405.

Simon, W. and Gagnon, J. H., "A sexual scripts approach" in J. H. Geer and W. T. O'Donoghue (eds.), *Theories of Human Sexuality* (London, Plenum Press, 1987).

Smith, P. B. and Pederson, D. R., "Maternal sensitivity and patterns of infant-mother attachment" (1988) 59 *Child Development* 1097–1101.

Socarides, C. W., *Homosexuality* (New York, Jason Aronson, 1978).

Stagnor, C. and Ruble, D. M., "Development of gender role knowledge and gender constancy" in L. S. Libent and M. L. Signorella (eds.), *Children's Gender Schemata: New Direction for Child Development* (San Francisco, Jossey-Bass, 1987).

Stern, M. and Karraker, K. H., "Sex stereotyping of infants: A review of gender labelling studies" (1989) 20 *Sex Roles* 501–522.

Stevenson, M. R. and Black, K. N., "Parental absence and sex role development: A meta-analysis" (1988) 59 *Child Development* 793–814.

Tasker, F. and Golombok, S., "Adults raised as children in lesbian families" (1995) 65(2) *American Journal of Orthopsychiatry* 203–215.

Tasker, F. and Golombok, S., *Growing Up in a Lesbian Family* (New York, Guilford Press, 1997).

Tiefer, L., "Social Constructionism and the Study of Human Sexuality", in Shaver, P., and Hendrick, C., (eds) *Review of Personality and Social Psychology, 7, Sex and Gender* (London, Sage, 1987).

Vuchinich, S., Hetherington, E. M., Vuchinich, R. *et al.*, "Parent-child interaction and gender differences in early adolescents' adaptation to stepfamilies" (1991) 27(4) *Developmental Psychology* 618–626.

Wallerstein, J. S. and Kelly, J. B.. *Surviving the Breakup: How Children and Parents Cope With Divorce* (New York, Basic Books, 1980).

Zimmerman, M. A. and Arunkumar, M. A., "Resiliency research: Implications for schools and policy", *Social Policy Report: Society for Research in Child Development, Volume 8* (1994), pp. 1–17).

10

Parents : A Children's Perspective

ALLISON JAMES*

1. INTRODUCTION

Teacher: "Who's still at home?"
Carla: "Jeannie."
Teacher: "How old's she?"
Carla: "Three."
Teacher: "What will your mum do when she's off to school?"
Carla: "Go out I suppose. . . Go out and get rid of us. That's what she says she's gonna do. And she's not going to come back and she's going to leave my dad, do all the work and he's got to go up and down to school. And she said and if she does come back she's going to come back on one condition, my dad's got to buy her a new car."
(Steedman 1982, p.23)

In her conclusion to "The Tidy House"—a book which relates the writing of a play by three working-class eight-year-old girls—Steedman argues that what the play provides is a valuable insight into children's knowledge of the workings of family life, of parent and sibling relationships and of the little girls' vision of their future lives as adult women. Its particular value lies in the fact that:

> "A few working-class women over the last century have described, how in childhood, they *worked it out*, saw the hollowness of social and sexual expectation and achieved, momentarily, a radical revision of circumstances. But adult, then, they could not describe *how* this came about. 'The Tidy House' is a small piece of evidence, an example of how, taking the circumstances of their own life and the materials to hand, people can, without the benefit of theory or the expectations of others, critically confront the way things are and dimly imagine, out of those very circumstances, the way they might be."
> (Steedman 1982, p. 157)

It is precisely this paucity of knowledge about what children know or think about family life in general, and about parents in particular, that this chapter addresses. Despite the wealth of sociological and anthropological literature on child-rearing practices and systems of socialisation, and despite the abundance

* Thanks to Adrian James, Pia Christensen and Jenny Hockey for their comments and advice on earlier drafts of this chapter.

of work within developmental psychology accounting for the role of parents in children's social, emotional and cognitive development, in fact we know relatively little about how "parenting" is actually experienced by children themselves or what children think about parents. As Hill and Tisdall (1997, p. 74) observe, "systematic accounts of children's own views are rare" when compared with the array of studies which portray parenting from the adult viewpoint.

The task of this chapter is thus twofold: first to explore why it is that we know so little about what children think about parents; secondly, to examine the little that we *do* know in order to begin to document a "children's perspective" on parents and parenting. In undertaking these twin tasks, this chapter therefore takes up Brannen and O'Brien's (1996) point that family research needs to refocus itself on *children in families* rather than on *families with children*, a distinction which addresses the imbalance noted by Qvortrup (1996), namely that the study of parents and parenting has become synonymous with the study of the family. This conceptual equation, embedded in any number of conventional policy-led, welfarist initiatives—"it is the task of the family to care for its children"—has had, Qvortrup notes, the rather strange effect of separating "children from families, despite their contrary intent, *expresses verbis*, to be more concerned with children" (1996, p., xii).[1] This is a point well made and echoed, for example, in Day-Sclater's (1998) account of children and divorce in England. Despite the promise of the Children Act 1989, the legal framework still often fails to provide many children with an arena within which their own interests in and views about their parents' divorce can be effectively articulated, particularly in relation to private, as opposed to public law proceedings.[2]

Such examples serve, therefore, to underline the suggestion made above that the Western cultural concept of "parenting", made visible in social policy and family law, is essentially adult-centric and welfarist—that is, it is broadly conceived as something primarily done to children, a view which takes little, if any, account of children's own subjectivity; and that from within this model of "parenting", children are regarded as being fundamentally vulnerable, dependent and in need of protection.

As this chapter explores, that such a model of parenting also pervades the sociological literature helps explain why its rendering of the relationships *children* have with their parents, rather than those that parents have with their children, is both patchy and selective. For the most part, as we shall see, a children's perspective on parenting is represented by accounts of family life in the "exceptional", rather than "ordinary", circumstance of divorce, serious illness or family breakdown. Two explanations for this can be offered. First, if as suggested, "parenting" is conventionally viewed as largely the concern of adults, rather

---

[1] This chapter is concerned with the models of parents and parenting which are central to Western nuclear family structures and which receive ideological backing via family law and welfare policy.

[2] My thanks to Adrian James for pointing out the differential effectiveness of the Children Act for children involved in divorce with respect to these different domains.

than children, then only when this is under threat—through marital break-down, child illness or death—might it seem pertinent for adult researchers to explore the nature of the relationship which children have with their parents. Secondly, by definition, a welfarist and adult-centric model of parenting in itself excludes the significance of children's views. Within such a model children can only be envisaged as the passive recipients or "outcomes" of the process of parenting. Thus, only with the recent and radical recognition from within the new social studies of childhood that children might have their own perspectives on the social world (James and Prout, 1990; James, Jenks and Prout, 1998) has it become possible to envisage parenting as being as much a *child-parent*, as a parent-child, relationship (see for example, Morrow 1998; Neale *et al.*, 1998) through the growing realisation that children do have their own views on family life in general and on the role of parents in particular.

It is, however, towards an explanation of the relative dearth of children's views of parents and parenting that this chapter first turns through a consideration of what, ironically, might be called "the absent parent" in studies of childhood.

2. THE "ABSENT" PARENT

In his discussion of sociology's theoretical engagement with the body, Shilling (1993) argues that it has been an "absent presence"—something assumed and naturalised, rather than held up for inspection. This is, I suggest, a useful analogy for explaining why it is that children's perspectives on parents are, with a few recent exceptions, notably Morrow (1998), largely absent from the sociological literature, save for those of children living in "exceptional" circumstances (see below). Quite simply, for those conducting research with children and seeking to understand children's social worlds, parents are naturalised and taken-for-granted.

Thus, within the new social studies of childhood (James *et al.*, 1998) in circumstances where there is no family breakdown or family pathology to remark, researchers have tended to regard both parents and "the family" as simply part of the backdrop against which children's social lives—the main focus of such studies—are seen to unfold. For example, the now burgeoning literature on children's friendships and social relations—their play and leisure, their participation in schooling and so on—has, in large part, taken as an unacknowledged standpoint that, although children obviously do have parents, the child-parent relationship is of only minimal significance for an understanding of the child's social world or children's relationship with their peers. In such studies of peer group culture or children's social worlds (see for example, James (1993), Corsaro (1985), Pollard (1985) Thorne (1993)) rarely is any mention made of the relationships children have with their parents or of their familial lives at home and little, if any, information seems to have been volunteered by the children themselves about their family backgrounds.

This is a somewhat curious omission, for children's families (as noted, represented usually by parents) *are* in policy terms regarded as one of the key social indicators of what kind of people children are or are likely to become.[3] As Qvortrup (1997) notes:

> "when we find children described it is practically always done with reference to their parents' situation. Children are ordered in accordance with parents' income, with (mostly) father's occupation, with the education of *parents* and so on. The socio-occupational background of children, as we may call it in a generalised way, is in fact a description of their *parents'* status" (1997, p. 90).

Such correlations are both widespread and commonly drawn as I have discussed elsewhere (James, 1998) when describing the pre-school entry visits made by primary school teachers to children's homes. The teachers carefully observed and remarked upon not only the parents' actions during their visit, and those of mothers in particular, but also the material circumstances of the domestic environment, and used these observations to make an initial evaluation of the kind of child who was about to enter their care at school. That Donna's mother was "very pushy" while Sally's mother "still wants to keep her a baby", that Maxine's home was "chaotic, with her running about and her mother saying nothing" signalled, to the teachers, that Donna, Sally and Maxine might present them with particular problems when they started school. It would seem, then, that the child-parent relationship must be regarded as a critical and constitutive part of the understanding offered of children's own social relationships for, at the very least, it provides the "social context" which colours the perceptions and actions of those, such as teachers or social workers, who have the power to shape the everyday lives of children.

However, it remains rare to find much account given of it in the new child-focused studies. In part this can be explained by the context within which the research has been largely conducted. Many contemporary studies of childhood take place as the study of peer relations in schools, so that "parents and the family", if mentioned at all, are the taken-for-granted contextual descriptors of children's lives. With a few exceptions, to be discussed below, studies of childhood are rarely conducted in the more private domestic world of the family. Somewhat ironically, therefore, this new exclusion of *parents* from childhood studies mirrors the somewhat longer exclusion of children from studies of the family (James and Prout, 1996) where, traditionally, children's interests were assumed to be congruent with those of the family represented, in turn, as being the interests of their parents.

---

[3] Journals such as *Children and Society* make this link explicit. Many articles centre on the parent-child relation as a decisive factor in children's social lives.

3. PARENTING UNDER THREAT: REVEALING A CHILDREN'S PERSPECTIVE

As noted, the sociological literature which does deal explicitly with children's views on parents is a literature which has been, with a very few exceptions to be discussed below, concerned with those children for whom parenting is in some way under threat. Thus, two classic studies which offer clear accounts of children's views about their parents and of their experience of being parented are Mitchell's (1984) study of children's experiences of divorce and Bluebond-Langner's (1978) account of dying children.[4] Though clearly the experiences of these children and parents relate to very different life circumstances, that both studies do offer us rare and almost unique accounts of children's views of being parented is not without significance: for both these groups of children the potential rupture and recasting of the parenting relationship means that it can no longer be taken for granted, albeit for rather different reasons and in rather different ways.

More recently, Neale *et al.* (1998) provide us with further evidence that children involved in divorce have much to say about the parenting process which is invaluable for our understanding of family life during separation and divorce. However, that such work continues the tradition serves to confirm Mitchell's earlier suspicion that children's opinions about parenting may usually only be solicited by adults when, through disruption or dysfunction, that relationship itself becomes visible and explicit. The "black box" of familial relations is broken open, with the result that "only those children who come to the notice of professionals have their feelings recorded" (Mitchell, 1984). Until the recent shift in emphasis in the Children Act 1989, children were regarded in law as objects over which parents had rights, rather than responsibilities. Arguably, then, it was only when those *parental* rights were seen to be under threat that children were made visible in the parenting relationship and their subjectivity addressed by welfare practitioners and researchers.

The explicit articulation of a children's perspective on parenting has largely been prompted, therefore, by a concern to explore the potential rupture of the parenting relationship through divorce and/or separation, a situation comparable, in many ways, with the threat to parenting which a child with a serious illness is understood to represent (Bluebond-Langner, 1978). It is clear, for example, that for very sick children and for those involved in the divorce of their parents the experience of "being parented" involves, in part, the daily iteration of the concept of childhood itself.[5] The research accounts reveal that, in their

---

[4] See also Wallerstein and Kelly (1980); Walczak and Burns (1984). Sharpe's *Fathers and Daughters* (1994) is, however, a discussion of the parenting relationship written by fathers and their *adult* daughters. Thus, these accounts have to be seen as a remembering of the parenting relationship and thus tempered by time and maturity.

[5] In this process, and in these circumstances, the theme of children's dependency may receive a considerable and heightened emphasis—possibly because, in both cases, of parents' need to establish and insist on a child's dependency to retain an effective parenting role in contexts where the

everyday social practices within the family, parents in these difficult circumstances drew heavily on the welfarist discourses of protection, innocence and dependency to shape their relations with their children. These discourses the children themselves were aware of and, while acknowledging their value for other children, for themselves as children involved in particular relationships with their parents they were disregarded. The children actively challenged and resisted them.

Thus, for example, both Mitchell and Bluebond-Langner describe how parents worked to maintain their children's dependence on them by limiting their access to knowledge about impending divorce or death. The children themselves were, however, conscious that this information was being withheld through growing awareness of subtle changes in their parents' behaviour and in their own relationships with them. Such awareness occurred very early on in the changed relationship, as Bluebond-Langner describes for children recently diagnosed with leukemia:

> "The children remarked on the sudden deluge of gifts . . . They talked about what they received, things they did not ask for, how they did not have certain things anymore and how their fathers often would not go to work. They spoke in hushed tones about the conversations they had tried to listen in on, but could not hear. They announced how people cried and looked sad when seeing them: 'Mommy cries when she sees me'; 'Nanny stares and shakes her head at me.' " (1978, p. 173).

Having realised that their parents were deceiving or misinforming them, the children then adopted active strategies to obtain knowledge about their changed situation.

The desire to keep children in ignorance of issues such as parental disputes and serious illness reflects a second and linked feature of adult constructions of parenting as a one way dependent relationship: the need to protect children. However, in both Mitchell's and Bluebond-Langner's accounts, the children describe how, once they became aware of their parents' prospective divorce or the gravity of their own illness, it was *they* who worked hard to protect their *parents*, thereby reversing the protective role which is usually held to constitute good parenting. The children, for example, wanted to shield their parents from further upset and thus did not openly reveal their own feelings as Mitchell describes, during the divorce proceedings:

> "some of these children had cried alone and deliberately out of sight of their parents, whom they had not wanted to upset even further . . . They had never told their parents how upset they were" (1984, p. 94).

future of that role is unclear and their position as parents may become undermined. A greater insistence by parents on children's dependency in these circumstances may explain why it is, therefore, that it is in these particular accounts that the interdependence of child-parent relationships is so remarked by children. From the children's point of view, it may be that their own contribution to that relationship has become marginalised or unacknowledged and that therefore children have been forced to articulate that which in normal circumstances remains implicit. These ideas are currently being developed for a study of children, parenting and divorce (James, A. and James, A. L., forthcoming).

Bluebond-Langner, in a comparable passage, describes how children did not wish to upset their parents by talking about their approaching death and would engage in a mutual pretence, adopting distancing strategies which were, in part, designed to give parents an excuse:

"they would withdraw from family and friends, either through expressions of anger or through silence. Then she [Mother] won't cry so much and be sad" (1978, p. 196).

Thus in situations when parenting is at risk, it would seem that children actively strive to minimise the harm which their own position as "children at risk" might pose for their parents. As Neale *et al*'s study of children in post-divorce and separation families shows:

"One of the most striking aspects of children's own discourse about their family lives . . . is that they speak in terms of an ethic of care. This is not merely a one way process, focusing on the care they receive. They also try to work within this ethic in a way that is supportive of their parents" (Neale *et al*., 1998, p. 45).

Other recent, smaller scale studies (Borland, 1996) and Lindon (1996) provide additional confirmation that, at times of stress, children see themselves as sources of support for their parents and act in a caring way towards them:

"I knew my mum was really upset because Grandad died. I said to her in the end 'It's alright, Mum, I know you've been crying. You don't have to pretend.' " (Lindon, cited in Hill and Tisdall (1997, p. 76)

These accounts highlight the themes of dependency and protection through which childhood is conventionally described. However, from the point of view of the children themselves, these qualities speak less about the traditional hierarchical status relationship of parent-child, than about the qualities pertinent to any caring familial relationship, of which parenting is simply a particular version.[6] Morrow's (1998) study shows for example that, for children, the concept of the family is constituted through sets of *mutually* caring relationships. One thirteen-year-old girl puts it this way:

"A family is a group of people which all care about each other. They can all cry together, laugh together, argue together and go through all the emotions together. Some live together as well. *Families are for helping each other through life*" (Morrow 1998, p. 27, emphasis added).

These examples suggest, therefore, that children hold views about parents and the parenting relationship which may differ markedly from those of adults. For example, while for parents divorce clearly does not terminate the biological relationship with their children, it may well radically recast the social aspect of the parenting role through the denial of contact or through the adoption of a new status as a lone or co-parent. From children's point of view, however,

---

[6] In referring to caring here I pass no judgement on the more emotional or psychological aspects of such relationships. Caring here is taken to refer to forms of *social* action rather than emotional intent.

divorce may be regarded somewhat differently for, as Morrow points out, from their perspective "there is no such thing as a single parent" (1994, p. 130). Children may see their relationships with their mums and dads as enduring beyond the socio-legal and temporal confines of marriage and the family. This view is confirmed by the children in Neale *et al*'s (1998) study for whom the *quality* of the loving relationships they have with their parents post-separation and divorce, rather than the structure of the family itself, is what will continue to make a parent a "proper" parent.

A more general point to note to be drawn from this literature, therefore, is that children do not see or conduct themselves as passive partners in the child-parent relationship. Children see themselves as active contributors to it. This is in strong contrast to how that relationship is conventionally depicted from an adult perspective where it is regarded as a fundamental and one-way dependency such that dependent old age can often only be effectively managed through infantilising metaphors of childhood (Hockey and James, 1993). As such, therefore, this literature on children's experience of parenting in "exceptional" circumstances turns out to provide not only a shared consensus amongst children about what parenting is or should consist of but a highly particularised condensation, as Mies notes for women involved in divorce:

> "In the 'experiences of crises' . . . and rupture with normalcy, women are confronted with the real social relationships in which they had unconsciously been submerged as objects without being able to distance themselves from them" (1983, p. 71)

These studies of divorce and illness are, I suggest, therefore instructive about children's perspectives on parenting in less exceptional circumstances in being able to reveal that which is normally obscured: that, more generally, children see themselves as participants in, rather than simply the recipients of, the parenting relationship and that parenting is visualised by children as more of an interdependent, than a dependent relationship.

4. "BEING PARENTED": PATTERNS OF INTERDEPENDENCE AND CARE

The studies considered so far have been instrumental in forcing a reconsideration of parenting as that which is simply done *to* children. From a children's perspective, parenting is regarded as a two-way process. Other studies of children living in "ordinary" rather than exceptional circumstances provide additional confirmation.

Mayall's (1996) study, for example, looks at children's lives across the twin sites of home and school in an attempt to explore the ways in which "children's lives are lived through childhoods constructed for them by adult understandings of childhood and of what children are and should be" (1996, p. 1). In this study, children's view of parents are briefly explored as an integral part of how parenting is experienced, parenting here being seen as integral to that process of constructing a particular kind of childhood for children, or what Mayall terms, children's "understandings of their social position at home" (1996, p. 91). Thus, for example, she depicts how the youngest children of five and six years old derived pleasure and pride in their gradual achievement of independence from their parents in relation to self-care. Older children, those of eight and nine years, placed more emphasis on the ways in which parents work to instill in them particular moral codes in relation to health care and their personal responsibility for the adoption or rejection of these codes:

> "Both 5- and 9-year olds indicated their understanding that their mothers (and in some cases their fathers) provided the moral order, with which they negotiated. Both groups identified parental control over personal care and home maintenance as structuring their daily lives, though the older children experienced parental control as stronger and more irksome. They also perceived that parents regulated the home and children in the interests of adult agendas" (1996, p. 97)

A second study, Solberg's (1997) account of children's family lives in Norway, provides further evidence of the ways in which children's relationships with their parents is a negotiated, rather than imposed, feature of family life. It provides further support for the suggestion that, from children's points of view, parenting is regarded as an interdependent relationship and not a one-way dependency of children upon their parents. Solberg depicts the different types of relationships twelve-year-old Norwegian children have with parents through the use of a four-fold model. These relationships range from the one extreme in which the child is seen by the parent as immature and in need of overt and visible care, to the other in which a child of the same age is given many domestic responsibilities and expected to perform a great deal of self-care. These varied experiences of twelve-year-old children, while clearly reiterating the themes of innocence, protection and dependency noted earlier as characteristic of a welfarist model of childhood, nonetheless also underscore the notion that childhood has a social and contextual character which permits variation in and differences between children's experiences. But what is perhaps more interesting, is the suggestion in this piece of research that it is the children themselves who have been instrumental in shaping the specific way in which the child-parent relationship is performed in each household.

Thus Solberg argues, for example, that in carrying out her housework tasks independently and performing them well without her mother's supervision, Anne is regarded by her parents as a big twelve-year-old who is competent in self-care and in making an equal contribution to the household tasks. This contrasts with Carl who, although he does some housework, performs it under the watchful eye of his mother. Thus children like Anne are able to negotiate some parent-free time at home, time which they see as valuable due to the absence of parental constraint and restriction.

Solberg's account is instructive. Children's independence from their parents arises out of the *interdependent* character of the child-parent relation which, through negotiation, is changed from an hierarchical to a more equal relationship:

> "The negotiating parties do not of course have the same social rank. Parents have authority and power to punish and reward their children. Children do not have the corresponding means at their disposal. But by using the term 'negotiate' I wish to emphasise the fact that although in many ways children's position is a weak one, they do not passively adapt themselves to what their elders say and do. In everyday life, . . . children have and make use of a considerable freedom of action. They are in a position to influence the outcome of the negotiating process in directions which they perceive to be favourable to themselves" (Solberg 1997, p. 127).

A children's perspective on "being parented" is thus somewhat at odds with the more conventional adult-centred, one-way, welfarist model of parenting described earlier, through an insistence on its negotiated and interdependent character, an interdependency made possible through the particular qualities of the parenting relationship which enable children, as we have seen, to realise their own subjectivities. Thus, as this chapter now goes on to explore, in discussions about parents and parenting, it is significant that children emphasise the importance of the "quality" of the relationship, as they experience and participate in it, over and above its structural form. On occasions, then, the relationship between how children view parents—people with whom they have a particular biological and social relationship—and parenting—the experience or enactment of that relationship- turns out to be somewhat equivocal.

A first important point to note is that, conceptually, "parenting" for children can only ever be experienced subjectively: it is the process of "being parented". However, this potentially subjected and passive status does not square readily with children's own understanding and everyday experiences of family life. Few children, for example, would volunteer the nomenclature "parent" to refer to those who parent them—in either its biological or social renderings. It is, instead, "my mum" or "my step-dad" who attend parents' evening at school, who see Johnny's pictures on the wall and talk to his teacher. Additionally, the generalised concept of "parent" may have little value; as Morrow's (1998) study suggests, particularly for younger children, a child's "parent" is regarded as person specific, as "my mum" and "my dad".

Similarly, the term "family" is an inclusive term, often used by adults to refer to those with whom children live in their households: mums and/or dads, step-dads and mums, alongside brothers and sisters, half-siblings, sometimes nana and grandad, or cousins, aunts and uncles (Levin, 1995). However, Morrow (1998) and Neale *et al.* (1998) point out, from a children's perspective, "the family" can also include those who do not physically share the same physical space. Many of the children they talked with included in their pictures of family life those biological parents who lived elsewhere and with whom, sometimes, they had relatively infrequent contact. In addition, "family" may embrace a mother or father's new partner, depending upon the quality of the relationship between a particular child and a particular adult. Thus, from a children's perspective "parenting" (by mums and dads or whoever) is contextualised as a special and particular relationship of care and set of roles distinctive among those in the larger set of familial, social relations. As Neale, Wade and Smart note:

"whether children feel they have good or poor relationships with a parent does not depend on how often they see them . . . Children attach a great deal of importance to the quality of kin relationships, in particular to having 'proper' parents who will provide them with love, care and respect in their own right" (1998, p. 22).

Whether or not an additional biological link can be claimed to "my mum" or "my dad", it is the quality of the relationship which pertains between those adults who parent them and the children who are parented which, for children, matters most. Here again, then, the literature on children living in exceptional circumstances is instructive for our understanding of a more general children's perspective on parents. It draws a clear distinction between the concept of "parent" and the actions of "parenting". A "proper" parent is a person with whom one has a good relationship such that the experience of being parented involves "a profound sense of being loved and valued" even if that parent is not in contact regularly (Neale *et al.*, 1998).

For the majority of children living in "ordinary families", however, such a distinction may be elided in the practical daily round of family life. In these circumstances "parent" and "parenting" are constituted within the same persons in the household and thus the quality and content of that child-adult relationship may not normally be questioned or held up for inspection.[7] It is simply taken-for-granted. Thus it may be only those children who experience the disjunction between "parent" and "parenting" who are prompted to reflect or offer commentary on their experiences of "being parented".

However, the little research that has been carried out on children's perspectives on parenting in ordinary family circumstances supports the findings which emerge from the literature on children and divorce as regards what "parenting" involves. Morrow's (1998) study of children's perspectives on families pinpoints love, care, mutual respect and support as the key characteristics, for children, of the experience of being parented. Borland's *et al.* (1996) small Scottish study similarly found that "the quality children valued most in parents was love" and that this was seen as the "job of parenting" (cited in Hill and Tisdall, 1997, p. 75). Allat's (1996) study of older children's concepts of parenting provides similar confirmation. Teenagers have come to see parents as:

"the guardians of the social and moral order, who . . . would ensure the maintenance of such key familial values as equity and the statuses embedded in sibling hierarchies

---

[7] Interestingly, this may help explain why it is that some children may continue to submit to abuse within families. The emotional, social and physical power invested in the "parent-child" relationship, through which abusive practices may be promulgated, may be conceived of by the child as a kind of parental right associated with the status of "parent" (Kitzinger, 1990).

. . . Parents were also seen as those to turn to first when in trouble or in need of support, who would be upset if children turned elsewhere" (1996, p. 142).

From a children's perspective this experience of "being parented"—of being cared for and cared about—is part and parcel of the act of parenting. Regarded by children as an interdependent relationship, their own active experience of receiving such "care" is, however, seen by them as fundamental to the proper enactment of parenting. It is, however, one which can often only be described, particularly by younger children, through those concrete forms of social action which, for them, make tangible the act of parenting and their own related experience of being parented.

Thus young children cite the provision of meals and gifts, wrapping children up warm when they are ill, providing succour and comfort when they are sick or accompanying them to places which are dangerous, as signs of parental "care", of a relationship in which they themselves have an active investment and involvement (Hill and Tisdall 1997, p. 75). A participant in Morrow's (1998) study describes family life as follows:

"Families are for giving me stuff: food, clothes, presents. Loving, caring for me and *for giving things back to*" (1998, p. 26 emphasis added).

Similarly, in an on-going study of children's use of time (Christensen *et al.*, 1999) when asked about the time they spend with their family, many of the ten-year-old children refer to the "things" that parents do for them—trips out to the seaside or theme parks, buying clothes and so on—as both an indication of the quality of family life and of the kinds of parenting they, as children, receive and participate in.

From these examples, then, it is clear that the love and care which parenting brings is experienced by children concretely through the ebb and flow of everyday activities in which they also have a part to play and, in this respect, children may make a distinction between mothers and fathers as regards the kinds of care they provide. Morrow's (1998) study, for example, reveals that while both parents are central figures in children's lives, mothers are often seen as the parent who is the main source of physical and emotional care, and particularly by older girls, as the parent in whom they can confide; fathers may be seen as caring through their adoption of a more task-oriented stance towards their children—as someone to do things with. In our study (Christensen *et al.*, 1999) children similarly commented explicitly on the different roles adopted by parents in the parenting process: whether it is mum or dad who tells you off, by whom a child gets "grounded" and for how long; who shouts the most in families, Mum or Dad, and which parent can be called upon to sort out fights between siblings.

From a children's perspective, then, parenting has a number of different features and some aspects of parental care are experienced by children as a form of control. The essential interdependence of the child-parent relationship means, however, that in ordinary regimes of caring-control, children are nonetheless still able to see themselves as active participants in that relationship. In our on-going study, for example, the children revealed that although parenting may be sometimes experienced as irksome in placing restrictions upon their activities, they nonetheless see themselves as being able to negotiate a way through. Two children, Barry and Tom, express such a view. They have been asked their opinion about decision-making at home and they compare notes about using the telephone. From their conversation it is clear that, for both boys, mum exerts some kind of control, but it is however a control which can be challenged as Tom explains:

> Barry: "My mum says you're wasting, you're gonna have to pay with your own money".
> Tom: "Oh yeah, my mum says that and I say I can't, I haven't got any money."

In this example, defiant though Tom's presentation of self is, and controlling although his mother appears, the interdependent character of the parenting relationship provides the basis for negotiation rather than conflict between them.

Parental "control" can, of course, be experienced by children as excessive when the authority of parents becomes authoritarian, rather than authoritative or democratic. In such circumstances, as Coleman and Coleman (1984) argue in relation to adolescents, the parenting relationship may become problematic. But, equally, excessive permissiveness by parents is not valued for what "adolescents themselves most require of parents and other authority figures is *support* rather than freedom" (Bainham, 1992). Here then is further confirmation of the interdependent character of child-parent relationships. As Morrow's study confirms, children wish to "be talked to and consulted, and given information, and to be able to give their point of view and have their opinions taken into account" (1998, p. 45). Parenting is not just what parents do to children but a relationship in which children see themselves as active participants.

5. CONCLUSION

In her study of adolescent attitudes towards their parents, Allat observes that "in their representation of parenting, these young people saw themselves as central to their parents' lives, as constituting a major parental achievement" (1996, p. 142). However, we still know relatively little about how this interdependent and negotiated relationship develops through the life-course; neither do we have much empirical evidence for it. What is needed, therefore, is research into a still essentially uncharted territory within childhood studies, one which asks further questions about the ways in which children's views on parenting are silenced and then work to give voice to their views.

Why is it, for example, that the information which children *voluntarily* exchange with one another, seems rarely to include details about their life at home? In previous research (James, 1993) it was apparent that young children's knowledge of others' home lives, or their relationships with their parents, was sparse, something which is currently being confirmed in our on-going project.

Interviewed in friendship groups about how they spend their time, not infrequently, it appears that in these discussions children are for the first time sharing details of their lives at home. This is sometimes the case even among close friends who may spend time in each other's houses. For example, it clearly came as a surprise to Laurence's school friends that his father did not live with him, while some of Kerry's friends were to discover that she often lived with her grandmother during the week while her mother went to work.

Is it that children actively exclude or filter the information they wish to share about their families, and about their parents in particular? Or is it that views on parents and knowledge about family life at home may simply not be pertinent to children's relationships with other children? Is it only those children whose living arrangements are different from their peers or who experience a sudden change in family life who are drawn to reflect upon the nature of the parenting they experience? Or is "parenting" simply so taken-for-granted as a loving relationship of care and regarded as so fundamental by children that to speak of it is unnecessary? Whatever questions arise one thing is certain: only if the interdependent character of the child-parent relationship is acknowledged by researchers will any progress towards answering them be made.

REFERENCES

Allat, P., "Conceptualizing parenting from the standpoint of children: relationship and transition in the life course" in J. Brannen and M. O'Brien (eds.), *Children in Families: Research and Policy* (London, Falmer, 1996).

Bainham, A., "Growing up in Britain: Adolescence in the post-Gillick era" (1992) *Juridical Review* 155–176.

Bluebond-Langner, M., *The Private Worlds of Dying Children* (Princeton, Princeton University Press, 1978).

Borland, M., Brown, J., Hill, M. *et al.*, *Parenting in Middle Childhood* (Glasgow, Report to Health Education Board for Scotland, 1996).

Brannen, J. and O'Brien, M. (eds.), *Children in Families: Research and Policy* (London, Falmer, 1996).

Christensen, P., James, A. and Jenks, C., Project entitled "Changing Times: children's understanding and perception of the social organisation of time", part of the ESRC Children 5–16 Programme, 1999.

Coleman, C. and Coleman, E. Z., "Adolescent attitudes to authority" (1984) 7 *Journal of Adolescence* 131–141.

Corsaro, W. A., *Friendship and Peer Culture in the Early Years* (Norwood, NJ, Ablex, 1985).

Day-Sclater, S., "Children and Divorce- Hidden Agendas?", paper presented at the Children and Social Exclusion Conference, University of Hull, March 1998.

Hill, M. and Tisdall, K., *Children and Society* (London, Longman, 1997).

Hockey, J. and James, A., *Growing Up and Growing Old* (London, Sage, 1993).

James, A., *Childhood Identities: Self and social relationships in the experience of the child* (Edinburgh, Edinburgh University Press, 1993).

James, A., "Imaging children 'at home', 'in the family' and 'at school': movement between the spatial and temporal markers of childhood identity in Britain", in N. J. Rapport and A. Dawson (eds.), *Migrants of Identity* (Oxford, Berg, 1998).

James, A., Jenks, C. and Prout, A., *Theorising Childhood* (Cambridge, Polity Press, 1998).

James, A. and Prout, A. (eds.), *Constructing and Reconstructing Childhood* (Basingstoke, Falmer Press, 1990) (2nd edn., 1997).

James, A. and Prout, A., "Strategies and structures: towards a new perspective on children's experiences of family life" in J. Brannen and M. O'Brien (eds.), *Children and Families: Research and Policy* (London, Falmer Press, 1996).

Kitzinger, J., "Who are you kidding? Children, Power and the struggle against sexual abuse" in A. James and A. Prout (eds.), *Constructing and Reconstructing Childhood* (Basingstoke, Falmer Press, 1990) (2nd edn. 1997).

Levin, I., "Children's perceptions of their family" (1995) *Annale dell'Instituto di Dirritto e Procedura penale 55–74.*

Lindon, J., *Growing Up: From Eight Years to Young Adulthood* (London, National Children's Bureau, 1996).

Mayall, B., *Children, Health and the Social Order* (Buckingham, Open University Press, 1996).

Mies, M., "Towards a methodology for feminist research" in G. Bowles and R. D. Klein (eds.), *Theories for Women's Studies* (London, Routledge & Kegan Paul, 1983).

Mitchell, A., *Children in the Middle* (Tavistock, London, 1984).

Morrow, V., "Responsible children? Aspects of children's work and employment outside school in contemporary UK" in B. Mayall (ed.), *Children's Childhood, Observed and Experienced* (London, Falmer Press, 1994).

Morrow, V., *"Understanding Families: Children's Perspectives"* (London, National Children's Bureau, 1998).

Neale, B., Wade, A. and Smart, C., *"I just get on with it: Children's experiences of family life following parental separation and divorce"* (Leeds University, Centre for Research on Family Kinship and Childhood, 1998).

Pollard, A., *The Social World of the Primary School* (London, Holt, Rhinehart and Winston, 1985).

Qvortrup, J., Foreword to J. Brannen and M. O'Brien, (eds.), *Children in Families: Research and Policy* (London, Falmer, 1996).

Qvortrup, J., "A voice for children in statistical and social accounting: a plea for children's right to be heard" in A. James and A. Prout (eds.), *Constructing and Reconstructing Childhood*, 2nd edn. (Basingstoke, Falmer Press, 1997).

Shilling, C., *The Boy and Social Theory* (London, Sage, 1993).

Solberg, A., "Negotiating childhood: changing constructions of age for Norwegian children" in A. James and A. Prout (eds.), *Constructing and Reconstructing Childhood*, 2nd edn. (Basingstoke, Falmer Press, 1997).

Steedman, C., *The Tidy House* (London, Virago, 1982).

Thorne, B., *Gender Play: Girls and Boys in School* (New Jersey, Rutgers University Press, 1993).

Walczak, Y. and Burns, S., *Divorce: The Child's Point of View* (London, Harper and Row, 1984).

Wallerstein, J. and Kelly, J., *Surviving the Break-up: How Children and Parents Cope with Divorce* (London, Grant McIntyre, 1980).

11

State Intervention and Parental Autonomy in Children's Cases: Have We Got the Balance Right?

BRIDGET LINDLEY

1. INTRODUCTION

The primary role of the state in relation to promoting the welfare of children is to provide support to families with children in need, and to intervene in family life to protect children who are at risk of harm. These functions reflect the requirements of two international Conventions. On the one hand, the United Nation Convention on the Rights of the Child establishes a clear expectation that whilst parents have the primary responsibility for bringing up children, the State must provide supportive and protective services for them (Articles 18 and 19).[1] On the other hand, the European Convention on Human Rights and Fundamental Freedoms establishes the right to privacy and family life (Article 8), which effectively guarantees against unwarranted State intrusion into family life, on behalf of both adults and children.[2]

The classification of children "in need", and at risk of "harm", will vary from time to time according to current ideological and societal definitions.[3] These variations will determine the extent and level of service provision and intervention at different times.[4] However, they do not affect the underlying challenge for

---

[1] This Convention was ratified by the United Kingdom Government in December 1991. Although not enforceable (because there is no international court), it is binding on English law to the extent that every ratifying country confirms that it is prepared to meet the provisions and obligations set out in the Convention. It therefore provides a benchmark for the legal framework relating to children in England and Wales.

[2] The United Kingdom Government is a signatory to this Convention and has now effectively made its provisions binding on domestic courts by the enactment of the Human Rights Act 1998, which, once implemented, will require domestic courts to ensure that decisions do not breach 'Convention Rights' which include the right to family life.

[3] See for example the recent linking of domestic violence and child protection on the social work agenda (Social Services Inspectorate, Domestic Violence and Social Change, Department of Health, 1995).

[4] The current Government has stated clearly that it is committed to strengthening family life. However there is policy confusion between government departments as to how this should be achieved. Its policy on youth justice aims to achieve this by placing responsibility for young people firmly with the family, by means of punitive measures if necessary (as discussed elsewhere in

the State to ensure that the process of delivering these services achieves the right balance between identifying, supporting and protecting children in need of such services, whilst simultaneously avoiding unnecessary and unwarranted intrusion into family life. These two perspectives can be regarded as being on a continuum, without necessarily being mutually exclusive. It is the task of the State to ensure that the degree of support, coercion and compulsion occur at the right point on that continuum.

The Children Act 1989 (CA) provides a comprehensive and integrated legal framework for dealing with children's cases in England and Wales so as to promote children's welfare. The Act establishes a baseline of parental autonomy, and also makes provision for the State to provide support for families with children in need, with compulsory intervention being confined to cases where particular criteria are satisfied. The aim of this chapter is to review these provisions from a public law perspective, and, a decade after the Act was passed by Parliament, to consider whether they achieve an appropriate balance of these two competing perspectives, both in law, and as the provisions are implemented in practice by child-care professionals. It will also identify certain tensions which exist between the two agencies of the State (namely the courts and local authorities) in achieving effective State intervention on behalf of children, and will briefly consider policy aspects of the provision of children's services in the future. It does not seek to discuss current or likely future definitions of child welfare and maltreatment, nor how these should be assessed by practitioners.

2. HISTORICAL BACKGROUND

There is no doubt that the legislative framework which existed before the Children Act 1989 was passed contained serious defects, which often left children's welfare seriously compromised. The Act was therefore preceded by a very thorough review of the law relating to children. This review identified a number of factors which influenced the way the Children Bill was drafted (Ryan, 1994). First, the House of Commons Social Services Committee published the Short Report (House of Commons, 1984) on children in care recommending urgent reform of child-care law so as to rationalise and simplify the existing complex legal framework for dealing with children's cases. In response, the government of the day set up an inter-departmental working party to carry out a detailed consultation exercise on all aspects of child-care law. Simultaneously, the Law Commission issued consultation papers on custody, guardianship and wardship. During this parallel consultation process, a wide

this book (Gelsthorpe, Chapter 12 below). However, its policy on promoting the welfare of children shows a commitment to developing services which will advise and support families in their child-rearing tasks, increasing the degree and availability of support for those who need it, and reducing the level of compulsory intervention to those cases where there is a risk of abuse (Department of Health, 1998a; Department of Health, 1998b).

range of views was sought from relevant child-care organisations, professionals and researchers. They raised other important factors which influenced the reform including the conclusions and recommendations of a number of public enquiries which were set up in response to a particular set of cases at both ends of the continuum (for example the Beckford and Cleveland enquiries);[5] a number of cases in the European Court which successfully challenged the legal position in the United Kingdom on access to children in care, emphasising that parents should be able to participate in planning and decision-making concerning their children;[6] and the findings of a number of research studies which identified the impact of poor planning for children removed into the public care system (DHSS, Social Work Decisions in Child Care, HMSO, London 1985*b*). This consultation process resulted in the publication of two influential reports,[7] which were followed by a White Paper issued in 1987 (DHSS, 1987), and the Children Bill being introduced into Parliament in 1988. There were many late amendments to the Bill and it only reached the statute book in 1989 following a guillotine motion.

The problems under the previous legal system which this process identified (see Lindley, 1994) compromised both reasonable parental autonomy[8] and effective State intervention. The Children Act aimed to redress these problems. It was firmly based on the principle that a child's welfare is likely to be best promoted by services being provided for him/her (whether on a voluntary or compulsory basis) which involve consultation with his/her family in the decision-making and planning process. Such family involvement is particularly important given the evidence (which was available when the Children Bill was drafted) that contact between children in care and their families is the key to children returning home from the care system (Millham *et al.*, 1985); and the evidence that by far the majority of children who are looked after in the care system (both on a voluntary and compulsory basis), return to their families or home communities when they leave the care system (86 per cent within 5 years, and an estimated 92 per cent eventually) (Bullock *et al.*, 1993). Although not specifically mentioned in the Act itself, the principle of the State working in partnership with families to provide services for children is central to the philosophy underpinning the public law provisions of the Act (Department of Health,

[5] On the one hand these provided extreme examples of the State's failure to protect children at risk of serious harm from their families resulting in allegedly preventable child deaths (for example, the Beckford Enquiry); and on the other hand examples of excessive and unwarranted State intervention into family life in which the parents lacked adequate legal means of challenging the actions of the local authority (for example, the Cleveland Enquiry).

[6] *O,H,W,B & R v United Kingdom*, Cases Nos 2/1986/100/14826/1986/104/152, *The Times* 9 July 1987, and *R v the United Kingdom* [1988] 2 FLR 445.

[7] DHSS, *Review of Child Care law: Report to Ministers of an Inter-departmental Working Party* (1985*a*). This contained 223 recommendations for the improvement, consolidation and clarification of child-care law; and Law Commission, *Review of Child Care Law, Guardianship and Custody* (1988). This contained a draft Bill which eventually formed the basis of the Children Bill when it was introduced into Parliament.

[8] Parental autonomy is used to include any person with parental responsibility for the child.

1991a). This principle seeks to respect parental autonomy, without compromising the child's welfare and need for protection (if any).

3. THE LEGAL FRAMEWORK FOR PARTNERSHIP

In spite of the absence of the term "partnership" in the Act, it contains a number of provisions which, together, require that child-care cases are conducted as far as possible in a partnership between State and family. These requirements provide for parental autonomy as well as compulsory intervention by the State. The extent to which these co-exist in a balanced, working partnership varies depending on the degree of compulsion being exercised by the State.

(a) Parental autonomy

One of the central tenets of partnership is the notion of continuing "parental responsibility" (PR). It includes "all the rights, duties, powers, responsibilities and authority which by law a parent of a child has in relation to the child and his property" (CA, s.3).[9] As such it is the cornerstone of parental autonomy. More than one person can have PR simultaneously (s.2(6)). Each can exercise their PR independently of the other (s.2(7)), and although a person with PR may not surrender it, s/he may arrange for it to be exercised by someone else (s.2(9)). Mothers and married fathers automatically have parental responsibility for their children (s.2(1), (2)), and for them it is inalienable, unless their child is adopted. Non-married fathers can acquire parental responsibility by agreement or court order (s.4). Others caring for, or seeking to care for, children (with the exception of local authority foster carers to whom certain restrictions set out in section 9(3) apply) can acquire parental responsibility by way of a residence order (s.8) (provided leave to make the application is granted by the court), a guardianship order (s.5) or through an adoption order. Wherever PR is acquired by court order (other than in adoption cases), it is revocable.

In general, this notion of continuing PR ensures that parental autonomy is guaranteed in relation to all decision-making and other aspects of a child's life, save where the child him/herself is competent to make decisions for him/herself (as determined by the principle established in the case of *Gillick v West Norfolk and Wisbech Area Health Authority*),[10] and where there are statutory exceptions in the field of private law. For example a child may only be removed from the jurisdiction for a period of longer than one month if all those with PR have consented (Child Abduction Act 1984, section 1).

---

[9] The section numbers quoted in this article all refer to the Children Act 1989 unless otherwise specified.
[10] [1986] AC 112.

This parental autonomy is even absolute when the State is involved in providing services to children in need and their families, on an agreed basis. Such services are provided as a result of the general duty on every local authority to: "safeguard and promote the welfare of children in need[11] in their area by providing services which will promote the upbringing of such children by their families" (s.17(1)). The services which may be provided include, amongst other things, the provision of "accommodation" for a child in the care system where certain statutory criteria are established, for example that: "the person who has been caring for him/her is prevented for whatever reason from continuing to do so" (s.20(1)). This accommodation may only be provided with the agreement of those with PR (s.20(7)). The local authority does not acquire PR for the child during the period of accommodation, and those with PR have a veto on any of the plans for the child.[12] The latter may remove the child from accommodation at any time and there is no notice requirement for this removal. Whether there should be a notice requirement was the subject of specific debate when the Bill was passed through Parliament, but any provision to this effect was specifically rejected by the government because accommodation was viewed as part of a package of support services provided under Part III of the Act to help families care for their children who were in need, without undermining their autonomy to make decisions for their children.[13] Thus where there is agreement about the provision of services, the legal framework and the principle of partnership aims to ensure that parental autonomy is guaranteed.

(b) Compulsory state intervention

Parental autonomy may be, and usually is, circumscribed once the local authority takes compulsory measures to protect children who are at risk of significant harm, although the degree to which this occurs depends on the level of intervention. The latter is determined by particular statutory criteria which relate to three tiers of intervention.[14]

[11] A child is in need if:
"(a) he is unlikely to achieve or maintain . . .a reasonable standard of health or development without the provision of services for him . . .;
(b) his health or development is likely to be significantly impaired, or further impaired without the provision . . . of services; or
(c) he is disabled" (s.17(10)).
[12] This veto arises by virtue of the duty on the local authority to agree with one person with PR the plan for every child (under 16) who is in accommodation to be found in Regulation 3, Arrangements for Placement of Children (General) Regulations 1991 (SI 1991 No. 890), reg. 3.
[13] See Hansard HL, vol. 502 cols. 1337, 1342–4 Children Bill Committee stage; vol. 503 cols. 1411–13 Report Stage, vol. 512 cols. 737–9 Consideration of Commons Amendments.
[14] It is no longer possible for the local authority to intervene in family life so as to remove a child into care, without these statutory criteria being established, either in wardship proceedings or under the inherent jurisdiction of the court (s.100). This was a common practice prior to the Act. The inherent jurisdiction can no longer be exercised unless the leave of the court is granted according to the criteria set out in s.100(4).

The first relates to child protection investigations. The local authority is under a duty to make enquiries where they have reasonable cause to suspect that a child may be suffering from significant harm (s.47). Each local authority must draw up detailed child protection procedures to provide for inter-agency co-operation during such enquiries, and to ensure that decisions are made about whether the child's name should be placed on the child protection register and whether an application for an order under Part IV of the Act should be made. In cases where the local authority decides, as a result of these enquiries, not to apply for any compulsory order, but the child's name is placed on the child protection register, there is an obligation to review the case at a later date (s.47(7)). The local authority is obliged to see the child during such enquiries, unless they are satisfied that they already have sufficient information about him/her (s.47(4)). Where they are denied access to the child, they are obliged to apply for an emergency protection order (EPO), a child assessment order (CAO) or a care order (CO), unless they are satisfied that the child's welfare can be satisfactorily safeguarded without doing so (s.45(7)).

The local authority does not acquire PR during the course of the enquiries, and there is a strong emphasis in the government guidance on child protection procedures in *Working Together* (Department of Health, 1991b) that the local authority should work in partnership with the family and involve them fully in the investigation, decision-making and planning process in order best to protect and promote the welfare of their child. However, it is implicit in the wording of section 47(4), and clear from the guidance in *Working Together*, that there is an expectation that the child's family will co-operate fully with the enquiries and allow the child to be seen, on request, in order not to risk an application being made to the court for a compulsory order. Thus, whilst parental autonomy is generally respected where there is a suspicion of significant harm, the guidance on partnership in child protection raises a presumption that the parents and other relevant family members should be involved in the child protection process. This means that their autonomy may be subject to coercive pressure, where necessary, to ensure effective State intervention. Where this fails to achieve what the State considers to be effective protection for the child, the degree of intervention will progress to the next level, introducing greater compulsion to supersede parental autonomy.

The second tier of intervention relates to emergency measures in the court process. The court is empowered to make an EPO where there is reasonable cause to believe that the child will suffer significant harm if he is not removed to accommodation provided by the local authority, or if he does not remain in the place where he is already being accommodated, or where the local authority is making enquiries under section 47 and that those enquiries are being frustrated by access to the child being unreasonably refused (s.44). An EPO may be made for up to eight days and may be renewed on application for a further seven days (s.45(1), (5)). Where any parent or other person with PR opposes the making of an EPO, they may either oppose the initial application for it if they are given notice of it, or they may apply to discharge the order after seventy-two hours, provided they were not present at the initial application (s.45(8)).

An EPO gives the applicant PR for the child, and also authorises the removal of a child to accommodation provided by the applicant, or the prevention of removal from accommodation already being provided, and also operates as a direction to comply with any request to produce the child (s.44(4). However, these powers are limited: the applicant is under an obligation to return the child to (or allow him to be removed by) the person from whom he was removed or his family, where s/he has either seen the child or taken protective measures, and it appears to him/her that it is safe for the child to be returned (s.44(10)). Throughout the duration of the EPO, those who already have PR retain it, but their autonomy to make decisions about their child's care will be subject to complying with the terms of the EPO. Thus, although there is a legal means to challenge the making of such an order, once an EPO is made by the court, parental autonomy will be overridden as is necessary to ensure the child's immediate safety and protection.

The third tier of intervention relates to the longer term. The court may make a care order on application where it *is satisfied* that a child under seventeen is suffering, or is likely to suffer, significant harm,[15] and that that harm is attributable to the care given to the child, or likely to be given to him, not being what it would be reasonable to expect a parent to give him, or the child being beyond parental control (s.31(2)). The civil burden of proof, whether an event has occurred on the *balance of probabilities* applies. However, recent case law has given further guidance on how this should be interpreted in children's cases, which has a direct bearing on parental autonomy. In the case of *Re H & R (Child Sexual Abuse: Standard of Proof)*,[16] the House of Lords held that the "more improbable the event, the stronger must be the evidence that it did occur before, on the balance of probability, its occurrence would be established". However, it went on to state that it was open to a court to conclude that there was a real possibility that a child would suffer harm in the future although harm in the past had not been established. This would occur in cases where although the alleged maltreatment was not proved, the evidence did suggest a combination of profoundly worrying features affecting the care of the child within the family. This second part of the judgment relates to the fact that the threshold criteria include not just proven harm, but also likelihood of harm. The impact of this decision may have a direct bearing on parental autonomy in individual cases: when the allegation of abuse is serious, it may be very difficult for families living in disadvantaged circumstances to argue that the threshold criteria are not established, even if the allegation that abuse has occurred is not proven.

---

[15] "Harm" means ill-treatment or the impairment of health or development (s.31(9)). Where the question of whether the harm suffered by the child is significant turns on the child's health or development, his health or development must be compared with that which could reasonably be expected of a similar child (s.31(10)).

[16] [1996] 1 FLR 80.

When interpreting "significant harm", the guidance issued in conjunction with the Children Act refers to the dictionary definition of "significant" as being "considerable, noteworthy or important" (Department of Health, 1991c, para 3.19). This received judicial endorsement soon after the Act was implemented,[17] but there has been little other case law interpretation of what constitutes significant harm. Another House of Lords case (*Re: M (A Minor) (Care Order: Threshold Conditions)*[18] has confirmed that the interpretation of "is suffering" relates to the period immediately before the protective arrangements (if any) were initiated by the local authority, rather than the date of the hearing, where applicable. Even after these threshold criteria are established, a care order will only be made if such an order will positively promote the child's welfare as determined by the welfare principle, the welfare "checklist" and the "no order" principle in section 1.

The effect of a care order is that the local authority is obliged to keep the child in its care for the duration of the order, which is normally until the child is eighteen unless it is discharged at an earlier date (s.33(1)). The order confers PR on the local authority. The latter is under a duty to make plans for the child which will promote its welfare (Arrangement for Placement of Children (General) Regulations 1991, reg. 3 and CA, s.22(2)), and there is an obligation to place the child with a member of his family unless that would not be consistent with his welfare (s.23(6)). Parents (and others) retain their PR for the duration of the order, and the authority is expected to work in partnership with them when making and reviewing plans for their child, seeking their agreement and co-operation wherever possible (Department of Health, 1991d, paras 2.49–2.50). Indeed there is a specific duty on local authorities to "ascertain" and "give due consideration" to the wishes and feelings of those with PR (and indeed a father without PR), as well as the child's race culture, language and religion, in relation to all decisions about the child throughout the time that s/he is looked after (ss.22(4), (5)).

Where it is not possible to reach agreement, the authority may determine the extent to which a parent/guardian can exercise their PR (s.33(3)). The Act does not afford parents any legal means to challenge this restriction because a prohibited steps order and a specific issue order (both of which pertain to the exercise of PR) may not be made in relation to a child in care (s.9(1)). The only possibility for parents to challenge a restriction of their PR would therefore be an application for judicial review if grounds of unreasonableness could be established, which is likely to be in exceptional circumstances only. In effect, this means that the local authority has the power to make whatever plans it considers are necessary to protect the child from significant harm and promote his future welfare, including placing the child for adoption, against the wishes of the parents/others with PR.[19] Therefore, although the principles of parental

---

[17] *Humberside County Council v B* [1993] 1 FLR 257.

[18] *Re M (A Minor) (Care Order: Threshold Conditions)* [1996] 2 FLR 257.

[19] There is provision in the draft adoption Bill, published by the last government for consultation as part of a longer process of the review of adoption law, to circumscribe the power of the local

autonomy and partnership ensure consultation between parents and State about decisions and plans for the child in cases of long-term compulsory intervention, they do not, in theory, compromise the local authority's ability to make decisions which will, in its view, promote and safeguard the welfare of a child in the care system.

4. IS THE BALANCE RIGHT IN LAW?

In order to evaluate critically whether the balance is right in law, we need to examine whether there are any circumstances in which the State is prevented from taking action to protect and safeguard the welfare of a child as a result of which the child may be at risk of further harm in the future; and whether family members are unreasonably denied the opportunity of challenging the local authority's decisions and plans in respect of their child.

(a) Compulsory state intervention

The task of protecting children from harm on behalf of the State falls to two main agencies: local authorities and courts. The Act places clear duties on local authorities to take positive steps to make enquiries where there is a suspicion that a child is suffering significant harm, and establishes clear criteria which the local authority must prove in order for the court to make compulsory orders under Part IV. These steps must be taken, and compulsory orders may be applied for, in respect of all children. This even applies to children who are already receiving support services from the local authority, with the agreement of the family, under Part III of the Act, including children in accommodation. Although the local authority does not have PR for such children, they may still make enquiries and apply for an EPO or CO in respect of them where the level of risk to the child merits such intervention. Indeed, one of the grounds for making an emergency protection order is that there is reasonable cause to believe that an accommodated child will suffer significant harm if he does not remain in the place where he is already accommodated (s.44(1)). Therefore, the existence of prior agreement between the local authority and the family about the provision of services, in respect of which there is a parental veto, will not prevent the local authority from taking protective measures in respect of a child who may subsequently become at risk of suffering significant harm, provided the statutory criteria can be established to merit the level of intervention. On the contrary, it has been argued that the lack of notice period for removing children

authority to place a child in care for adoption without having previously obtained a placement order to authorise placement. However, there is no indication currently that this Bill will be introduced into Parliament in the foreseeable future (either in its current or a revised form) which means that local authority powers in relation to a child in care are currently unfettered.

from accommodation may precipitate the local authority to take compulsory measures in accommodation cases which might otherwise have been avoided, simply in order that the local authority can supervise a phased return home (Eekelaar, 1991). This means that there are no children who fall outside the scope of the State's protective legislative framework.

However, it is clear from a number of reported cases that there are recurring areas of tension between the two agencies of the State (local authorities and the courts) as to how the protective function of the State should be interpreted in particular cases (Smith, 1997). This is not surprising given that the function of the court is not to rubber stamp the local authority's application, but to evaluate the evidence submitted in support of the application, to decide whether on the balance of probabilities the statutory criteria are established, and only to make orders which will positively benefit the child's welfare (s.1). Yet, this tension arises in circumstances in which the unfettered discretion of the local authority is, arguably, inappropriate, and may merit future statutory reform.

First, the court lacks the ability to direct a local authority to apply for a compulsory order: this problem was highlighted by the case of *Nottinghamshire County Council v P*,[20] in which the father of three girls admitted sexually abusing them. The local authority applied for an EPO. Following an investigation of the children's circumstances under section 37, the local authority decided that they should remain with their mother, but with the father excluded from the home and from having contact with the children. The local authority sought to achieve this by seeking a prohibited steps order under section 8 to restrict the father in this way, rather than applying for a care order under section 31. The Court of Appeal held that there was no power for the local authority to apply for, or for the court to make, a prohibited steps order on the application of the local authority. This was because an order for no contact fell within the scope of a contact order which the local authority was expressly prohibited from applying for by section 9(2), and the same result as a contact order could not be achieved by making a prohibited steps order (s.9(5)). The court expressed considerable concern that the local authority had decided not to apply for a care order to protect these children, and that it lacked any power to require it to do so. In the absence of any power to make a care order of its own motion, it became apparent to the court that the operation of the Children Act 1989 in relation to protecting children was entirely dependent on the full co-operation of the local authority; and that, where the latter doggedly resisted taking steps which it considered were appropriate to protect children at risk of suffering from significant harm, the court was powerless.

Secondly the court lacks the power to attach conditions to a care order, and to make any direction about the care plan for the child once a care order is made. This has caused tension between local authorities and courts in a number of

---

[20] [1993] 2 FLR 134.

reported cases in which the latter have attempted to interfere with the former's discretion.

When applying for a care order, the local authority must submit a detailed care plan for scrutiny by the court outlining its plans for the child if a care order is made (*Re: T (Minors)(Care: Care Plans)*)[21]. This will indicate to the court the local authority's plans for the child if a care order is made. But what happens if the court considers that a care order should be made, but does not agree with the local authority's care plan? Case law has established that the courts may have some influence where an *interim* care order exists. The CA provides that the court may make directions about medical or other assessments of children who are under an EPO (s.44(6)), or an interim CO (s.38(6)). The House of Lords case has recently confirmed in the case of *Re: C (Care: Residential Assessment)*[22] that such assessments can include a residential assessment of a child with his/her parents at a specified establishment. In that case, in which the local authority opposed a residential assessment of the family on financial grounds, Lord Browne-Wilkinson said:

> "The purpose of s.38(6) [the power to make directions under an interim care order] is to enable the court to obtain the information necessary for its own decision, notwithstanding the control over the child which in all other respects rests with the local authority. I therefore approach the subsection on the basis that the court is to have such powers to override the views of the local authority as are necessary to enable the court to discharge properly its function of deciding whether or not to accede to the local authority's application to take the child away from its parents" (at 7).

In other cases, the Court of Appeal has confirmed that a return home can be ordered under an interim care order (see for example the cases of *Buckinghamshire County Council v M*[23] and *Re: T (A Minor) (Care Order: Conditions)*,[24] although this has been the subject of academic criticism for blurring legal principles (Hayes, 1996). In addition, Ward J held in the case of *C v Solihull MBC*[25] that courts should not abdicate responsibility to the local authority by making a final order when not in possession of all the facts.

Thus, courts retain the power to influence local authority plans and practice in the case prior to the final order. However, once a care order is made, case law has clearly established that the court may not interfere with the local authority's exercise of its discretion. It has no power to impose a care plan for the child on the local authority. It has the option of not making a care order (Children Act Advisory Committee, 1995), but in so doing, it denies the child the potential protection of compulsory care, which gives the local authority the right to make plans for the child against the wishes of the parents and others with PR. In cases

---

[21] [1994] 1 FLR 253. A clause was included in the draft adoption Bill to amend the Children Act so as to place this requirement on a statutory footing, but to date this has not been pursued.
[22] *Re: C (Interim Care Order: Residential Assessment)* [1997] 1 FLR 1, HL.
[23] [1994] 2 FLR 506.
[24] [1994] 2 FLR 423.
[25] [1993] 1 FLR 290.

where the *threshold criteria* have been established, this course may be too risky. It is therefore not a realistic option. The court may have no choice but to make the care order applied for, and hope for the best that the local authority will heed any comments made by the judge about the appropriate plan for the child in the future. This tension has been evident in particular cases where the parties have invited the court to make directions about the future care of the child within the protective framework of a care order. However, rulings on appeal have clarified that the pre-Children Act principle[26] that courts may not interfere with local authority discretion to make plans for a child under a care order is still binding[27] (see for example the case of *Re T (A Minor) (Care Order: Conditions)*[28] and *Re: J (A Minor) (Care: Care Plans)*.[29]

(b) The ability of parents and other family members to challenge local authority decisions

On the face of it the Children Act seems to provide an effective framework for ensuring that parents and others with PR enjoy an appropriate level of autonomy in public law cases. They retain their PR throughout the time that their child is looked after, whether s/he is in compulsory care or not (s.2(6)), and although their exercise of their PR may be curtailed where a CO is in force (s.33(3)), parents (irrespective of PR) and "significant others" are consulted and involved in planning for their children's future care (s.22(4), (5)). In contrast to the pre-Children Act position, parents are now automatically parties to care proceedings and other relatives may apply to be joined as parties. They are entitled to advance disclosure of the evidence in support of the local authority's application which gives them an opportunity to prepare their case.[30] Parents and others with PR have a legal means by which they may challenge local authority decisions or actions, for example by being able to apply for a contact order (s.34), the discharge of a care order (s.39) and an emergency protection order after seventy-two hours (s.45(8), (9)). Relatives may apply for a residence order (s.8)[31] to authorise them to care for a child where they do not agree with the local authority's plans and can prove to the court that the care they will offer

---

[26] Prior to the Children Act 1989, the House of Lords held that where Parliament has entrusted the local authority with discretion to make decisions in respect of children in care, it is not for the courts to interfere with that discretion (*A v Liverpool City Council* [1982] AC 363, [1982] 2 FLR 22, [1982] 2 All ER 385, HL).

[27] There is one exception to this: the court does have the power to make contact orders following a care order (provided the child's welfare demands it) even where this may interfere with the local authority's long term plans for a child because the power to make contact orders in relation to children in care has been specifically conferred on the courts by CA, s.34 (*Re: B (Minors) (Care: Contact: Local Authority's Plans)* [1993] 1 FLR 543).

[28] [1994] 2 FLR 423.

[29] [1994] 1 FLR 253.

[30] Family Proceedings Courts (Children Act 1989) Rules 1991 (SI 1991 No. 1395), rr. 14, 17.

[31] They will need to apply for leave first unless they have a right to apply under CA, s.10(4), (5).

will best promote the child's welfare (s.1). There is also a statutory requirement for local authorities to consider complaints about the provision of services for children in need under Part III of the Act (s.26(3)).

All these provisions appear to provide parents and other family members with an opportunity for consultation, and a fair hearing, in relation to compulsory intervention, with an opportunity for legal redress where they disagree with local authority decisions or actions. However, there are still aspects of the legal framework which could be improved to enhance parental autonomy, without jeopardizing any protective measures for children in need of state protection.

First, there are practical problems which can, and often do, undermine the family's ability to challenge local authority actions through the courts. There is some evidence that parents and others with PR are not exercising their right to apply to discharge EPOs (Hunt and McLeod, 1996), nor challenging interim care order applications (Lindley, 1994). For those that do make an application to court, the limited range of orders available to the court may reduce their chances of success. Where the threshold criteria have been established, few courts would be willing to take the risk of ordering a phased return home by way of other orders (for example a contact order, building up to a residence order coupled with a supervision order). Most would want to know that any return home was being undertaken within the safe framework of a care order. Yet they cannot order it (other than under an interim order, the legality of which is unclear). They are therefore left with little choice but to grant the care order, and hope that their views about future plans will be heeded.

By way of example, this scenario might occur in a case in which the court considers that a care order should be made in order to give the local authority ultimate control in planning the child's future, but that an attempt should be made to place the child with his grandparents. The court may not attach a condition to the care order to this effect. It can simply make a care order, and trust, or hope, that the local authority will do this. Alternatively, it could make a residence order in favour of the grandparents, coupled with conditions attached and a supervision order, but neither of these orders would give the local authority PR for the child and therefore the authority would not be in the driving seat in the planning process. Thus, although parents and others with PR have a right to oppose an application for a care order and to apply to discharge such an order, they cannot take advantage of it very effectively in practice because the court may not stray into the forbidden territory of post-care order decision-making.

Secondly, there are potential shortcomings in the way that complaints procedures are established. The statutory requirement for local authorities to establish such procedures to consider complaints made about the provision of services under Part III of the Act (s.26(3)), includes a requirement that the complaint is considered by an independent person (s.26(4)). In theory, this procedure should enhance parental autonomy by making the local authority more accountable for decisions it makes about the exercise of its powers and duties.

However, this avenue of accountability may be flawed in practice, because the local authority only has to have "due regard" to the findings of those considering the complaint (s.26(5)), which means that even where a complaint is upheld, the authority may ignore the findings and still proceed with their original plan for service delivery.

Thirdly, accommodation may not always be as voluntary an arrangement as it was originally intended to be. On the face of it, parental autonomy should be absolute in cases in which children are looked after in accommodation, because anyone with PR who is not in agreement with the local authority's plans for their child can simply remove him or her from accommodation. However, there is some evidence that accommodation is used on a coercive rather than an agreed basis by local authorities as an alternative to applying to the court for a compulsory order to authorise actions they wish to take in respect of the child (Freeman and Hunt, 1996), which can have detrimental effects on the child (Children Act Advisory Committee, 1997). This means that those with PR may feel unable to exercise their right to remove a child from accommodation for fear of precipitating an application for a compulsory order.

5. IS THE BALANCE RIGHT IN PRACTICE?

Having considered the legal framework and its shortcomings, the real substance of the question of whether the balance is right lies in how these provisions are implemented in practice. There have been, since implementation of the Act, reports of a number of tragic and allegedly preventable child deaths at the hands of their parents or carers. Such cases are always shocking and deserve the extensive public enquiries they trigger to establish causes, so that lessons can be learnt from such cases about how to prevent similar tragedies in the future. However, these are a tiny minority of cases in which there is a gross failure on the part of the State to protect children at risk of harm; and given their rarity, it would be wrong to judge the efficacy of State intervention by numbers of such deaths. More appropriate would be to consider recent research evidence on how the child protection system is working overall.

(a) Research evidence

Following implementation of the Children Act, the Department of Health commissioned, and disseminated the research findings of, a number of research studies on the effectiveness of the child protection system since implementation of the Act (Department of Health, 1995). These findings highlight the importance of not only identifying more accurately families in which there is a real risk of abuse, but also of working in partnership with families, and supporting them when there is compulsory intervention by the State.

First, the referral process which triggers a child protection investigation under section 47 may currently be over-zealous. A national survey of statistics of children on the child protection register, and a more detailed study of all significant referrals to eight local authorities over a four-month period, revealed that for the majority of cases drawn into the process, there is an over-emphasis on child protection. In this study, this emphasis obscured the need for support services to be provided to the majority of families who have been, and will continue to care for, their children in the future. Indeed, three-quarters of the children "netted" in the child protection system received no protective intervention, and a high proportion received no help of any kind (Gibbons *et al.*, 1995). Many families are therefore being unnecessarily and inappropriately drawn into the child protection process. This is of particular concern given that another survey of 583 child protection cases in one local authority, and a detailed study in two authorities of thirty cases caught up in the early stages of enquiry, found that the impact of a child protection investigation can be devastating for a family: the disintegration of marital relationships and the relocation of children is marked, whilst professional attention rapidly moves elsewhere when the allegations are unsubstantiated (as they are in many cases) (Cleaver and Freeman, 1995).

Secondly, when the investigation is appropriate, the evidence seems to suggest that the outcomes for children are generally better when the local authority works in partnership with the family. One study of 220 consecutive child protection cases (and a sub-sample of thirty-three cases identified for more detailed study) in seven local authorities found that there was a clear link between good outcome and the greater involvement of parents in child protection cases. It also found that there was no evidence that things ever turned out badly for children or parents from working in partnership (Thoburn *et al.*, 1995). Another prospective study of 120 child protection cases in which a conference was held, found that there was a close link between the adequacy of the initial child protection plan (where the child's name was registered) and the child's safety; and that the protection plan had the most enduring influence when the social worker was new to the case at the time of registration. Professionals often underestimated the impact of the allegations and of the investigation on parents, and the withdrawal of support from non-abusing parents adversely effected their ability to assist in their child's recovery. Social workers who kept in constructive contact with the family were valued and this relationship contributed to good outcome (Farmer and Owen, 1995).

In disseminating these research findings, the Department of Health (1995) emphasised the importance of working in partnership with families. It states:

"the most important condition for success [in child protection work] is the quality of the relationship between a child's family and the professionals responsible . . . an alliance is needed which involves parents and, if possible, children, actively in the investigation, which takes account of their views and incorporates their goals into plans. Failure to achieve this level of cooperation helps to explain why some children remain safe when others do not" (p.45).

It cites evidence that a recurrence of abuse was less common in those families where some agreement had been reached between professionals and family members about the legitimacy of the enquiry and the solutions adopted. It concludes that:

> "an approach based on the process of Section 47 enquiries and the provision of Section 17 services might well shift the emphasis in child protection work more toward family support . . . a more balanced service for vulnerable children would encourage professionals to take a wider view. There would be efforts to work alongside families rather than disempower them, to raise their self-esteem rather than reproach families, to promote family relationships where children have their needs met, rather than leave untreated families with an unsatisfactory parenting style. The focus would be on the overall needs, rather than the narrow concentration on the alleged incident" (p.55).

(b) The refocusing debate

This review of research, and the Department of Health's conclusions about it, has triggered a new debate in the field of child protection. It highlights the need to refocus the provision of services towards greater family support for the majority of children drawn into the child protection process, and a more specialised child protection system for those cases of serious risk. This has necessarily raised questions about the thresholds for compulsory intervention, as set out in section 31 and section 44 of the Act. Proposals have been made for raising the threshold for section 47 investigations to ensure that it is only those cases where children are really at risk of harm that are drawn into the child protection process, thereby releasing greater resources to be provided for those children for whom the provision of support services are more appropriate but who are currently receiving a less than adequate service.

The Government's consultation paper on new proposals for inter-agency co-operation in child protection (Department of Health, 1998a) reflects this view by stating: "we no longer wish to see children being routed inappropriately into the child protection system as a way of gaining access to services"(p.iii). It also states that:

> "revised guidance now needs to promote a change of focus of SSD's work to ensure that the emphasis in future is on assessing needs and intervening earlier when children and families are first in need of support, rather than waiting until concerns about abuse mean that a s.47 enquiry becomes necessary. In this way, families should be better supported and the number of unnecessary child protection enquiries reduced" (p.21).

In order to achieve this, it proposes that agencies should adopt a more "needs-led" approach in the provision of services for children, whether or not they are drawn into the child protection system, with the emphasis on identifying what can be done to help families. However, it does not make any concrete proposals for increasing the resources available to enhance the supportive role of the State, nor does it give any clear guidance on how the threshold for compulsory intervention should be more specifically targeted at cases of serious risk. To date this is only a consultation exercise, and the revised guidance is currently being drafted. If the Government is serious about implementing aspects of its stated policy of supporting families, it should ensure that the revised guidance is very directive in this area, reinforced with resources to make a refocus of services towards effective support meaningful. Without it, there is likely to be wide variation of interpretation by service providers with the result that the support available to individual families will be subject to local policy priorities and other regional differences between agencies.

6. CONCLUSION

International conventions establish clear principles that the State should respect family life but must also provide supportive and protective services for children. The Children Act provides the legal framework in England and Wales to implement these principles in a balanced way. At their respective ends of the continuum, parental autonomy and State intervention are more or less unfettered, albeit that there is room for minor statutory reform to enhance each notion without compromising the other. Not surprisingly, it is the grey area in the middle that deserves closer scrutiny, since it is in this grey area that the balance between the two perspectives is the most delicate.

The principle of partnership, although present throughout the continuum, is most challenged in the grey area. When the State intervenes in family life to provide services for children, the degree of consultation with parents, which respects parental autonomy as far as possible, will be superseded by coercion wherever necessary to ensure the child's safety and protection. In principle, this seems entirely appropriate. The only difficulty seems to be deciding where an individual case falls on the continuum, and as a result, the level of coercion which should be exercised alongside consultation. This is largely a matter for practitioners to decide in their professional opinion. However, given the understandable caution exercised by many practitioners who investigate referrals to social services in ensuring that a child's need for protection is not overlooked, there is also scope for local and/or central government policy to direct more clearly the appropriate way to assess such referrals. In particular, there is a need for clear guidance as to how the thresholds for compulsory intervention should be interpreted so that child protection services are restricted to those cases where there is real evidence of risk rather than inappropriately "netting" children in need of support rather than protection into this process, with often devastating personal consequences for the child and family. The current revision of government guidance on child protection in *Working Together* provides a good opportunity to do this. The effect would be to allow greater numbers of families with children in need to keep their parental autonomy intact, with coercion being restricted to those cases in which there is clear evidence of a risk of significant harm.

REFERENCES

Brent London Borough, *A Child in Trust*, Report of the Panel of Enquiry into the Circumstances Surrounding the Death of Jasmine Beckford (London, London Borough of Brent, 1985).

Bullock, R., Little, M. and Millham, S., *Going Home* (Dartmouth Press, Aldershot, 1993).

Children Act Advisory Committee, *Annual Report* (1995).

Children Act Advisory Committee, *Final Report* (1997).

Cleaver, H. and Freeman, P., *Parental Perspectives in Cases of Suspected Child Abuse* (London, HMSO, 1995).

Cleveland Report, *Report of the Enquiry into Child Abuse in Cleveland* (London, HMSO, 1987).

Department of Health, *The Care of Children: Principles and Practice in Guidance and Regulations* (London, HMSO, 1991) (1991a).

Department of Health, *Working Together Under The Children Act* (London, HMSO, 1991) (1991b).

Department of Health, *The Children Act Regulations and Guidance, Volume 1, Court Orders* (London, HMSO, 1991) (1991c).

Department of Health, *The Children Act Regulations and Guidance, Volume 3* (London, HMSO, 1991) (1991d).

Department of Health, *Child Protection: Messages from Research* (London, HMSO, 1995).

Department of Health, *Working Together to Safeguard Children: New Government Proposals for Inter-agency Co-operation Consultation Paper* (London, HMSO, 1998) (1998a).

Department of Health, *Supporting Families: A Consultation Document* (London, HMSO, 1998) (1998b).

Department of Health and Social Security, *Review of Child Care Law: Report to Ministers of an Inter-Departmental Working Party* (London, HMSO, 1985) (1985a).

Department of Health and Social Security, *Social Work Decisions in Child Care* (London, HMSO, 1985) (1985b).

Department of Health and Social Security, *The Law on Child Care and Family Services* (London, HMSO, 1987).

Department of Health and Social Security, *Domestic Violence and Social Care* (London, HMSO, 1995).

Edwards, D., "Children first" (1997) *Community Care* (April).

Eekelaar, J., "Parental responsibility: state of nature or nature of the state?" (1991) *Journal of Social Welfare Law*, p. 37.

Farmer, E. and Owen, M., *Child Protection Practice: Private Risks and Public Remedies Decision-making, Intervention and Outcomes in Child Protection Work* (London, HMSO, 1995).

Freeman, P. and Hunt, J., *Parental Perspectives on Care Proceedings* (University of Bristol 1996).

Gibbons, J., Conroy, S. and Bell, C., *Operating the Child Protection System: A Study of Child Protection Practices in English Local Authorities* (London, HMSO, 1995).

Gibbons, J., Gallagher, B., Bell, C. *et al.*, *Development after Physical Abuse in Early Childhood: A Follow-Up Study of Children On Child Protection Registers* (London, HMSO, 1995).

Hayes, M., "The proper role of the courts in child care cases" (1991) 8 *Child and Family Law Quarterly* 3.

House of Commons, *Children in Care: Second Report from the House of Commons Social Services Committee* (London, HMSO, 1984).

Hunt, J. and McLeod, A., *Statutory Intervention in Child Protection Research Project: Thematic Summary* (University of Bristol, 1996).

Law Commission, *Review of Child Care Law, Guardianship and Custody, Law Commission,* No. 172 (London, 1985).

Lindley, B., *On the Receiving End* (London, Family Rights Group, 1994).

Millham, S., Bullock, R., Hosie, K. *et al.*, *Children Lost in Care: The Family Contact of Children in Care* (Gower, 1985).

Ryan, M., *The Children Act 1989: Putting it into Practice* (Aldershot, 1994).

Smith, C., "Judicial power and local authority discretion—the contested frontier" (1997) 9 CFLQ 3.

Thoburn, J., Lewis, A. and Shemmings, D., *Paternalism or Partnership? Family Involvement in the Child Protection Process* (London, HMSO, 1995).

12

Youth Crime and Parental Responsibility

LORAINE GELSTHORPE

1. INTRODUCTION

Recent pronouncements from the Labour Government which focus on youth crime give a clear message that parental responsibility for crimes of young people cannot be avoided. The title of the 1997 White Paper *No More Excuses* which led to a major revamping of the youth justice system, for example, is a telling clue to popular sentiments and to the direction of criminal justice policy in this regard. The purpose of this chapter is to chart attempts to promote parental responsibility for crime and to examine critically recent shifts in thinking which indicate that the "war on crime" is sometimes tantamount to a "war on parents".

Throughout the 1990s there have been widely proclaimed assumptions about the demise of childhood, the ill-discipline of children and the lawlessness of youth. Indeed, such assumptions have dominated popular discourses and political reaction. Of course, such claims are not new. Geoffrey Pearson (1983), for one, has described the periodic panics about youth crime, hooliganism, and lawlessness over time and claims made about "out of control youth" in the 1990s could easily have been voiced in the 1600s, 1700s , or 1800s. But the claims were recently refuelled by two significant events: the Bulger case and fears about persistent young offenders.

The murder of two-year old James Bulger by two ten-year old boys on 12th February 1993 in Bootle, Merseyside, received massive national and international media coverage and generated an enormous amount of public and private debate. The event inspired a kind of national collective agony, evidenced both within the media and within individuals' discussions. It was variously seen in terms of being symptomatic of social decay, the decline of morality, a cause of the swelling of parents' fears for their children and a spur to government policy relating to juvenile crime. Other media inspired discussions revolved around the "loss of innocence" of childhood marked by the revealing of the "evil" within two ten-year-old boys. More recently, the case has generated extensive debate about the role of the executive (that is, the Home Secretary) in sentencing, following his handling of judicially recommended tariffs and his pronounced intention to take public opinion into account in fixing the final tariff. Lord Justice Morland, dealing with the case, had ordered the boys to be detained at Her Majesty's Pleasure (the equivalent of a life sentence—in effect, meaning that their release from custody would be discretionary once a "tariff" period had been served). In January 1994 it was discovered that the judge had recommended a "tariff" of a minimum detention period of eight years for Jon Venables and ten years for Robert Thompson, with the overseeing Lord Chief Justice recommending a minimum period of ten years. Michael Howard, Home Secretary for the then Conservative Government, eventually ordered the two boys to serve a minimum of fifteen years, a decision which was criticised by some for making political capital out of the event. Interestingly, in May 1996, two judges in the Divisional Court declared Howard's decision to fix a minimum sentence of fifteen years in custody for the two boys as unlawful—since he had treated them as "adult murderers" rather than as children. Despite challenge in the higher courts, there is obvious support from the European Court of Human Rights in Strasbourg for the criticism of the Home Secretary since the boys' general treatment (including the trial in an adult court and in public) is seen to have breached the European Human Rights Convention.[1]

There are two particular points that merit further attention here. The first concerns the alleged influence of video nasties on the boys' behaviour, and the increasing tendency for children to remain unsupervised. As Alison Young has put it:

> "In addition to the comforting possibility that exposure to violent films might provide the answer to the question that the media had been asking for months (why did these boys do it?. . .), the focus on violent films is linked to the issue of parental care and the breach in the maternal relation" (1996, p. 133).

After the jury had returned their verdict the judge presiding in the case made a plea for a public debate on parenting and on the exposure of children to violent films and videos:

> "In my judgement the home background, upbringing, family circumstances, parental behaviour and relationships were needed in the public domain so that informed and worthwhile debate can take place for the public good in the case of grave crimes by young children. This could include exposure to violent video films, including possibly *Child's Play 3*, which has some striking similarities to the manner of the attack on James Bulger" (quoted in *The Guardian*, 27 November 1993).

A debate was thus sparked off between politicians, film critics and theorists, and psychologists. Some twenty-five psychologists signed a report entitled *Video Violence and the Protection of Children*, by Elizabeth Newsom, Professor

---

[1] I would add that the Bulger case was seemingly used by the Government as a pretext for a number of criminal justice initiatives, including the building of 170 additional places in secure units for 12 to 16-year-olds. For further deatils of the case see *R v Secretary of State for the Home Department, ex parte Thompson and Venables* [1997] 2 FLR 471.

of Developmental Psychology at Nottingham University, which pointed to direct effects on children's behaviour where they were repeatedly "exposed to images of vicious cruelty in a context of entertainment and amusement" (*The Guardian*, 1 April 1994). Despite evidence which suggests that children prefer soap operas to video nasties (Hagell and Newburn, 1994a) the Newsom Report was taken up with alacrity across the political divide. In April 1994 the Home Secretary stipulated that a new clause was to be inserted in the Criminal Justice Bill 1994 (now an Act) placing a duty on the British Board of Film Classification in granting licences to take account of the psychological impact of videos on children. Uncertain of its ability to regulate the behaviour of children, it seems, the Government has chosen to regulate the hire of video films to parents and children. Beneath all this there is perhaps a sense in which the Bulger case rocked, disturbed and disquieted the public's notion of childhood innocence, a notion which reflects the cultural and social investment in childhood (Warner, 1994). Bad children are thus seen to be a symptom of modernity and the grief for James Bulger is grief for the loss of an ideal of children. Parents (and particularly lone parents) are implicated in all of this.

The second and connected event concerned fears about children's *persistent* offending behaviour. Fears about the potentially damaging impact of video nasties and television violence following the Bulger case ran alongside fears that youth were persisting in criminal behaviour and that somehow youth was out of control. It is almost as if the Bulger case triggered alarm about the nature, extent and persistence of youth crime. Indeed, in the weeks following the Bulger case there was a gradual transition in newspaper reports from a focus on the horror of a single event to the horror that hordes of young people were marauding the country—making a mockery of any attempts to control them on the part of schools or criminal justice agents. Hagell and Newburn (1994b) were quick off the mark to test out the proposition. Based on a sample of several hundred young people who had been arrested three or more times in one year, they considered the nature and extent of their offending and their experiences of the criminal justice system. Contrary to political and public discourse (ably assisted by the media) however, they did not find a distinct group of very frequent offenders: they found only twenty-five offenders who met the secure training order criteria. Moreover, the persistent offenders they did find were not disproportionately engaged in serious offending.

Whatever the realities of events, however, it is clear that these two "crises" contributed to renewed emphasis on fears about young people and crime, and the part that parents can or should play in preventing it. But the notion of parental responsibility for crime is certainly not new.

2. PARENTAL RESPONSIBILITY FOR CRIME: CRIMINOLOGICAL THEMES

Research conducted by Cyril Burt in the early 1920s indicated that the home of the delinquent was often one particularly characterised by "defective family relationships" and "defective discipline" (1925, p. 101), and he argued in favour of detention for delinquents on the basis that "the shock of sharp separation will often rouse the casual offender to his senses, *and bring his family to a feeling of their own responsibility and blame"* (1925, p. 107; my emphasis).[2] Recent Home Office research on young offenders involving a self-report survey of some 2,500 young people aged fourteen to twenty-five suggests that 42 per cent of juveniles who had low or medium levels of parental supervision offended, but only 20 per cent of juveniles with a high level of supervision. The same research showed that the relationship between parent and child is crucial and that poor relationships with fathers were more prevalent among offenders than poor relationships with mothers (Graham and Bowling, 1995). A higher rate of offenders from single parent families was associated with less parental supervision, a greater likelihood of a poor relationship with at least one parent and greater poverty. Such a finding rehearses the findings of other studies on similar themes, for example, Harriet Wilson on parental supervision (1987) and David Farrington (1978, 1991) on parental discipline. The research findings here suggest that those parents who are harsh or erratic in disciplining their children are twice as likely to have children who offend. Extensive reviews of families, parenting skills and delinquency undertaken in 1974 by Power *et al.* and in 1983 by Rutter and Giller reveal that the research into the causes of juvenile delinquency amongst different social and ethnic groups has persistently shown that children who begin offending at an early age and who become serious offenders, or show serious conduct disorders, tend to come from large families (although the effect here is probably not due to size alone, but to the greater stresses and increased risk of family discord to which larger families are exposed); to have parents with a criminal record; to experience erratic or harsh discipline at home, particularly if combined with parental cruelty or neglect or poor parental supervision.

Similarly in the Cambridge-Somerville study in Boston, McCord (1979) reported that poor parental supervision was the best predictor of both violent and property crimes. In a Birmingham study, Wilson (1980) followed up nearly four hundred boys in one hundred and twenty large, intact families and concluded that the most important predictor of convictions, cautions and self-reported delinquency was lax parental supervision at age ten. A national survey of juveniles aged fourteen to fifteen came to a similar conclusion, noting that poor parental supervision was the most important correlate of self-reported delinquency for girls, and that it was the second most important for boys (after delinquent friends) (Riley and Shaw, 1985). Generally speaking, the parents of troublesome children have been found to be more punitive, more prescriptive, more likely inadvertently to reward delinquent behaviour, and more likely than others to issue vague and conflicting commands (see the reviews by Loeber and Stouthamer-Loeber (1986) and Farrington (1998)). The most recent com-

---

[2] Despite certain suggestions that some of Cyril Burt's research findings may have been fabricated (see Hearnshaw, 1979 and Mackintosh, 1995, for example) it is worth noting that he placed considerable emphasis on environmental and family conditions that gave rise to delinquency.

mentary on anti-social behaviour by young people (Rutter *et al.*, 1998) confirms all the above.

The family, or more specifically the "parenting", theme, therefore, is one which has been well rehearsed within debates about juvenile crime in various attempts to persuade, encourage, support, cajole, or coerce, young people, and their parents, in the fight against crime. As a result of these general findings, there has been considerable emphasis on family intervention initiatives (see, for example, Utting *et al.*, *Crime and the Family. Improving Child-rearing and Preventing Delinquency* (1993) and *Misspent Youth*, Report of the Audit Commission (1996)). A whole raft of initiatives ranging from "parent management training", "intensive home visiting programmes", and "community programmes" have made "families" as opposed to individual delinquents, a legitimate focus for attention (Utting, 1997; Wyness, 1997; Scheinwort and Weikart, 1993).[3] Before reviewing the recent governmental strategies to involve parents in the prevention of delinquency, however, it is important to outline earlier strategies.

3. HISTORICAL BACKGROUND

The need for special jurisdiction over juvenile offenders was first mooted in the early nineteenth century, but for present purposes we may begin this historical outline with the Children Act 1908 which firmly established the principle of dealing with juvenile offenders separately from adult offenders. Juvenile courts (a branch of the magistrates' courts) were formally created in this Act, with dual jurisdiction: partly criminal (as for adults, but with some procedural, substantive and sentencing variations) and partly a care jurisdiction (civil) for "children in need" (i.e. neglected children, those beyond the control of their parents, those in "moral danger", etc.). The juvenile courts were to sit at a different place, and/or time from the adult magistrates' court for the same area and offenders were to receive treatment differentiated to suit their special needs. The public were excluded; newspaper reporting was allowed, but with anonymity for defendants and their parents; and crucially, the imprisonment of juveniles was to be abolished. Nonetheless, it is arguable that the introduction of the juvenile court reflected a primarily *symbolic* change in attitudes towards the juvenile offender. Juvenile courts remained *criminal* courts and the procedures were essentially the same as for adults.[4] Moreover, Herbert Samuel, introducing the changes, argued that parents were to be made more responsible for the

---

[3] There was a striking example of this earlier in the century when out of concern for the nation's health, following a disastrous perfomance in the Boer War and a declining birth rate, children were seen to belong not merely to the parents, but to the community as a whole as a national asset. Education for motherhood was set in train as a way of ensuring that children were protected for the good of the country (Davin, 1978). Thus not only are "parenting classes" not new, but echo an earlier "family strategy" to deal with a broad social problem.

[4] The numbers processed through the care jurisdiction were usually fairly small relative to the number of criminal proceedings brought.

wrong-doing of their children. The age of criminal responsibility remained—as historically in England—at seven, with the upper age limit of the juvenile court's jurisdiction being (normally) the sixteenth birthday.

The English juvenile court was fully reviewed by an official committee in 1927 (Home Office, 1927). This committee carefully considered, but rejected, the possibility of reforming the system along American "welfare" lines (Faust and Brantingham, 1979). Significantly, however, it was recommended (and subsequently enacted in the Children and Young Persons Act 1933) that magistrates were to have regard to "the welfare of the child". The juvenile court was to act in *loco parentis,* establishing itself as the forum capable of adjudicating on matters of family socialisation and parental behaviour, even if no "crime" as such had been *committed* (my emphasis) (see Morris and McIsaac, 1978; Rutherford, 1986) .

The recommendations of the 1927 Committee also led, in the 1933 Act, to the raising of the age of criminal responsibility from seven to eight, and indicated that there was to be a specially selected panel of magistrates to deal with juveniles. A combination of crime control and welfare perspectives thus informed juvenile justice. Whilst we can see the interplay of these two approaches throughout, there were few other formal changes in the system for dealing with young offenders until the 1960s.

4. JUVENILE JUSTICE DEVELOPMENTS IN THE 1960S: THE DEVELOPMENT OF A WELFARE PERSPECTIVE

One feature of the broad political consensus at the end of the Second World War was the creation of a post-war "welfare state" which involved state intervention in the economy in order to maintain full employment, with supporting policies on housing, unemployment and sickness benefit, health and child-care (Marshall, 1975; Marwick, 1982; Halsey, 1988). Nevertheless, despite the emergence of a welfare perspective in general and a sympathetic, child-oriented perspective in particular (Rose, 1989), the war years had seen a new clamour for an unequivocally punitive perspective towards young offenders. A concern for the welfare of the child co-existed with a tougher outlook.

As Bottoms and Stevenson (1992) point out, the key events of the post-war history of juvenile justice can be traced back to a letter to *The Times*, 16 March 1955, signed by, among others, the wife of the Archbishop of Canterbury, an eminent child psychiatrist, a celebrated penal reformer and a leading social work thinker. Their theme was "the urgent need for re-orienting the social services towards the maintenance of the family", not least because they believed juvenile crime often resulted from "family breakdown". They called for the setting up of a Committee of Enquiry whose terms would be broad enough "to include all causes of family breakdown, with positive recommendations for their prevention and alleviation".

At the same time, the Magistrates' Association pressed the Home Office for a review of the procedure in juvenile courts and the treatment of juveniles coming before them. The Home Office responded by setting up, in 1956, a Departmental Committee, (the Ingleby Committee) to consider the issues posed by both groups. The Ingleby Report (Home Office, 1960) largely endorsed the existing structure of the juvenile court, but included recommendations to strengthen the powers of the court by allowing magistrates to sentence young persons directly to borstal. The Committee also proposed that the age of criminal responsibility be raised from eight to twelve, thereby replacing criminal with care proceedings for the younger age group. In 1963, as a legislative compromise, the age of criminal responsibility was raised to ten in the Children and Young Persons Act. Whilst the same Act placed local authorities under a duty to promote the welfare of children by reducing the need to receive them into care, with powers to provide preventive assistance to relevant families, left-wing critics focused primarily on the missed opportunity for creating a unified family service. Subsequent reports of the Labour Party (Labour Party, 1964) continued the critical theme with the claim, amongst other things, that juveniles had no personal responsibility for their offences. There was a clear aspiration to take juveniles out of the criminal courts and the penal system and to treat their problems in a family setting through the establishment of family advice centres, a family service and, for a minority, a family court.

The Labour Government's White Paper, *The Child, the Family and the Young Offender* (Home Office, 1965) thus proposed the abolition of the juvenile court and its replacement by a non-judicial "family council", linked to a unified "family service". But there was concerted opposition to these proposals from magistrates, lawyers, and probation officers, whom commentators believe did not want to lose the chance of working with young offenders in their fast developing professional service (Rutherford, 1986; Harris and Webb, 1987; Pitts, 1988). In response to this opposition, the Labour Government produced a second White Paper, *Children in Trouble* (Home Office, 1968). In this renewed attempt to promote reforms, the Government leaned heavily on the expertise of the Home Office Child Care Inspectorate (Pitts, 1988) and, as a result, the language used changed (though not all of the underlying sentiments). The response was one which depended on "observation and assessment", "a variety of facilities for continuing treatment", "increased flexibility" and "further diagnosis." And this White Paper, whilst retaining some of the more radical features of the earlier attempt at reform, managed to produce proposals which were largely acceptable to political, administrative and professional constituencies. The cost of this, however, was the retention of the juvenile court.

The culmination of this period of activity was the Children and Young Persons Act 1969. The 1969 Act dictated that juveniles under fourteen were not to be referred to the juvenile court solely on the grounds that they had committed offences (thus bringing Britain into line with many other European countries). Rather, it was proposed that "care and protection" proceedings should be brought, where it could be established that such juveniles were not receiving the care, protection and guidance "*a good parent might reasonably be expected to give*" (my emphasis). Overall, the general aim of the Act was to make the commission of an offence no longer a sufficient ground for intervention—that is, to "decriminalise" the court's jurisdiction. Put very simply, the juvenile court was to become a welfare providing agency, but also an agency of last resort: referral to the juvenile court was to take place only where voluntary and informal agreement could not be reached between social workers, juveniles and, crucially, their parents (Morris and McIsaac, 1978).

5. JUVENILE JUSTICE IN THE 1970S: THE ECLIPSE OF WELFARE?

Having witnessed the development of a consensus, albeit a fragile one, the 1969 Act appeared to bring latent tensions to the surface. The breakdown of this specific consensus reflected the breakdown in the broader political consensus achieved in the immediate post-war years. The stage was set for a very different conception of social order and of the appropriate response to juvenile offenders in 1970 when there was a change of government from Labour to Conservative. The writings of the Conservative Party (see, for example, Cooper and Nicholas, 1963 and 1964) depict the law-breaker as choosing to commit offences and as doing so from personal iniquity and from "demands" or "desires" exacerbated by the welfare state rather than from social inequality.[5] Neither psychological nor social conditions were viewed as relevant to understanding criminal behaviour. Consequently, juvenile offenders were viewed as personally responsible for their actions, although, depending on their age, parents might share in this responsibility in having failed both to discipline their young and to inculcate "basic values" in them. Thus a key role in preventing and controlling crime was assigned to the family which, it was believed, had been systematically undermined by socialism because it had taken away the responsibility from families to provide for its members. "Family responsibility" was given a different force and meaning to that found in comparable Labour Party writings. Deficiencies in the family were to be remedied through discipline and external controls not through support and services. Parents were to be held responsible for the offences of their children by making them pay, quite literally. The appropriate response to the delinquent was correction through discipline and punishment. The role of the courts—and the actual and symbolic powers of the magistracy— were also viewed as important in preserving respect for the law, ensuring parental responsibility and making juvenile offenders accountable for their

---

[5] The Conservative Central Office published two influential reports in the 1960s which are clear statements of Conservative Party policy on crime. These are *Crime and Punishment* published in 1961 and *Putting Britain Right Ahead* in 1965. In addition, the Conservative Political Centre also published a number of reports and papers in the 1960s on crime which, though not official Conservative Party policy, can be broadly taken as indicative of Party thinking.

actions. Sections of the Conservative Party were always opposed to the philosophy underlying the Longford Report (Labour Party, 1964), the 1960s White Papers and the subsequent legislation.[6]

When the Labour Party was re-elected in 1974, it was no longer politically or popularly viable to implement the Act in full. Thus new welfare measures supplemented but did not replace the old punitive ones. By the mid-1970s, the perspective underlying the 1969 Act was deemed to have failed; in reality, it had never been tried. But its "moment" had gone (Gelsthorpe and Morris, 1994).

6. JUVENILE JUSTICE IN THE 1980s: THE "MOMENT OF CRIME CONTROL"

In the 1980s in England and Wales, as elsewhere, there was an explicit revival of traditional criminal justice values. It is no accident that this coincided with and was fuelled by the electoral campaigns and eventual election of a Conservative Government with a large majority. The "need to stand firm against crime" was especially apparent in the electoral campaigns of the Conservative Party in 1979. To the electorate it presented itself as the Party who could and would take a strong stand against crime, in contrast to the Labour Party who were presented as excusing crime and as being sympathetic to offenders.

The messages in this 1979 campaign were the need to protect victims from offenders irrespective of their age[7] and the need to reduce the high level of recorded crime and the allegedly increased seriousness of crime, particularly among juveniles. Specifically, the political rhetoric referred to "young thugs" who were to be sent to detention centres for a "short, sharp shock". And later that year, after they had won the election, the new Home Secretary made good some of the electoral promises: two detention centres were, on an experimental basis, to have tougher regimes. A few years later, a White Paper, *Young Offenders* (Home Office, 1980), set the scene for further changes.

Both this White Paper and the ensuing legislation—the Criminal Justice Act 1982—hit at the root of the social welfare perspective underlying the 1969 Act and represented a move away from treatment and lack of personal responsibility to notions of punishment and individual and parental responsibility. They also represented a move away from executive (social workers) to judicial decision-making and from the belief in the "child in need" to the juvenile criminal. The Act attempted to toughen and tighten up the provisions of the 1969 Act—

---

[6] In making sense of Conservative ideology about crime, we find its roots in the core values of Conservatism. In essence, Conservative societies are believed to be better off, both materially and morally, with only limited state control (Durham, 1989). Substantial government intervention is viewed as socially disruptive (because "wants" get translated into "rights"), as wasteful of resources (because it stimulates false "demands"), as promoting economic inefficiency (through weakening competition) and as removing individual freedom. There is an acceptance of the government's role in the provision of certain services but this is as a last resort, a safety net, and only for those in "real" need.

[7] It is no accident that the growth of the "victims movement" also dates from around this period.

including the provision of youth custody, provision for short periods in detention centres, and it was to become normal practice to fine parents rather than the juvenile. The actual operation of juvenile justice turned out rather differently (Gelsthorpe and Fenwick, 1997), but that is not germane to discussion here.

We can sum up the 1980s in this way. In 1979, the Conservative Party made crime a major election issue. The emphasis was on re-establishing "Victorian values" in opposition to the legacy of the supposed permissiveness of the 1960s and its "soft" approach to crime. Indeed, as McLennon (1987) has argued, it was not merely that left-wing and liberal writers failed to see the problems inherent in "soft" approaches to crime, discipline, education and so on, but that those "soft" approaches were seen as contributing to permissiveness with all its unwelcome, politically unpalatable effects (see also Taylor, 1981). In such a supposedly de-moralising culture, crime and violence were seen as "out of control": hence the need for "law and order" policies to reassert the virtue and necessity of authority, order and discipline and attempts to realign relationships between the state and civil society as a whole. Parental responsibility for crime was to become an increasingly important theme in all of this.

7. JUVENILE JUSTICE IN THE 1990S: THE RETURN TO CONSENSUS?

The first significant event of the 1990s was the implementation of the Children Act 1989 which came into force in October 1991. As will be clear from other chapters in this volume, this represented a major structural alteration to the law concerning the welfare of juveniles and covers an enormous range of matters previously dealt with in different legislation. The law affecting juveniles who offend is only touched upon, but the resulting changes, together with the Act's underlying sentiments about the nature of the relationship between the State, children and their parents, have significant implications for juvenile offenders.

The most important of these is the cessation of the use of the care order as a disposal available to the court in criminal proceedings and the removal of the offence condition in proceedings justifying state intervention in the life of a family. This change at once recognises the enormous decline in the use made of the care order, the inappropriateness of a care order in criminal proceedings, the principle of determinacy in sentencing and the importance that the government gives to parental responsibility (Harris, 1991). New rules also provide for the transfer of care proceedings from the juvenile court. These are now heard in a renamed "family proceedings" court; the newly-named youth court deals only with criminal proceedings. Hence the Children Act 1989 *separates* criminal and "care" issues. This is in stark contrast to the Children and Young Persons Act 1969 which sought to blur the distinction in its promotion of a welfare philosophy and policy for all young people "in trouble" of one sort or another.

The Criminal Justice Act 1991 contained three distinct powers to identify parents more closely with the criminal activity of their children. The powers requiring parents to attend court with their children, and making parents responsible for payment of fines, were attempts to strengthen measures which already existed under previous statutes. The third and most important change was the introduction, in section 58, of a completely new duty upon magistrates to bind over the parents of a child under sixteen so as to "take proper care and exercise proper control over the child" (s.58(2)(b)). The rationale for this approach to parental responsibility was set out clearly by the then Minister of State at the Home Office, John Patten, who claimed that the parents of young offenders were individuals "who could cope, but simply chose not to . . . these are the families which have failed not through misfortune or misjudgement, but through wilful neglect by parents of their responsibilities" (Hansard, vol.49, col.767).

"Binding over" is an ancient court power which dates back to Saxon times; it allows the courts to obtain a promise from an individual to keep the peace or to be of good behaviour for a fixed period of time. If the promise is broken, the person concerned can be ordered to forfeit a sum of money no greater than a maximum set at the time of the original decision. An individual does not have to be convicted of a criminal offence to be bound over. A recent Law Commission report has argued the case for the abolition of the bind over powers on the grounds that they offend against modern notions of justice and human rights (Law Commission, 1994). Nevertheless, in the Criminal Justice Act 1991 it was stated that if the court does not bind over the parents, it must state why it is not doing so in open court. The parent is bound over in a specified sum of money up to £1,000, and, if the child reoffends, the parent is liable to forfeit that amount. Binding over requires the parent's consent, but, as the Act empowered the courts to fine parents who refuse to be bound over, in reality parents have little choice in the matter. In effect, we could say that a bind over amounts to a suspended fine.

The binding over requirements of the 1991 Act were highly controversial. Magistrates already had the power to bind over parents, but rarely used it because they considered that in most cases it would do more harm than good. Moreover, whereas requirements for parents to pay fines and compensation orders imposed on children applied only in cases where a court decided to impose a financial penalty, the binding over provisions of the 1991 Act were to apply in all cases, whatever other penalty was imposed on a juvenile. During the passage through Parliament of the Criminal Justice Act 1991, the proposal was strongly criticised by organisations representing magistrates, justices' clerks, probation officers and social workers . The Magistrates' Association, in particular, made known its strong opposition. In its comments on the White Paper, *Crime, Justice and Protecting the Public* (1990), which preceded the 1991 Act, the Association referred to the "harmful effect these proposals could have in hastening a breakdown of family relationships" and said that "parents may feel that they are being punished twice for one offence of their child". The Justices'

Clerks' Society also opposed the proposal. The widespread strength of feeling against the then Conservative Government's approach was reflected in an editorial in the Magistrates' Association Magazine *The Magistrate* (December 1990/January 1991) which said:

> "It is felt by a wide range of organisations, including the Magistrates' Association, that if implemented these proposals are not only unlikely to achieve the government's objective, but are likely in many instances to damage such little cohesion as may survive in already fraught and vulnerable families. One of the most extreme of these proposals concerns the binding over of parents for their children's good behaviour . . .
>
> Magistrates have daily experience of sentencing offenders. Those who sit in the juvenile court will be only too well aware of the high incidence of already difficult family circumstances amongst the children and young people before them. Why, one wonders, is the Home Secretary so determined to refuse to listen not only to all the agencies and voluntary organisations working in the juvenile justice field, from many of whom he might expect opposition on ideological grounds, but also to this Association's Juvenile Courts Committee's very clear rejection of the proposal that courts should be required to bind over parents?"

Similarly, a leading article in *The Times* (10 November 1990), commented:

> "This is the kind of proposal that makes perfect sense to middle class Ministers, who generally leave the taming of adolescence to their children's boarding schools. For, say, the single mother in Brixton, struggling against odds to keep a young person on track, they represent only a threat."

The powers were nevertheless implemented on 1 October 1992 and although their use has been sporadic, and somewhat tempered by the absence of any practical steps which courts can take to enforce the orders, the punitive ethos towards parents has had powerful symbolic impact in terms of diminishing sympathy towards struggling parents. The Criminal Justice and Public Order Act 1994 extended the bind over provisions introduced by the 1991 Act by empowering courts binding over a parent or guardian to ensure that the child complies with the requirements of a community sentence. Whereas under the 1991 Act parents could be required to forfeit up to £1,000 if their children reoffended, under the 1994 Act they may also be required to do so even if the child does not reoffend but fails to comply with the requirements of a sentence. This provision was implemented in February 1995.

It is arguable that this power is subject to the same objections as the original, that it could unfairly punish parents who have genuinely but unsuccessfully tried to improve their children's behaviour. Such parents are often at their wits' end to know how to control their children and prevent them from offending (Penal Affairs Consortium, 1995). Clearly, the threat of financial penalties, if their children do not comply with requirements, is unlikely to help them do so better. Such a threat may well exacerbate already difficult relationships between parents and children, and it may accelerate the trend for parents to throw their children out of the home. In any case, such threats will undoubtedly increase the degree of pressure and hardship on families which are already struggling, and have the potential to send out the rather confusing message that young people can slough off responsibility on to their parents.[8]

It might be argued that the sections of the Criminal Justice Act 1991 which deal with young people must be viewed in conjunction with the provisions of the Children Act which had been contemporaneously part of the legislative programme of the same Government. As Andrew Ashworth *et al.* (1992), chief commentators on the Act, put it: "the 1989 Act provides a crucial statutory backcloth to the new youth court". And yet nothing could be more different than the approach to parental responsibility adopted in the two pieces of legislation. Far from lauding the advantages of the minimalist State, and, in sharp contradistinction to the idea that parents act most responsibly when left to get on with things, the Criminal Justice Act 1991 proceeds on the basis that "responsible" behaviour can only be achieved by punishing the parents of young people in trouble. The effect of recent changes has thus been to "publicly implicate parents in the criminality of their children by requiring them to take their place alongside their child in court" (Edwards, 1992, p. 117).

There are other significant events which mark the increasing emphasis on parental responsibility. The first concerns the publication of a major review of government policy in this area. The Audit Commission's report, *Misspent Youth* (Audit Commission, 1996), essentially argued that the present youth justice (with all its emphasis on control, punishment, and law and order) is expensive, inconsistent, and ineffective. Additionally, the report increased the volume of calls for renewed emphasis on "criminality prevention", and, in particular, interventions in early life which research suggests hold out the greatest promise of reducing youth crime. The report was welcomed by critical academics, experienced policy-makers and practitioners alike. The Commission was clearly putting its weight behind schemes for diverting offenders from court, where possible, and, if not, developing more constructive schemes for dealing with them in the community. The need to support parents is part of this constructive strategy for dealing with young offenders.

A second event concerns the publication of a Green Paper entitled *Tackling Youth Crime* (a consultative document) in March 1997, on juvenile offending, by the Conservative Government of the day—a paper which might be seen as an official response to the enlightened views of the Audit Commission Report. The Green Paper, however, whilst nodding sympathetically in the direction of early prevention (without promises of further resources to accomplish this), endorsed the punitive theme the Government had been promoting. "Parental

---

[8] Another concern here relates to the fact that there is no provision for parents to have separate legal representation in the proceedings. Bind overs are made without the parents' own representative addressing the court on their behalf. While the child's legal representative may be of assistance, there may be a conflict of interest between parents and child over the question of the extent to which responsibility for the offending behaviour lies with the parents rather than the child.

responsibility" was the major headline following publication of the report—
with the notion of "Parenting Orders" for example, to induce parents to exert
greater authority and control over their children. The first sketches of such
orders were developed in the subsequent White Paper, *No More Excuses* (1997).
As the Secretary of State (Mr O'Brien) announced in Committee in the House of
Commons, the Parenting Order:

> "is designed to help and support parents to control the behaviour of their children by
> requiring them to attend counselling and guidance sessions and, if necessary, to com-
> ply with specific requirements . . . We believe, until now, insufficient help or attention
> has been given to parents to change their children's behaviour" (Official Report,
> Standing Committee B, 7 May 1998, col. 255).

Section 8 of the Crime and Disorder Act 1998[9] provides that the court may
make a Parenting Order where (i) a child safety order is made,[10] (ii) an anti-
social behaviour order or a sex offender order is made in respect of a child or a
young person,[11] (iii) a child or young person is convicted of an offence, or (iv) a
person is convicted of offences under sections 443 or 444 of the Education Act
1996. In essence, the Parenting Order requires a parent to attend counselling or
guidance sessions no more than once a week for a maximum of twelve weeks
(but this can, on a discretionary basis, be waived where the parent has previously been through a parenting course). The Parenting Order may also include
additional requirements (for example, to ensure that the child regularly attends
school; ensure that the child is home by a certain time each night) for a period
up to twelve months. Parents may be fined for failing to comply with any
requirements in a Parenting Order. Where a person under sixteen is convicted
of an offence, the court *shall* make a Parenting Order (if the desirability condition is fulfilled), or, if no order is made, the court shall state in open court why
an order is not being made. The parental bind over powers of the 1991 Act are
retained at present alongside the Parenting Order (but the Government has said
that the case for maintaining the bind over powers will be reconsidered in the
light of experience of piloting the Parenting Order).[12]

---

[9] Details of the Act are described in Padfield (1999).

[10] A child safety order is available in the Family Proceedings Court for children under 10 who
have committed what would be an offence if 10 or over, *or* where such an order is considered necessary to prevent such actions.

[11] The anti-social behaviour order (s.1 of the 1998 Act) is a community-based order which can be
applied for by the police or local authority in consultation with each other against an individual or
several individuals whose behaviour is anti-social (causing distress, alarm or harassment to one or
more people not in the same household). The order, which has effect for a minimum of two years,
and which imposes prohibitions to prevent further anti-social acts, is expected to be used mainly
against adults, although it can be used for family members aged 10 upwards, who may be participating with the adults in the anti-social behaviour. The sex offender order (s.2) is similarly a community-based order, applied for by the police, against any sex offender whose present behaviour in
the community gives reasonable cause to believe that an order is necessary to protect the public from
serious harm. The order, which applies to all those over the age of criminal responsibility, has effect
for a mimimum of five years.

[12] The piloting of such orders began on 30 September 1998 and will last for 18 months.

The Government's proposal for this method of increasing parental responsibility has by no means found widespread support. The Bishop of Hereford, for example, summed up many people's concerns in the first debate in the House of Lords:

"I believe that parenting orders are a doubtful method of coping with the problems that we face. By definition, they come into effect, if they work at all, too late in the day to prevent young people being caught up in bad company and acquiring bad habits. They seem to be contrary to the spirit of partnership, which is at the heart of the Children Act. The threat of financial penalties on parents who are often already poor, inadequate and sometimes in despair is unlikely to achieve very much which is positive" (HL Official Report, vol. 585, no. 95, col. 557–558).

Such criticisms were pushed aside. Put simply, we are now left with an order embodied in the Crime and Disorder Act 1998 which flies in the face of expert views. In response to Home Secretary Jack Straw's announcement of plans for a National Family and Planning Institute to oversee parent classes and help-lines, *The Guardian* feature writer Heather Welford, drawing heavily on the Save the Children (Scotland) Report, *Positive Parenting* (1998), questioned the Government's strategy on parenting (*The Guardian*, 9 September 1998). She pointed out some of the dangers of dictating to people how they must raise their children, arguing that informal support groups and networks are more likely to have impact with parents than didactic approaches. As the Save the Children (Scotland) Report indicates, "some parents have been deterred from attending because they associate 'parenting courses' with 'bad parenting' and feel that attendance would be stigmatising" (1998, p. 39). The parents did not want a pre-set curriculum, or the feeling of obligation to attend. But they did want access to expertise and the chance to set their own priorities.

Parenting Orders involve ordering parents of convicted children to go on corrective courses so that they learn their responsibilities to keep their offspring out of trouble, exert control and authority over them—operating curfews where appropriate, and ensure school attendance (see Ministerial Group on the Family, 1998). Threats of punishment accompany the orders—where parents fail to comply. Whilst the supportive aspects of this theme may be attractive, it is surely questionable as to whether enforcing child curfews and using compulsion and threats of fines and imprisonment will change the behaviour of parents. On the contrary, the stigmatisation and potential resentment may well exacerbate matters; the measures may well undermine and embitter those upon whom they are imposed.

Other difficulties with the notion of the Parenting Order include the fact that apart from reference to previous legislation which indicates that the orders can be imposed on "a person who is a parent or guardian of the child or young person" in question,[13] nowhere does it clearly state in the legislation what is meant

[13] The Crime and Disorder Act 1998, Sch. 7, para. 1.3, amends s.55 of the Children and Young Persons Act 1933 (which empowers courts to order parents or guardians to pay fines or

by "a parent" in a practical sense—an issue which is central to this volume. Is the Parenting Order to be imposed on the legal parent or guardian? the parent with whom the child resides? What if mum lives with her boyfriend—is the Parenting Order to be imposed on him too? Or on the "distant" parent who sees the child once a month? Also, is the parent who is denied contact under the Children Act 1989 to be held responsible under the Crime and Disorder Act 1998? It is conceivable that the child or young person might be engaging in criminal behaviour because of a lack of contact with a parent.

Whatever the legal difficulties, we know that the parents of young people in trouble are disproportionately drawn from homes where all responsibilities have been devolved to one remaining adult (see, for example, Rutherford, 1986; Hagell and Newburn, 1994b). As women so overwhelmingly occupy this position, where parents are punished for failing, these punishments inevitably fall upon them in similarly unequal proportions. A cynic might determine that there was an element of "feminist backlash" in all of this; at the very least, we should note that the courts' harsh treatment is sometimes reserved for "failed mothers" (Carlen, 1988; Worrall, 1990; Hedderman and Gelsthorpe, 1997). Indeed, Juliet Mitchell and Jack Goody have drawn attention to the placing of the mother centre-stage in "parenting" elsewhere in this book, and the theme of "problem children of problem mothers" is a common one when discussing juvenile crime (Mann and Roseneil, 1994). Initially, the panic about the Jamie Bulger case concerned juvenile crime; later it transpired that at least part of the moral panic was about an underclass in which lone mothers featured very largely (Halsey, 1992; Murray, 1990). Interestingly, the whole issue of Parenting Orders coincides with a broad social policy thrust regarding not only general support for parents (for example, better financial support), but support for marriage (Ministerial Group on the Family, 1998; Utting, 1995). One can discern in preparatory debates a distinct image of what a "proper family" and "proper parents" do. As Jack Straw, then Shadow Home Secretary, and Janet Anderson, then Shadow Minister for Women, describe in their consultation paper on Parenting:

> "In the 1990s we expect modern parents to engage with their children on at least the following: Respect for others; Lying; Stealing; Family and personal relationships; Personal care and hygiene; Diet and exercise; Sex education; Drinking; Smoking; Drugs; Education—school and homework; TV, video and cinema violence; Bullying; Truancy; Vandalism; Household participation; Work and career motivation" (Straw and Anderson, 1996).

Thus, Lord Thomas of Gresford seemed to put his finger on the issue in relation to Parenting Orders in a very perceptive way:

compensation on behalf of their offspring) so that the definition of "parent" in the Family Law Reform Act 1987 applies to that section; but this definition of "parent" is not applied to "parent" in Section 8 of the 1998 Act. "Guardian" in the 1998 Act has (by virtue of s.117) the same meaning as in the Children and Young Persons Act 1933, s.107. It would surely have been helpful to state the definition of parents and guardians in a straightforward way (alongside other definitions) in order to resolve any ambiguities.

"The orders seem to be wonderfully idealistic. We have before us the template of the new Labour family where no doubt the mother smilingly greets her children as they come from school with her arms covered in flour from baking scones for their tea, and the father is ready to help with the homework, and so on—and if they are not, we shall jolly well make them so because we shall train them in the proper duties of how to be a mother and father. People are not like that. The puritanical, almost Cromwellian, zeal with which the order is introduced is typical of other measures which may be found with the Bill" (HL Official Report, 10 February 1998, col. 1068–70).

The reality of parenthood in many cases where young people are in trouble, undoubtedly involves vulnerability and poverty (Drakeford, 1996), with many parents (especially mothers) living on State benefits and experiencing housing problems often including overcrowding. We should acknowledge, however, that the statistically significant predictors of delinquency (*inter alia* social status, family size, suffering a broken home before the age of five, low family income, a parent with a criminal record, poor parenting skills, birth order) rarely approach the realms of certainty (Utting *et al.*, 1993). There *are* clear signs that what seems to happen is that adverse social and environmental factors, combined with family management practices, educational under-achievement, conflict in the home and so on, add stresses that *may well* result in delinquency, but any intervention strategies that set about stigmatising individual children or their parents known to be statistically "at risk" would arguably have as many dangers as benefits. What is particularly worrying, in the light of the extensive evidence on links between family factors and delinquency, is the 1998 Crime and Disorder Act's architects' inherent assumption of "wilful neglect" on the part of parents.[14]

There is obvious need for support and encouragement for the parents of young offenders. The binding over provisions are unmistakably punitive. The chief problem with the Parenting Order revolves around the context in which such "support" is to be delivered, that is, a punitive, court-room context. There is an irony here in the fact that whilst "care" and "control" issues relating to the offenders themselves have been separated because of the complexities and tensions (the Children Act 1989/Criminal Justice Act 1991 divisions) the issues become blurred in relation to the parents. Whilst some of the thinking underlying the Parenting Order is laudable (the underlying recognition that poor parenting skills may contribute to delinquency), there appears to have been too little thought given to the context of its delivery and to recognition elsewhere (Sparks and Bottoms, 1995) of notions of legitimacy, i.e., the need to sustain the

---

[14] The punitive approach taken towards parents reflects wider thinking about personal responsibility within the Crime and Disorder Act 1998, e.g., the abolition of the presumption of *doli incapax* (s.34). Following lengthy debate on the issue the Government declared that there was no case for retaining the presumption on the grounds that a child under fourteen clearly does know the difference between right and wrong and therefore does not need protection from the harshness of criminal punishment. Similarly, changes in pre-court decision-making, with the introduction of a limitation on reprimands and warnings (as opposed to open-ended cautions) reflects personal responsibility for crime (see Padfield, 1999).

faith and support of "consumers" of the criminal justice system in order to create effective practice. In other words, actions have to be perceived as "legitimate" in order to carry weight. In view of this, the idea of delivering "supportive" parental programmes in a punitive context is likely to be alienating. There is also an increasingly persuasive literature on the effectiveness of modern notions of rehabilitation which emphasise the possibilities of increasing the effectiveness of practice in a voluntary context, where there is consent (see McIvor (1992); McLaren (1992), and McGuire (1995) for instance). In this sense, the new Parenting Order goes against the grain.

Ironically, the White Paper, *No More Excuses* (1997) rehearses other, arguably rather more positive, family and parental themes: for example, in proposals for the reform of court structures so that there is more direct engagement of participants in proceedings. One such suggestion involves the use of a single table around which participants might sit; another concerns a reduction of the emphasis on adversarial proceedings. Some of the discussion here reflects interest in Family Group Conferences (Morris and Maxwell, 1997; Marsh and Crow, 1998) and, arguably, the Scottish Hearing System which has long since directly involved parents in proceedings (Lockyer and Stone, 1998).

Family Group Conferences were developed in New Zealand and are based on the traditional systems of conflict resolution in Maori culture. Family Group Conferences involve a professional co-ordinator inviting the young offender and their extended family to a "network conference" along with the victim. The aim is to provide a forum to discuss all aspects of the problem caused by the young person and to propose a mutually acceptable plan which addresses the needs of both the young person and the wider community.[15] The New Zealand model of Family Group Conferences is not readily transferable to the youth justice system in England and Wales, but a number of pressure groups involved in penal reform have urged agencies to see how elements of Family Group Conferences might be incorporated. The key relevance of all this here revolves around the notion of constructive co-operation with parents and other kin to ensure an outcome which deals with the victim's feelings and rights as well as the need to control crime.

The system for dealing with young offenders (between eight and sixteen) in Scotland is essentially a welfare "Hearing System" (involving a Reporter—a legally trained official—and a lay panel of members of the public) and similarly involves "constructive co-operation" with parents.[16] Significantly, the Scottish system has always been seen as a "welfare" system in contrast to the more punitive system in England and Wales. Changes within the Children (Scotland) Act

[15] In England and Wales the Family Rights Group (a national voluntary organisation) have been responsible for promoting and supporting a number of pilot projects in family group conferencing that have been particularly concerned with the care, protection and welfare of children.

[16] For reasons of space it is obviously not possible to do justice to the Scottish system in this chapter, but essentially, the system involves a complete separation between the judicial and disposition functions so that young offenders are initially referred to a Reporter whose function it is to decide on the basis of reports, whether or not the juvenile referred to him/her by the police, social work

1995 (particularly those relating to the provision to place "public protection" above that of the "best interest of the child" in certain cases) allied with moves to tie parental rights more closely with responsibilities, have led to a clarion call from some commentators to protect the traditional welfare principles and resist punitive populism (McAra and Young, 1997; Asquith, 1998) but there is optimism that welfare principles will prevail.

8. CONCLUSION: FROM A WAR ON CRIME TO A WAR ON PARENTS

The arguments about youth justice are no longer about "welfare", "crime control" or "justice" it seems, and the new philosophies cannot be allied to the political right or left as they once could. A "populist punitiveness" reigns (Bottoms, 1997) which fosters consensus around issues where dissent or moral pluralism exists, and whilst Labour have pressed the case for being "tough on crime *and the causes of crime*" (my emphasis)[17] there seems to be a reluctance to institute changes which involve a wholesale shift from repression to prevention. The Government is hedging its bets and going for both, but the fall-out from this not only makes parents responsible but blurs the boundary between support and punishment.[18]

The notion of parental responsibility has increasingly exercised government ministers then, and over a wider field of social policy than criminal justice. For example, the broad thrust of Thatcher governments to "roll back the frontiers of the state" had, as one of its corollaries, the replacement of public and State activity by private and family activity (Hudson, 1992) and it has been strongly argued that the preservation of family autonomy in child-rearing (see Freeman, 1987), increases "personal choice". The belief in the past has been that the State might legitimately increase and reinforce parental responsibilities, but the exercise of these responsibilities is best left as unregulated as possible. The practical embodiment of this approach is most fully realised perhaps in the Children

agencies, or education departments, is in need of compulsory measures of care (a supervision requirement which may include residential conditions). If the juvenile or parents deny the commission of an offence the case is referred by the Reporter to the Sheriff Court for the offence to be proved. If referred through the Hearing System, the panel can discharge the referral by the Reporter or impose a compulsory measure of care. The panel has no power to fine the juvenile or his/her parents, to impose a custodial penalty, or to remit the juvenile to the Sheriff Court for sentence. Interested readers may like to consult Asquith (1998). The early development and functioning of the Scottish system is described in Martin *et al.* (1983).

[17] This slogan, in fact written by Gordon Brown, encapsulates the attempt to move the argument about crime beyond the choice between personal and social responsibility (Tony Blair, interview on BBC Radio 4 "The World This Weekend" programme, 10 January 1993).

[18] There is a fascinating account of Jack Straw and the shaping of home affairs policy in Anderson and Mann (1997), ch. 7. It is clear that Tony Blair has had a strong hand in the shaping of policy and that he himself has used the ideas of the American Communitarian movement—particularly the ideas of Amitai Etzioni—(that is, the need to create a new moral, social and public order based on restored communities) to provide intellectual credibility. From this one can see how the notions of "stakeholders" and "individual duties and responsibilities" emerge.

Act 1989. John Eekelaar (1991) cites "parental responsibility" as the "pivotal conception" of the Act locating responsibility for child-rearing firmly with the parents rather than the State. Minimum State intervention, it was argued, would lead to maximum parental responsibility: "The Bill's obligation on the primary function of parenthood will . . . highlight the obligation on parents to care for their children and bring them up properly" (House of Commons Debates 1988, *Hansard*, vol. 151, col. 767). But the Labour Party appears to have moved to the right and there seems to be a new, shared realism amongst Party members of different persuasions that punishment and responsibility (including parental responsibility) are at the core of concerns about juvenile justice. The Criminal Justice Act 1991, in particular, reinforced the social and moral duties of parenthood, and there is explicit finger pointing at parents for not upholding their end of an implicit social contract, to produce moral upstanding citizens (Wyness, 1997) and "good families". It is arguable that the Crime and Disorder Act 1998 merely transforms the finger pointing into "finger wagging" through paternalistic parenting classes delivered in the punitive context of the court-room. What is so very frustrating at present, is the apparent belief that a "populist punitiveness" (encapsulating a belief that harsh penalties deter offenders, a belief that increased punitiveness may strengthen moral consensus in society against certain kinds of activity, and a belief that the adoption of such a punitive stance will satisfy a particular electoral constituency) is in the ascendency. This is to do both our understanding of crime, and the parents of young offenders, an injustice. Whilst the need for early intervention in the lives of children to prevent delinquent behaviour and to protect those at risk is overwhelmingly convincing, the need to punish already vulnerable parents is not.

REFERENCES

Anderson, P. and Mann, N. (eds.), *Safety First. The Making of New Labour* (London, Granta Books, 1997).
Ashworth, A., Cavadino, P., Gibson, B. *et al.*, *The Youth Court* (Winchester, Waterside Press, 1992).
Asquith, S., "Children's hearings in an international context" in A. Lockyer and H. Stone (eds.), *Juvenile Justice in Scotland. Twenty-Five Years of the Welfare Approach* (Edinburgh: T & T Clark, 1998).
Asquith, S., "Scotland" in J. Mehlbye and L. Walgrave (eds.), *Confronting Youth in Europe* (Forlage, Denmark, AKF, 1998).
Audit Commission, *Misspent Youth* (London, Audit Commission, 1996).
Bottoms, A. E., "The philosophy and politics of punishment and sentencing" in C. Clarkson and R. Morgan (eds.), *The Politics of Sentencing Reform* (Oxford, Oxford University Press, 1997).
Bottoms, A. and Stevenson, S., "What Went Wrong? Criminal justice policy in England and Wales, 1945–1970" in D. Downes (ed.), *Unravelling Criminal Justice* (London, Macmillan, 1992).

Burt, C., *The Young Delinquent* (London, University of London Press, 1925).

Carlen, P., *Women, Crime and Poverty* (Buckingham, Open University Press, 1988).

Conservative Political Centre, *Crime and Punishment* (London, CPC, 1961).

Conservative Political Centre, *Putting Britain Right Ahead* (London, CPC, 1965).

Cooper, B. and Nicholas, G., *Crime in the Sixties* (London, CPC, 1963).

Cooper, B. and Nicholas, G., *Crime and the Labour Party* (London, The Bow Group, 1964).

Davin, A., "Imperialism and Motherhood" (1978) 5 *History Workshop* (Spring) 9.

Drakeford, M., "Parents of young people in trouble" (1996) 35 *The Howard Journal of Criminal Justice* 242.

Durham, M., "The right: The Conservative Party and conservation" in L. Tivey and A.Wright (eds.), *Party Ideology in Britain* (London, Routledge, 1989).

Edwards, S., "Parental responsibility: an instrument of social policy" (1992) 22 *Family Law* 113.

Eekelaar, J., "Parental responsibility: state of nature or nature of the state?" (1992) 37 *Journal of Social Welfare and Family Law* 37.

Farrington, D., "The family backgrounds of aggressive youths" in L. Hersov, M. Berger, and D. Shaffer (eds.), *Aggression and Antisocial Behaviour in Childhood and Adolescence* (Oxford, Pergamon, 1978).

Farrington, D., "Childhood aggression and adult violence: Early precursors and later life outcomes" in D. Pepler and K. Rubin (eds.), *The Development and Treatment of Childhood Aggression* (Hillsdale, N.J., Erlbaum, 1991).

Farrington, D., "Using Risk Factor Research to Shape Crime Prevention Policy", paper given at the 12th International Congress on Criminology in Seoul, Korea, August 1998.

Faust, F. and Brantingham, P. (eds), *Juvenile Justice Philosophy* (St. Paul, Minnesota, West Publishing Co., 1979).

Freeman, M., "Freedom and the welfare state: child rearing, parental autonomy and state intervention" (1987) 20 *Journal of Social Welfare Law* 70.

Gelsthorpe, L. and Fenwick, M., "Comparative juvenile justice: England and Wales" in J. Winterdyk (ed.), *Comparative Juvenile Justice* (Toronto, Canadian Scholars' Press, 1997).

Gelsthorpe, L. and Morris, A., "Juvenile justice 1945–1992" in M. Maguire, R. Morgan and R. Reiner (eds.), *The Oxford Handbook of Criminology* (Oxford, Oxford University Press, 1994).

Graham, J. and Bowling, B., *Young People and Crime* (Home Office Research Study No 145, London, Home Office, 1995).

Hagell, A. and Newburn, T., *Young Offenders and the Media: Viewing Habits and Preferences* (London, Policy Studies Institute, 1994a).

Hagell, A. and Newburn, T., *Persistent Young Offenders* (London, Policy Studies Institute, 1994b).

Halsey, A., *British Social Trends Since 1900*, 2nd edn. (London, Macmillan, 1988).

Halsey, A., "Foreword" to N. Dennis and G. Erdos, *Families Without Fatherhood* (London, IEA Health and Welfare Unit, Choice in Welfare No.12, 1992).

Harris, R., "The life and death of the Care Order (Criminal)" (1991) 21 *British Journal of Social Work* 1.

Harris, R. and Webb, D., *Welfare, Power & Juvenile Justice* (London, Tavistock, 1987).

Hearnshaw, L., *Cyril Burt. Psychologist* (London, Hodder & Stoughton, 1979).

Hedderman, C. and Gelsthorpe, L. (eds.), *Understanding the Sentencing of Women* (Home Office Research Study 170, London, Home Office, 1997).

Holman, B., *Children and Crime* (Oxford, Lion Publishing, 1995).

Home Office, *Report of the Departmental Committee on the Treatment of Young Offenders* (Cmd. 2831, London, HMSO, The Maloney Committee, 1927).

Home Office, *Report of the Committee on Children and Young Persons* (Cmnd. 1191, London, HMSO, The Ingleby Report, 1960).

Home Office, *The Child, The Family and the Young Offender* (Cmnd 2742, London, HMSO, 1965).

Home Office, *Children In Trouble* (Cmnd. 3601, London, HMSO, 1968).

Home Office, *Young Offenders* (Cmnd. 8045, London, HMSO, 1980).

Home Office White Paper, *Crime, Justice and Protecting the Public* (London, Home Office, 1990).

Home Office Green Paper, *Tackling Youth Crime* (London, Home Office, 1997).

Home Office, *No More Excuses—A New Approach To Tackling Youth Crime In England And Wales* (Cm. 3809, London, HMSO, 1997).

Hudson, B. L., "Family trends and public policy" (1992) 65 *Health Visitor* 20.

Jarvis, G., Parker, H. and Sumner, M., "An ambivalent service" (1987) 34 *Probation Journal* 103.

Labour Party, *Crime: A Challenge to Us All*, Report of a Labour Party Study Group—The Longford Report (London, The Labour Party, 1964).

Lockyer, A. and Stone, F. (eds.), *Juvenile Justice In Scotland. Twenty-Five Years of the Welfare Approach* (Edinburgh, T & T Clark, 1998).

Law Commission, *Binding Over* (Report No. 222, London, HMSO, 1994).

Loeber, R. and Stouthamer-Loeber, M., "Family factors as correlates and predictors of juvenile conduct problems and delinquency" in M. Tonry and N. Morris (eds.), *Crime and Justice, Volume 7* (Chicago, University of Chicago Press, 1986) 29.

Mackintosh, N. (ed.), *Cyril Burt: Fraud or Framed?* (Oxford, Oxford University Press, 1995).

Mann, K. and Roseneil, S., "Some mothers do 'ave 'em: backlash and the gender politics of the underclass debate" (1994) 3 *Journal of Gender Studies* 317.

Marsh, P. and Crow, G., *Family Group Conferences in Child Welfare* (Oxford, Blackwell Science Ltd, 1998).

Marshall, T., *Social Policy* (London, Heinemann, 1975).

Martin, F., Fox, S. and Murray, K., *Out of Court* (Edinburgh, Scottish Academic Press, 1983).

Marwick, A., *British Society Since 1945* (Harmondsworth, Penguin, 1982).

McAra, L. and Young, P., "Juvenile justice in Scotland" (1997) 15 *Criminal Justice Matters* 8.

McCord, J., "Some child-rearing antecedents of criminal behaviour in adult men" (1979) 37 *Journal of Personality and Social Psychology* 1477.

McEwan, J., "In search of juvenile justice: The Criminal Justice Act 1982" (1983) 20 *Journal of Social Welfare Law* 112.

McGuire, J., *What Works: Reducing Offending* (Chichester, John Wiley, 1995).

McIvor, G., *Sentenced to Serve* (Aldershot, Gower, 1992).

McLaren, K., *Reducing Reoffending: What Works Now?* (Report, Wellington, Department of Justice, 1992).

McLennon, G., "Sociological theories of crime: from disorganisation to class and beyond" in Open University Course Booklet *Thinking About Crime: Theories of Crime and Justice* (Milton Keynes, The Open University, 1987).

Mehlbye, J. and Waldergrave, L. (eds.), *Confronting Youth in Europe* (Forlaget, Denmark, AKF, 1998).

Ministerial Group on the Family, *Supporting Families*, A Consultation Document (London, Home Office, 1998).

Morris, A. and Maxwell, G., *Family Group Conferences and Convictions*, Occasional Papers in Criminology no.5 (Wellington: Victoria University of Wellington, 1997).

Morris, A. and McIsaac, M., *Juvenile Justice?* (London, Heinemann, 1978).

Murray, C., *The Emerging British Underclass* (London, IEA Health and Welfare Unit, 1990).

Newsom, E., *Video Violence and the Protection of Children* (Nottingham, University of Nottingham, 1994).

Padfield, N., *A Guide to the Crime and Disorder Act 1998* (London, Butterworths, 1999).

Pearson, G., *Hooligan: A History of Respectable Fears* (Basingstoke, Macmillan, 1983).

Penal Affairs Consortium, *Parental Responsibility, Youth Crime and the Criminal Law* (London, NACRO, 1995).

Pitts, J., *The Politics of Juvenile Justice* (London, Sage, 1988).

Power, M., Ash, P., Shoenberg, E. *et al.*, "Delinquency and the family" (1974) 4 *British Journal of Social Work* 13.

Riley, D. and Shaw, M., *Parental Supervision and Juvenile Delinquency* (London, Home Office, 1985).

Rose, N., *Governing the Soul: The Shape of the Private Self* (London, Routledge, 1989).

Rutherford, A., *Growing Out of Crime: Society and Young People in Trouble* (Harmondsworth, Penguin, 1986).

Rutter, M. and Giller, H., *Juvenile Delinquency: Trends and Perspectives* (Harmondsworth, Penguin, 1983).

Rutter, M., Giller, H. and Hagell, A., *Anti-Social Behaviour By Young People* (Cambridge. Cambridge University Press, 1998).

Save the Children, Scotland, *Supporting Parents, Supporting Parenting. Positive Parenting, First Year Report* (London, Save the Children, 1998).

Scheinwort, L. and Weikart, D., *A Summary of Significant Benefits: the High/Scope Perry Pre-School Study Through Age 27* (Michigan, High/Scope Press, 1993).

Sparks, R. and Bottoms, A. E., "Legitimacy and order in prison" (1995) 46 *British Journal of Sociology* 45.

Straw, J. and Anderson, J., *Parenting. A Discussion Paper* (London, The Labour Party, 1996).

Taylor, I., "Crime waves in post-war Britain" (1981) 5 *Contemporary Crises* 43.

Tildesley, W. and Bullock, W., "Curfew orders: the arguments for" (1983) 30 *Probation Journal* 139.

Utting, D., *Family and Parenthood* (York, Joseph Rowntree Foundation, 1995).

Utting, D., *Reducing Criminality Among Young People: A Sample of Relevant Programmes in the UK* (Home Office Research Study No. 161, London, Home Office, 1997).

Utting, D., Bright, J. and Henricson, C., *Crime and the family. Improving child-rearing and preventing delinquency* (London, Family Policy Studies Centre, NACRO and Crime Concern, 1993).

Warner, M., *Making Monsters* (London, Vintage, 1994).

Wilson, H., "Parental supervision: A neglected aspect of delinquency" (1980) 20 *British Journal of Criminology* 203.

Wilson, H., "Parental supervision re-examined" (1987) 27 *British Journal of Criminology* 275.

Worrall, A., *Offending Women: Female Lawbreakers and the Criminal Justice System* (London, Routledge, 1990).

Wyness, M., "Parental responsibilities, social policy and the maintenance of boundaries" (1997) 45 *Sociological Review* 305.

Young, A., *Imagining Crime: Textual Outlaws and Criminal Conversations* (London, Sage, 1996).

Part III
Parenting Post-Divorce

13

The Parent-Child Relationship in Later Life: the Longer-Term Effects of Parental Divorce and Remarriage

WENDY SOLOMOU, MARGARET ELY, CAROL BRAYNE and
FELICIA A. HUPPERT*

1. INTRODUCTION

In this chapter we consider the long-term effects of divorce from the point of view of the divorced parent. Whilst most of the research in this area has focused on outcomes for the child and indicates that the parent-child relationship can be adversely affected (Rodgers and Pryor, 1998), here we focus on the divorced parents themselves. We analyse data collected from a large sample of elderly people to describe the patterns of contact that people aged sixty-five and over have with their adult children and to ascertain whether earlier divorce does, in fact, have an adverse effect on the availability for them of supportive contact from their adult children and others. If this is the case, and our data suggest that it is, we can expect to see a continuing rise in the number of elderly people who have poor levels of supportive contact with their adult children as the effects of increases in divorce rates over recent decades feed through to the older population.

2. BACKGROUND

Results from a number of quantitative studies published in the 1990s, mainly conducted in North America, suggest that, in general, divorce does have long-term adverse effects on the quality and amount of contact between parents and their adult children. These studies use various measures to assess the quality of parent–child relations, including frequency of contact, levels of intergenerational exchange of practical, financial and emotional support, perceptions of

* We wish to acknowledge the invaluable input to the Healthy Ageing Study of our colleagues, Kevin Morgan and Pamela Sussams. We also thank Jennifer Brookes, Valerie Jackson and Judith Nickson for their administrative support on the Study. The project was funded by a grant from the Economic and Social Research Council, with additional funding for analyses provided by a grant from the Nuffield Foundation.

support available, and ratings of felt obligations towards parents. Some studies base their analyses on national survey data that include parents, who are mostly in middle, rather than old, age. However, the patterns of contact and support reported appear to be consistent with those observed between adult children and older divorced parents and it is important to note that these patterns appear to be set relatively early on and then persist in old age.

In general, there is a stronger likelihood of a breakdown of the parent and adult-child relationship, in terms of frequency of contact and levels of supportive exchange, for parents who divorce compared to parents who do not divorce. This negative effect is stronger for divorced fathers than it is for divorced mothers (Cooney and Uhlenberg, 1990, 1992; Amato and Booth, 1991; Bulcroft and Bulcroft, 1991; Umberson, 1992; White, 1992; Booth and Amato, 1994; Cooney, 1994; Millward, 1997). An exception to the general finding, although not inconsistent with the weaker effects reported for divorced mothers, is Choi's (1995) comparative study of long-term widows and divorcees (on their own for more than twenty years and aged seventy years and over). In terms of proximity to, and contact with adult children the study reports no major differences between the two groups of women, other than widows having more telephone contact.

Studies that consider the effect of living apart from children following divorce find that this is particularly detrimental to subsequent relations for fathers. Seltzer and Bianchi (1988) note a steady decline in interaction of children with the absent parent over time as typical, but with non-custodial mothers having more frequent contact with their children than non-custodial fathers. Seltzer (1991) also describes a steady decline in non-custodial fathers' involvement with children over time after separation. Aquilino (1994b) reports that relationships with custodial mothers and fathers remained positive among young adults raised in single-parent households, both in terms of quality of relationship and amount of contact with parents. Non-custodial mothers had nearly as good a relationship with their adult children as custodial mothers did, providing the custodial father did not remarry. However, for the fathers, becoming the non-custodial parent was likely to result in severe deterioration of the father–child relationship. Adult children were also more likely to live at a greater geographical distance from a non-custodial parent than from a custodial parent or parents who had not divorced. Geographical proximity itself was an important predictor of parent-child contact and thus custody also had an indirect negative effect on contact via this factor.

The number of fathers who live with or have custody of their children is relatively small. In an attempt to assess whether parental gender might also be an important factor, some studies have focused on divorces taking place when children have already reached adulthood. Cooney (1994) examined the influence of recent parental divorce on contact and affective relations between young men and women, aged eighteen to twenty-three, and their parents, from the perspective of the adult child. (The affective dimension of the relationship with each parent was assessed using a 15-item scale of adult child-parent intimacy that included statements such as "he thinks of your best interest", "you respect each other".) Despite the fact that custody was not at issue as the children were grown up, this study found that compared to young adults whose parents remained married, adult children of divorced parents reported similar levels of contact with their mother, but significantly lower levels of contact with their father. Divorced fathers were also worse off in terms of affective relations with their daughters, but not with their sons. However, in a sample of young people aged nineteen to thirty-four with parents mostly aged between forty and sixty-four, Aquilino (1994a) also finds significant negative effects for divorced mothers, although these effects were much smaller than the divorce effects on father-child relations. Later-life parental divorce was also associated with greater geographical distance between adult children and fathers, thus adding an indirect negative effect on levels of contact for divorced fathers, but not for divorced mothers. Aquilino's study supports the conclusion that in terms of both relationship quality and frequency of contact, the relationship of father and daughter suffers somewhat more than that of father and son.

There is evidence to suggest that the longer the non-custodial parent lived with their children prior to divorce the more positive the effect on subsequent relations. Bulcroft and Bulcroft (1991) report that the reduction in contact between divorced men and their adult children was less severe when parental divorce occurred in later life. Aquilino (1994b) notes that the older the age of the child at final separation from the non-custodial parent the more positive the relationship with that parent in adulthood in terms of relationship quality and amount of contact.

There is no clear evidence that remarriage of the custodial parent has an adverse effect on subsequent relations between parents and their adult children. White (1992) reports that intergenerational support patterns were similar for those families where the parents remarried and for those where the parents remained divorced. Aquilino (1994b) finds no difference in mother–child relationship quality (as reported by the adult child) between those children whose custodial mothers remarried and those children whose custodial mothers remained single-parent, although remarriage did slightly reduce frequency of contact with adult children. Similar results were found for custodial fathers and Aquilino concludes "that the custodial parent's remarriage has only a weak influence at best on adult children's relations with their custodial parent". Aquilino (1994b) also considers the effect of remarriage of the custodial parent on relations with the non-custodial parent and reports that non-custodial mothers were more severely affected than non-custodial fathers. Whilst the custodial mother's remarriage appeared to have no impact on relationship quality between adult children and non-custodial fathers and led to only moderately lower levels of contact, if the custodial father remarried both the quality of the relationship and amount of contact with the non-custodial mother was greatly impaired.

The gender differences in the amount and type of contact that divorced men and women have with their adult children may reflect the way that men and women relate to their adult children in general. Aquilino (1994a) reports that widowhood had no impact on adult children's relations with mothers—relationship quality and contact were similar to that of mothers whose husbands remained alive. However, in comparison to fathers with wives, adult children reported much lower levels of contact with their widowed fathers and this negative effect was significantly stronger for daughters. In terms of quality of relationship with the widowed father, a significant negative effect was observed for daughters, but not for sons.

To summarise, parental divorce appears to have an adverse effect on the long-term relationship between some parents and their adult children and, as a group, non-custodial fathers are the most likely to experience this deterioration. There is also evidence that affective relations between father and daughter suffer somewhat more than that of father and son. However, even when divorce takes place in later life and custody is not an issue, fathers are more likely than mothers to have less contact and support from their adult children. This may reflect a general pattern of behaviour between men and their children; among parents who have not divorced, widowed fathers have less contact with their adult children than widowed mothers and the father–daughter relationship appears to suffer the most. More generally, at least within couples, it is women who are the "kin-keepers" or emotional housekeepers and tend to take the initiative in maintaining social contact with relatives on both sides of the family.

3. DESCRIPTION OF A BRITISH SAMPLE

We used data from a study of healthy ageing conducted in Cambridgeshire and Nottingham to examine whether the intergenerational patterns of contact and support described in the USA and elsewhere can be also observed in a British sample. The sample consists of 2,041 people aged sixty-four and over, living independently in the community in a relatively good state of mental and physical health. A more detailed description of the study and sample selection is given in the appendix to this chapter. The advantage of using a sample that excludes those who are mentally or physically frail is that any effects that the onset of physical or mental impairment may have on family relationships do not influence our findings. If people become frail in old age, the pattern of their social networks changes, as they move from living independently to a reliance on informal forms of support (providing it is available to them) and then, for some, to living dependently in an institution.

4. PREVALENCE OF DIVORCE AND REMARRIAGE

From our initial sample, 2,032 respondents answered questions about divorce. Table 13.1 describes the sample by age group and gender, giving percentages of

Table 13.1: Marital history by age group and gender

Age group and gender	N	Marital history		
		Married, never divorced (%)	Married, have divorced* (%)	Always single (%)
64–69	652	83.4	10.6	6.0
Men	315	82.9	11.4	5.7
Women	337	84.0	9.8	6.2
70–74	482	84.9	11.2	3.9
Men	231	86.1	10.4	3.5
Women	251	83.7	12.0	4.4
75–79	493	85.6	9.5	4.9
Men	231	86.6	9.5	3.9
Women	262	84.7	9.5	5.7
80 and over	405	86.9	4.9	8.1
Men	175	89.7	5.7	4.6
Women	230	84.8	4.3	10.9
Total**	2032	85.0	9.4	5.7
Men	952	85.8	9.7	4.5
Women	1080	84.3	9.1	6.7

* Includes four men and six women who give current marital status as "separated".
** Excludes five men and four women who did not answer questions on divorce.

those who have experienced marriage and divorce. The majority (85 per cent) had been married and never divorced, a small percentage (nearly 6 per cent) had always remained single and just over 9 per cent (190 respondents) had either experienced divorce or were currently separated.[1] Eighteen respondents had divorced twice. This means that for those who had married, almost one in ten had experienced divorce at some stage in their life. The proportion of respondents who had experienced divorce is higher for people in the 64–79 age group (10.6 per cent) than for those aged eighty and over (4.9 per cent), reflecting the rising divorce rate for this population. It is interesting to note that, with the exception of the group of women aged eighty and over where a relatively high proportion (10.9 per cent) remained single, a larger proportion of respondents had experienced divorce than had remained bachelors or spinsters.

For the 190 respondents who had divorced, 36 per cent had not remarried, 44 per cent were currently in a second or third marriage, 16 per cent had remarried but were now widowed, and 4 per cent had remarried but were now divorced for a second time. Rates of divorce and remarriage were similar for men and women.

[1] Ten respondents gave current marital status as "separated" and, for simplification, are included in the "divorced" category.

5. FAMILY SIZE AND COMPOSITION

All respondents were asked to provide information about their living children. At the time of interview, 85 per cent (1,721) of respondents, including five respondents who had never married, had children, yielding data on 3,956 children. Family size ranged from one to ten children with a mean of 2.3. From Table 13.2 we can see that the proportion of respondents who had children is similar for the group who had never divorced (89 per cent) and the group that had experienced divorce (92 per cent). However, the number of children was larger among respondents who had divorced than among those who had not (the mean number of children per family is 2.8 for the divorced group and 2.3 for the non-divorced group)[2]. This difference is explained by the fact that whilst the numbers of biological children reported was similar for the ever-divorced and never-divorced respondents, respondents who had experienced divorce were more likely to have step-children. We can explore this phenomenon in more detail by looking at family type by marital history (see Table 13.3). By "family type" we mean whether respondents described the children in their family as "biological", "step", "adopted", or a mixture of these. (Respondents were asked if a child was their "*natural,* biological child". There was no evidence that respondents had any problem with a question framed in this way and, in this chapter, we shall use the term "biological" to indicate that the relationship between the respondent and child was assumed, by the respondent, to be genetic.) None of the thirty-nine respondents who had adopted children had ever been divorced. Among respondents who had remained married, 94 per cent described all of the children in their family as "biological", compared to 80 per

Table 13.2: Percentage of sample with children and family size by marital history

Marital history	N	Have children (%)	Family size		
			mean	median	range
Married, never divorced	1,727	89	2.3	2	1–10
Married, have divorced	190	92	2.8	2	1–10
Always single	115	4	1.2	1	1–2
Total*	2,032	85	2.3	2	1–10

* Missing data for one man who did not provide details about his children and five men and four women who did not answer questions on divorce.

[2] Test of difference between number of children in divorced and not divorced groups: Mann-Whitney U, P = 0.0019.

Table 13.3: Family type by marital history

Family type	Marital history*			
	*never divorced***		*ever divorced*	
	N	*% of group total*	N	*% of group total*
All "biological"	1446	93.8	140	80.0
All step	31	2.0	6	3.4
All adopted	17	1.1	0	0
"Biological" and step	23	1.5	29	16.6
"Biological" and adopted	21	1.4	0	0
"Biological" and adopted and step	1	0.1	0	0
Group total	1539		175	

* Excludes four respondents who were always single and nine respondents who did not answer the questions about divorce.
** Missing data on relationship of child for two respondents who had never divorced.

cent of those who had divorced. Twenty per cent of the divorced group had step-children (compared to 3.6 per cent of the remained married group) and the divorced group were more likely to have a mixture of step- and biological children in their family (16.6 per cent) than those who had never divorced (1.6 per cent). There is, of course, another kind of "mix" that we are, unfortunately, unable to identify from our data; that is, whether all of the children in a family who are described as "biological" share the same set of biological parents. If one parent or both have been married before then it is quite possible that while the respondent describes the children as "biological", the reconstituted family consists of half-siblings, as well as step-siblings.

6. FREQUENCY AND QUALITY OF CONTACT WITH CHILDREN FOLLOWING DIVORCE

Three-quarters (143) of those who had experienced divorce had children by their divorced spouse. These respondents were asked further questions concerning the quality of their relationship with these children, whether there was any current contact, and whether these children could be relied on in an emergency. Responses to these questions were generally positive: 74 per cent said that the divorce had not lessened the quality of their relationship; 81 per cent maintained contact; and 77 per cent thought that the children of a divorced spouse could be relied on in an emergency. If, however, we look at these responses for mothers and fathers and depending on whether children lived with the respondent or the divorced spouse, interesting differences become apparent (see Table 13.4). We should first note that in response to the question, "Did your children mainly live with you or mainly with your spouse after the divorce?" a far higher proportion (87 per cent) of women reported that their children lived with them in comparison to the proportion for men (22 per cent). In only one case was residence shared between both parents.

Table 13.4: Contact between children and divorced parents

Questions respondents were asked about their children from an earlier marriage	Whom the child mainly lived with after the divorce* (% answering yes)			
	Respondent		Respondent's ex-spouse	
	Men N=13	Women N=55	Men N=46	Women N=7
Do they come to see you, write to you, and/or assist you in any way?	100	91	52	86
Could you rely on them in an emergency?	92	86	44	86
Has divorce lessened the quality of your relationship with your children?	23	13	61	43

* Of the 143 respondents who had children by their divorced spouse, 122 respondents answered the question, "Did your children mainly live with you or mainly with your spouse after the divorce?" Data for one respondent who reported that the child had lived with both himself and his former spouse is omitted.

** 20 respondents who reported that their eldest child was at least 19 years of age at the time of divorce, did not answer the question about whom the child lived with following the divorce. This group gave a high proportion of positive responses: 100 per cent (men and women) to the first question; 85 per cent (men), 88 per cent (women) to the second; and 0 per cent (men), 11 per cent (women) to the third.

The group that suffers most in terms of the continuing parent–child relationship is men who did not live with their dependent children following divorce. Only 52 per cent of this group had continuing contact, 44 per cent felt able to rely on these children in an emergency, and 61 per cent felt that divorce had lessened the quality of their relationship with these children. This is in sharp contrast to the group of men who had lived with their dependent children following divorce (100 per cent maintained contact; 92 per cent were able to rely on their children in an emergency; and only 23 per cent felt that their relationship had been impaired by divorce).

For the women, the issue of continuing contact with, and support from, their children does not appear to be related to whether the children lived with them following divorce. However, the quality of their relationship was affected; 43 per cent of the women whose children had not lived with them felt that the divorce had lessened the quality of their relationship, compared to only 13 per cent of women who had lived with their children. We should note, though, that the former group consists of only seven cases.

Twenty respondents who reported that their eldest child was at least nineteen years of age at the time of divorce did not answer the question about whom the children lived with following the divorce. This group gave high proportions of positive responses to the questions about their continuing relationship with their children (see note to Table 13.4).

For the respondents who remarried following divorce, remarriage appears to have little effect on the continuing relationship with children of the previous marriage. (Similar proportions of men and women remarried following divorce, 66 per cent and 61 per cent respectively, and the likelihood of remarriage was the same for those who had children and those who did not.) For men, remarriage did not affect the level of contact with children of a divorced spouse. However, whilst all of the women who had not remarried had maintained contact with their children, 13 per cent of those who remarried had not.[3] All six of the women (4 per cent of the total) who thought that the quality of the relationship with their children had suffered because of the divorce had remarried.

7. FACTORS ASSOCIATED WITH CONTACT

We have seen how the experience of divorce is associated with relatively lower levels of supportive contact with adult children for the group of male respondents who did not reside with those children following divorce. We now wish to consider to what extent contact with adult children may differ for men and women and may also depend on marital history, for the whole sample. All respondents with children were asked about the frequency of contact with each child (both face-to-face contact and by letter or telephone) as well as whether each child lived locally, in the United Kingdom or abroad. Table 13.5 summarises the data on frequency of contact in the following four ways: frequent contact with at least one child; frequent contact with all children; no contact with at least one child; and no contact with any children. We define "frequent contact" as either seeing a child or having contact by telephone or letter, at least once a week and "no contact" as never seeing nor having any telephone or written contact with any child. We are thus able to examine both extremes—frequent contact with all children and no contact with any children—as well as the factors associated with having frequent on-going contact with at least one child or losing contact completely with at least one child. While frequency of contact does not necessarily imply a supportive relationship, some degree of contact is necessary for the possibility of a supportive relationship.

[3] Pearson Chi-square, p=0.08

Table 13.5: Contact between parent and child by gender and marital history

Amount of contact	Marital history and gender*					
	Never divorced		Divorced, did not remarry		Divorced and remarried	
	Men	Women	Men	Women	Men	Women
	N = 729	N = 812	N = 28	N = 32	N = 58	N = 55
	%	%	%	%	%	%
Frequent contact with at least one child	91	92	61	84	69	75
Frequent contact with all children	66	66	21	47	14	36
No contact with at least one child	3	3	29	16	35	20
No contact with any children	1	1	21	3	10	0

* Excludes four respondents who were always single nine respondents who did not answer the questions about divorce and two respondents who had never divorced and who did not supply any information on children.

Table 13.5 describes the proportions of respondents falling in each of these four categories by marital history and gender. Respondents who had never divorced had the highest levels of contact and, for this group there were no differences between men and women: 91 per cent of the men and 92 per cent of the women had frequent contact with at least one child and 66 per cent of both men and women had frequent contact with all of their children. Respondents who had divorced fared worse in levels of contact, although the women had better levels of contact than the men. However, the majority of divorced respondents (remarried and not remarried combined) did have frequent contact with at least one child (66 per cent of men and 78 per cent of women), but smaller proportions maintained frequent contact with all of their children (16 per cent of men and 40 per cent of women). The percentage of men who had frequent contact with at least one child was larger for those who had remarried (69 per cent) than those who remained on their own after their divorce (61 per cent). This may be partially attributed to the differences in family size mentioned earlier (remarriage is associated with having a larger number of children). Cooney and Uhlenberg (1990), using similar categories for frequency of contact, report that the more children in a family, the less likely it is both to have frequent contact with all children and to have no contact with any children. There will also be an increased likelihood of having both frequent contact with at least one child and completely losing contact with at least one child. The only exception to this expected general pattern in our data is the group of women who divorced and remarried, where the percentage having contact with at least one child is actually lower (75 per cent) than for the divorced, not remarried group (84 per cent). This may add support to our suggestion (in the description of divorced women's relationship with children of a divorced spouse) that remarriage may have an adverse effect on women's relations with their children from an earlier marriage. But it may also say something about the difference in the levels of contact that men and women have with their step-children—women who marry divorced men who did not live with their children following divorce, will share the same low level of contact with those children as their partner. Similarly, men who remarry women who have children from a previous marriage will share the same high level of contact with those children as their partner. Further analyses of our data (not presented) supported this hypothesis—levels of contact with step-children were higher for men who were living with a spouse, than for those who were no longer living with the biological mother of their step-children, and for women, in general.

It was relatively unusual for parents who remained married to lose contact with at least one or with all of their children (3 per cent and 1 per cent, respectively for both men and women). Divorced women were highly unlikely to have no contact with any of their children (1 per cent), although a good proportion had lost contact with at least one child (18 per cent). Divorced men were more likely than any other group to lose contact with at least one child (33 per cent) and also more likely to have no contact with any of their children (14 per cent).

In order to assess whether differences in levels of contact might in some way be attributable to the way in which men and women relate to their children in the absence of a spouse due to widowhood (or incapacity of the spouse necessitating institutional care), rather than as a consequence of divorce, we looked at the levels of contact with adult children for the parents who had not experienced divorce. Table 13.6 describes the same four categories of frequency of contact by gender and whether or not the respondent was living with their spouse, for all respondents who had children and had not experienced divorce. For the women, there was little difference between the group that lived with the spouse and the group that did not for each of the four categories of frequency of contact. For the men, however, there were differences between the two groups. Whilst men who lived with their spouse had similar levels of contact for all four categories as the women, significantly higher percentages of men who did not live with their spouse reported no contact with at least one child (1.9 per cent of those living with a spouse; 10.1 per cent of those not living with a spouse)[4] and no contact with any children (0.3 per cent of those living with a spouse; 2.2 per cent of those not living with a spouse).[5]

---

[4] Fisher's Exact test, p=0.00004.
[5] Fisher's Exact test, p=0.05.

Table 13.6: Contact between never-divorced respondents and children by gender and living arrangements

Amount of contact	Living arrangements and gender			
	Men		Women	
	Lives with spouse		Lives with spouse	
	Yes	No	Yes	No
	N = 575	N = 139	N = 381	N = 430
	%	%	%	%
Frequent contact with at least one child	91	87	91	93
Frequent contact with all children	67	60	65	67
No contact with at least one child	1.9	10.1	2.6	2.6
No contact with any children	0.3	2.2	0.3	0.7

8. CONCLUSIONS

The patterns of contact between parents and their adult children that we observe in this British sample are consistent with those reported in other studies carried out in the USA and elsewhere. We find that respondents who remained married had the highest levels of contact with their adult children. In comparison, respondents who had experienced divorce had less contact, although women had more than men. We have used similar ways of classifying frequency of contact to that of Cooney and Uhlenberg (1990) in their study comparing ever-divorced and married fathers and the percentages in each category for the men in our sample and theirs from the USA are strikingly similar.

Looking specifically at the group of men and women who had experienced divorce, again, our findings are consistent with those of other studies. The men who did not live with their children following divorce were less likely to have continuing contact with, and to be able to rely on, their children in an emergency. They were also more likely to feel that divorce had lessened the quality of their relationship with these children. However, divorced fathers who lived with their children did not differ from divorced mothers on these three measures of contact and support. Not living with children following a divorce does not appear to have the same adverse effects on the mother-child relationship as it does for the father-child relationship. However, the numbers of women who did not live with their children following divorce was relatively small in this cohort.

Our data do not allow us to assess the effect of the timing of divorce. However, the twenty respondents who reported that their eldest child was at least nineteen years of age at the time of divorce[6] gave high proportions of positive responses to the questions about their on-going relationship with their children. Although the numbers are too small to allow us to draw a strong conclusion, this finding is consistent with the hypothesis that the parent-child relationship is less likely to be impaired, the later the timing of the parents' divorce (Bulcroft and Bulcroft, 1991; Aquilino, 1994b).

For men, remarriage did not affect the risk of losing contact with the children of a divorced spouse. However, the patterns observed at the aggregate level may be the result of different underlying processes; for example, remarriage of the non-residential father facilitates contact, if the presence of a step-mother allows the residential mother to feel more confident about allowing the children to visit, but reduces contact if remarriage is the source of further conflict (Emery, 1988). Whilst remarriage did not appear to have an effect for men, our data suggest that there is possibly a negative effect for women (see Chapter 14 in this volume). Given that most of the divorced mothers in our sample lived with their children, we might expect to see remarriage having some impact on subsequent relations as a step-father, and possibly step-siblings and half-siblings, are added to the family. The relationship between step-father and children can be problematic and possibly lead to tensions in the mother-child relationship. In our sample, 20 per cent of the respondents who had been divorced had step-children. We do not have information on the previous marital status of the spouse of respondents in the study or on the timing of remarriage, but these would be important factors in explaining the patterns and quality of contact with step-children. If step-children have a long-term and emotionally close relationship with a step-parent, particularly in the absence of a biological parent, then it seems reasonable to assume that they will be more likely to maintain contact in the long-term. In a study of attitudes about obligations to assist an older parent or step-parent following later-life remarriage, Ganong *et al.* (1998) find that adult children felt more obligated to lend assistance to a parent than to a relatively new step-parent. Perceived obligations to help step-parents, particularly step-mothers, were further weakened if the relationship with that step-parent was not close.

For the respondents who had been married and never divorced, we found no differences between men and women in terms of the levels of contact they had with their adult children, provided that the respondent was currently living with their spouse. However, for men who were living alone, we observed significantly higher percentages for the two categories, no contact with at least one child and no contact with all children. Aquilino (1994a) speculates that mothers play a role in facilitating contact between fathers and their children and when the mother dies, "father and children may have a harder time connecting with each other". In his study he found that the death of the mother had only a small

---

[6] These 20 respondents did not answer the question about with whom their children lived following divorce, suggesting that they did not have other, dependent children at the time of the divorce.

effect on children's ratings of general relationship quality with their father, but a much larger impact on contact. This suggests that children do not necessarily feel less affection toward their widowed father, but feel less wish or obligation to maintain the previous level of contact. This in turn raises interesting questions about whether widowed fathers are less needy in practical or emotional terms than widowed mothers, even if one assumes the same degree of closeness of the parent-child relationship.

Our data have allowed us to examine some general patterns of parent–child contact in a large sample and to identify which groups may most often lose contact. In this sample of people aged sixty-five and over in 1991, we found that whilst current marital status indicated that 2.9 per cent of respondents were currently divorced or separated, 9.4 per cent had experienced divorce. Much of the current available data on elderly people includes information on current marital status, but not of past experience of divorce and remarriage. Depending on the purposes for which data are used, it may be important to have such information. With rising divorce rates the percentage of elderly people who have experienced divorce will rise as successive cohorts reach old age. Increasing proportions of elderly people will experience the long-term "costs" of divorce in a number of ways. On measures of life satisfaction and social engagement, for example, people who remain divorced and did not marry into old age, fared worse. This was especially true for men (Askham, 1994; Solomou et al., 1998). In terms of economic resources divorce has been shown to have adverse effects for both men and women (Uhlenberg et al., 1990; Everett, 1991; Maclean, 1991; Askham, 1994; Solomou et al., 1998). As we have indicated from our data and our review of other studies, divorce has a negative impact on supportive contact with adult children. The informal support of close family is an important resource for many people who become frail in old age; without it, larger numbers of elderly people will be more dependent on the care-giving services or institutions provided by private agencies or the State.

APPENDIX: DESCRIPTION OF SAMPLE

The Healthy Ageing sample is a selected subset from the population studied in the Cambridgeshire and Nottingham centres of the Medical Research Council Multi-centre Study of Cognitive Function and Ageing (CFA Study), a longitudinal study of population samples in England and Wales (Chadwick, 1992; MRC CFAS, 1998). The original random sample was stratified by age in order to achieve equal sample sizes in the age ranges of 64–74 and 75-and-over. The Cambridgeshire sample was drawn from Ely and its surrounding rural area in East Cambridgeshire and the Nottingham sample was drawn from the city.

The CFA Study involved an initial screening interview that collected basic socio-demographic information and assessed cognitive function, past and current physical health, and activities of daily living. Following this, approximately

20 per cent of the sample were selected for a more detailed psychiatric assessment interview. In addition, a further sub-sample was selected to participate in the Resource Implication Study (RIS). This included all respondents who were physically frail, as well as respondents who were cognitively impaired (Resource Implication Study Group of the MRC CFAS, 1998). Respondents not selected for the above interviews comprised the target sample for the Healthy Ageing Study. Thus, the target sample excluded all respondents who were physically frail and/or cognitively impaired.

The CFA Study achieved a response rate of 80 per cent in Cambridgeshire and 83 per cent in Nottingham. The CFA sample was representative of the population when compared to the 1991 census data in terms of overall gender distribution, age distribution by gender (stratified by the two age groups, 65–74 and 75+), and marital status distribution (MRC CFAS, 1998). During 1991 to 1992 the Healthy Ageing Study recruited and interviewed 2,041 respondents (1,021 in Cambridgeshire and 1,020 in Nottingham), giving a re-interview response rate of 85 per cent for Cambridgeshire and 90 per cent for Nottingham. The Healthy Ageing sample differed in its distribution of gender from that of the population. Both the Cambridgeshire and Nottingham samples included slightly more men and slightly fewer women than would be predicted from the 1991 Census (OPCS, 1991). This is expected given the age stratification of the CFAS sample resulting in higher proportions of women in the older age groups who had a greater likelihood of exclusion from the Healthy Ageing Study on the grounds of physical and/or mental fragility. However, the percentage currently divorced in the sample was similar to the 1991 Census for both the Nottingham and Cambridgeshire samples (OPCS, 1991).

REFERENCES

Amato, P. R. and Booth, A., "Consequences of parental divorce and marital unhappiness for adult well-being" (1991) 69 *Social Forces* 905–914.

Aquilino, W., "Later life parental divorce and widowhood: impact on young adults' assessment of parent-child relations" (1994) 56 *J. Marriage and the Family* 908–922.

Aquilino, W., "Impact of childhood family disruption on young adults' relationships with parents" (1994) 56 *J. Marriage and the Family* 295–313.

Askham, J., "Marriage relationships of older people" (1994) 4 *Reviews in Clinical Gerontology* 261–268.

Booth, A. and Amato, P., "Parental marital quality, parental divorce, and relations with parents" (1994) 56 *J. Marriage and the Family* 21–34.

Bulcroft, K. and Bulcroft, R., "The timing of divorce: effects on parent-child relationships in later life" (1991) 13 *Research on Aging* 226–243.

Chadwick, C., "The MRC multicentre study of cognitive function and ageing: a EURODEM incidence study in progress" (1992) 11 *Neuroepidemiology* (Suppl 1) 37–43.

Choi, N. C., "Longterm elderly widows and divorcees: similarities and differences" (1995) 7 *J. Women and Ageing* 69–92.

Cooney, T., "Young adults relations with parents: the influence of recent parent divorce" (1994) 56 *J. Marriage and the Family* 45–56.

Cooney, T. and Uhlenberg, P., "The role of divorce in men's relations with their adult children after mid-life" (1990) 52 *J. Marriage and the Family* 677–88.

Cooney, T. and Uhlenberg, P., "Support from parents over the life course: The adult child's perspective" (1992) 71 *Social Forces* 63–84.

Emery, R. F., *Marriage, Divorce and Children's Adjustment* (Sage, California, 1988).

Everett, C. A. (ed.), *The Consequences of Divorce: Economic and Custodial Impact on Children and Adults* (Haworth Press, New York, 1991).

Ganong, L., Coleman, M., Kusgen Mcdaniel, A. *et al.*, "Attitudes regarding obligations to assist an older parent or stepparent following later-life remarriage" (1998) 60 *J. Marriage and the Family* 595–610.

Maclean, M., *Surviving Divorce: Women's Resources After Separation* (Macmillan, London, 1991).

Millward, C., "Divorce and family relations in later life" (1997) 48 *Family Matters* 30–33.

MRC Cognitive Function and Ageing Study, "Cognitive function and dementia in six areas of England and Wales: the distribution of MMSE and prevalence of GMS organicity level in the MRC CFA Study" (1998) 28 *Psychological Medicine* 319–335.

Office of Population Censuses and Surveys, *Census data for East Cambridgeshire*, table 2, p.52; *Census data for Nottingham*, table 2, p.55 (HMSO, London, 1991).

Resource Implication Study Group of the MRC Cognitive Function and Ageing Study, "Mental and physical frailty in older people: the costs and benefits of informal care" (1998) 18 *Ageing and Society* 317–354.

Rodgers, B. and Pryor, J., *Divorce and Separation: The Outcome for Children* (York, Joseph Rowntree Foundation, 1998).

Seltzer, J., "Relationships between fathers and children who live apart. The father's role after separation" (1991) 53 *J. Marriage and the Family* 79–101.

Seltzer, J. and Bianchi, S., "Children's contacts with nonresidential parents" (1988) 50 *J. Marriage and the Family* 663–677.

Solomou, W., Richards, M., Huppert, F. A. *et al.*, "Divorce, current marital status and well-being in an elderly population" (1998) 12 *Int. J. Law, Policy and the Family* 321–342.

Uhlenberg, P., Cooney, T. and Boyd, R., "Divorce for women after midlife" (1990) *J. Gerontology: Social Sciences* S3–S11.

Umberson, D., "Relationships between adult children and their parents: the psychological consequences for both generations" (1992) 54 *J. Marriage and the Family* 664–74.

White, L., "The effect of parental divorce and remarriage on parental support for adult children" (1992) 13 *Journal of Family Issues* 234–250.

14

Parents and Divorce: Changing Patterns of Public Intervention

MAVIS MACLEAN and MARTIN RICHARDS

1. INTRODUCTION

This chapter will look at the development of public intervention in the relationship between parents and their children when a marriage ends. Family structures within which the parental relationship lies have become more complex over time with the development of serial monogamy. We argue that this, combined with the continuation of parental relationships across household boundaries and the more flexible and complex arrangements, will need to be supported by the legal framework (Bastard and Voneche, 1996). We suggest, however, that there will be an inevitable tension in policy development between, on the one hand, the wish to affirm the responsibility of individual parents for their children, whatever their living arrangements, and, on the other, the concern to support children and their parents as they move through what may be only one in a series of family changes and help them to sustain the most favourable living arrangements they can.

(a) The legal frame: custody and access to residence and contact

Family law debates have traditionally centred around the degree of public intervention in family life. Is the family to be considered as a private sphere within which the State has only a residual role to play offering protection from abuse or neglect, matters which may be dealt with through the criminal law? Or do we have a view about what family life should offer by way of moral and social education for the coming generation, and legislate to this end? The former view is unacceptable to those concerned with gender imbalance and the rights of children, as withdrawal of public intervention tends to result in the continuation of the status quo in which existing power balances remain unchecked in favour of the strongest members. In such a regime the wage earner with access to the outside world, almost always the man, is held to assume a dominant role. If on the other hand we move towards the other end of the scale and look to the State to

decide on the value system to be endorsed within the family we face unacceptable curtailment of individual choice, for example concerning contraception
and abortion, separation and divorce, or the requirement in former socialist
republics to raise good socialist children for the State. Such limitations become
increasingly difficult to accept in a multi-cultural society, such as our own
(Kurczewski and Maclean, 1997).

In the United Kingdom we have sought the middle ground in our regulatory
framework for parenting after divorce, culminating in the Children Act 1989.
We have come a long way since issues related to children were referred to as
"ancillary matters" in divorce proceedings, that is, the issues to be settled once
the main issue of whether or not there was to be a divorce had been decided.
Historically the father was the child's natural guardian, and he had wide legal
powers supporting his authority over the child. While children were workers,
and a source of immediate economic advantage, or others in wealthy families
would inherit the family wealth, legal custody after separation or divorce
remained with the father. As children began to have an extended period of education and dependency, their physical custody began more often to fall to the
mothers. The Custody of Infants Act 1839 permitted the Lord Chancellor to
allow a mother who had not committed adultery access to her children if they
were with the father, and even to grant her legal custody of a child up to the age
of seven. In 1873 the age was increased to sixteen, and the adultery bar could be
lifted. But mothers did not attain full equality with fathers in their rights as parents until the Guardianship Act 1973.

Divorce became more common and broadly distributed in socio-economic
terms after the Second World War as legal aid became available and jurisdiction
to grant divorce was extended to county court judges sitting "as" High Court
judges, giving general access to the divorce jurisdiction. Thus remarriage
became a possibility for a wider population. This same period saw the development of procedures at divorce intended to safeguard the well-being of children.
The welfare principle, long established in law, began to be heard in private law
disputes about which parent children should live with and to whom they should
have access, and the judge was required to scrutinise the arrangements which
had been made. With the development of the welfare state and child protection
services, came an increased interest in the "best interests of the child" as a guid-
ing principle in law. This welfarism was associated with a higher degree of
supervision of the outcomes for children in divorce cases. Alongside the concept
in law of divorce as a trial, with guilty and innocent parties, there had been a
need to protect the child from the guilty and reward the innocent with custody
of their offspring. The children could be used as a bargaining chip in the divorce
struggle. In this context we see the development of the courts' own service to
assess and advise on the needs of children in divorce, the Divorce Court Welfare
Officers, now known as Family Court Welfare Officers (James and Hay, 1993).
But although the "best interests of the child" became the paramount concern of
the courts, the child was still seen almost as the "property" of the parents to be

allocated to one or other, or more latterly to be shared by both in joint custody. The court still requires a statement of arrangements for the child with which it must be satisfied before a divorce can be granted.

The early 1960s saw the beginning of the sustained rise in the number of divorces which continued until the late 1970s, and which led to many changes in the law and procedures to deal with the growing numbers. By the end of this period we had reached the present position in which about one in three of all new marriages in England and Wales are projected to end in divorce. This rise has been accompanied by major transitions in family life: a continuing decline in fertility and marriage rates, and a very substantial rise in cohabitation and births outside marriage (now over one-third of all births are to parents not married to each other). The focus of marriage has shifted from an institution to a relationship. Some (e.g. Reibstein and Richards, 1992) have argued that this represents the culmination of the growing trend towards companionate marriage with a new form of individualism focused on the nuclear family. Marriage is now but one form of a committed personal relationship which persists only as long as the relationship provides emotional satisfaction for both parties.

Until the Children Act 1989, orders for custody and access were general at divorce. That is to say, in effect, the divorce dissolved the formal shared arrangements for responsibility for children which were part of the marriage and reassigned these in terms of custody and access to the two divorced parents. The Children Act ended that dissolution of parenthood and so separated marriage and parenthood. The presumption thereafter is that the parental position within marriage is not changed by divorce and orders are only granted when there are particular reasons to change the basic arrangement. The terms were also changed: "custody" and "access" became "residence" and "contact", and more generally the Act represents a shift from parental rights to parental duties. The Children Act 1989 affirmed the responsibility of parents towards their children largely irrespective of their civil status, i.e. whether they were married, cohabiting, separated, divorced, or alone, and that this responsibility was lifelong, though in extreme cases of neglect or abuse it might be interrupted or shared with a welfare authority. The result at divorce was to end the necessity for the court to award custody to one parent or the other, as both retained parental responsibility. The court need only approve the arrangements made by the parents for their children, intervening only in case of a dispute over where a child should live, whether it should be in contact either face to face or indirectly with a parent or other relative or close friend, or to agree that a specific course of action should not be permitted under the prohibited steps order or specific issue order which might for example prevent one parent from taking the child out of the country. However, unlike the situation in some other English-speaking jurisdictions, the separation of marriage and parenthood is not quite complete. For that substantial minority of children born outside marriage while the concept of illegitimacy has been largely abolished, a legal distinction remains in that, although their fathers (genetic, as the DNA test is the legal test of paternity) do have a duty to support them financially, they are not yet otherwise regarded fully as parents unless they seek a parental responsibility agreement or order under the Children Act. As Ros Pickford describes (Chapter 8 above), this situation is unsustainable and is likely to be changed to something akin to the concept of parenthood within marriage in the future.

The degree of public protection for children through supervision of the living arrangements made for them by their parents at divorce to be included in the new divorce law, the Family Law Act 1996, is still unclear. The current provision for the court to look at a statement of arrangements is likely to remain, though perhaps in a modified form. The welfare of children whose parents divorce is a central concern of the Act, although the legislation does not deal directly with the children as the legal regulation of their position is located firmly within the Children Act 1989. However, the Family Law Act 1996 when implemented will offer mandatory information sessions to parents which will address the needs of children at this time, and may encourage the use of parenting plans (Richards, 1999). These documents provide an agenda for discussion of the way both parents will care for their children when they live separately, covering not only residence and contact but asking the parents to think about such practical matters as possible causes of tension such as Christmas and birthday celebrations, and also the impact of new partners and step-children on their children. A rather simpler version of such a plan is in use in Australia, where it can be given formal status by being registered with the court. However, it has been suggested that this has not been helpful in that it has made the plans the occasion for further dispute rather than a focus for thinking ahead in a flexible and constructive way. It is unlikely that the plans will be used in this formal way in England and Wales but would form a part of the support for planning ahead which the Family Law Act seeks to provide. A slightly modified version of these parenting plans are being used on a trial basis in New Zealand and Alberta.

During the parliamentary discussion of the Family Law Bill arguments were put forward that the voice of the child should be heard directly. However, while some small concessions were promised to allow children to be independently represented in certain probably rather rare situations, the general thrust of the legislation is to endeavour to safeguard the well-being of children through emphasising their needs in the information given to parents and supporting continued relationships between them and their parents. Given that the legal regulation of the position of children remains based on the Children Act, the long-standing difference between the ways in which children are treated under the public and private law procedures remains (Timms, 1997). In the private law (divorce) situation when there is a dispute and court welfare officers are reporting to the court children may not be seen directly (Trinder, 1997) and there is evidence of reluctance of solicitors to raise issues about children's wishes and needs (Piper, 1997). In the matter of children, the balance remains firmly tilted toward the non-interventionist pole (James and Richards, 1999).

(b) The legal frame: child maintenance

The first part of this chapter has discussed the ways in which the legal frame-work is developing to meet the need to protect children after parental divorce. We have indicated how the State has withdrawn from making prescriptive rules about the ways in which the gender or conduct of the parents, or the age of the child, should determine where the child should live. Instead the parents respon-sibility for their child is affirmed, irrespective of their relationship to each other, and the legal framework now encourages and supports this responsibility while withdrawing from any further intervention unless the parents are grossly failing to care for their child or have a dispute about a specific matter. The second part of the chapter turns to the other side of the picture. We have so far looked at how the law supports the largely private activity of parenting. We turn now to how the State has become more active in regulating and enforcing the aspect of parenting which impinges on the public purse; the financial support of children who live apart from a parent. The second piece of recent legislation to affect parents at divorce is the Child Support Act 1991, which addressed the economic needs of children living with one (birth) parent. This form of regulation, though widely criticised, fits alongside the Children Act in that while accepting the free-dom to make a wide variety of choices about living arrangements, this legisla-tion gives the child the right to a defined level of financial support whatever the relationship between the (birth) parents. Formerly, financial support for chil-dren tended to be derisory for children whose parents had never lived together, or had lived together without marriage. And even in divorce cases the financial arrangements made tended to focus on the needs of the former wife, or on her needs together with those of her children. Under the Child Support Act the needs of the child are given the first call on the non-resident parent's resources. The calculation of the amount required is complex, based on the potential cost to the State for the social security payments which would be made to the child's house-hold in the absence of parental support, with some allowances to the payer based on his/her own basic social security entitlement. The implementation has been under-resourced, and has suffered from being in the vanguard of the Next Steps agency movement, under which the Child Support Agency (CSA) was bur-dened with unrealistic targets exacerbated by a failure to understand the differ-ence between administering a benefit and entering into a dispute between parties. When making assessment of entitlement to benefit the Benefits Agency is applying rules and assessing information provided by the applicant. In assess-ing child support liability, the CSA enters into a dispute between two parties about the earnings of the absent parent, his housing costs and other responsi-bilities. This takes time, whether formerly as a court-based activity or, in the current scheme, located within an administrative structure. The amounts of money sought have also proved painful in a society accustomed to serial part-nerships but low levels of child support, where the mobile parent, usually the father had formed a second family and was unable to support two households, our system had allowed him to support the family he currently lived with rather than requiring him to divert resources back to a household he had left. The CSA suddenly reversed these priorities, and has proved unable to satisfy either the parents living with the children by diverting sufficient resources or those elsewhere who felt pursued for unrealistic amounts. Nor has the CSA collected sufficient revenue to appease the Treasury. Modification of the scheme is under discussion. The consultation paper published in July 1998 proposes making the assessment process much simpler, requiring a proportion of gross income related to the number of children concerned, as is the case in Australia. In doing this the paper recognises that a more rough and ready rule will not be able to justify demanding the relatively high level of support sought under current rules. Amounts will be lower. The changes contemplated also include giving higher priority in the assessment to the presence of children in the payer's household. However, it will be some years before any changes filter through into practice.

2. THE LEGAL FRAME

On divorce, children's interests are now the primary concern of the family justice system. Parents are now required to tell the court what arrangements they have made for their children in the new circumstances, even though these plans may change. The court is not expected to interfere in these arrangements, as the parents remain responsible for their children. The court will only become involved if a specific dispute arises. In the past the financial arrangements made on divorce centred around the duty of a man to support his former wife, and orders for child maintenance were either included in spousal support or added as the final part of any settlement. The financial needs of the children are now given primacy in the making of periodical payments by the CSA. Furthermore in dealing with the allocation of property, as opposed to income, research (Jackson *et al.*, 1993) has shown how the need to house the children is the starting point for most property settlements, including the disposal of the family home.

It appears that children have attained a central role in the divorce process. The new Family Law Act 1996 is predicated on the need of parties who divorce to try to save their marriages. But failing that, it is hoped that they will make the best efforts they can to avoid conflict which it is thought could damage their children's development, and to look forward and make realistic plans for their children rather than to look back to the reasons for the breakdown of the marriage.

Within the legal framework, children appear to be in pole position. The parental relationship is taking over from marriage and divorce as the focus for legal and other forms of regulation. Traditional arguments were concerned with whether a good divorce was better or worse for children than a bad marriage.

We then moved on to the idea that divorce is damaging for at least some children, and we searched for ways of ameliorating this damage. The latest generation of child-focused studies place emphasis on the similarities rather than the differences between children of intact marriages or other stable committed relationships, and the children of couples who separate (Rodgers and Pryor, 1998).

This new emphasis sits well with the discovery of the complexity of household formations within which children live, and of the kinds of pathways they take through a number of different family structures. It is this diversity and fluidity which makes if difficult to continue to think in the old "broken family" versus "intact family" dichotomy, so beloved of those seeking to identify ways of improving the quality of social control. And it is this diversity which is calling forth new ways of supporting children and their parents through not one traumatic divorce, but through a number of complex and often stressful changes. However a number of issues remain unresolved, and a number of new issues are emerging.

In the third part of this chapter, before turning to these new issues, we will present some information from a recent study on the experience of parenting after divorce across households.

3. PARENTING AFTER DIVORCE: THE PRACTICE

In a recent study carried out in Oxford with the support of the ESRC, Mavis Maclean and John Eekelaar looked at the experience of a sample of parents screened out from the general population using the Child Support Agency's identifying question "are you the parent of a child whose other parent lives elsewhere?" If the answer was yes, they were asked permission for a longer interview about the family history and current relationship between the child in question and both the parents, and with any new partners of either parent. The aim was to identify patterns of parental involvement across household boundaries, and whether we could define what constituted a continuing meaningful active parenting relationship (Maclean and Eekelaar, 1997). The findings of this study changed our perspective on the position of the children of divorced parents. In earlier research we had found, as others had, among the children of divorced parents higher levels of poverty at least in the short term, combined with lower educational attainment and subsequent lower earning capacity (Rodgers and Pryor, 1998). But it is helpful to look more widely at the range of parenting experiences which children in complex families pass through, including living only with one parent, but never both, or with parents who cohabit and separate, as well as those whose parents marry but later divorce. Furthermore these parents who do not continue to live with the child's other birth parent may re-partner, re-separate and partner again. Any of these relationships may bring children of a new partner into the family group, as well as new children born to a parent and a new partner. It is important therefore to look across these different situations and make comparisons not as a dichotomy between separated and intact families, but between the different kinds of family situations where one parent of a child lives elsewhere. If we do so, a very different picture emerges. In this context, when comparing the children of divorcing parents with those of separating cohabitants or with those whose mothers never shared a home with the father, the children of divorced parents appear in a more favourable position. They have fewer economic difficulties, more contact with the non-resident parents, and live in better housing.

If we look only to levels of financial support available to these children from their mother's former husband the picture is not encouraging. But there was far more on-going active and regular parental involvement than we had anticipated. We found that 69 per cent of the 152 formerly married parents whom we interviewed reported continuing contact between the child and the non-resident parent. Only 5 per cent said that there had never been any contact established, and 27 per cent said that contact had been interrupted or had ended. The most common arrangement was for the child to see the outside parent once or twice a week, but overnight stays were regular in one in four of the families. We looked for factors associated with the establishment and continuation of contact and had expected factors such as geographical distance between the households or the formation of a new partnership and the arrival of new babies to be important determinants. We were surprised, however, by the lack of impact of distance, though perhaps we should not have been in the light of the numbers of fathers asking for travel costs to be taken into account in the CSA calculations. And new partners could have a positive or negative impact on contact. Though some fathers became preoccupied with new families and less interested in their first family, and some new partners wished to end a step-child's involvement elsewhere or to exclude a child of former partner from a new relationship, it was also the case that a new and liked partner might make a mother more confident about access visits to a formerly irresponsible father. The factor which best predicted the survival of active parental involvement was the age of the child at the separation, which indicates the length of time for which the child and the now outside parent had lived together. Sharing a home seemed to create a relationship which could survive high levels of conflict between the two biological parents around the time of the divorce, which sometimes interrupted the meetings but did not end them. Contact was re-established, sometimes at the initiative of the child, in several cases two years after the separation. The former finding seems to fit with common sense expectations, but the second is more surprising and encouraging. We found a slight improvement in the relationship between the parents when contact continued. Contact which began when the relationship was poor was associated with slight improvement in the relationship over time. There is evidence (Buchanan and Ten Bricke, 1997) that the quality of the relationship between the adults does not necessarily affect the relationship between the outside parent and the child. We suggest that the continuation of contact may even help to reduce hostility between the parents over time. We were also surprised by the amount of movement between households, particularly of older children. In particular, as a boy grew older there were mothers who sought to send a difficult child over to the father for at least a while to have discipline exercised.

Other chapters in this volume address the nature of parenting in its various forms and situations, including those assisted by reproductive technology. But after separation or divorce there is a change in the parental relationship from social combined with biological parenthood, to a split between these two functions for one parent, usually the father. In addition it is common for at least one parent to repartner and so for two new social parental relationships to come into the picture. We know that children are adept at adding people (and animals) to their "family" and find this easier than coping with loss. It is less clear how adults add to and subtract from the family definition in emotional terms, and it would be interesting to learn of differences between adults and children in this respect. One way of identifying adult priorities is by seeing how they approach the allocation of scarce monetary resources when there are conflicting claims from children in the household and children elsewhere, or children of a first and second partner. In the Oxford study we attempted to address this issue by presenting a small vignette to each parent. This described a man who had been married with a child, had divorced and now lives with a new partner and her child. We then added to the picture a new child born to the man and his new partner. The interviewer than asked who should come first for him, his biological child living elsewhere or his step-child with whom he lived. 73 per cent of the mothers in our sample put his own child living elsewhere first, compared with 59 per cent of the fathers. When we asked whether the step-child should affect the amount of money to be sent to the first child, the gap between the views of mothers and fathers increased, as 46 per cent of the mothers and 18 per cent of the fathers said no. And when the final question was asked about whether the subsequent biological child of the second partnership should affect the amount sent to the first family 58 per cent of mothers and 40 per cent of fathers said no. We suggest that fathers are more able to relate support obligations to social parenthood than mothers, which is not surprising when we consider that only the fathers are likely to have experienced social parenthood which is not combined with biological parenthood. Mothers rarely separate from their children and therefore may find it difficult to conceptualise the nature of the bond outside day-to-day life in a common household, even though many of them repartner and experience the attachment of their new partner to their own children.

These conflicting demands on not only the financial resources but also the time and emotional energy of parents with more than one set of children form one of the key issues now emerging which will need to be resolved in the new forms of family life after divorce or separation. Earlier work (Simpson and Walker, 1993) has indicated how difficult it is for non-resident fathers (as well as mothers) to combine maintaining a strong relationship with children and at the same time developing a new relationship with a partner, especially if she already has children.

A second set of issues surrounds the question of the circumstances in which we wish to support contact with the outside parent when either the child or the resident parent are reluctant to take part. Research has documented how the law has found itself in the contradictory position of demanding that an outside parent should have access to a child while at the same time requiring him/her to stay away from a former home and partner as a result of violence (Hester and Radford, 1996). These are difficult issues to deal with, particularly when clouded by the emotional turmoil associated with separation and repartnering. What is encouraging however is the new interest in support for children, however problematic the CSA may be. We suggest that as a society we are now more willing to debate the needs of children and the responsibilities of parents and less concerned with marital fault and whether men or women are doing better out of divorce than we were twenty years ago. Furthermore, new forms of professional intervention are emerging to offer help with these newly-defined issues. Counselling for children is developing and is now thought to be most helpful if it can include an element of peer group work. Mediators are now working on reframing or perhaps reducing conflict in order to minimise problems for the children, and are considering ways of taking account directly of the wishes and feelings of the child rather than working only through the parents. There are moves to bring together the family court welfare officers with the guardian *ad litem* service. And there is increased energy and enthusiasm behind the development of providing contact centres, places where outside parents can spend time with their children with some supervision or support. Here the professional development is rapid, with complex discussion about whether the relationship between child and outside parent should be worked on directly, or whether this can only develop well if the relationship between the conflicted parents is addressed (Bastard, 1998). However, as suggested elsewhere (James and Richards, 1999) the perspective of children may still be underplayed.

To conclude, we return to our original question, what do we seek from the law in the regulation and management of parents involved in the divorce process? We would suggest that the law is able to regulate financial relationships after divorce, and that there is a strong case for it do so if there is a political imperative to protect the public purse from the demands which serial monogamy (which produces more children than partnerships) could make on it through the social security system. These demands would not be limited only to the needs of dependent children of divorcing couples, but also to the needs for public provision of care to the divorced parents when they reach old age (see Solomou and colleagues, Chapter 13 above). It could also be argued that there is a need for the law to protect children from violence, not only directly experienced but also indirectly through exposure to violent incidents between their parents which may not directly harm the children. Finally we seek from the law a framework for resolving disputes about their care. But perhaps we do not seek firm prescription to go further. Indeed we seem to be developing a fuzzy area of law where the Family Law Act exhorts rather than prescribes, by offering information, encouraging alternative dispute resolution rather than legal remedies, with the aim of reducing the difficulties associated with divorce for many children. This model may mistakenly assume a rational and well-disposed divorcing population, rather than the historical model of a highly deviant group going for trial with assertions of guilt and innocence to be tried. Perhaps the Parenting Plan (Richards, 1999) is the key indicator to the way ahead for the legal framework for divorce, in that it provides a clear steer towards looking ahead in order to promote the best interests of the child, but without prescription. But while a Parenting Plan may encourage parents to listen to their children and hear their views on what they want to happen, it cannot guarantee that their voice will be heard.

REFERENCES

Bastard, B., unpublished paper to RCSL Onati, July 1998.
Bastard, B. and Voneche L., "Interprofessional tension in the divorce process in France" (1996) 9 *International Journal of Law and the Family* 275–285.
Buchanan, A. and Ten Bricke J. A., *What Happened When They Were Grown Up? Outcomes From Parenting Experiences* (York, Joseph Rowntree Foundation, 1997).
Fermi, E. and Smith K., *Step-Parenting in the 1990s* (London, Family Policy Studies Centre, 1998).
Jackson, E., Wasoff, F. and Maclean, M., "Financial support on divorce" (1993) 7 *International Journal of Law and the Family* 230–254.
James, A. and Hay, W., *Court Welfare in Action* (Hemel Hempstead, Harvester Wheatsheaf, 1993).
James, A. L. and Richards M. P. M., "Further reflections on family policy: adult thinking and sociological tinkering", (1999) *J. Social Welfare and Family Law*, 23–39.
Kurczewski, J. and Maclean, M. (eds.), *Family Law and Family Policy in the New Europe* (Aldershot, Dartmouth, 1997).
Hester, M. and Radford, L., *Domestic Violence and Child Contact Arrangements in England and Denmark* (Bristol, The Policy Press, 1996).
Maclean, M., "Delegalisation of family obligation" in J. Kurczewski and M. Maclean (eds.), *Family Law and Family Policy in the New Europe* (Dartmouth, Aldershot, 1997).
Maclean, M. and Eekelaar, J., *The Parental Obligation. A Study of Parenthood across Households* (Oxford, Hart Publishing, 1997).
Piper, C., "Ascertaining the wishes and feelings of the child" (1997) *Family Law* 769–800.
Reibstein, J. and Richards M. P. M., *Sexual Arrangements: Marriage and Affairs* (London, Heinemann, 1992).
Richards, M. P. M., "The Family Law Act 1996 of England and Wales and The Welfare of Children", (1999) *Butterworth's Family Law Journal* (forthcoming).
Rodgers, B. and Pryor, J., *Divorce and Separation: The Outcomes for Children* (York, Joseph Rowntree Foundation, 1998).

Simpson, B. and Walker, J., *Post Divorce Fatherhood* (Newcastle, Family and Community Dispute Resolution Centre, 1993).

Timms, J., "The tension between welfare and justice" (1997) *Family Law* 38–47.

Trinder, L., "Competing constructions of childhood: children's rights and children's wishes in divorce" (1997), 19 *J. Social Welfare and Family Law* 291–305.

15

The Psycho-Politics of Post-Divorce Parenting

SHELLEY DAY SCLATER and CANDIDA YATES*

1. INTRODUCTION

Divorcing parents are in an impossible position. Caught, on the one hand, between the desire to end the marriage, to break away and to assume separate and independent lives, and the apparent "need" for their children to have parents who keep in touch; caught, on the other hand, between the ambivalences of loss (the sadness, bewilderment, the guilt, the hostilities) and the powerful rhetoric of the "harmonious" divorce, it is perhaps not surprising that they find it hard to arrive at "good enough" solutions. This chapter is about how mothers and fathers negotiate these conflicts. It draws upon empirical work (see Day Sclater (1999a), (1999b)) in which divorcing parents gave accounts, in their own words, of their experiences. Using extracts from the case studies, we examine the ways in which women's and men's interpretations of the welfare discourse may be said to be "gendered", and we explore the psychological constellations which are implied by these gendered interpretations.

A brief word about the welfare discourse would perhaps be helpful at this early stage. In decisions under the Children Act 1989, which are made on divorce, the "welfare principle" states that the "welfare of the child" is of "paramount importance". As Maclean and Richards point out in Chapter 14 above, children's interests are now the primary concern of the family justice system.[1] As has frequently been pointed out, however, the principle is an indeterminate

* Earlier versions of this chapter have been presented at the British Psychological Society, Psychology of Women Section Conference, Birmingham, June 1998, and the British Psychological Society, London Conference, Symposium on "The Family" (convenor Prof. Anne Woollett), December 1998. We are indebted to the participants at these venues for their valuable feedback. The research was supported by a grant from the ESRC in 1996–1997, (award number R000236323) for which we are grateful. We would also like to thank those men and women whom we interviewed, without whose willing participation, none of our work would have been possible, and to those solicitors and mediators who assisted with the recruitment of participants to the study. We are also grateful to Barry Richards and to the members of the Cambridge Socio-Legal Group for their comments on an early version of this chapter.

[1] They argue this has to be seen against the backdrop of broader social changes in "the family" and the increasing tendency for parenthood to replace marriage as the basis for family life.

one; it lacks specific content but, arguably, it is this very indeterminacy which permits decisions to be made which are in accord with the specific interests of individual children in each case which comes before the courts. However, there does exist some consensus around the broad parameters of what it is that best furthers the interests of children in general. It is widely thought, for example, that children's adjustment to divorce is best facilitated if they can maintain relationships with two parents who are in harmonious contact with each other (Lord Chancellor's Department, 1993, 1995). These assumptions are reflected in both research into the "effects" of divorce on children[2] and divorce dispute resolution practices. The organisation of these ideas into a framework for understanding, and a basis for legal decision-making, is what we refer to as the discourse of welfare. The welfare discourse has become a dominant one in divorce; its prominence is supported by a pervasive political rhetoric and it forms a central strand in the vocabularies of the professionals involved in divorce dispute resolution.

Importantly, for our purposes, the discourse of welfare implies a "vulnerable" child[3] who is "at risk" of "harm", particularly if the parents cannot manage the divorce in a co-operative way or if the child cannot maintain good quality relationships with both parents (see Kaganas, 1999).[4] The discourse thus positions children as vulnerable but, in so doing, it also provides a repository for the parents' feelings of vulnerability which they find difficult to "own" for themselves (Day Sclater, 1998b; Day Sclater and Piper, 1999). In other words, the welfare discourse permits parents to focus on children's vulnerability (in a process psychoanalysts call "projection") and so to experience their own vicariously, at one step removed.

The discourse of welfare is also often invoked by divorcing parents who give accounts of what they have done and why they have done it. This should not be surprising, since divorcing couples are commonly exhorted to put their own feelings and interests to one side for the sake of the children (see, for example, Magnus, 1997). But, as with a range of other discourses, it transpires that divorcing people do not just accept, unquestioningly, either the premises of the welfare discourse or its prescriptions for behaviour and feelings. Discourses are not determining of the conduct of human actors; rather, people may negotiate or even actively resist being "positioned" by them.[5] In this chapter, we explore the different interpretations made of the welfare discourse by mothers and fathers. Our finding that these gendered interpretations may be being made routinely by divorcing women and men flies in the face of the gender-neutrality of family law and its central concept of "parental responsibility". It also raises

---

[2] For a recent review of this literature, see Rodgers and Pryor (1998).

[3] Piper (1996) argues that it is an image of the child as the "victim" of divorce that is implied in the provisions of the Family Law Act 1996.

[4] The emphasis on children's welfare in family law leads to powerful prescriptions for "responsible" parenting (see, for example, Neale and Smart (forthcoming)).

[5] On the concept of "discursive positioning", see Davies and Harre (1990).

questions about the psychological investments that women and men make in disputes about children on divorce. We explore these questions in this chapter, using psychoanalytic ideas about the psychic roots of masculinities and femininities to guide our analysis.

In our study, we found that mothers and fathers both commonly invoke the welfare discourse in giving their accounts of divorce. In mothers' talk, however, the prominence of the welfare discourse is frequently challenged by what we have called the "independence discourse". Often considerable tensions exist between the two, as they pull in opposite directions. The welfare discourse emphasises the priority to be given to children's interests and their apparent need for parents who are in harmonious contact with each other. The independence discourse, on the other hand, emphasises the needs of the woman for a final and complete separation from the former partner, and the pursuit of personal autonomy after divorce as a valued and motivating goal. The existence of the independence discourse in mothers' narratives mitigates the impact of the welfare discourse and, we argue, results in particular interpretations of it being made. In their narratives, fathers also invoke the welfare discourse, but they do so in a different way and they make different interpretations of it.

The existence of these gender differences, however, should not surprise us as marriage itself remains, in many ways, an institution organised around gender. More than twenty-five years ago, Jessie Bernard (1973) alerted us to the fact that, within every marriage, there are two: his and hers. What she meant was that, not only do the expectations and experiences of women and men in marriage differ, but also that those differences are deeply rooted both structurally and psychologically; gender was identified as an important organising category which pervades experience at all levels. More recently, as Segal (1994) argues: "Over the last decade . . . the household/family has become more than ever a site where dramatic social inequalities have been deepening and reproducing themselves" (p.312).

In the arena of divorce, however, gender differences tend to have been submerged under a pervasive rhetoric of gender neutrality in family law. There have, of course, been a wealth of feminist criticisms over the years,[6] but these have always remained marginal in the public debate; the power of the dominant discourses[7] has been such that feminist voices which have sought to move "gender" to centre stage have rarely been heard. Nevertheless, there are powerful arguments to be made that, even in these days of formal equality before the law, substantive inequalities continue to exist along gender lines (Fineman, 1995), that gender remains an important organising category in all our lives (Butler,

---

[6] For example, in relation to family law generally, see Brophy and Smart (1985); Smart (1989); Smart and Sevenhuijsen (1989); O'Donovan (1993). In relation to "no fault" divorce provisions, see Fineman (1991). In relation to conciliation/mediation, see Bottomley (1985); Grillo (1991). On the issue of domestic violence, see Mullender and Morley (1994); Hester and Radford (1996); Hester *et al.* (1997); Burton *et al.* (1998). See also the regular bulletins from Rights of Women.

[7] On the question of the dominance of some discourses over others see, for example, Fairclough (1989), (1992) and Plummer (1995).

1990), and that our culture is pervaded by gendered discourses which are continually present (Probyn, 1993). Thus, the gender neutrality of family law's notion of "parental responsibility" sits uneasily alongside the gendered discourses and practices of motherhood and fatherhood which pervade our culture.[8]

Our focus in this chapter is on the ways in which, at a psychic level, masculinities and femininities both derive from and feed into a whole range of competing discourses and cultural narratives about women and men (Probyn, 1993), as the normative parameters set by culture both activate and respond to a range of expressions and repressions of different aspects of ourselves (Hollway, 1989). We are concerned to produce an understanding of the ways in which gender is both implied and constructed in relation to post-divorce parenting. The focus is a dual one: first, on the discourses mothers and fathers invoke in talking about their experiences and, secondly, on the psychic constellations which both underpin and result from these discursive engagements.

2. THE WELFARE DISCOURSE IN MOTHERS' AND FATHERS' NARRATIVES

Without exception, the mothers in the study invoked the welfare discourse in constructing their divorce stories. This involved, in most cases, a conscious and explicit attempt, at least in the early stages, to progress the divorce with the minimum of acrimony, despite the emotional pain (including feelings of loss, abandonment and betrayal) which many women were experiencing. Helen, for example, went to mediation rather than to a solicitor, because she was acutely aware that she wanted to do what she thought would be best for her children. When asked the reason she had gone to mediation, she said:

> "You know, to see if we could do it *painlessly because of the children* . . . I didn't want to go to a solicitor who would take it all over and be very sort of, um, well I think they just go for the kill at times, and I didn't want that, because I don't want to antagonise my ex-husband, um, because we *don't want to have that sort of relationship as far as the kids are concerned*" (Helen, first interview, emphasis added).

These mothers tended to persist in their efforts to put their own feelings to one side for the sake of the children, but many described the contact times as particularly painful. Here is Jill talking about how she felt around contact times:

> "It totally chokes me, knowing that when she sort of goes to him, she cries when she goes in the car, and I think it will upset me for a long, long time. A lot of people say

---

[8] As Juliet Mitchell and Jack Goody argue in Chapter 6 above, a very particular image of the "good mother" emerged during the years after the Second World War; fathers were all but absent from the psychological theorising and remedial social practices of the time. This has left a lasting legacy in which motherhood has been equated with nurturance and fatherhood with progenesis and financial provision. Whilst recent social and economic changes are undoubtedly blurring the boundaries between what women and men do in the family, the process of change is slow.

that I have got to try to sort of succumb to that and get used to it, but it's—but I just feel that it's early days really" (Jill, second interview).

What Jill is describing here is a feeling of acute emotional pain when her baby daughter goes to see her father. But she seems ready to persist with the arrangement, in accordance with the idea that the baby needs a relationship with her father, however painful that might be for Jill; she is thus able to position herself as a "good" mother within the welfare discourse.

However, in mothers' divorce narratives, there are contrary discourses in operation too. Perhaps the most important of these is what we call the "independence discourse", which describes a set of ideas that most mothers invoked to express their own needs for independence and autonomy. Helen expressed it like this:

"And I suppose I just need something more for me, rather than constantly thinking about the children all the time" (Helen, second interview).

Alison felt that continued contact with her ex-husband was so painful that she couldn't wait to move far away:

"It's just like he is blowing everything away . . . I will never forgive him, not ever . . . And he doesn't seem to—he just isn't the least bit concerned, he doesn't see how much he hurt me, and how much it still hurts when I think about it, because it still does, and I suppose it will go on hurting until I am out of this town and I don't have to see him and I can put a space between us" (Alison, third interview).

By the time of the second interview, Jill was thinking about her desire for her own needs to be met, but her ambivalence about expressing them is clear: here she is invoking the doctor's authority in support:

"Yes, I have got her [baby] but, you know, I have got my own needs that aren't being met, you know . . . [my doctor] said look, you have got to start thinking of yourself and be happy" (Jill, second interview).

Inevitably, there are tensions between the welfare discourse and the independence discourse; one pushes towards a harmonious relationship with the ex-partner, the other pulls for severance of that relationship altogether. Mothers talked about these tensions in the interviews and it is apparent that they are far from easy to resolve:

"I wish that he would just get out of my hair and leave me alone, but with her [daughter], I can't. He is always going to be there" (Jill, third interview).

"If I see him, I hate him. My idea would be to have nothing more to do with him whatsoever. Then I could start getting on with my life. But I cannot do that because of the children" (Laura, third interview).

"I really don't want to have any contact with him any more. I don't want to have to consider his needs. It would be much better if we could move completely to the other end of the country or something like that and never see him again" (Helen, third interview).

"I need to go through this, this bereavement that I can't quite get over now, that I can't quite work through, because the body has not yet been buried. It has mentally in my mind, but not actually. And I am not too sure how I can achieve the degree of separation until my youngest has sort of left home . . . he [ex-husband] has still got to be part of my life . . . I feel inextricably knotted, whatever the law states our position to be" (Gina, third interview).

Helen's own need for independence eventually led her to re-think the premises of the welfare discourse:

"I think it is not really clear to the children why people, why the parents have split up, um, you know, we went to mediation thinking that it would be—that what we were doing was best for the children. And to me the answers just aren't very clear, because the children seem to have a confused message now about, um, you know, we both tend to have quite a good relationship in their eyes, why can't we live together? They can't see it . . . I think, you know, if we had had a very stormy break up, and just left it at that, the children might have been affected slightly differently, but I don't think they'd be quite as confused as they are now. You know, I don't think it's very clear to them why our relationship didn't work, and I don't think mediation has made that clearer, and I don't know if what is considered to be best for the children is actually what is best for them. I think it's a very grey area" (Helen, third interview).

In expressing these sentiments, Helen has moved a long way from the idealisation of mediation as a "painless" process that she voiced in the first interview. What has intervened are her own needs for autonomy, and her experience of the realities of post-divorce parenting. But it is probably significant that she, like other mothers in our study, continues to justify her thoughts on the basis of the welfare discourse. Importantly, though, she is reinterpreting it from her own perspective. In their different ways, these women are negotiating the tensions between the prescriptions of the welfare discourse and their own needs for autonomy in ways that permit them to maintain positioning as "good enough" mothers. As others have identified (see, for example, Gilligan (1982)), these women's priorities are relational, and they seem particularly intent on doing the best that they can for their children, even at an emotional cost to themselves.

The fathers in our study also invoked the welfare discourse, but they tended to give it a different interpretation. Here is Harry talking about his 2-year-old daughter:

"There have been times when I wished that I didn't want to see my daughter. But the only reason I'm hanging on is because, look, I need to see my daughter, I'm not going to lose contact with my daughter. The whole way I've fought this case and whatever, I've always had one thing in the back of my mind. I always imagine my daughter when she's twenty turning round to me saying, 'Dad, was it your fault, what happened?' And I have always wanted to be able to put my file in front of my daughter and say, right, read it, this is what happened. And that's why I've always done it, and I've said to my lawyer, once the whole thing finishes, you have one last job. You can photocopy that whole file for me" (Harry, first interview).

Here Harry is talking about his own need to see his daughter, which he admits is bound up with his need to be vindicated. However, it is not the case that Harry is simply "using" his daughter for his own ends, as he obviously feels close to her, as the following quotation illustrates:

"I am very close to her because I took six months off when she was born. And we were really close. And that was the other thing which hurt, I mean, I used to sit there and wish I wasn't close to my daughter, this wouldn't hurt so much. But it's because of my daughter I've stuck it out, I've tried to fight it, I've tried to get some rights. It's only because of my daughter, 'cause if it had just been me and her [ex-wife], it would have been, go away, I don't want to know you, and I haven't got a solicitor, and you don't know where I live" (Harry, first interview).

Here Harry is making a particular interpretation of the welfare discourse and using it as an opportunity to claim "rights" in respect of his daughter. He is making it clear that, were it not for his daughter, he would have disengaged completely from his ex-wife. One of Harry's major worries was that his daughter would grow up to be like his hated ex-wife:

"That's what's worrying me more than anything, that she will end up being like her, that's that's, what I'm worried about. I don't like to think about it because, you know, you break down in tears, thinking what's going to happen to my daughter, you know. I'd die for that girl, you know. She is my life. Simple as that. And that's what's hurting, the fact that she is so perfect, and she's not with me . . . I've got one major regret and one major worry which is my daughter. If she [ex-wife] continues with life the way she is now, I dread to think how my daughter's going to be brought up, morals whatever and everything else. I would do anything to have my daughter live with me, anything" (Harry, first interview).

It should be said that Harry had not taken any legal steps to obtain an order for residence in respect of his daughter, which perhaps makes the sentiments he expresses more interesting and powerful. Harry talks about his daughter as "his life"; the acute emotional pain he experiences in respect of her and the concerns he has about her future are closely linked with his deep feelings of anger and hatred about his ex-wife. These feelings, however, extend beyond Harry's feelings for his own ex-wife and extend to women in general:

"I'm wary. I meet people, I meet an attractive woman, um, but at the same time I'm— The other day—this is how my mind thinks—I see an attractive woman, she's beautiful. She's a bitch. That's the only way. She's going to be a bitch. She's attractive, she's a manipulative bitch. I don't hate women, but I am very untrusting now with women, untrusting that if they get involved with me, they are going to take me for everything I've got" (Harry, first interview).

Harry sees himself as having "lost everything" through the divorce; he has even "lost" his business because he wound it up and registered as unemployed in order to become eligible for legal aid. "Losing everything" because of the actions of an untrustworthy woman was a common theme expressed in the fathers' narratives. James too characterised his experience in this way:

"I've lost my marriage, I've lost my kids, I've lost my house" (James, first interview).

What is interesting in James' case was that he had not, in fact, "lost everything"; on the contrary, he had remained in the former matrimonial home with the two children, and Pamela had moved out. At the time of the first interview, nine months had gone by without any indication at all that Pamela was going to try to alter that situation in any way, and they remained on reasonably amicable terms with no obvious difficulties. But James clearly had a sense of having "lost everything", accompanied by a fear that his ex-wife might have the ability (even if not the intention) to "clean him out" financially:

"She isn't out to get all she can get, or so she keeps telling me. Um, I don't suppose she is but, um, we shall see . . . I feel, what have I got out of this? You know, I've spent 23 years of my life working, and I suppose, you know, I think well, I could have spent 23 years and all this money on myself. Um, because ultimately she could have been the sort of person that was determined to, you know, clean me out of every penny that she could. And what am I going to be left with?"

It seems that what is at stake here are powerful feelings of vulnerability; against a background of these feelings, issues of rights and justice loom large, and one has a real sense in talking to these men that they do feel themselves to be the "victims" of divorce that Collier (1999) and others have talked about. The "system" is seen as favouring women, which facilitates the generalisation of hostile feelings for the ex-wife to women in general. Similarly, Richard felt himself to be an "easy target" and retained an enduring sense of injustice, particularly in relation to financial matters:

"But like I said, I have got fifty thousand [£50,000 was the proposed capital settlement in this case] reasons to hate her. And they are going to go up by £450 a month, £450 a month which I have got to pay until my daughter is 18, so that is another nine years (Richard, second interview).

For Richard, questions about his relationship with his daughter were closely linked to his angry feelings about having to pay maintenance for her, which in turn were linked to his resentment at having to make any capital settlement at all. He saw himself as having "bought out" his responsibilities for his daughter in the capital settlement:

"She is getting £50,000 in cash from me, and I am buying off all the responsibilities for her. She wanted the daughter, she can now have her, seven days a week, 365 days a year for the rest of her life . . . She is getting 50 grand plus £450 a month. She is *getting* a daughter, and she is *getting* out of my life. She said to me the other day, 'when me and Katy walk out of that front door, when we go to our own house, you will be really happy.' And I said, 'no, I won't be really happy'. I said, 'what would make me really happy, if you walked out of that front door with Katy and you both got knocked down by a bus, because you would save me 50 grand, save me £450 a month, and I get your life insurance policies paid out because we are not divorced yet' " (Richard, second interview, emphasis Richard's).

In his narrative, Richard did not talk about his daughter separately from his concerns about money and other aspects of the divorce. His interpretation of the welfare discourse was such that he saw his daughter's needs as being adequately met by her mother alone. Most often, Richard's words conveyed a strong sense of his anger and hostility, but he was also aware of co-existing vulnerabilities; these he saw as "grey areas" that he was striving to avoid:

"I don't like grey areas. The daughter, and access to the daughter, and maintenance to the daughter, seeing the daughter, is a grey area. It is a painful and emotional scenario. And if I feel any emotions for her, I am going to be hurt. So it is not going to happen. So I am just not going to see her" (Richard, first interview).

In fact, Richard did go on seeing his daughter, albeit not on a regular basis; this was undoubtedly problematic for him because he blamed the birth of his daughter, and the attention his ex-wife Jennifer gave to her, for the breakdown of the marriage. Richard's angry feelings were not just about Jennifer; he had lost trust and respect for women in general:

"Your gender hurts me, I hurt you back, all of you, not just the person who has actually done it. And men and women are not really compatible, it is one of God's little jokes, you know" (Richard, second interview).

The anger and hostility here are clearly mixed up with a profound pain. Here is Richard talking about the "biggest hurt" he has felt in relation to the divorce:

"The lies that society puts upon us, that tells your gender to play with little dolls, go out and have little girls, and tells my gender that they have got to be macho and hard and not cry, all those things. And then puts us together, and lets us loose, and it doesn't work like that, and we wind up hurting each other. And anything that I do to my wife, to my child, to your gender, is simply a cry of pain. When I told my wife that if she didn't get it [financial settlement] sorted, and she took everything away from me, I was going to clump my daughter with a sledgehammer one day. That was the loudest cry of pain she would ever hear from me. There were no tears involved, no shouting. And she will never know it, she will never know it" (Richard, second interview).

As others have pointed out, men and women seem to have different emotional vocabularies (see, for example, Riessman (1990); Craib (1998)). In the extract above, it is clear that Richard is using his anger as the medium through which to express his pain and vulnerability.

3. GENDERED DIVORCE EXPERIENCES

There are common themes among the accounts of women and men, aspects of the divorce experience that they both share; the emotional trauma, the sense of loss, the problems around parenting generally and contact in particular, the conflict and the ambivalences, the desire for detachment, the need to build a new life (Day Sclater, 1999a,1999b; Brown and Day Sclater, forthcoming). These are the aspects of the divorce experience which women and men share, but which we argue impact upon parenting in different ways. There are also places where the accounts of mothers and fathers diverge. It is of course very difficult to make generalisations when dealing with such rich and detailed case study material. Nevertheless, it is a worthwhile exercise to try to compare the themes which emerge from our discussion with those which others have identified as aspects of the experience which are differentiated along gender lines.

The central theme which united the mothers' narratives was a tension between the welfare and independence discourses which the women sought to resolve in a range of ways. For the most part, our case studies show these resolutions to have been achieved in ways that maintained the priority of welfare, enabling the women to retain a sense of themselves as "good enough" mothers in the face of the prescriptions of the discourse. But this accommodation was by no means easy to achieve, and involved considerable emotional work. The problems these women were concerned with were primarily relational ones, their own needs and their own worries about finances were secondary in every case. By contrast, the theme which unites the narratives of fathers in this study is a strong sense of vulnerability and loss which is overlaid, from time to time, with angry appeals to justice and rights in an attempt to salvage something for themselves. The fathers in this study made different interpretations of the welfare discourse; for some, ironically, it presented them with an opportunity to pursue a rights-based discourse, for some it was inseparable from financial issues and all felt a profound sense of injustice *vis-à-vis* women in general. We might conclude that both women and men are "doing gender'(see Butler, 1990) in relation to post-divorce parenting.

In this context, Neale and Smart (forthcoming) draw a useful distinction between parental care ("caring for") and parental authority ("caring about") in relation to the parenting activities of women and men. They argue that recent legislative change in family law has had the effect of extending father's rights in relation to children[9], and that this has been based on a conflation of "parental care" with "parental authority"; the law has provided fathers with new opportunities to exercise parental authority, without regard to its implications for mothers' exercise of parental care. In their study of sixty parents, the majority of separated and divorced parents did not practice co-operative co-parenting of the kind envisaged by the Family Law Act; Neale and Smart found a remarkable persistence of "custodial" parenting where one parent alone exercised parental authority and accepted the responsibilities for day-to-day care of the children. Further, they found that co-parenting could fuel conflicts, particularly where it

---

[9] Similarly, Standing (1998) argues that legal definitions of parental responsibility allow fathers to make choices and exercise control even where the father has little or no knowledge of the child in question. Standing sees this as a "reassertion of private patriarchy" whose effect is to extend the surveillance of mothers. Recent proposals for a change in the law to extend automatic parental responsibility to certain categories of unmarried fathers (see Ros Pickford, Chapter 8 above) arguably takes this process a stage further.

was the product, not of a shared ideology, but of legal, financial or physical coercion or unresolved tension over who is to be the custodial parent.[10]

Neale and Smart go on to examine the range of moral codes which underlie different parenting arrangements. They found that the dominant ethical framework articulated by most mothers in the study was an "ethic of care" which defined moral situations as neither right nor wrong, but in terms of the interdependence and value of relationships, the avoidance of harm, and the preservation of the dignity and worth of others, whilst the model articulated by most fathers was one of "justice", which was quickly invoked at times of conflict. The fathers in their study spoke in terms of their status as fathers, their "natural" rights to their children, their right to "equal" treatment with mothers, and in terms of the mothers' duties to respond to these rights. Changes in arrangements for the children thus became, for many fathers, struggles over parental authority whilst, for mothers, they were negotiations over parental care.

In a study of ninety-one divorced fathers, Simpson *et al.* (1996) reported that the "loss of control" experienced by many fathers on divorce is felt at many levels. That "loss of control" should be an issue at all relates to the continued pervasiveness of gendered ideologies in which *paterfamilias* rules; as Simpson *et al.* point out, the role of the father in our culture remains integrally linked with power, authority and masculinity, which are in turn associated with the maintenance of order in both "the family" and society as a whole. We have only to witness the moral panic which has been occasioned by the increasing number of "single" mothers and by the spectre of a rising tide of "families without fatherhood" (Dennis and Erdos, 1992)[11] to understand that the apparent decline in men's authority is extremely anxiety-provoking for both individual men and for society as a whole.

Arendell (1995), in her study of seventy-five divorced fathers, suggests that it is a primary concern of most divorcing men to seek to preserve a sense of masculine identity; for them, divorce was seen in terms of a battle of the sexes: "[T]hey expended major efforts to re-establish and reassert their identities as men" (Arendell, 1995, p.14). The story shared by a large majority of the fathers in Arendell's sample was one of perceived injustice, discrimination, resistance, frustration and discontent.

---

[10] Similarly, Bailey Harris *et al.* (1998), in a study which monitored applications under the Children Act 1989, found that, since the implementation of the Act (and contrary to its ideology and expectations), litigation is increasing and cases are taking longer to resolve. The authors speculate that one reason for this may be the predominantly settlement orientation being fostered by the Act, such that courts are reluctant to make decisions in unmeritorious cases at an early stage and instead prefer to encourage the parties to reach some form of agreement. However, in this context it is worth mentioning the findings of a study by Maccoby and Mnookin (1992); they found that highly conflicted parents were unlikely to become more co-operative over time, and that in these cases the welfare of the child is perhaps best served by allowing the parents to disengage from each other.

[11] A parallel situation appears to exist in the USA: see Blankenhorn (1995). He argues that "paternal disinvestment" is the major cause of declining child well-being and the underlying source of the most important social problems, especially those rooted in violence.

Collier (1999) talks about the ways in which some men have begun to see themselves as the new "victims" of divorce.[12] Many men seem to be feeling that "[t]he pendulum has swung too far in favour of women—it's time for men to demand their rights" (Brosnan, 1995, p.16). The implementation of the Child Support Act produced a strong reaction on the part of many divorced fathers; the demand for what seemed like excessive amounts of money undoubtedly fuelled men's perception of their vulnerability *vis-à-vis* their former partners, and the sustained campaign against the Act's provisions bears testimony to the sense of injustice which many men are feeling. Collier (1999) argues that the so-called "crisis of the family" has been formulated against a backdrop of changes in gender relations and has been closely linked to a "crisis in masculinity": "[A] zero-sum calibration of power relations between men and women has been invoked, whereby legislation perceived as empowering women has been seen as simultaneously *dis*empowering men" (Collier, 1999).

As Arendell (1995) points out, divorcing men clearly feel that their very masculinity is under threat. Collier raises the question about *why* this should be, given that there continues to be objective evidence of men's continued economic, cultural and social empowerment relative to women. These arguments raise a crucial question about the gendered psychological constellations that support the different experiences, concerns and understandings of mothers and fathers in the divorce process.

4. GENDER AND SOCIAL CHANGE

We have seen how there is a sense in which the welfare discourse, with its emphasis on the vulnerability of children, provides a convenient repository for the vulnerabilities of divorcing adults which they find difficult to "own" for themselves. Gender, however, plays a central part in this process of adult denial. The ordering of gender in patriarchal culture has traditionally rested on a constructed binary opposition in which masculinity has been defined in opposition to femininity. These constructions are not fixed, but are subject to historical change and hegemonic contestation in the social and psychic context of men and women's relations (Segal, 1990). The duality of gender has historically found expression in the ways in which men and women are socially and psychologically positioned differently as emotional beings. For example, women have traditionally been the "dependent" sex, for whom it has been socially acceptable to be emotional and to express vulnerability. However, as Richard (above) aptly observed, men by contrast, have traditionally been seen as independent and strong. The strong psychological investment which, in the past, has helped to sustain this gendered division of emotional experience should not be underestimated. As Maguire (1995) argues, the

---

[12] See also Arditti and Allen (1993) for a discussion of fathers' perceptions of inequities post-divorce based on a study of 81 "distressed" fathers. The perception that "the man loses everything after divorce" is an increasingly common one.

gendering of emotions, together with their different modes of expression, have deep psychic roots; traditionally, women's strength and independence was projected onto men, leaving men as a sex to carry those burdens. Conversely, men's vulnerabilities and their dependence has traditionally been carried by women. However, since at least the 1960s, there has been rapid social change in the area of gender relations. The changing social and economic realities, together with the challenges presented by feminism, have pushed and tested the boundaries that maintained this male-female opposition. The various cultural shifts associated with the processes of late modernity, which have contributed to the changing hegemonic climate of men and women's social relations, and the emotional struggles and dilemmas that have emerged as a consequence, have been well documented (Elliott, 1996; Frosh, 1991,1994; Giddens, 1992; Minsky, 1998). Women have increasingly come out of the "private" sphere to participate in the "public" world, and most now have opportunities for economic independence. In this context of social and political change, women can no longer so readily be positioned as dependent or vulnerable; women have been (re)claiming for themselves qualities traditionally associated with masculinity. The reverse process has not been so straightforward, owing to the cultural premium placed upon masculine qualities; men have found it much harder to begin to own their own "feminine" qualities, in a situation where women are increasingly refusing to accept men's projections of vulnerability.

The uncertain and changing sphere of gender relations, provides the broader context for the emotional challenges presented for divorced parents today. As the interviews illustrate, the contestation and blurring of the psycho-social boundaries which once marked out the gendered division of emotional experience, often sit uncomfortably with the contemporary welfare discourse of divorce that denies the space to articulate the social and emotional dilemmas of gender difference, and the conflictual feelings of loss, guilt and anger, which almost inevitably accompany the process of divorce and the break up of family relationships (Brown and Day Sclater, 1999).

This contradiction is reflected in the gendered ways in which the interviewees re-interpret the apparently neutral language of welfarism, and struggle to reconcile the latter with their own confusions regarding their competing needs and vulnerabilities. The preferred message of welfarist discourse regarding post-divorce parenting is one of harmony and a denial of gender conflict, and the contradictory feelings in this context are managed by a displacement that emphasises the vulnerability of children. It may be no accident, therefore, that we are currently witnessing a reconstruction of childhood where children's vulnerabilities and their need for protection are being emphasised, and where calls for children's "rights", or even for their voices to be heard, meets with such opposition.[13] As adults, we *need* children to be vulnerable, because the social "space" for adult vulnerabilities is getting smaller all the time.

[13] See, for example, Roche (1999). In the context of divorce, Piper (1999) has pointed out that, despite the provisions in the Children Act for the wishes and feelings of children to be taken

5. GENDERED EXPERIENCES OF LOSS AND POSSESSION: A PSYCHODYNAMIC
PERSPECTIVE

Psychoanalytic understandings of subjectivity provide useful insights into the powerful and unconscious psychological roots of adult vulnerability in this context, and its relationship to the gendered division of emotional experience, in which femininity becomes the psychic "other" of masculinity. Psychoanalysis points to the need to develop an emotional capacity to tolerate internal conflicts and ambivalent feelings, which have their roots in very early childhood, when humans are at their most vulnerable. For Freud and Lacan, the dominant narrative around this emotional struggle is one that centres around the conflicts of bisexuality and the identificatory dilemmas that are stirred up around the parental objects during the Oedipal crisis and the castration complex (LaPlanche and Pontalis, 1988, p.26).This experience is overdetermined by feelings of separation and loss as it marks the child's transition away from the exclusivity of the mother, into patriarchal culture and the internalisation of norms associated with the "law of the father".

A central outcome of this process is the establishment of gendered subjectivities. In developmental and structural terms, the child moves into another psychic space or positioning, in which the more primary modes of bisexual identification and desire are given up and channelled in a socially acceptable way (Minsky, 1996; Mitchell, 1975). As feminist interpretations of the Oedipal crisis emphasise, this process is fraught with difficulty and its "resolution" is achieved at the psychic cost of denying one part of ourselves (the sexual other), which in later situations may be projected onto others (Rose, 1987).

Boys and girls experience a different set of losses and insecurities in relation to the Oedipus complex and the phantasies around castration. In traditional Freudian discourse, it is argued that the male Oedipal process is instigated by a fear of castration from the rivalrous father, who demands that the boy give up his incestual love for the mother and also the qualities of femininity identified with her, and instead identify with him and the patriarchal order he represents (Freud, 1905). At this time, boys learn the limits of their own omnipotence, and that they cannot be everything that the mother desires. This disillusionment may turn to contempt and a profound distrust of femininity more generally. In learning to repudiate their femininity, women become objects of derision and fear and are pushed "out there" (Benjamin,1988, p.164). In this way, woman becomes a signifier of difference and the un-mourned "other" men can never be, or fully possess (Butler, 1990).

It is commonly argued that while boys are likely to exhibit a fear of dependency and intimacy (because of their repudiation of femininity and their identification with a masculine other), girls and women seek intimacy and have more

account of in divorce, in practice, this rarely happens. See also Maclean and Richards, Chapter 14 above.

"relational" selves, because they are unconsciously driven by a longing to return to mother (Fenichel, 1946; Riviere, 1932). For girls, the Oedipal crisis is not instigated by a fear of castration, but rather, by an awareness that they already lack the prized penis and the symbolic power it represents. In this way, girls have less to lose in staying with the first maternal love and so the pre-Oedipal bond between mother and daughter remains less repressed (Freud, 1931; Moi, 1987). Toril Moi (1987, p.144) sums up the implications of this for women in the following way: "Women's later experiences . . . will be influenced by their ambivalent, preoedipal relationship to their mother. This is culturally reinforced by the physical contact between the girl and her mother and among girls in general. The dominant force in woman's psyche is not castration anxiety but fear of loss of love".

It is likely that these gendered modes of relating, with their associated anxieties about loss and possession, underpin the ways in which the interviewees interpret and use the welfare discourse to articulate their own anxieties about post-divorce parenting. From the psychoanalytic perspective of the castration complex, the potential transgression of gender boundaries in this context necessitates a crisis around the return of repressed psychic material associated with more primary bisexual modes of identification and the losses of the Oedipus complex. However, these anxieties may also be reinforced and given meaning by more primary phantasies associated with the pre-Oedipal mother. The earlier and more primitive conflictual feelings and phantasies that are stirred up in the first infantile relationship with the mother, have been explored in more depth by feminist psychoanalysts who challenge the centrality Freud gave to the father in the construction of gendered subjectivities.

Karen Horney (1924, 1926) was extremely influential in this respect and was perhaps the first to challenge Freud's concept of "penis envy" with her idea of "womb envy" as the basis for sexual difference. Her emphasis on the importance of the mother was taken up by British Object Relations theorists,[14] who saw the pre-Oedipal period as crucial for the development of gendered subjectivities. At this stage of development, the mother is all-powerful and the emerging identity of the infant is closely merged with hers. In order to achieve an independent identity, babies have to undergo a psychological separation from this early one-ness with the mother, and herein lies the psychological origins of gendered subjectivities.

In this process of separation, the little girl separates from her mother but remains identified with her in important ways. By contrast, the little boy must cut himself off from this all-powerful woman and renounce his own feminine features, in order to attain a masculine identity. But his envy and fear of woman and her reproductive power lives on in the unconscious, and the devalued feminine parts of himself are experienced at one step removed, through projection

[14] Various authors have explored Object Relations theory in relation to the sociology of gender. See, for example, Chodorow (1978); Dinnerstein (1977); Maguire (1995); Minsky (1996), (1998); Sayers (1986), (1991); Segal (1990).

on to the female sex. In this way, masculinity is forever tinged at an unconscious level with a deep sense of insecurity, loss and envy and there can be a deep unconscious fear and hatred of women. Maguire (1995) sees the cultural dominance of "the masculine" as a way in which society, as a whole, organises the fear and envy associated with the mother's power. Thus, she argues that social structures, institutions and discourses provide men with real opportunities to deny their dependency needs, whilst forcing women into confrontation with infantile aspects of their own experience.

6. THE CRISIS OF GENDERED SUBJECTIVITY AND ITS RELATIONSHIP TO CULTURE

We have argued that the traditional gendered duality of emotional experience has been pushed and tested by men and women in the troubled context of post-divorce parenting. The more conscious processes of contestation that have contributed to the blurring of gender boundaries are made all the more anxiety-provoking for the people concerned because of their interaction with the deeper psychic processes which shape and continue to inform masculine and feminine subjectivities. The original Oedipal conflicts around possession and loss, together with the more primary feelings of envy and aggression, are never fully overcome but may return to haunt us later on, especially when faced (as in divorce) with the experience of separation and the threatened loss of possession. In having to "let go" of one's primary wishes and desires, we are "reluctant mourners" and the ambivalent feelings continue to surface and subvert our conscious lives in a variety of ways (Richards, 1989a).

In utilising defensive unconscious strategies to cope with the "tragedies" and intolerable feelings of early loss (for example in the forms of projection, splitting and denial) (see Brown and Day Sclater, 1999), it is this that makes them "tolerable" (Richards, 1989a, 1989b). However, one can argue that the unconscious management of "intolerable" feelings now appears to be in crisis. For example, the contemporary "crisis" or uncertainty around masculinity indicates that the traditional gendered relations of "possession" and "lack" appear to have shifted, and that the possessive Oedipal father is not getting it all his own way. One can argue that the defensive and even paranoid reaction of certain groups of men to the challenges presented by feminism, and the imagined loss of male power or "rights", suggests that these responses may also, at a deeper psychic level, represent the crisis-management of repressed intolerable feelings associated with the fiction of phallic power and the forbidden un-mourned territory of the forbidding pre-Oedipal mother.

It is this defensive response against the "return of the repressed" that underpins the current gendered interpretations of welfare discourse, where for example, men attempt to use it, often in an overly defensive way, to reinforce traditional notions of paternal authority and possession. A language that points to a chronic mistrust and envy of women and what they represent, is also a theme of these interviews. However, men's use of the welfare discourse in this context is mixed and often contradictory. For example, there is also evidence in some of the interviews that the broader social blurring of gender lines has helped to produce a questioning on the part of certain men, and an acknowledgement of their own fragility and emotional suffering, which draws on a discourse of vulnerability usually associated with femininity. The male struggle to find a language to articulate the emotional risks and dilemmas in this context, signifies a shift from more traditional fatherly modes of "caring about" to what Richard, in his interview, defined as "a grey area", where the positive wish to communicate with one's child and build a meaningful relationship with him or her, is nevertheless in tension with a resistance based on a reluctance to let go of the more traditional male defences associated with the fear of loss.

The central theme in the feminine appropriation of the welfare discourse, is the need to maintain a harmonious relationship for the sake of the children. The meanings of good-enough mothering in this context are bound up with the specific experiences of feminine subjectivity where, in contrast to men, women possess a more relational definition of the self. As discussed above, the specific psychic wounds and losses which underpin the construction of feminine identity are dealt with and managed on a daily basis through the search for intimacy and a sense of positive narcissistic affirmation, through merging and bonding with another. However, as the mothers in this study indicate, women have begun to challenge the social and psychic boundaries of femininity, to open up a new imaginary space, in which to redefine the meanings of maternal "parental care". This shift is reflected in what we termed the "independence discourse", where mothers struggle to assert their need for autonomy and separation and a less relational way of being. One can argue that what is occurring here is the re-gendering of the maternal space and what it means to be a mother.

Clearly, this is a brave enterprise and a process fraught with guilt and emotional tensions, not only because it involves a negation of what has previously underpinned dominant social definitions of femininity and ideas about the "good" mother, but also because, at a deeper psychic level, it signifies a refusal of the very identifications upon which femininity is founded. From a psychodynamic perspective, this represents a rejection of the maternal inheritance associated with the mother and also a disillusionment with the father, and all he represents. It is not surprising then, that the women in the study express guilt and anxiety about a wish for the kind of autonomy previously associated with men. These tensions, between the wish for autonomy and more traditional notions of good-enough mothering, appear at times to produce an impossible dilemma for the women interviewed who (as with the men discussed above) feel emotionally pulled in a number of different directions. Paradoxically, the desire for independence, may produce so much anxiety, that their own deeper dependency needs may re-surface and be felt all the more keenly; something which is then displaced and projected onto the children.

7. CO-PARENTING: THE WAY FORWARD?

In the extracts from the case studies we have examined, the psychic patterning of power and vulnerability described above, intersects in complex ways with cultural discourses of gender and of divorce. Contemporary divorce discourses emphasise men's nurturing capacities; in the ideology of co-parenting, implicit in the concept of Parental Responsibility, parents are positioned as gender-neutral: fatherhood becomes synonymous with motherhood, and fathers are encouraged to "share" caring activities with mothers. On the face of it, this proposition appears attractive, because it implies a greater degree of equality between men and women, and an opportunity for fathers to move beyond the more restrictive modes of parental "caring about", to one in which they can communicate more fully with their children and ease some of the responsibilities formerly carried by mothers. However, in reality, what actually happens is something rather different. In practice, fathers do not share day-to-day caring responsibilities with mothers. Rather, the very gender neutrality of the welfare discourse, and of the notion of Parental Responsibility, seems to encourage an envious competition on a terrain that was previously the province of women. Insofar as the dominant discourses conflate "mothering" and "fathering" in a gender-neutral concept of "parent", they deny the fundamental facts of gender difference and fail to carve out new spaces for women and men to carry out their parenting activities. So whilst there are those who would see the idea of gender-neutral parenting as none other than a positive development, one can also argue that this it is fraught with tensions and difficulties, because it signifies a denial of the conflictual social realities and power-dynamics of gender difference and the specific psychological constellations which under-pin them.

At a symbolic level, one can interpret this denial as representing a narcissistic refusal to accept the limits and boundaries of difference and the inevitable losses that accompany human development and the construction of gendered subjectivity. The refusal to acknowledge the gendered implications of post-divorce parenting is potentially dangerous, because it promotes a situation whereby men and women are invited to occupy a more regressive psychic space, associated with the more "primitive" pre-Oedipal anxieties described by Horney.[15] It is perhaps not surprising, in the conflictual context of post-divorce parenting, that phantasies about the loss of phallic power appear all the more real. Fathers may resort to envious and destructive patterns of behaviour as a means to cope with the uncertainties of their situation and the threatened loss of male possession.

The task facing contemporary parents is to recreate a new terrain of fatherhood that does not simply "colonise" motherhood. It is important to avoid any

---

[15] Juliet Mitchell (personal communication) has suggested that, drawing on the work of Winnicott, the dominant discourse of harmony in divorce also promotes a "false self" at a social level.

further expression of men's unconscious need to dominate women. Notwith-standing the rhetoric of the "new man" ideology, there are undoubtedly some men who are genuinely trying to care better for their children, which involves developing their own feminine and nurturing capacities, but which is based on an acknowledgement of sexual difference and of their own vulnerabilities.

However, as we have seen, and is amply illustrated by some of the fathers in other studies (see, for example, Neale and Smart, 1999), this is not what all fathers who become involved in disputes over children are doing. For some, the operation of the welfare discourse in law provides them with an opportunity, not to come to terms with their own emotional needs, but to formulate new sets of "rights" and to pursue retributive agendas against the women they feel have abandoned them.[16] In the light of the kind of psychic backcloth we have described, the new emphasis on gender neutral parenting, far from being a pro-gressive development, as it can appear to be, seems more like a new opportunity for the expression of the old patriarchal powers.

Just as men are threatened by women's mothering activities, many divorcing women are threatened by the continued involvement of their ex-partners as fathers. Only when women attain full substantive equality with men, which involves men coming to terms with their own psychic vulnerabilities which they are currently encouraged to deny, will the groundwork have been laid for parenting to be truly gender neutral. In existing conditions, the construction of children in the welfare discourse as the vulnerable victims of divorce, simply provides a new socially condoned opportunity for fathers to deal with their own infantile humiliation by triumphing over "mother" whom they have experi-enced as all-powerful. The dominant discourses which are currently structuring post-divorce parenting thus provide an institutionalised means of defence against male anxieties about loss of masculine identity and female anxieties about achieving separation and independence and asserting autonomy. As Benjamin (1988) argues, it should be possible for both boys and girls to identify with a psychic masculinity that does not involve denigrating the feminine or dominating woman.

Thus we would argue that there will have to be political change, cultural change *and* psychic change before mothers and fathers can become "equal" par-ents; parenting probably never will be gender-neutral, and it is indeed question-able whether such gender neutrality is desirable. When this equality has been achieved, gender difference can be recognised as a source of richness and diver-sity, rather than a source of pain or a basis for oppression. Psychoanalytic the-ory is useful in this respect, because it argues that while emotional ambivalence lies at the heart of subjectivity, a central ontological tension of human develop-ment and experience, is about learning to live with and cope with conflict, rather than to deny or entirely remove it. As Maguire (1995) argues, the envy, fear and vulnerability generated by the fact of sexual difference can only be resolved if

---

[16] On contemporary issues in masculinities and fatherhood, see Lupton and Barclay (1997); Hill (1997); Balbus (1998) and Kaganoff and Spano (1997).

both sexes can identify with the psychological qualities of the other. In a changing world, both parents need to find new places for themselves, but this should not be done through either an assertion of control or a denial of difference, for that would be merely to perpetuate existing relations of domination, to the detriment of us all.

REFERENCES

Arditti, J. and Allen, K., "Distressed Fathers' Perceptions of Legal and Relational Inequities Post-Divorce" (1993) 31 *Family and Conciliation Courts Review* 461–476.

Arendell, T., *Fathers and Divorce* (London, Sage, 1995).

Bailey-Harris, R., Davis, G., Barron, J. *et al.*, *Monitoring Private Law Applications Under the Children Act: A Research Report to the Nuffield Foundation* (University of Bristol, 1998).

Balbus, I. D., *Emotional Rescue: The Theory and Practice of a Feminist Father* (London, Routledge, 1998).

Baumgart, H., *Jealousy; Experiences and Solutions* (London, The University of Chicago Press, 1990).

Benjamin, J., *The Bonds of Love: Psychoanalysis, Feminism and the Problem of Domination* (London, Virago, 1988).

Bernard, J., *The Future of Marriage* (New York, Souvenir Press, 1973).

Blankenhorn, D., *Fatherless America: Confronting Our Most Urgent Social Problem* (New York, Basic Books, 1995).

Bottomley, A., "What is happening to family law? A feminist critique of conciliation" in J. Brophy and C. Smart (eds.), *Women in Law* (London, RKP, 1985).

Brophy, J. and Smart, C. (eds.), *Women in Law* (London, RKP, 1985).

Brosnan, J., "Men behaving sadly" (1995) *New Statesman* (4 August) 16–17.

Brown, J. and Day Sclater, S., "Divorce: a psychodynamic perspective" in S. Day Sclater and C. Piper (eds.), *Undercurrents of Divorce* (Aldershot, Ashgate, forthcoming).

Burton, S., Regan, L. and Kelly, L., *Domestic Violence: Supporting Women and Challenging Men* (Bristol, The Policy Press, 1998).

Butler, J., *Gender Trouble: Feminism and the Subversion of Identity* (New York, Routledge, 1990).

Chodorow, N., *The Reproduction of Mothering: Psychoanalysis and the Sociology of Gender* (Berkley, University of California Press, 1978).

Collier, R., "From women's emancipation to sex war: heterosexuality and the politics of divorce" in Day Sclater, S. and Piper, C. (eds.), *Undercurrents of Divorce* (Aldershot, Ashgate, forthcoming).

Craib, I., "Thinking About Feeling", paper presented at the Modern Feelings Symposium, University of East London, 1998.

Davies, B. and Harre, R., "Positioning: the discursive production of selves" (1990) 20 *Journal for the Theory of Social Behaviour* 43–63.

Day Sclater, S., *The Psychology of Divorce: A Research Report to the ESRC* (London, University of East London, 1998) (1998a).

Day Sclater, S., "Children and Divorce: Hidden Agendas?", paper presented at the Children and Social Exclusion Conference, Hull University, March 1998 (1998b).

Day Sclater, S., *Divorce: A Psychosocial Study* (Aldershot, Ashgate, forthcoming) (1999a).

Day Sclater, S., "Experiences of divorce" in S. Day Sclater, and C. Piper, (eds.), *Undercurrents of Divorce* (Aldershot, Ashgate, forthcoming) (1999b).

Day Sclater, S. and Piper, C., "The Family Law Act 1996 in context" in S. Day Sclater, and C. Piper, (eds.), *Undercurrents of Divorce* (Aldershot, Ashgate, forthcoming).

Dennis, N. and Erdos, G., *Families Without Fatherhood* (London, Institute of Economic Affairs, 1992).

Dinnerstein, D., *The Rocking of the Cradle and the Ruling of the World* (New York, Souvenir Press, 1977).

Elliott, A., *Subject To Ourselves; Social Theory, Psychoanalysis and Postmodernity* (Cambridge, Polity Press, 1996).

Fairclough, N., *Language and Power* (London, Longman, 1989).

Fairclough, N., *Discourse and Social Change* (Cambridge, Polity Press, 1992).

Fenichel, O., *The Psychoanalytic Theory Of Neurosis* (London, Tavistock/Routledge, 1946/1990).

Fineman, M. A., *The Illusion of Equality: The Rhetoric and Reality of Divorce Reform* (Chicago, University of Chicago Press, 1991).

Fineman, M. A., *The Neutered Mother, the Sexual Family and Other Twentieth Century Tragedies* (New York, Routledge, 1995).

Freud, S., "Three essays on the theory of sexuality", *The Pelican Freud Library, Volume 7* (Middlesex, Penguin Books, Harmondsworth, 1905/1977).

Freud, S., "The ego and the id", *The Pelican Freud Library, Volume 11* (London, Pelican Books, 1923/1984).

Freud, S., "Female Sexuality", *The Pelican Freud Library, Volume 7* (Middlesex, Penguin Books, Harmondsworth, 1931/1977).

Frosh, S., *Identity Crisis: Modernity, Psychoanalysis and the Self* (London, Macmillan, 1991).

Frosh, S., *Sexual Difference: Masculinity and Psychoanalysis* (London, Routledge. 1994).

Giddens, A., *The Transformation Of Intimacy* (Cambridge, Polity Press, 1992).

Gilligan, C., *In a Different Voice* (Cambridge, MA, Harvard University Press, 1982).

Grillo, T., "The mediation alternative: process dangers for women" (1991) 100 *Yale Law Journal* 1545–1610.

Hester, M., Pearson, C. and Radford, L., *Domestic Violence: A National Survey of Court Welfare and Voluntary Sector Mediation Practice* (Bristol, The Policy Press, 1997).

Hester, M. and Radford, L., *Domestic Violence and Child Contact Arrangements in England and Denmark* (Bristol, The Policy Press, 1996).

Hill, D., *The Future of Men* (London, Phoenix, 1997).

Hollway, W., *Subjectivity and Method in Psychology* (London, Sage Publications, 1989).

Horney, K., "On the genesis of the castration complex in woman" (1924) 5 *International Journal of Psychoanalysis* 50–65.

Horney, K., "Flight from womanhood" (1926) 7 *International Journal of Psychoanalysis* 324–339.

Kaganas, F., "Contact, conflict and risk" in S. Day Sclater and C. Piper (eds.), *Undercurrents of Divorce* (Aldershot, Ashgate, 1999).

Kaganoff, P. and Spano, S. (eds.), *Men on Divorce: The Other Side of the Story* (London, Harcourt and Brace, 1997).

Laplanche, J. and Pontalis, J. B., *The Language of Psychoanalysis* (London, The Institute of Psychoanalysis, Karnac Books, 1988).

Lord Chancellor's Department, *Looking to the Future: Mediation and the Ground for Divorce, A Consultation Paper* (Cm 2424, London, HMSO, 1993).

Lord Chancellor's Department, *Looking to the Future: Mediation and the Ground for Divorce, The Government's Proposals* (Cm 2799, London, HMSO, 1995).

Lupton, D. and Barclay, L., *Constructing Fatherhood: Discourses and Experiences* (London, Sage Publications, 1997).

Maccoby, E. and Mnookin, R., *Dividing the Child: Social and Legal Dilemmas of Custody* (Cambridge, MA, Harvard University Press, 1992).

Magnus, S. M., "For Better or For Worse", *The Guardian,* 10 September 1997, pp. 10–11.

Maguire, M., *Women and Men: Passion and Power* (London, Routledge, 1995).

Minsky, R. (ed.), *Psychoanalysis and Gender: A Reader* (London, Routledge, 1996).

Minsky, R., *Psychoanalysis and Culture* (Cambridge, Polity Press, 1998).

Mitchell, J., *Psychoanalysis and Feminism* (Middlesex, Penguin, Harmondsworth, 1975).

Moi, T., "Jealousy and sexual difference" in Feminist Review (eds.), *Sexuality: A Reader* (London, Virago, 1987).

Mullender, A. and Morley, R. (eds.), *Children Living with Domestic Violence: Putting Men's Abuse of Women on the Child Care Agenda* (London, Whiting and Birch, 1994).

Neale, B. and Smart, C., "In whose best interests? Theorising family life following separation and divorce" in S. Day Sclater and C. Piper (eds.), *Undercurrents of Divorce* (Aldershot, Ashgate, 1999).

O'Donovan, K., *Family Law Matters* (London, Pluto Press, 1993).

Piper, C., "Divorce reform and the image of the child" (1996) 23 *Journal of Law and Society* 364–382.

Piper, C., "The wishes and feelings of the Child" in S. Day Sclater and C. Piper (eds.), *Undercurrents of Divorce* (Aldershot, Ashgate, 1999).

Plummer, K., (1995) *Telling Sexual Stories* (London, Routledge, 1995).

Probyn, E., *Sexing the Self: Gendered Positions in Cultural Studies* (London, Routledge, 1993).

Richards, B., *Images of Freud: Cultural Responses to Psychoanalysis* (London, Dent, 1989) (1989a).

Richards, B. (ed.), *Crises of The Self: Further Essays On Psychoanalysis and Politics* (London, Free Association Books, 1989) (1989b).

Riessman, C. K., *Divorce Talk: Men and Women Make Sense of Personal Relationships* (London, Rutgers University Press, 1990).

Riviere, J., "Jealousy as a mechanism of defence" (1932) 13 *International Journal of Psychoanalysis* 414–424.

Roche, J., "Children and divorce: a private affair?" in S. Day Sclater and C. Piper (eds.), *Undercurrents of Divorce* (Aldershot, Ashgate, 1999).

Rodgers, B. and Pryor, J., *Divorce and Separation: The Outcomes for Children* (York, Joseph Rowntree Foundation, 1998).

Rose, J., "Femininity and its discontents" in Feminist Review (eds.), *Sexuality: A Reader* (London, Virago, 1987).

Sayers, J., *Sexual Contradictions* (London, Tavistock, 1986).

Sayers, J., *Mothering Psychoanalysis: Helene Deutsch, Karen Horney, Anna Freud and Melanie Klein* (London, Hamish Hamilton, 1991).

Segal, L., *Slow Motion: Changing Masculinities, Changing Men* (London, Virago, 1990).

Segal, L., "A feminist looks at the family" in J. Muncie, M. Wetherell, R. Dallos *et al.* (eds.), *Understanding the Family* (London, Sage Publications, 1994).

Simpson, B., McCarthy, P. and Walker, J., *Being There: Fathers After Divorce* (University of Newcastle, Relate Centre for Family Studies, 1995).

Smart, C., *Feminism and the Power of Law* (London, Routledge, 1989).

Smart, C. and Sevenhuijsen, S. (eds.), *Power and the Politics of Child Custody* (London, Routledge, 1989).

Standing, K., "Reasserting Fathers' Rights? Parental Responsibility in Education and Lone Mother Families", paper presented at the Gender, Sexuality and Law Conference, Keele University, June 1998.

Index

Printed in the United Kingdom
by Lightning Source UK Ltd.
126879UK00001B/229-231/A